Guide to Firewalls and VPNs

Third Edition

Michael E. Whitman

Herbert J. Mattord

Andrew Green

COURSE TECHNOLOGY
CENGAGE Learning

Australia • Brazil • Japan • Korea • Mexico • Singapore • Spain • United Kingdom • United States

COURSE TECHNOLOGY
CENGAGE Learning

**Guide to Firewalls and VPNs,
Third Edition**
Michael E. Whitman, Herbert J. Mattord,
Andrew Green

Vice President, Editorial: Dave Garza

Executive Editor: Stephen Helba

Acquisitions Editor: Stephen Helba

Managing Editor: Marah Bellegarde

Senior Product Manager: Michelle Ruelos
Cannistraci

Developmental Editor: Kent Williams

Editorial Assistant: Jennifer Wheaton

Vice President, Marketing: Jennifer Ann
Baker

Marketing Director: Deborah S. Yarnell

Marketing Manager: Erin Coffin

Marketing Coordinator: Erica Ropitzky

Production Manager: Andrew Crouth

Senior Content Project Manager: Andrea
Majot

Senior Art Director: Jack Pendleton

For product information and technology assistance, contact us at
Cengage Learning Customer & Sales Support, 1-800-354-9706

For permission to use material from this text or product,
submit all requests online at **cengage.com/permissions**
Further permissions questions can be emailed to
permissionrequest@cengage.com

Library of Congress Control Number: 2011927669

ISBN-13: 978-1-111-13539-3

ISBN-10: 1-111-13539-8

Course Technology
20 Channel Center Street
Boston, MA 02210
USA

Cengage Learning is a leading provider of customized learning solutions with office locations around the globe, including Singapore, the United Kingdom, Australia, Mexico, Brazil, and Japan. Locate your local office at:
international.cengage.com/region

Cengage Learning products are represented in Canada by
Nelson Education, Ltd.

For your lifelong learning solutions, visit
www.cengage.com/coursetechnology

Purchase any of our products at your local college store or at our preferred online store **www.cengagebrain.com**

Visit our corporate website at **www.cengage.com**

Printed in the United States of America
3 4 5 6 7 12 11

To Rhonda, Rachel, Alex, and Meghan, thank you for your loving support.

— MEW

To Julianna and Ellie, the future starts with you.

— Grampy

For Tammy: The best is yet to come.

— A

Brief Contents

Table of Contents

CHAPTER 3
Authenticating Users **67**

PART 2
Firewalls

CHAPTER 4
Introduction to Firewalls **97**

PART 3
VPNs

Introduction

This book provides an introduction to firewalls and certain network security components that can work together to create an in-depth defensive perimeter around a Local Area Network (LAN). Firewalls are among the best-known security tools in use today, and they are growing in popularity among the general public as well as among Information Technology professionals. However, firewalls work most effectively when they are backed by effective security planning and a well-designed security policy as well as when they work in concert with other tools.

Accordingly, this book examines firewalls within the context of the other elements needed for effective perimeter security and security within a network. These elements include packet filtering, authentication, proxy servers, encryption, bastion hosts, virtual private networks (VPNs), and log file maintenance.

Approach

Guide to Firewalls and VPNs, Third Edition provides faculty and students with a single resource that combines the managerial background for successful network security administration with the technical knowledge needed to design, select, and implement many common networking defenses. This book covers the policy, procedures, and managerial approaches needed to build a network defense program as well as the technical background essential to networking, and then progresses through the technical controls needed for network defense, such as firewalls and VPNs.

This book's approach to information security includes the following features:

Certified Information Systems Security Professional's Common Body of Knowledge—Because two of the authors hold the Certified Information Systems Security Professional (CISSP) credential, the CISSP knowledge domains have had an influence in the design of this book. Although care was taken to avoid producing another CISSP study guide, the authors' backgrounds have ensured that the book's treatment of information security integrates, to some degree, much of the CISSP Common Body of Knowledge (CBK).

Running Cases—Each chapter opens with a vignette that features a fictional organization encountering information security issues that are commonly found in real-life organizations. At the end of the chapter, there is a brief follow-up to the opening vignette.

Hands-On Learning—At the end of each chapter, there is a Chapter Summary and a set of Review Questions as well as a set of Real World Exercises that give students the opportunity to examine the information security arena outside the classroom. Here, students are asked to research, analyze, and write responses to questions that are intended to reinforce learning objectives and deepen their understanding of the text. These exercises are followed by a set of Hands-On Projects, which offer students the chance to explore the technical aspects of the theories presented in the chapter. Each chapter ends with a Running Case Project that lets the student practice the technical skills needed to gain mastery of the concepts presented in the chapter. This will enable students to gain practical experience using the firewall software tools as they are encountered in practice.

New to This Edition

This third edition of *Firewalls and VPNs* is a sequel to *Guide to Firewalls and Network Security: With Intrusion Detection and VPNs, Second Edition*. It features a tightened focus on the core subject matter, provides a stronger emphasis on hands-on applications, and updates the content in the following areas:

- **Revised Sections on Information and Network Security**—Core background content necessary for understanding how network security can be achieved using firewalls and VPNs.

- **Reorganized Section on Security Policy and Standards**—Improved coverage of policy as a guide for the deployment of security technologies. This version also introduces major security standards organizations, which can guide enterprise security efforts.

- **Incorporated Standards Materials from NIST**—Best practices and standards from *SP 800-41 Rev. 1, September, 2009 Guidelines on Firewalls and Firewall Policy* are included. This document, which serves as guidance for thousands of public and private organizations, contains numerous recommendations for the installation and configuration of firewalls.

- **Revised and Improved Section on Firewalls**—Revised and improved flow of the firewall material with no loss of relevant content.

- **Revised and Expanded Section on VPNs**—Discussion of firewalls both distinct from and integrated with the material on VPNs, each section containing relevant applied material as well as theoretical foundations.

- **General Updates**—Topics updated throughout the book, with revised examples and references to maintain currency and relevance.

Author Team

Michael E. Whitman, Herbert J. Mattord, and Andrew Green have jointly developed this text, merging their collective knowledge from the world of academic study with practical experience from the business world.

- Michael E. Whitman, Ph.D., CISM, CISSP, is a Professor of Information Security in the Information Systems Department, Coles College of Business at Kennesaw State University, Kennesaw,

Georgia, where he is also Director of the KSU Center for Information Security Education (*infosec.kennesaw.edu*) and the coordinator for the Bachelor of Science in Information Security and Assurance. Dr. Whitman is an active researcher in Information Security, Fair and Responsible Use Policies, and Ethical Computing. He currently teaches graduate and undergraduate courses in Information Security. He has published articles in the top journals in his field, including *Information Systems Research*, *Communications of the ACM*, *Information and Management*, *Journal of International Business Studies*, and *Journal of Computer Information Systems*. He is a member of the Information Systems Security Association, the Association for Computing Machinery, (ISC)2, ISACA, and the Association for Information Systems. Dr. Whitman is also the coauthor of *Principles of Information Security, Fourth Edition*; *Management of Information Security, Third Edition*; *Principles of Incident Response and Disaster Recovery*; *Readings and Cases in the Management of Information Security*; *Readings and Cases in Information Security: Law and Ethics*; and *Hands-On Information Security Lab Manual, Third Edition*, as well as the predecessor to this text, all published by Course Technology, a division of Cengage Learning. Prior to his career in academia, Dr. Whitman was an armored cavalry officer in the United States Army.

- Herbert J. Mattord, M.B.A., CISM, CISSP, completed 24 years of IT industry experience as an application developer, database administrator, project manager, and information security practitioner before joining the faculty at Kennesaw State University in 2002. Professor Mattord is the Operations Manager of the KSU Center for Information Security Education and Awareness (*infosec.kennesaw.edu*) as well as the coordinator for the KSU Information Systems Department of Certificate in Information Security and Assurance. During his career as an IT practitioner, he has been an adjunct professor at Kennesaw State University; Southern Polytechnic State University in Marietta, Georgia; Austin Community College in Austin, Texas; and Texas State University in San Marcos, Texas. He currently teaches undergraduate courses in Information Security. He was formerly the Manager of Corporate Information Technology Security at Georgia-Pacific Corporation, where much of the practical knowledge found in this textbook was acquired. Professor Mattord is also the coauthor of *Principles of Information Security, Fourth Edition*; *Management of Information Security, Third Edition*; *Principles of Incident Response and Disaster Recovery*; *Readings and Cases in the Management of Information Security*; *Readings and Cases in Information Security: Law and Ethics*; and *Hands-On Information Security Lab Manual, Third Edition,* all published by Course Technology, a division of Cengage Learning.

- Andrew Green, M.S., has been involved in information security for nine years, offering consulting services that focus primarily on the needs of small and medium-sized businesses. Prior to becoming a full-time information security consultant, Mr. Green worked in the healthcare IT field, where he developed and supported transcription interfaces for medical facilities throughout the United States. In addition to his consulting work, Mr. Green is a faculty member at Kennesaw State University, where he teaches classes in information security and information systems.

Structure

Guide to Firewalls and VPNs addresses three subject areas. First, it presents an introduction to and overview of information security and network security, with an emphasis on the role of data communications in network security. Second, it addresses firewalls. Third, it addresses VPNs, with a primer on encryption to further the student's understanding of VPNs.

The book is divided into three sections and ten chapters, with an appendix that offers students a supplemental firewall lab experience:

Part I: Introduction to Information Security

Chapter 1 Introduction to Information Security This chapter lays the foundation for network security by providing a primer in information security and an understanding of the terminology used throughout the text and the discipline. The text also discusses the threats and attacks the reader can expect to encounter while dealing with network security and firewalls.

Chapter 2 Security Policies and Standards This chapter couples the need for a policy-driven approach with an understanding of modern security standards organizations like ISO, NIST, and the IETF. Relevant security programs like security education, training and awareness, and planning for contingencies are also presented.

Chapter 3 Authenticating Users This chapter presents an examination of access controls used in most servers and network security appliances. It covers modern access control approaches and methodologies, security tools and techniques, and security issues associated with administering access controls.

Part II: Firewalls

Chapter 4 Introduction to Firewalls This chapter provides an introduction to firewalls. The reader is introduced to the various generations and categories of firewalls and shown how these firewalls are deployed in an organization. The chapter also introduces other security technologies—specifically, VPNs—and other remote connection protection.

Chapter 5 Packet Filtering This chapter provides a detailed explanation of how most modern firewalls work—that is, by using a series of encoded rules to assess network traffic. It covers both traditional static packet-filtering firewalls and the more modern stateful packet-inspection firewalls, as well as their assorted rule sets.

Chapter 6 Firewall Configuration and Administration This chapter examines the rule sets used to configure firewalls. It also discusses the requirements for ongoing administration of firewall appliances, with specific attention to remote management, log management, and advanced firewall functions.

Chapter 7 Working with Proxy Servers and Application-Level Firewalls This chapter examines the use and deployment of proxy servers and application-level firewalls, which are used to support the operations of an enterprise.

Chapter 8 Implementing the Bastion Host This chapter examines firewalls in greater detail, including the specifications for installing, configuring, and protecting the bastion host firewall architecture. The unique requirements for this architecture are discussed along with recommendations for the hardware/software and networking components.

Part III: VPNs

Chapter 9 Encryption—The Foundation for the Virtual Private Network This chapter examines the use of encryption to support firewall functions, and the incorporation of VPN technologies. It also serves both as a primer on encryption and as a transition to a more detailed examination of VPN operations in the following chapter.

Chapter 10 Setting Up a Virtual Private Network This chapter examines in detail the implementation, configuration, and use of virtual private network technologies. It also discusses how VPNs use tunneling to support their functions as well as the security issues involved in deploying VPNs.

Appendix A Setting Up and Operating a Software Firewall At the end of each chapter, students are given a series of Hands-On Running Case assignments using the Vyatta software-based firewall. The appendix provides a consolidated reprise of these firewall learning activities using the Endian Community Firewall as an alternative software solution.

End Matter

- **Glossary**: A complete compendium of the acronyms and technical terms used in this book, with definitions.
- **Index**: An alphabetical list of key concepts with page references.

Text and Graphic Conventions

Wherever appropriate, additional information and exercises have been added to this book to help you better understand what is being discussed in the chapter. Icons throughout the text alert you to additional materials. The icons used in this textbook are described in the following paragraphs.

 Notes present additional helpful material related to the subject being described.

 Tips highlight suggestions on how to attack problems you may encounter in a real-world situation.

 Hands-On Projects offer students the chance to explore the technical aspects of the theories presented in the chapter.

 Running Case Projects provide the opportunity for technical practice through the use of extended labs.

Instructor's Materials

The following supplemental materials are available for use in a classroom setting. All the supplements available with this book are provided to the instructor on a single CD-ROM (ISBN: 0840024215) and online at the textbook's Web site.

Please visit *login.cengage.com* and log in to access instructor-specific resources.

To access additional course materials, please visit *www.cengagebrain.com*. At the *CengageBrain .com* home page, search for the ISBN of your title (from the back cover of your book) using the search box at the top of the page. This will take you to the product page where these resources can be found.

Additional materials designed especially for you might be available for your course online. Go to *www.cengage.com/coursetechnology* and search for this book title periodically for more details.

Electronic Instructor's Manual—The Instructor's Manual that accompanies this textbook includes additional instructional material to assist in class preparation, including suggestions for classroom activities, discussion topics, and additional projects.

Solution Files—The Solution Files include answers to selected end-of-chapter materials, including the Review Questions and some of the Hands-On Projects and Running Case Projects.

ExamView—This textbook is accompanied by ExamView, a powerful testing software package that allows instructors to create and administer printed, computer (LAN-based), and Internet exams. ExamView includes hundreds of questions that correspond to the topics covered in this text, enabling students to generate detailed study guides that include page references for further review. The computer-based and Internet testing components allow students to take exams at their computers; they also save the instructor time by grading each exam automatically.

PowerPoint Presentations—This book comes with Microsoft PowerPoint slides for each chapter. These are included as a teaching aid for classroom presentation. They can also be made available to students on the network for chapter review, or they can be printed for classroom distribution. Instructors, feel free to add your own slides for additional topics you introduce to the class.

Coping with Change on the Web

Sooner or later, all the specific Web-based resources mentioned in this book will go stale or be replaced by newer information. In some cases, the URLs you find here may lead you to their replacements; in other cases, the URLs will lead nowhere, leaving you with the dreaded 404 error message: "File not found."

When that happens, don't give up! There's always a way to find what you want on the Web, if you're willing to invest some time and energy. To begin with, most large or complex Web sites offer a search engine. As long as you can get to the site itself, you can use this tool to help you find what you need.

Don't be afraid to use general search tools like *www.google.com*, or *www.bing.com* to find related information. Although certain standards bodies may offer the most precise and specific information about their standards online, there are plenty of third-party sources of information, training, and assistance. If you can't find something where the book says it is, start looking around. It's got to be around there somewhere!

Acknowledgments

The authors would like to thank their families for their support and understanding during the many hours that were dedicated to this project—hours taken away, in many cases, from family activities. Special thanks to Dr. Carola Mattord whose reviews of early drafts and suggestions for keeping the writing focused on the student resulted in a more readable manuscript.

Reviewers

We are indebted to the following individuals for their respective contributions of perceptive feedback on the initial proposal, the project outline, and the chapter-by-chapter reviews of the text:

- Wasim A. Al-Hamdani, Ph.D, Kentucky State University, Frankfort, KY
- Dan Guilmette, Cochise College, Sierra Vista, AZ
- Pam Schmelz, Ivy Tech Community College, Columbus, IN
- Nick Symiakakis, Branford Hall Career Institute, Springfield, MA

Special Thanks

The authors wish to thank the editorial and production teams at Course Technology. Their diligent and professional efforts greatly enhanced the final product:

- Michelle Ruelos Cannistraci, Senior Product Manager
- Kent Williams, Development Editor
- Steve Helba, Executive Editor
- Andrea Majot, Senior Content Project Manager
- John Bosco, Technical Editor

Our Commitment

The authors are committed to serving the needs of the adopters and readers of this book. We would be pleased and honored to receive feedback on the textbook and its supporting materials. You can contact us through Course Technology.

Lab Requirements
To the User

The labs prepared for use with this text are designed to expose you to the configuration and operation of a software firewall. Although every effort has been made to make the lab steps function properly, be aware that operating system patches and application software versions cause things to change. You may need to develop a spirit of improvisation when faced with these small differences in how things work over time.

Hardware and Software Requirements

To complete the project at the end of each chapter as well as the appendix, you will need a computer running Windows XP, Vista, or Windows 7 that is configured with TCP/IP on a network with other properly configured TCP/IP computers. We recommend and provide instructions for using Sun's VirtualBox software, but you may substitute any virtualization platform that can support the applications being used. The hardware system should meet the following minimum specifications:

- 1 GHz processor
- 512 MB RAM
- 8 GB HD
- 2 Network cards, minimum 10/100

You will need an additional, separate system to function as an internal network client. You will also need a hardware switching device to connect the internal network client to the firewall. Alternatively, you can connect the internal network client directly to the internal NIC on the firewall through the use of a crossover cable.

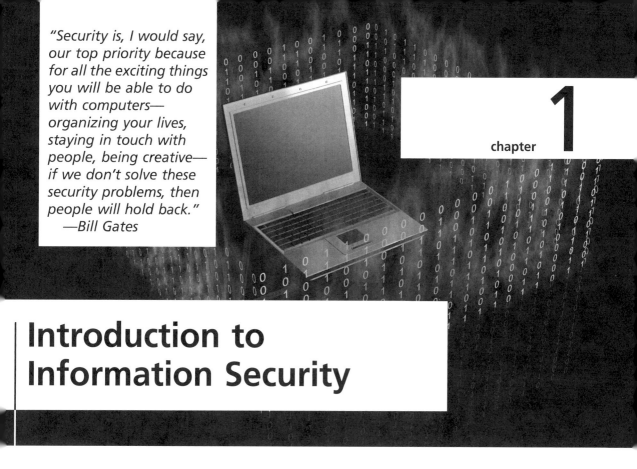

"Security is, I would say, our top priority because for all the exciting things you will be able to do with computers—organizing your lives, staying in touch with people, being creative—if we don't solve these security problems, then people will hold back."
—Bill Gates

Introduction to Information Security

After reading this chapter and completing the exercises, you will be able to:

- Explain the component parts of information security in general and network security in particular
- Define the key terms and critical concepts of information and network security
- Describe the organizational roles of information and network security professionals
- Discuss the business need for information and network security
- Identify the threats posed to information and network security, as well as the common attacks associated with those threats
- Differentiate threats to information within systems from attacks against information within systems

Running Case: You Must Be Joking

Meghan Sanders couldn't believe her eyes. She blinked twice, and then looked back at Alex to be sure it wasn't a joke.

"Well, do you think you can help me?" Alex Truman asked, with a hint of desperation in his voice.

"This is your current perimeter defense?" Meghan asked, hesitantly. "Have you reconfigured the device in any way?"

"Yes, that's it, and no, it was installed out of the box," Alex replied. "I bought the best one they had on the shelf at the time! We know we need to consider an upgrade, but it's been working pretty well so far."

That's the understatement of the year, Meghan thought. She took a deep breath. "Okay, I think I know what we need to do, but it's going to take some time and effort. Let me check in with my team and I'll send over an estimate."

As she walked back to her car, Meghan mulled over the issues at hand. Her company, Onsite Security Services, was doing well so far. She'd built a small but solid base of customers, including several small businesses, work-at-home professionals, and even a few local retail chain vendors. But this was going to be the most challenging job yet. Most of her work involved helping clients update and secure computers, servers, printers, and the occasional network configuration. She'd worked with small firewalls for the home users, but had never really gotten involved in commercial-grade security appliances. "I guess it's time I upgraded my service offerings," she told herself.

What Meghan couldn't believe was that a local data center, with over 50 servers providing data collection and data mining services for local businesses, was protected at the perimeter with a residential-grade firewall, the same inexpensive device most people used at home. All that data, residing behind a piece of technology bought on sale for $49.99, she thought to herself.

Meghan called her office manager. "Rachel?" she said, "I just left Data Mart. I need you to see if Mike can schedule an appointment with Alex Truman to start educating him on effective security profiles. This job is going to take some real work, and I think we need to start with the basics."

Introduction

Network security is a critical activity for almost every organization, and for some organizations it may be *the* critical activity that defines their business. The cornerstone of most network security programs is an effective perimeter defense. Perimeter defense is the protection of the boundaries of the organization's networks from the insecurity of the Internet. The heart of any good perimeter defense is an effective firewall that has been properly configured to be safe and efficient. However, before you can start the processes used to plan, design, and build effective firewall defenses, you should have an understanding of information security and how network security and an effective firewall fit into that context. Learning about the overall topic of information security helps you become aware of each of the many factors that affect network security and firewall management. The field of information security has matured rapidly in the past 20 years. Those who don't understand the conceptual basis of information security risk being unable to make the best business decisions regarding network security. This chapter offers an overview of the entire field of information security and of how that broader field influences current trends in network security.

What Is Information Security?

Information security (InfoSec) is the protection of information and its critical elements, including the systems and hardware that use, store, and transmit that information.[1] To protect information and its related systems, each organization must implement controls such as policy, awareness training, security education, and technical controls. These security controls are organized into topical areas, and any successful organization will be able to integrate them into a unified process that encompasses the following:

- **Network security**—The protection of networking components, connections, and contents (the broader topic within which this textbook falls)
- **Physical security**—The protection of the physical items, objects, or areas of an organization from unauthorized access and misuse
- **Personnel security**—The protection of the people who are authorized to access the organization and its operations
- **Operations security**—The protection of the details of a particular operation or series of activities
- **Communications security**—The protection of an organization's communications media, technology, and content

Modern information security has evolved from a concept known as the C.I.A. triangle. The **C.I.A. triangle**, an industry standard for computer security since the development of the mainframe, is based on the three characteristics of information that make it valuable to organizations: confidentiality, integrity, and availability. These three characteristics of information are as important today as they have always been, but the model of the C.I.A. triangle no longer adequately addresses the constantly changing environment of the information technology (IT) industry. The current environment has many emerging and constantly evolving threats. These threats may be accidental or intentional. The resulting losses may be from damage or destruction to IT systems or data, or they may involve theft, unintended or unauthorized modification, or any one of the many other ways that IT systems can experience loss. This has prompted the expansion of the C.I.A. triangle into a more robust model that addresses the complexities of the current information security environment. This expanded list of critical characteristics of information is described in the next section.

Critical Characteristics of Information

The value of information comes from the characteristics it possesses. A change to one of the characteristics of information changes the value of that information. The value either increases or, more commonly, decreases. Although information security professionals and end users have the same understanding of the characteristics of information, tensions can arise when the need to secure the confidentiality or integrity of information conflicts with the end users' need for unhindered access to the information (availability). The following are some of the important characteristics of information you should know when discussing the security and integrity of information[2]:

- **Availability**—The information is accessible by authorized users (persons or computer systems) without interference or obstruction, and they receive it in the required format.

- **Accuracy**—Information is free from mistakes or errors, and it has the value that the end user expects.

- **Authenticity**—The information is genuine or original rather than a reproduction or fabrication. Information is authentic when it is the information that was originally created, placed, stored, or transferred.

- **Confidentiality**—The information is protected from disclosure or exposure to unauthorized individuals or systems. This means that only those with the rights and privileges to access information are able to do so. To protect against a breach in the confidentiality of information, a number of measures can be used:

  - Information classification
  - Secure document storage
  - Application of general security policies
  - Education of information custodians and end users

- **Integrity**—The information remains whole, complete, and uncorrupted. The integrity of information is threatened when the information is exposed to corruption, damage, destruction, or other disruption of its authentic state.

- **Utility**—The information has value for some purpose or end. To have utility, information must be in a format meaningful to the end user. For example, U.S. Census data can be overwhelming and difficult to understand; however, when properly interpreted, it reveals valuable information about the voters in a district, what political parties they belong to, their race, gender, age, and so on.

- **Possession**—The information object or item is owned or controlled by somebody. Information is said to be in one's possession if one obtains it, independent of format or other characteristics.

CNSS Security Model

The definition of information security presented earlier is based in part on a document from the U.S. Committee on National Systems Security (CNSS) called the National Training Standard for Information Security Professionals NSTISSI No. 4011 (*www.cnss.gov/Assets/pdf/nstissi_4011.pdf*). This document presents a comprehensive model for information security and is becoming the evaluation standard for the security of information systems. The model, known to most information security professionals as the **McCumber Cube**, was created by John McCumber in 1991; it provides a graphical description of the architectural approach widely used in computer and information security.[3] As shown in Figure 1-1, the McCumber Cube uses a representation of a 3 x 3 x 3 cube, with 27 cells representing the various areas that must be addressed to secure today's information systems. For example, the cell that represents the intersection of technology, integrity, and storage calls for a control or safeguard that addresses the need to use technology to protect the integrity of information while it is in storage. One such control is a system for detecting host intrusion that protects the integrity of information by alerting the security administrators to the potential modification of a critical file. What is commonly left out of a model like the McCumber Cube is the need for guidelines and policies that provide direction for the practices and implementations of technologies. The need for policy is a critical element for all organizations, and you will find that it is mentioned frequently throughout this textbook.

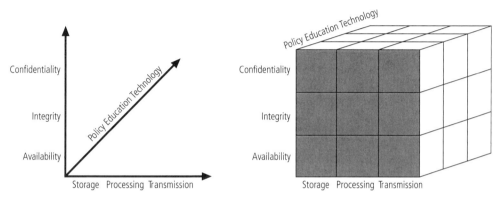

Figure 1-1 The McCumber Cube
© Cengage Learning 2012

Balancing Information Security and Access

Even with the best efforts of planning and implementation, it is not possible to achieve perfect information security. Information security is a process, not an end state. Information security must balance protection of information and information assets with the availability of that information to its authorized users. It is possible to permit access to a system so that it is available to anyone, anywhere, anytime, through any means—that is, maximum availability. However, this poses a danger to both the confidentiality and the integrity of the information. On the other hand, to achieve the maximum confidentiality and integrity found in a completely secure information system would require that the system not allow access to anyone.

To achieve balance—that is, to operate an information system that meets the high level of availability sought by system users as well as the confidentiality and integrity needs of system owners and security professionals—the level of security must allow reasonable access, yet protect against threats. An imbalance between access and security often occurs when the accessibility needs of the end user fall short due to requirements for protecting the information or when security has been neglected to improve accessibility. Both sides in this trade-off must exercise patience and cooperation when interacting with the other, as both should recognize that they have the same overall goal—to ensure that the data is available when, where, and how it is needed, with minimal delays or obstacles. Using the principles of information security, it is possible to address that level of availability, even with consideration of the concerns for loss, damage, interception, or destruction.

Business Needs First

Information security performs these four important organizational functions:

1. Protects the organization's ability to function

2. Enables the safe operation of applications implemented on the organization's IT systems

3. Protects the data the organization collects and uses

4. Safeguards the technology assets in use at the organization

Protecting the Functionality of an Organization

Both general management and IT management are responsible for implementing information security to protect the organization's ability to function. Although many managers shy away from addressing information security because they perceive it to be a technically complex task, information security has more to do with management than with technology. Just as managing payroll has more to do with management than with mathematical wage computations, managing information security has more to do with policy and enforcement of policy than with the technology of its implementation.

Enabling the Safe Operation of Applications

Organizations are under immense pressure to acquire and operate integrated, efficient, and capable information systems. They need to safeguard applications, particularly those that serve as important elements of the infrastructure of the organization, such as operating system platforms, electronic mail (e-mail), instant messaging (IM), and all the other applications that make up the current IT environment.

Protecting Data That Organizations Collect and Use

Almost all organizations rely on information systems to support their essential functions. Even if a transaction is not online, information systems and the data they process enable the creation and movement of goods and services. Therefore, protecting data in motion, data at rest, and data while it is being processed is a critical aspect of information security. The value of data motivates attackers to steal, sabotage, or corrupt it. An effective information security program directed by management is essential to the protection of the integrity and value of the organization's data.

Safeguarding Technology Assets in Organizations

To perform effectively, organizations must provide secure infrastructure services to meet the needs of the enterprise. In general, as the organization's network grows to accommodate changing needs, it may need more robust technology solutions. An example of a robust solution is a firewall, a device that keeps certain kinds of network traffic out of the internal network. Another example is caching network appliances, which are devices that store local copies of Internet content, such as Web pages that employees frequently refer to. The appliance displays the cached pages to users rather than accessing the pages on the remote server each time.

Security Professionals and the Organization

It takes a wide range of professionals to support the complex information security program needed by a moderate or large organization. Senior management is the key component for a successful implementation of an information security program. But administrative support is also needed to develop and execute specific security policies and procedures, and technical expertise is needed to implement the details of the information security program.

We will now describe the various professional positions that are involved in a typical organization's information security.

The **chief information officer (CIO)** is often the senior technology officer. Other titles, such as vice president (VP) of information, VP of information technology, or VP of systems, may be used. The CIO is primarily responsible for advising the chief executive officer, president, or company owner on the strategic planning that affects the management of information in the organization.

The **chief information security officer (CISO)** is the individual primarily responsible for the assessment, management, and implementation of information security in the organization. The CISO may also be referred to as the manager for IT security, the security administrator, information security officer (ISO), chief security officer (CSO), or by a similar title. The CISO usually reports directly to the CIO, although in larger organizations it is not uncommon for one or more layers of management to exist between the two.

The information security **project team** consists of a number of individuals experienced in one or more facets of the vast array of required technical and nontechnical areas. Many of the same skills needed to manage and implement security are also needed to design it. Members of the security project team assume the following roles:

- **Champion**—A senior executive who promotes the project and ensures that it is supported, both financially and administratively, at the highest levels of the organization.
- **Team leader**—An individual, perhaps a departmental line manager or a staff unit manager, who understands project management, personnel management, and information security technical requirements.
- **Security policy developers**—Individuals who understand the organizational culture, existing policies, and requirements for developing and implementing successful policies.
- **Risk assessment specialists**—Individuals who understand financial risk assessment techniques, the value of organizational assets, and the security methods to be used.
- **Security professionals**—Specialists in all aspects of information security, both technical and nontechnical.
- **Systems, network, and storage administrators**—Individuals with the primary responsibility for administering the systems, storage, and networks that house and provide access to the organization's information.
- **End users**—Those who will be most directly affected by new implementations and changes to existing systems. Ideally, a selection of users from various departments, levels, and degrees of technical knowledge will help the team focus on realistic controls applied in ways that do not disrupt the essential business activities they seek to safeguard.

Data Management

Every information asset and piece of data used by the organization was developed by someone for a particular purpose. The use of that data involves three categories of data managers, whose very specific responsibilities with regard to the protection and use of that data are as follows:

- **Data owners**—Data owners own the data and are responsible for the security and use of a particular set of information. They are usually members of senior management and are usually business division managers. Data owners are responsible for determining who can access the data, and under what circumstances. Data owners work with data custodians to oversee the day-to-day administration of the data.

- **Data custodians**—Data custodians work directly with data owners and are responsible for the storage, maintenance, and protection of the information. Depending on the size of the organization, the custodian may be a dedicated position, such as the CISO, or it may be an additional responsibility of a systems administrator or other technology manager. The duties of a data custodian often include overseeing data storage and backups, implementing the specific practices and procedures specified in the security policies and plans, and reporting to the data owner.

- **Data users**—Data users are those in the organization who are allowed by the data owner to access and use the information to perform their daily jobs supporting the mission of the organization. Data users therefore share the responsibility for data security.

Key Information Security Terminology

In order to effectively support any information security effort, including the design, implementation, and administration of an effective perimeter defense, the security professional must be familiar with certain common terms.

Threats and Attacks

In general, a **threat** is a category of object, person, or other entity that poses a potential risk of loss to an asset—that is, the organizational resource that is being protected. Examples of threats are presented later in this chapter.

An **asset** is anything that has value for the organization. It can be physical, such as a person, computer system, or other tangible object. Alternatively, an asset can be logical, such as a computer program, a Web site, or a set of information. An **attack** is an intentional or unintentional action that could represent the unauthorized modification, damage, or loss of an information asset. Some common attacks are presented later in this chapter.

When considering the security of information systems components, it is important to understand that a computer can be the subject of an attack or the object of an attack. When a computer is the **subject of an attack**, it is used as an active tool to conduct the attack. When a computer is the **object of an attack**, it is the entity being attacked. Figure 1-2 illustrates computers as the subject and object of an attack. There are also two types of attacks: direct attacks and indirect attacks. A **direct attack** is when a hacker uses a personal computer to break into a system. An **indirect attack** is when a system is compromised and used to attack other systems, such as in a botnet (a collection of software programs that operate autonomously to attack systems and steal user information) or other distributed denial-of-service attack. Direct attacks originate from the threat itself. Indirect attacks originate from a system or resource that itself has been attacked and is malfunctioning or working under the control of a threat. A computer can, therefore, be both the subject and object of an attack when, for example, it is first the object of an attack and then compromised and used to attack other systems, at which point it becomes the subject of an attack.

Internet

Stolen information

Hacker request

Hacker using a
computer as the
subject of an attack

Remote system that is
the **object** of an attack

Figure 1-2 Computer as the Subject and Object of an Attack
© Cengage Learning 2012

Vulnerabilities and Exploits

A **threat agent** is a specific instance of a general threat. As an example, an act of electronic trespass could be considered a general threat, whereas the threat agent would be a particular hacker. The threat agent exploits vulnerabilities in the controls that protect an asset. A **vulnerability** is a weakness or fault in the mechanisms that are intended to protect information and information assets from attack or damage. Vulnerabilities that have been examined, documented, and published are referred to as **well-known vulnerabilities**. Some vulnerabilities are latent, however, and thus are not revealed until they are later discovered.

There are two common uses of the term "**exploit**" in security. One use is for when threat agents attempt to exploit a system or information asset. For example, we may say a hacker exploits a known flaw in a program to complete a successful attack. The other use is for the specific recipe that an attacker creates to formulate an attack. For example, we might say that an elite hacker has posted an exploit for a new vulnerability on a Web site, thus allowing some script kiddies to make attacks otherwise beyond their skill level. Defenders try to prevent attacks by applying **controls, safeguards,** or **countermeasures**. These terms, all synonymous, refer to security mechanisms, policies, or procedures that can successfully counter attacks, reduce risk, resolve vulnerabilities, and generally improve the security within an organization.

Risk

Risk is the state of being unsecure, either partially or totally, and thus susceptible to attack, as in "at risk." Risk is usually described in terms of **likelihood**, which is the possibility or probability of unwanted action on an information asset. This is usually a concern for the loss, damage, unwanted modification, or disclosure of information assets. Dealing with risk is the task of **risk management**, which involves risk identification, risk assessment or analysis, and risk control. All organizations must live with some level of risk. The amount of risk an organization chooses to live with is called its **risk appetite** or **risk tolerance**. The amount of risk that remains after an organization takes precautions, implements controls and safeguards, and performs other security activities is termed **residual risk**.

Organizations control risk by implementing options from among the following four major strategies:

- Self-protection—Applying safeguards that eliminate or reduce the remaining uncontrolled risks. This is the main task of the information security professional: implementing effective controls to reduce risk. These steps are most often preventive in nature.
- Risk transfer—Shifting the risk to other areas or to outside entities, such as insurance companies or security management firms.

- Self-insurance or acceptance—Understanding the consequences and acknowledging the risk without attempting to control or mitigate it. Acceptance is a viable solution only if the organization has evaluated the risk and determined that the implementation of additional controls or strategies is not justified, due to cost or other organizational issues. Another aspect of this strategy involves reducing the impact should an attacker successfully exploit the vulnerability. This reduction in impact is done through the implementation of Incident Response, Disaster Recovery, and Business Continuity plans.

- Avoidance—Not engaging in certain types of activities to avoid the risk that those activities might bring with them. For example, a company that sells products using a catalog and mail-order model may choose not to engage in e-commerce because it wants to avoid the risks from operating an online business-to-consumer Web presence. If a company wanted to avoid the risks of handling credit card transactions, it might avoid that part of an e-commerce application by outsourcing it to another business entity, perhaps a bank or an online payment service.

Security Perimeter and Defense in Depth

An organization will often create a network **security perimeter**, which defines the boundary between the outer limit of an organization's security and the beginning of the outside network. A security perimeter attempts to protect internal systems from outside threats, as pictured in Figure 1-3. Unfortunately, the perimeter does not protect against internal attacks from employee threats or on-site physical threats. There can be both an electronic security perimeter, usually at the organization's exterior network or Internet connection, and a physical security perimeter, usually at the gate to the organization's offices. Both require forms of perimeter security.

Security perimeters may be implemented in multiple layers, with graduations in the level of security; they may also be implemented using multiple technologies (see the discussion of defense in depth that follows). These efforts seek to separate the protected information from potential

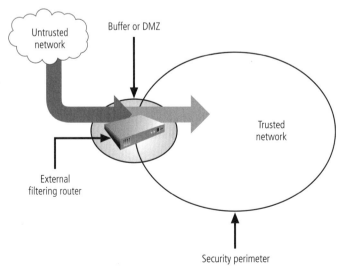

Figure 1-3 Security Perimeter
© Cengage Learning 2012

attackers. Within the established security perimeters, the organization may choose to set up security domains—that is, areas of trust within which users can freely communicate. In this approach, users with access to one system within a security domain have access to all systems within that particular domain. The security perimeter is an essential element of the overall security framework, and its implementation details are the core of the security blueprint. The key components of the perimeter include firewalls, DMZs, proxy servers, and intrusion detection systems. It should be noted that network endpoints are proliferating outside the usually defined perimeter. This includes mobile devices and remote computing solutions used by employees and business partners to gain increased availability to critical business data. This is a challenge to the traditional definition of an organization's perimeter.[4] Enterprises must carefully consider how these new technologies can redefine the location of the perimeter.

One of the basic tenets of security architecture is the layered implementation of security. This layered approach is called defense in depth. To achieve **defense in depth,** an organization must establish multiple layers of security controls and safeguards, which can be organized into policy, training and education, and technology, as per the CNSS model discussed earlier. While policy itself may not prevent attacks, it certainly prepares the organization to handle them; and coupled with other layers, it can deter attacks. This is true of training and education, which can also provide some defense against nontechnical attacks such as employee ignorance and social engineering. Social engineering occurs when attackers try to use social interaction with members of the organization to acquire information that can be used to make further exploits against information assets possible. It will be further discussed later in this chapter.

Technology is also implemented in layers, with detection equipment working in tandem with reaction technology, all operating behind access control mechanisms. Implementing multiple types of technology, thereby preventing one system's failure from compromising the security of information, is referred to as redundancy. Redundancy can be implemented at a number of points throughout the security architecture, such as firewalls, proxy servers, and access controls. Figure 1-4 illustrates the concept of building controls in multiple, sometimes redundant layers. The figure shows the use of firewalls and intrusion detection systems (IDS) that use both packet-level rules (shown as the header in the diagram) and data content analysis (shown as 0100101011).

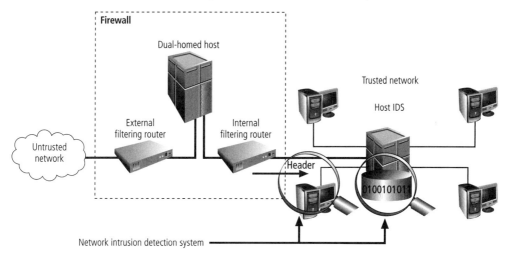

Figure 1-4 Defense in Depth
© Cengage Learning 2012

Threats to Information Security

Around 500 B.C., the Chinese general Sun Tzu wrote a treatise on warfare, *Art of War*. It contains military strategies still studied by military leaders and students today. In one of his most famous passages, Sun Tzu writes, "If you know the enemy and know yourself, you need not fear the result of a hundred battles. If you know yourself but not the enemy, for every victory gained you will also suffer a defeat. If you know neither the enemy nor yourself, you will succumb in every battle."[5] In the battle to protect information, you must know yourself—that is, be familiar with the information to be protected, and the systems that store, transport, and process it. You must also know the enemy. To make sound decisions about information security, management must be informed about the various threats facing the organization, its people, applications, data, and information systems—that is, the enemy.

As defined earlier, a threat poses a potential risk of loss to an asset—that is, the organizational resource that is being protected. Threats use attacks on information to cause damage to or otherwise compromise the information and/or the systems that support it. To understand the wide range of threats that pervade the interconnected world, researchers have interviewed practicing information security personnel and examined information security literature on threats. While the categorizations may vary, threats are relatively well researched and, consequently, fairly well understood.

The Computer Security Institute (CSI) Computer Crime and Security Survey, the results of which are shown in Table 1-1, is a representative study that reveals how many organizations have experienced the listed types of attack or misuse. As you can see, the line between threats and attacks is sometimes blurred, such as when a systems penetration also results in a loss of customer data. However, you can also see that a number of threats have been dominant for some time.

Type of Attack or Misuse	2009	2008	2007	2006	2005	2004	2003	2002	2001	2000	1999
Malware infection (renamed 2009)	64%	50%	52%	65%	74%	78%	82%	85%	94%	85%	90%
Laptop or mobile hardware theft or loss	42%	42%	50%	47%	48%	49%	59%	55%	64%	60%	69%
Being fraudulently represented as sender of phishing message (new category in 2007)	34%	31%	26%								
Insider abuse of Net access or e-mail	30%	44%	59%	42%	48%	59%	80%	78%	91%	79%	97%
Denial of service	29%	21%	25%	25%	32%	39%	42%	40%	36%	27%	31%
Bots within the organization (new category in 2007)	23%	20%	21%								

Table 1-1   CSI/FBI Computer Crime and Security Survey (continues)

Type of Attack or Misuse	2009	2008	2007	2006	2005	2004	2003	2002	2001	2000	1999
Financial fraud	20%	12%	12%	9%	7%	8%	15%	12%	12%	11%	14%
Password sniffing (new category in 2007)	17%	9%	10%								
Unauthorized access or privilege escalation by insider (alteredcategory in 2009)	15%										
Web site defacement (new category in 2004)	14%	6%	10%	6%	5%	7%					
System penetration by outsider (altered category in 2009)	14%										
Exploit of client Web browser (new category in 2009)	11%										
Theft of or unauthorized access to PII or PHI due to all other causes (new category in 2008)	10%	8%									
Instant Messaging misuse (new category in 2007)	8%	21%	25%								
Exploit of wireless network (new category in 2004)	8%	14%	17%	14%	17%	15%					
Theft of or unauthorized access to IP due to all other causes (new category in 2008)	8%	5%									
Exploit of DNS Server (new category in 2007)	7%	8%	7%								
Exploit of user's social network profile (new category in 2009)	7%										
Other exploit of public-facing Web site (new category in 2009)	6%										
Theft of or unauthorized access to IP due to mobile device theft or loss(new category in 2008)	6%	4%									

Table 1-1 CSI/FBI Computer Crime and Security Survey (continues)

Type of Attack or Misuse	2009	2008	2007	2006	2005	2004	2003	2002	2001	2000	1999
Theft of or unauthorized access to PII or PHI due to mobile device theft or loss (new category in 2008)	6%	8%									
Extortion or blackmail associated with threat of attack or release of stolen data (new category in 2009)	3%										
The following categories were replaced or dropped in subsequent years.											
Unauthorized access to information		29%	25%	32%	32%	37%	45%	38%	49%	71%	55%
Theft/loss of customer/ employee data (new category in 2007)		17%	17%								
System penetration		13%	13%	15%	14%	17%	36%	40%	40%	25%	30%
Misuse of public Web applications (new category in 2004)		11%	9%	6%	5%	10%					
Theft/Loss of proprietary information		9%	8%	9%	9%	10%	21%	20%	26%	20%	25%
Telecommunications fraud		5%	5%	8%	10%	10%	10%	9%	10%	11%	17%
Sabotage		2%	4%	3%	2%	5%	21%	8%	18%	17%	13%
Telecomm eavesdropping							6%	6%	10%	7%	14%
Active wiretap							1%	1%	2%	1%	2%

Table 1-1 CSI/FBI Computer Crime and Security Survey (continued)

Source: CSI/FBI surveys 1999–2009 (www.gocsi.com)

illustrates 12 categories that represent a clear and present danger to an organization's people, information, and systems.[6] Each organization must prioritize the dangers it faces, based on the particular security situation in which it operates, its organizational strategy regarding risk, and the exposure levels in which its assets operate. Keep in mind, while looking at Table 1-2, that many threats could be listed in more than one category. For example, an act of theft performed by a hacker would fall into the theft category, but because theft is often accompanied by defacement actions to delay discovery, it might also fall into the sabotage-or-vandalism category.

The TVA Triple

As part of risk management, mentioned earlier, the need to "know yourself" involves identifying and prioritizing your information assets, which is a complex process. The next step is identifying and prioritizing the threats to those assets. Finally, you need to identify the vari-

Category of Threat	Examples
1. Human error or failure	Accidents, employee mistakes, or failure to follow established policies or procedures
2. Compromises to intellectual property	Theft or unauthorized use of written documents, trade secrets, copyrights, trademarks, and patents, including software piracy
3. Espionage or trespass	Unauthorized access and/or data collection, hacking
4. Information extortion	Blackmail or information disclosure
5. Sabotage or vandalism	Destruction of systems or information
6. Theft	Illegal confiscation of equipment or information
7. Software attacks	Malicious code or malware attacks, including viruses, worms, macros, denial-of-service, and Trojan horses
8. Forces of nature	Fire, flood, earthquake, lightning, and electrostatic discharge
9. Deviations in quality of service	ISP, power, or WAN service issues from service providers
10. Hardware failures or errors	Equipment failure
11. Software failures or errors	Bugs, code problems, unknown loopholes
12. Obsolescence	Antiquated or outdated technologies

Table 1-2 Threats to Information Security[7]

ous vulnerabilities that each threat poses to each asset. This gives you a "TVA Triple" of Threat-Vulnerability-Asset that you can use to prioritize your work, each vulnerability being expressed as the intersection of a particular threat and a particular asset. Here are the first three examples, which could be continued indefinitely:

T1-V1-A1—Vulnerability 1 that exists between Threat 1 and Asset 1

T1-V2-A1—Vulnerability 2 that exists between Threat 1 and Asset 1

T1-V1-A2—Vulnerability 1 that exists between Threat 1 and Asset 2

These triples can be organized in a TVA worksheet, in preparation for adding the vulnerability and control information during risk assessment. Table 1-3, an example of such a worksheet, shows the placement of assets along the horizontal axis, with the most important asset at the left. The prioritized list of threats is placed along the vertical axis, with the most important or most dangerous threat listed at the top. The resulting grid provides a convenient method for examining the "exposure" of the various assets, allowing for a simple vulnerability assessment. We now have a starting point for our efforts—that is, addressing the highest prioritized TVA triple.

The next step in the risk management process is to examine whether or not the organization has sufficient controls to protect the assets in the triples from their corresponding threats, or at least mitigate the losses that may occur. Cataloging and categorizing these controls is the next step in the TVA worksheet. The final document becomes a valuable tool in planning the work effort in the security department.

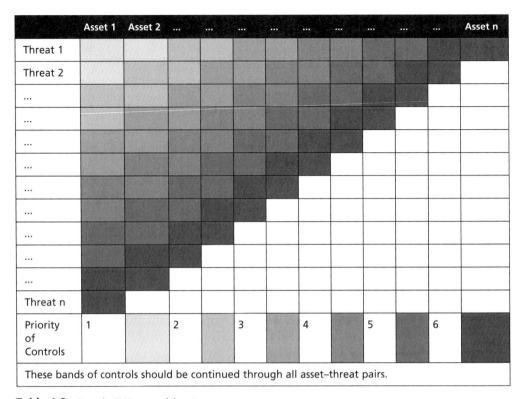

	Asset 1	Asset 2	...	...	...	...	...	...	...	...	...	Asset n
Threat 1												
Threat 2												
...												
...												
...												
...												
...												
...												
...												
...												
...												
Threat n												
Priority of Controls	1		2		3		4		5		6	
These bands of controls should be continued through all asset–threat pairs.												

Table 1-3 Sample TVA spreadsheet

Other Ways to View Threats

In addition to viewing threats from the perspective of the assets being attached, we can view them from the following perspectives:

- **Intellectual property**—The control of ideas and innovation, known as intellectual property, or IP, is an important part of the value of assets that organizations control. When organizations use the intellectual property of others under licensing or other arrangements, they should be mindful of the rights of the owner of that intellectual property. Whether or not we pay for the right to use the ideas of others, we "should always include proper credit to the source."[8]

- **Software piracy**—The most common IP breach; the unlawful use or duplication of software-based intellectual property

- **Shoulder surfing**—Observing another's password by watching system login activities

- **Hackers**—Individuals who gain access to information or systems without explicit authorization, often illegally. Hackers are often described by the skill levels they possess, with so-called elite hackers being the most skilled

- **Script kiddies**—Hackers of limited skill who use expertly written software to attack a system

- **Packet monkeys**—Script kiddies who use automated exploits to engage in distributed denial-of-service attacks

- **Cracker**—An individual who "cracks" (i.e., removes) software protection that is designed to prevent unauthorized duplication or use
- **Phreaker**—An individual who hacks the public telephone network to make free calls or disrupt services
- **Hacktivist or cyberactivist**—An individual who, sometimes working with others, interferes with or disrupts systems to protest the operations, policies, or actions of an organization or government agency
- **Cyberterrorist**—An individual who, sometimes working with others, hacks systems to conduct terrorist activities through a network or Internet pathway
- **Malicious code, malicious software,** or **malware**—Software components or programs designed to damage, destroy, or deny service to the target systems; examples include:
  - **Computer viruses**—Segments of code that perform malicious actions; examples include:
    - **macro virus**—A virus that is embedded in the automatically executing macro code common in word processors, spreadsheets, and database applications
    - **boot virus**—A virus that infects the key operating system files located in a computer's boot sector
  - **worms**—Malicious programs that replicate themselves constantly, without requiring another program to provide a safe environment for replication
  - **Trojan horses**—Software programs that reveal their designed behavior only when activated
  - **back door, trap door,** or **maintenance hook**—A component in a system that allows the attacker to access the system at will, bypassing standard login controls
  - **Rootkit**—A collection of software tools and a recipe used to gain control of a system by bypassing its legitimate security controls
- **Power irregularities**—Variations in the 120–volt, 60–cycle power provided to most businesses through a 15 or 20 amp circuit. Variations include:
  - **Spike**—A momentary increase in power
  - **Surge**—A prolonged increase in power
  - **Sag**—A momentary drop in voltage level
  - **Brownout**—A more prolonged drop in voltage level
  - **Fault**—A complete loss of power for a moment
  - **Blackout**—A lengthy loss of power

Attacks on Information Assets

As defined earlier, an attack is an act that takes advantage of a vulnerability to compromise a controlled system. A threat is brought closer to realization by a threat agent that attempts to damage or steal an organization's information or physical asset. Unlike threats, which are ever present, attacks occur through a specific act that may cause a potential loss. For example, the threat of damage from a thunderstorm is present during most of the summer in many places, but an attack and its associated risk of loss only exist for the duration of an actual thunderstorm. The following sections discuss each of the major types of attack used against controlled systems.

Malicious Code

Malicious code includes viruses, worms, Trojan horses, and active Web scripts that are executed with the intent to destroy or steal information. The state-of-the-art malicious code attack is the polymorphic (having many shapes), multivector (attacks in many ways) worm, which constantly changes the way it looks and then uses multiple attack vectors to exploit a variety of vulnerabilities in commonly used software. When malware is polymorphic, it is more difficult to detect and intercept. Likewise, when malware uses multiple attack vectors, it becomes more complicated and expensive to defend against. Table 1-4 outlines the six categories of attack vectors.

Vector	Description
IP scan and attack	The infected system scans a random or local range of IP addresses and targets any of several vulnerabilities known to hackers or left over from previous exploits such as Code Red, Back Orifice, or PoizonBox.
Web browsing	If the infected system has write access to any Web pages, it makes all Web content files (.html, .asp, .cgi, and others) infectious, so that users who browse to those pages become infected.
Virus	Each infected machine infects certain common executable or script files on all the computers to which it has write access with virus code that can cause infection.
Unprotected shares	Using vulnerabilities in file systems and the way many organizations configure them, the infected machine copies the viral component to all locations it can reach.
Mass mail	By sending e-mail infections to recipients in the address book, the infected machine infects many users, whose mail-reading programs also automatically run the program and infect other systems.
Simple Network Management Protocol (SNMP)	By using the common passwords that were employed in early versions of this protocol, which was widely used for remote management of network and computer devices, the attacker program can gain control of a device.

Table 1-4 Attack Vectors

Compromising Passwords

There are a number of attacks that attempt to bypass access controls by guessing passwords. Their methods range from attempting to make educated guesses based on the background of the individual to guessing every possible combination of letters, numbers, and special characters. The most common password attacks are cracking, the brute force attack, and the dictionary attack.

Cracking Attempting to guess a password is often called **cracking**. A cracking attack is a component of many dictionary attacks, which are discussed shortly. It is used when a copy of a system password file is obtained. The attacker then uses cracking techniques to search that file for a match. When a match is found, the password has been cracked.

Brute Force The application of computing and network resources to try every possible combination of options for a password is called a **brute force attack**. Since this often involves repeatedly guessing passwords for commonly used accounts, it is sometimes called a **password attack**. If attackers can narrow the field of target accounts, they can devote more time and resources to attacking fewer accounts. That is one reason to change account names for common accounts from the manufacturer's default.

While often effective against low-security systems, brute force attacks are often not useful against systems that have adopted the usual security practices recommended by manufacturers. Controls that limit the number of attempts allowed per unit of elapsed time are very effective at combating brute force attacks. Defenses against brute force attacks are usually adopted early on in any security effort and are thoroughly covered in the SANS/FBI list of the 20 most critical Internet security vulnerabilities.[9]

Dictionary The **dictionary attack**, which is a variation on the brute force attack, narrows the field by selecting specific target accounts and using a list of commonly used passwords (the dictionary) instead of random combinations. Organizations can use such dictionaries themselves to disallow passwords during the reset process and thus guard against easy-to-guess passwords. In addition, rules requiring additional numbers and/or special characters make the dictionary attack less effective. Another variant, called a rainbow attack, makes use of a precomputed hash using a time-memory tradeoff technique that uses a database of precomputed hashes from sequentially calculated passwords to look up the hashed password and read out the text version, with no brute force required.

Denial-of-Service (DoS) and Distributed Denial-of-Service (DDoS)

In a **denial-of-service** (DoS) attack, the attacker sends a large number of connection or information requests to a target (see Figure 1-5). So many requests are made that the target system cannot handle them along with other, legitimate requests for service. The system may crash, or it may simply be unable to perform ordinary functions. A **distributed denial-of-service**

In a denial-of-service attack, a hacker compromises a system and uses that system to attack the target computer, flooding it with more requests for services than the target can handle.

In a distributed denial-of-service attack, dozens or even hundreds of computers (known as zombies) are compromised, loaded with DoS attack software, and then remotely activated by the hacker to conduct a coordinated attack.

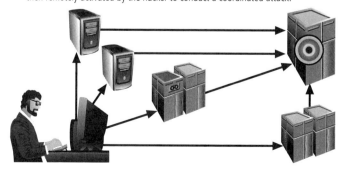

Figure 1-5 Denial-of-Service Attacks
© Cengage Learning 2012

(DDoS) launches a coordinated stream of requests against a target from many locations at the same time. Most DDoS attacks are preceded by a preparation phase in which many systems, perhaps thousands, are compromised. The compromised machines are turned into **zombies** (or **bots**), machines that are directed remotely (usually by a transmitted command) by the attacker to participate in the attack. DDoS attacks are the most difficult to defend against, and there are presently no controls that any single organization can apply. There are, however, some cooperative efforts to enable DDoS defenses among groups of service providers. (Among them is the "Consensus Roadmap for Defeating Distributed Denial of Service Attacks".[10]) To use a popular metaphor, DDoS is considered a weapon of mass destruction on the Internet.[11]

Any system connected to the Internet that provides TCP-based network services (such as a Web server, an FTP server, or mail server) is a potential target for denial-of-service attacks. Note that in addition to attacks launched at specific hosts, these attacks can be launched against routers or other network server systems if these hosts enable (or turn on) other TCP services (e.g., echo). Even though such attacks make use of a fundamental element of the TCP protocol used by all systems, the consequences of the attacks may vary, depending on the system.[12]

Spoofing

Spoofing is a technique used to gain unauthorized access to computers, wherein the intruder sends messages to IP addresses that indicate to the recipient that the messages are coming from a trusted host. To engage in IP spoofing, a hacker must first use a variety of techniques to find an IP address of a trusted host and then modify the packet headers (see Figure 1-6) to make it appear that the packets are coming from that host.[13] Newer routers and firewall arrangements offer protection against IP spoofing.

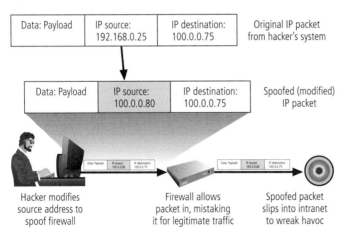

Figure 1-6 IP Spoofing
© Cengage Learning 2012

Man-in-the-Middle

In the well-known **man-in-the-middle** attack, the attacker monitors (or sniffs) packets from the network, modifies them using IP spoofing techniques, and then inserts them back into the network, which allows the attacker to eavesdrop as well as change, delete, reroute, add, forge, or divert data.[14] In a variant attack, the spoofing involves the interception of an encryption key exchange, which enables the hacker to act as an invisible man-in-the-middle—that is, an eavesdropper—in encrypted exchanges. Figure 1-7 illustrates these attacks by showing how a hacker uses public and private encryption keys to intercept messages.

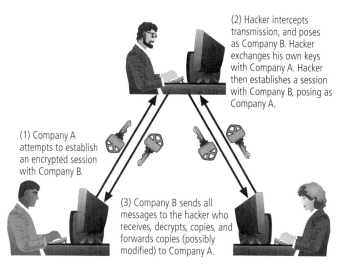

(2) Hacker intercepts transmission, and poses as Company B. Hacker exchanges his own keys with Company A. Hacker then establishes a session with Company B, posing as Company A.

(1) Company A attempts to establish an encrypted session with Company B.

(3) Company B sends all messages to the hacker who receives, decrypts, copies, and forwards copies (possibly modified) to Company A.

Figure 1-7 Man-in-the-Middle Attack
© Cengage Learning 2012

E-Mail Attacks

A number of attacks focus on the use of e-mail to deny service to the user (a form of denial of service), to exploit the inexperience of the user, or to trick the user into installing back doors or viruses. In general, e-mail is the vehicle for attacks rather than the attack itself. However, there are also specific e-mail attacks, which are described next.

Spam Spam, or unsolicited commercial e-mail, has been used as a means to make malicious code attacks more effective. In some cases, malicious code is embedded in MP3 files that are included as attachments to spam.[15] The most significant impact of spam, however, is the waste of both computer and human resources. Many organizations attempt to cope with the flood of spam by using filtering technologies to stem the flow. Other organizations simply tell users of their mail systems to delete unwanted messages.

Mail Bombing A **mail bomb** is an e-mail attack in which the attacker routes large quantities of e-mail to the target system. This can be accomplished through social engineering (to be discussed shortly) or by exploiting various technical flaws in the Simple Mail Transport Protocol. The target of the attack receives unmanageably large volumes of unsolicited e-mail. By sending large e-mails with forged header information, attackers can take advantage of poorly configured e-mail systems and trick them into sending many e-mails to an address chosen by the attacker. If many such systems are tricked into participating in the event, the target e-mail address is buried under thousands or even millions of unwanted e-mails.

Sniffers

A **sniffer** is a program or device that can monitor data traveling over a network. Sniffers can be used both for legitimate network management functions and for stealing information from a network. Unauthorized sniffers can be extremely dangerous to a network's security, because they are impossible to detect and can be inserted almost anywhere. This makes them a favorite weapon in the hacker's arsenal. Sniffers often work on TCP/IP networks, where they are sometimes referred to as **packet sniffers**.[16] Sniffers add risk to the network, because many systems and users send information on local networks in clear text. A sniffer program shows all the data going by, including passwords, the data inside files (such as word-processing documents), and screens full of sensitive data.

Social Engineering

Within the context of information security, **social engineering** is the process of using social skills to convince people to reveal access credentials or other valuable information to the attacker. This can be done in several ways and usually involves the perpetrator posing as a person higher in the organizational hierarchy than the victim. To prepare for this false representation, the perpetrator may have used social engineering against others in the organization by collecting seemingly unrelated information that, when used together, makes the false representation more credible. For instance, anyone can call the main switchboard of a company and get the name of the CIO, but an attacker may find it just as easy to get even more information by calling others in the company and asserting his or her (false) authority by mentioning the CIO's name. Social engineering attacks may involve individuals posing as new employees or as current employees desperately requesting assistance to avoid getting fired. Sometimes, attackers threaten, cajole, or beg in order to sway the target.

An example of a social engineering attack is the so-called Advance Fee Fraud (AFF), which is known internationally as the "4-1-9" fraud (named after a section of the Nigerian penal code). The perpetrators of 4-1-9 schemes often use fictitious companies, such as the Nigerian National Petroleum Company. Alternatively, they may invent other entities, such as a bank, a government agency, or a nongovernmental organization such as a lottery corporation. This scam is notorious for stealing funds from gullible individuals, first by requiring them to send money up-front in order to participate in a proposed money-making venture, and then by charging an endless series of fees. These 4-1-9 schemes have even been linked to kidnapping, extortion, and murder; and they have, according to the United States Secret Service, bilked over $100 million from unsuspecting Americans lured into disclosing personal banking information.

The infamous hacker Kevin Mitnick once stated: "People are the weakest link. You can have the best technology, [then] somebody call[s] an unsuspecting employee. That's all she wrote, baby. They got everything."[17]

Buffer Overflow

A **buffer overflow** is an application error that occurs when more data is sent to a buffer than it can handle. During a buffer overflow, the attacker can make the target system execute instructions, or the attacker can take advantage of some other unintended consequence of the failure. Sometimes, this is limited to a denial-of-service attack, when the attacked system crashes and is (until it's restarted) unavailable to users. In either case, data on the attacked system loses integrity.[18] In 1998, Microsoft revealed that it had been vulnerable to a buffer overflow problem, as described here:

> *Microsoft acknowledged that if you type a res:// URL (a Microsoft-devised type of URL) [that] is longer than 256 characters in Internet Explorer 4.0, the browser will crash. No big deal, except that anything after the 256th character*

can be executed on the computer. This maneuver, known as a buffer overrun, is just about the oldest hacker trick in the book. Tack some malicious code (say, an executable version of the Pentium-crashing FooF code) onto the end of the URL, and you have the makings of a disaster.[19]

Running Case: Connecting the Dots

Mike Edwards, Jr. looked across the table at Alex Truman, IT manager for Data Mart.

"And that's how you build a comprehensive security program, including an effective perimeter defense," he told Alex after several hours of explaining.

"Wow," Alex said, leaning back in his chair. "I thought I understood the terminology, but I never realized it was so complicated. You've laid everything out so well, I think I now understand why we're in such trouble."

Mike smiled. "That's what you pay us for, to help connect the dots."

"So where do we start?" Alex laughed.

"We'll start with risk management—identifying your information assets, and then looking at the threats to those assets. Then we'll look for vulnerabilities in those assets that could be attacked by those threats."

"Ah!" Alex nodded. "That I understand."

Chapter Summary

- Firewalls and network security have become essential components for securing the systems that businesses use to run their day-to-day operations. Before learning how to plan, design, and implement firewalls and network security, it is important to understand the larger issue of information security.

- Information security is the protection of information and its critical elements, including the systems and hardware that use, store, and transmit that information. The C.I.A. triangle is based on the confidentiality, integrity, and availability of information and the systems that process it.

- The value of information comes from the characteristics it possesses. When a characteristic of information changes, the value of that information either increases or, more commonly, decreases.

- The CNSS security model is known as the McCumber Cube and was created by John McCumber in 1991. It provides a graphical description of the architectural approach widely used in computer and information security.

- Securing information and its systems entails securing all components and protecting them from potential misuse and abuse by unauthorized users. When considering the security of information systems components, it is important to understand that a computer can be the subject of an attack or the object of an attack. There are also two types of attacks: direct attacks and indirect attacks.

- Information security cannot be an absolute: it is a process, not a goal. Information security should balance protection and availability. To achieve balance—that is, to operate an information system to the satisfaction of the user and the security professional—the level of security must allow reasonable access, yet protect against threats.

- Information security performs four important organizational functions: protecting the organization's ability to function, enabling the safe operation of applications implemented on the organization's IT systems, protecting the data the organization collects and uses, and safeguarding the technology assets in use at the organization.

- It takes a wide range of professionals to support the information security program: senior managers, system administrator support, and technical experts.

- A threat is an object, person, or other entity that represents a constant danger to an asset. Threats to information security fall into 12 categories: (1) human error or failure, (2) compromises to intellectual property, (3) espionage or trespass, (4) information extortion, (5) sabotage or vandalism, (6) theft, (7) software attacks, (8) forces of nature, (9) deviations in quality of service, (10) hardware failures or errors, (11) software failures or errors, and (12) obsolescence.

- An attack is an act that takes advantage of a vulnerability to compromise a controlled system. A vulnerability is an identified weakness in a controlled system. Attacks occur as a specific act that may cause a potential loss. There are major types of attacks, including: malicious code, back doors, password cracking, denial-of-service (DoS) and distributed denial-of-service (DDoS), spoofing, man-in-the-middle, spam, mail bombing, sniffers, social engineering, buffer overflow, and timing attacks.

- In order to most effectively secure its networks, an organization must establish a functional and well-designed information security program in the context of a well-planned and fully defined information policy and planning environment. The creation of an information security program requires information security policies, standards and practices, an information security architecture, and a detailed information security blueprint.

Review Questions

1. What is the difference between a threat agent and a threat?
2. What is the difference between vulnerability and exposure?
3. What is a hacker? What is a phreaker?
4. What are the three components of the C.I.A. triangle? What are they used for?
5. If the C.I.A. triangle no longer adequately addresses the constantly changing environment of the information technology industry, why is it still commonly used in security?
6. Who is ultimately responsible for the security of information in an organization?
7. What does it mean to discover an exploit? How does an exploit differ from a vulnerability?
8. Why is data the most important asset an organization possesses? What other assets in the organization require protection?

9. It is important to protect data in motion (transmission) and data at rest (storage). In what other state must data be protected? In which of the three states is data most difficult to protect?

10. How does a threat to information security differ from an attack? How can the two overlap?

11. List the vectors that malicious code uses to infect or compromise other systems. Which of these do you think is the one most commonly encountered in a typical organization?

12. Why do employees constitute one of the greatest threats to information security?

13. What measures can individuals take to protect against shoulder surfing?

14. What is the difference between a skilled hacker and an unskilled hacker (other than the lack of skill)? How might the defenses you create against each differ?

15. What is malware? How do worms differ from viruses? Do Trojan horses carry viruses or worms?

16. Why does polymorphism cause greater concern than traditional malware? How does it affect detection?

17. What is the most common way that intellectual property is violated? How does an organization protect against it?

18. What are the various forces of nature? Which type would be of greatest concern to an organization based in Las Vegas? Oklahoma City? Miami? Los Angeles?

19. How does obsolescence constitute a threat to information security? How can an organization protect against it?

20. What are the most common types of password attacks? What can a systems administrator do to protect against them?

21. What is the difference between a denial-of-service (DoS) attack and a distributed denial-of-service (DDoS) attack? Which is potentially more dangerous and devastating? Why?

22. For a sniffer attack to succeed, what must the attacker do? How can an attacker gain access to a network to use the sniffer system?

23. What is a buffer overflow, and how is it used against a Web server?

Real World Exercises

1. Assume that a security model is needed for the protection of information in your class. Using the CNSS model (McCumber Cube), write a brief statement on how you would address the three components represented in each cell.

2. Consider the most important item among all the categories of information stored on your personal computer. As it applies to that item of information (your information asset), identify an example of a corresponding threat, threat agent, vulnerability, exposure, risk, attack, and exploit.

3. Using the Web, identify the chief information officer, chief information security officer, and one systems administrator for your school. Which of these individuals represents the data owner? Data custodian?

4. Using the Web, find out who Kevin Mitnick is. What did he do? Who caught him? Write a short summary of his activities and why he is infamous.

5. If a hacker hacks into a network, copies a few files, defaces the Web page, and steals credit card numbers, identify the different threat categories encompassed by this attack.

6. The chapter discussed many threats to information security. Using the Web, find at least two other sources of information on threats.

Hands-On Projects

HANDS-ON PROJECTS

Project 1-1 Getting to Know Your Web Browser: Internet Explorer

Throughout this text, if not your entire academic and professional career, you will be using a Web browser with some expectation of protection. But how well configured is your Web browser? This project shows you how to look at your browser's security configurations.

Internet Explorer (IE) uses a number of settings to manage your security profile. One of the areas of configuration setting inside IE are Security Zones, which enable users to define sites they know to be safe as well as sites they know to be unsafe. It is possible to define lists of approved and/or disapproved sites, ones that are unique to a user's local network or intranet, as well as more general Internet (or external) sites. Other settings that can be configured include the acceptable encryption level, how cookies are used and/or stored, and a content rating system called Content Advisor. How you set them is up to you.

System Configuration: For this exercise, you need a computer with a version of Microsoft Internet Explorer installed. (*Note*: Versions will vary slightly since updates are released frequently.) This example uses I.E. 8.0.

1. Open an Internet Explorer window. Click **Tools**, **Internet Options**, and then click the **Security** tab. You see four distinct security zones listed. The Internet zone is the default for all sites not found in other zones. The Local intranet zone is for local network sites and files. The Trusted sites zone is for sites that the user explicitly defines, normally visited frequently and needing ActiveX controls or Flash animation, and so on. Finally, the Restricted sites zone is for sites that are known to have pop-up animations and windows, may contain malicious or corrupt content, and so on. These are also defined by the individual user. For each zone, there is a default level and a custom level. Browse through the various icons and options.

2. To begin an examination of how IE handles cookies, click **Tools**, **Internet Options**, and then click the **Privacy** tab. You should see a slider control with various settings. The default level for this setting is Medium. Move the slider up until the setting is High. Browse the Web and see how your system behaves differently. When finished, move the setting to a level you are comfortable with.

3. Click the **Advanced** button. Click the **Override automatic cookie handling** check box. You see the following three options: Accept, Block, or Prompt for each of the two classes of cookies (first-party and third-party). "First-party cookies" are cookies from the actual target domain, and "third-party cookies" are from any other domain. You may also choose an option to always allow "session cookies." Session cookies are not stored on your hard drive, whereas persistent cookies are. Now, click **OK**, and then click **OK** again.

4. In the open Internet Explorer window, click **Tools, Internet Options**, and then click the **Content** tab. The first area is labeled Content Advisor. Click the **Enable** button. You see a screen describing various categories and ratings. Click **Cancel** twice to exit Content Advisor and restore the computer to its original settings.

5. If needed, close all windows. (*Note*: You may want to turn off the Content Advisor or the next person who uses this computer may not be able to access the Microsoft site!)

Project 1-2 Getting to Know Your Web Browser: Firefox

Now that you've examined IE, it's time to look at another popular Web browser: Firefox. Firefox has a number of features that can be customized to increase the security of the browser. By default it is a very secure application. However, misconfiguration can reduce the application's security. There are a number of options in Firefox. Here, we will focus on those with a security impact.

System Configuration: For this exercise, you need a computer with a version of Mozilla's Firefox installed. (*Note*: Versions may vary slightly since updates are released frequently.) This example uses Firefox 3.6.13.

1. Open Firefox by clicking **Start, All Programs, Mozilla Firefox**, and then **Mozilla Firefox** again. Then open the Options menu by selecting **Tools, Options**.

2. Open the Content tab by clicking the **Content** icon at the top of the Options window. To prevent pop-up windows, check the **Block pop-up windows** box. (*Note*: I may be checked by default.) Other important boxes to have checked are:

   - **Load images automatically**
   - **Enable JavaScript**—If you are concerned about a problem similar to Active X malware, Firefox works differently with JavaScript and is inherently more secure.
   - **Enable Java**

3. Click the **Exceptions** button next to the Load images automatically option. Review the options contained here, and then click **Close**. Click the **Advanced** button to the right of Enable JavaScript. This reveals additional configuration options.

4. Uncheck the **Disable or replace context menus** option to prevent Web pages from disabling or changing the Firefox context menu. Click **OK** to continue.

5. Open the Privacy tab by clicking the **Privacy** icon at the top of the Options window. For shared computers, it is important to uncheck these options under the History section:

   - **Remember download history**
   - **Remember search and form history**
   - **Accept cookies from sites**
     Note: You can also set this option to:
   - **Keep until:** Select **I close Firefox**

6. Check the **Clear history when Firefox closes** box. This option prevents someone else from gaining access to information used during your session. The Settings button next to this preference allows you to specify what data is cleared. For shared systems, check all boxes except Cookies. For personal computers, check all boxes except Cookies and Saved Passwords. Click **OK** to close.

7. Open the Security tab by clicking the **Security** icon at the top of the Options window. Ensure these options are selected in the first box:

   • **Warn me when sites try to install add-ons**

   • **Block reported attack site**

   • **Block reported web forgeries**

8. In the Passwords box, if this is a shared computer (i.e., in a lab), uncheck **Remember passwords for sites**. If it is your personal computer, you can use this option, but it is recommended that you use a master password (the next option) to control access to the password files. This way, if someone else uses the computer and clicks the next option, Show Passwords, they will be prompted for the master password. The Settings button in the Warning Messages box allows you to specify what security warning you see while viewing Web pages. It is recommended that all options except **I am about to view an encrypted page** be selected. You can select the first if you want, but it doesn't represent a security threat. Click **OK** or **Cancel** to close this dialog box.

9. Open the Advanced tab by clicking the **Advanced** icon at the top of the Options window. Select the **Update** tab underneath. Under the **Automatically check for updates to:** option, ensure all three options are checked if this is a personal computer. If it is a lab computer, ask your instructor before selecting these options. If you have checked any of these options, specify when the updates are to be installed by selecting:

   • **Ask me what I want to do** (or)

   • **Automatically download and install the update.**

     We recommend selecting the second option and ensuring that the last option,

     Warn me if this will disable any of my add-ons, is checked.

10. Click **OK** to close the Options window.

Running Case Projects

CASE PROJECTS

Before you're ready to help Alex build his firewall, you need to create some key documents that outline what the network will do and how it will look. Use the information gleaned from the following case update (as well as from the chapter's opening and closing running case scenarios) to enhance your understanding of Data Mart and its information security needs. Then create the documents presented in the following Student Tasks section.

Data Mart was established in 2003 by Ann Lee, current owner and president. Ann started the business by providing secure off-site data backup for several small to mid-sized organizations in her hometown of Austin, TX. Business grew slowly but steadily over the next few years, with Ann hiring a number of employees, including her college friend Julie Matthews as VP of

Operations. Shortly afterward, Ann and Julie conducted an exhaustive search for a Chief Information Officer. With no true executives to choose from, they hired Alex Truman for the job. Alex's only experience was as a lab manager for the local community college; nevertheless, Ann and Julie reluctantly hired him, naming him Director of IT. They hoped that as Alex's skill set grew he might eventually be promoted to CIO.

In 2006, Julie recommended expanding the company's services from offering simple off-site data backups to offering data analysis and data mining, thereby helping their clients better understand the demographics of their customer bases. Ann agreed, and by 2010 the company had a staff of over 50 employees; its organizational structure is shown in Figure 1-8. The Operations section managed the data storage, and use of information entrusted to Data Mart by its customers. A group of 12 data and statistical analysts worked on identifying trends in marketing and sales data. A small customer support group handled customer requests for assistance in storing and accessing their data and in interpreting their reports.

In 2008, Matt Carola was hired as VP of Sales and Marketing, tasks which Ann had previously supervised herself. Matt's group included two managers, one responsible for sales, the other for marketing. Matt's shop includes coordinators for tech support and internal help desk functions. The heart of Data Mart's operations is a 1200-square-foot data center with over 200 rack-mounted servers. Most of the servers are accessed directly by customers for off-site data backup, providing both real-time transactional data transfers and off-peak data backup bulk transfer storage. The remaining servers are used for data and statistical analyses, and internal operations. Currently, the responsibility for managing the data center is shared between the Operations managers and Alex Truman, with Alex having final say on design, implementation, and maintenance issues. This

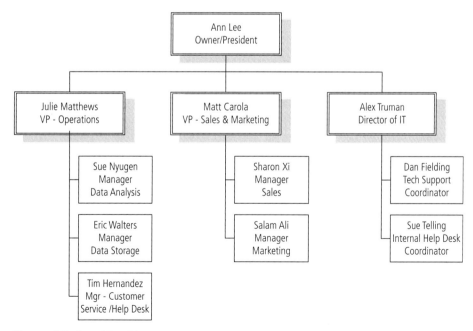

Figure 1-8 Data Mart Management
© Cengage Learning 2012

has proven to be a source of contention internally, with the loose compromise having been reached that "the software belongs to the managers, but the hardware belongs to Alex." The data, of course, belongs to the customers.

Student Tasks

1. Create a description of Data Mart's network, based on the information given. If you need to make assumptions, do so and state them in your description.

2. Create a list of the organization's information assets. Again, state your assumptions.

3. Create a list of the threats that Data Mart faces.

4. Create a prioritized TVA worksheet listing assets against threats, with the most valuable assets on the left and the most dangerous threats at the top. With this spreadsheet, what should Data Mart focus on first with regard to protecting its most important assets?

Endnotes

1. National Security Telecommunications and Information Systems Security, *National Training Standard for Information Systems Security (Infosec) Professionals*, 20 June 1994, file, 4011, Accessed 25 February 2010 from *www.cnss.gov/Assets/pdf/nstissi_4011.pdf*.

2. Parker, D. Fighting Computer Crime: A New Framework for Protecting Information. New York: Wiley (1998).

3. McCumber, John. *"Information Systems Security: A Comprehensive Model."* *Proceedings 14th National Computer Security Conference. National Institute of Standards and Technology.* Baltimore, MD. (October 1991).

4. Kadrich, M. *Endpoint Security*. Boston: Addison-Wesley (2007).

5. Sun-Tzu. "The Principles Of Warfare: The Art Of War" Chapter Three: Planning Attacks, Accessed 24 February 2010 from *www.sonshi.com/sun3.html*.

6. Michael Whitman, "Enemy at the Gates: Threats to Information Security," *Communications of the ACM*, 46(8) August 2003, pp. 91–96.

7. Michael Whitman, "Enemy at the Gates: Threats to Information Security," *Communications of the ACM*, 46(8) August 2003, pp. 91–96.

8. FOLDOC, "Intellectual Property," *FOLDOC Online* (27 March 1997) Accessed 25 February 2010 from *foldoc.doc.ic.ac.uk/foldoc/foldoc.cgi?query=intellectual+property*.

9. SANS Institute, "The Twenty Most Critical Internet Security Vulnerabilities (Updated): The Experts' Consensus," *SANS Institute Online* (2 May 2002). Accessed 25 February 2010 from *http://www.sans.org/top-cyber-security-risks/?ref=top20*.

10. SANS Institute, "Consensus Roadmap for Defeating Distributed Denial of Service Attacks: A Project of the Partnership for Critical Infrastructure Security," *SANS Institute Online*, (23 February 2000). Accessed 25 February 2010 from *www.sans.org/dosstep/roadmap.php*.

11. Paul Brooke, "DDoS: Internet Weapons of Mass Destruction," *Network Computing* 12, no. 1 (January 2001): 67.

12. CERT® Advisory CA-1996-21 TCP SYN Flooding and IP Spoofing Attacks, CERT, "TCP SYN Flooding and IP Spoofing Attacks," advisory CA-1996-21.

13. Webopedia, "IP spoofing," *Webopedia Online* (4 June 2002). Accessed 25 February 2010 from *www.webopedia.com/TERM/I/IP_spoofing.html.*

14. Bhavin Bharat Bhansali, "Man-In-The-Middle Attack: A Brief." *SANS Institute Online*, 16 February 2001. Accessed 25 February 2010 from *www.giac.org/practical/gsec/ Bhavin_Bhansali_GSEC.pdf.*

15. James Pearce, "Security Expert Warns of MP3 Danger," *ZDNet News Online* (18 March 2002). Accessed 25 February 2010 from *http://zdnet.com.com/2100-1105-861995.html.*

16. Webopedia, "sniffer," *Webopedia Online* (5 February 2002). Accessed 15 February 2004 from *www.webopedia.com/TERM/s/sniffer.html.*

17. Elinor Abreu, "Kevin Mitnick Bares All," *Network WorldFusion News Online* (28 September 2000). Accessed 25 February 2010 from *www.nwfusion.com/news/2000/ 0928mitnick.html.*

18. Webopedia, "buffer overflow," *Webopedia Online* (29 July 2003). Accessed 25 February 2010 from *www.webopedia.com/TERM/b/buffer_overflow.html.*

19. Scott Spanbauer, "Pentium Bug, Meet the IE 4.0 Flaw," *PC World* 16, no. 2 (February 1998): 55.

"The one who adapts his policy to the times prospers, and likewise that the one whose policy clashes with the demands of the times does not."
—Niccolo Machiavelli

chapter 2

Security Policies and Standards

After reading this chapter and completing the exercises, you will be able to:

- Define information security policy and describe its central role in a successful information security program
- Explain the three types of information security policy and list the critical components of each
- Define management's role in the development, maintenance, and enforcement of information security policy, standards, practices, procedures, and guidelines
- List the dominant national and international security management standards
- Describe the fundamental elements of key information security management practices
- Discuss how an organization institutionalizes policies, standards, and practices using education, training, and awareness programs

Running Case: Why Would We Need a Policy?

"…and that, Mr. Truman, is why policy is so important. It lays the foundation for appropriate behavior by the employees of your organization." Mike Edwards sat back down at the conference table after completing his presentation. Alex Truman, IT Director for Data Mart, looked across the table at Mike with a bit of a bored look on his face.

"Okay Mike, I see where in big companies you have to have these elaborate policies to control rogue employees, but here at Data Mart we only have 20 or so employees altogether. I know everyone by name, and everyone knows what you can and can't do at work," Alex said.

"Policy is important at any size company, Mr. Truman," Mike replied. "Otherwise, you won't have the legal recourse to protect the business from, say, employees who are shopping on the Web when they should be answering a phone call from a customer with a real emergency."

"But again, Mike, our employees know that they are not allowed to use the company systems for personal business, and that someone has to be on the help desk at all times, no exceptions," Alex said. He leaned forward, tapping the table. "Everyone here knows that, so why do we need a policy?"

Mike looked Alex straight in the eyes, and then he slowly shifted his gaze so that he was looking over Alex's left shoulder. With a puzzled look, Alex turned, looked behind him, and then slumped back into his chair. "Okay, okay, you're right!" he said. "Let's get started with the policies."

Behind Alex, just outside the clear glass wall of the conference room was Data Mart's customer support help desk, usually manned 24/7 with a team of two or more support technicians. The room was now illuminated by several phone lines flashing, which indicated there were several customers on hold, yet there was no one in the room to answer those calls. And the one computer monitor visible from the conference room was displaying a Web page from a popular online auction site.

Introduction

An organization is a collection of people working together toward a common goal. Most businesses are focused on profitability as a key measure of their success. To get groups of individuals to work toward a common purpose, the critical factor is a clear understanding of the rules of acceptable behavior. In the absence of such rules, an organization may lose focus; discord or even hostility may arise, disrupting progress and harmony. If an organization without clearly defined rules needs to control an individual whose behavior is disrupting the organization various legal issues may impede the organization's ability to implement some form of punishment. The aphorism "ignorance of the law is no excuse" applies in criminal courts, but pleading ignorance works quite well in civil court if an organization cannot demonstrate the presence and use of effective policy.

According to the National Institute of Standards and Technology (NIST):

"The success of an information resources protection program depends on the policy generated, and on the attitude of management toward securing information on automated systems. You, the policy maker, set the tone and the emphasis on how important a role information security will have within your agency. Your primary responsibility is to set the information resource security policy for the organization with the objectives of reduced risk, compliance with laws and regulations, and assurance of operational continuity, information integrity, and confidentiality."[1]

Policy also conveys management's intentions to its employees—not just what it considers approved or prohibited behavior, but the directions in which it wants the organization to head with regard to the implementation of technologies and services. For example, systems administrators cannot securely install a firewall unless they have received a set of clear information security policies. These policies need to stipulate the type of services that are permitted, how to authenticate users' identities, and how to log relevant events. An effective information security training and awareness effort cannot be initiated without the existence of written information security policies, because policies provide both the basis for and the actual content of the training and awareness material.

Also critical to the administration of an effective security program is the use of a formal plan to implement and manage security in the organization. Although the organization may choose to start a policy project from scratch, it will quickly realize that to use a recognized, tested, and recommended national or international standard for security management greatly improves the efficiency and effectiveness of its security management effort. National organizations such as NIST and international organizations such as the International Standards Organization (ISO) have published documents that provide templates for the structure of information security management programs. The use of these models, each of which includes specific requirements that information security policy be included in organizational practices, is examined in this chapter.

Information Security Policy, Standards, and Practices

A **policy** is a set of guidelines or instructions that an organization's senior management implements to regulate the activities of the organization members who make decisions, take actions, and perform other duties. Policies are the organizational equivalent of public laws in that they dictate acceptable and unacceptable behavior within an organization. Like laws, policies define what is right and what is wrong, what the penalties are for violating policy, and what the appeal process is. **Standards**, although they have the same compliance requirement as policies, are more detailed descriptions of what must be done to comply with policy. The standards may be an informal part of an organization's culture, what we call **de facto standards**. Or they may be published, scrutinized, and ratified by a group, what we call **de jure standards**. Practices, procedures, and guidelines effectively explain how to comply with policy. Figure 2-1 shows policies as the force that drives standards, which in turn drive practices, procedures, and guidelines.

Management must make policies the basis for all information security planning, design, and deployment. Policies direct how issues are addressed and how technologies are used. Policies do not specify the proper operation of equipment or software; this information should be placed in the standards, procedures, and practices of users' manuals and systems documentation. In addition, policy should never contradict law, because this can create a significant liability for the organization.

Because information security is primarily a management problem, not a technical one, quality security programs begin and end with policy.[2] Policy obliges personnel to function in a manner that adds to the security of information assets rather than threatens them. Security policies

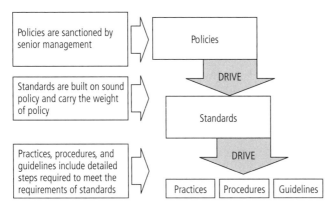

Figure 2-1 Policies, Standards, and Practices
© Cengage Learning 2012

are the least expensive control to design and disseminate—they require only the time and effort of the management team—but the most difficult to implement properly. Even if the management team hires an outside consultant to assist in the development of policy, the costs are minimal compared to those of technical controls.

For a policy to be considered effective and legally enforceable, it must meet the following criteria:

- Dissemination (distribution)—The organization must be able to demonstrate that the relevant policy has been made readily available for review by the employee. Common dissemination techniques include hard-copy and electronic distribution.

- Review (reading)—The organization must be able to demonstrate that it disseminated the document in an intelligible form, including versions for illiterate, non-English-reading, and reading-impaired employees. Often organizations develop versions of the policy in English and alternate languages and in audio-only format for their employees.

- Comprehension (understanding)—The organization must be able to demonstrate that employees understood the requirements and content of the policy. Common techniques include quizzes and other assessments.

- Compliance (agreement)—The organization must be able to demonstrate that employees agree to comply with the policy, through act or affirmation. Common techniques include logon banners that require a specific action (mouse click or keystroke) to acknowledge agreement, or requiring employees to sign a document clearly indicating that they have read, understood, and agreed to comply with the policy.

- Uniform enforcement—The organization must be able to demonstrate that the policy has been applied equally to all employees.

Policies are put in place to support the organization's mission, vision, and strategic planning. The **mission** of an organization is a written statement of its purpose. The **vision** of an organization is a written statement of the organization's long-term goals—where it expects to be in five years, ten years, etc. **Strategic planning** is the process of moving the organization toward its vision.

The meaning of the term **security policy** depends on the context in which it is used. For example, government agencies discuss security policy in terms of national security and national policies vis-a-vis foreign states. Security policy can also refer to, say, a credit card agency's method of processing credit card numbers. In general, a security policy is a set of rules that protects an organization's assets. An **information security policy** is a set of rules for the protection of an organization's information assets. Management must define three types of security policies, according to the widely referenced federal guideline on generally accepted information security practices, NIST SP 800-14:

1. Enterprise information security policies
2. Issue-specific security policies
3. Systems-specific security policies

Each of these types of policy is examined in greater detail in the sections that follow.

Enterprise Information Security Policy (EISP)

An **enterprise information security policy** (EISP) is also known as a general security policy, an IT security policy, or an information security policy. The EISP is based on and directly supports the mission, vision, and direction of the organization and sets the strategic direction, scope, and tone for all security efforts. The EISP is an executive-level document, usually drafted by or at least in cooperation with the organization's chief information officer. It is usually two to ten pages long and expresses the security philosophy within the IT environment. The EISP usually needs to be modified only when there is a change in the strategic direction of the organization.

The EISP guides the development, implementation, and management of the security program. It specifies the requirements to be met by the information security blueprint or framework. It defines the purpose, scope, constraints, and applicability of the security program in the organization. It also assigns responsibilities for the various areas of security, including systems administration, maintenance of the information security policies, and the practices and responsibilities of the users. Finally, it addresses legal compliance. According to NIST, the EISP should address an organization's need to comply with laws and regulations in two ways:

1. General compliance by ensuring the organization establishes suitable programs and assigns responsibilities to identified organizational units
2. Identification of specific penalties and disciplinary actions for deviations from policy[3]

When the EISP has been developed, the CISO begins forming the security team and initiating the necessary changes to the information security program.

EISP Elements   Although the specifics of EISPs vary from organization to organization, most EISP documents should include the elements shown in Table 2-1.[4]

Issue-Specific Security Policy (ISSP)

As an organization executes various technologies and processes to support routine operations, it must instruct employees on the proper use of those technologies and processes. In general, the **issue-specific security policy**, or **ISSP**, addresses specific areas of technology

Component	Description
Statement of Purpose	Answers the question, "What is this policy for?" Provides a framework that helps the reader understand the intent of the document. Here's a sample Statement of Purpose: "This document will: identify the elements of a good security policy explain the need for information security specify the various categories of information security identify the information security responsibilities and roles identify appropriate levels of security through standards and guidelines This document establishes an overarching security policy and direction for our company. Individual departments are expected to establish standards, guidelines, and operating procedures that adhere to and reference this policy while addressing their specific and individual needs."[5]
Information Technology Security Elements	Defines information security. For example: "Protecting the confidentiality, integrity, and availability of information while in processing, transmission, and storage through the use of policy, education and training, and technology...." This section can also lay out security definitions or philosophies to clarify the policy.
Need for Information Technology Security	Provides information on the importance of information security in the organization and the obligation (legal and ethical) to protect critical information about customers, employees, and markets.
Information Technology Security Responsibilities and Roles	Defines the organizational structure designed to support information security. Identifies categories of individuals with responsibility for information security (IT department, management, users) and their information security responsibilities, including maintenance of this document.
Reference to Other Information Technology Standards and Guidelines	Lists other standards that influence and are influenced by this policy document, perhaps including relevant laws (federal and state) and other policies.

Table 2-1 Components of the EISP

(as listed below), requires frequent updates, and contains a statement on the organization's position on a specific issue.[6] An ISSP may cover the following topics, among others:

- Use of company-owned networks and the Internet
- Use of telecommunications technologies (fax and phone)
- Use of electronic mail
- Specific minimum configurations of computers to defend against worms and viruses
- Prohibitions against hacking or testing organization security controls
- Home use of company-owned computer equipment
- Use of personal equipment on company networks
- Use of photocopy equipment

Table 2-2 shows an outline of a sample ISSP that can be used as a model. An organization should add to this structure any security procedures not covered by these general guidelines.

Component	Description

1. Statement of policy
  a. Scope and applicability
  b. Definition of technology addressed
  c. Responsibilities
	The policy should begin with a clear statement of purpose.

2. Authorized access and usage
  a. User access
  b. Fair and responsible use
  c. Protection of privacy
	This section addresses *who* can use the technology governed by the policy and *what* it can be used for. An organization's information systems are the exclusive property of the organization, and users have no general rights of use. Each technology and process is provided for business operations. Use for any other purpose constitutes misuse.

3. Prohibited usage
  a. Disruptive use or misuse
  b. Criminal use
  c. Offensive or harassing materials
  d. Copyrighted, licensed, or other intellectual property
  e. Other restrictions
	Unless a particular use is clearly prohibited, the organization cannot penalize its employees for using it in that fashion.

4. Systems management
  a. Management of stored materials
  b. Employer monitoring
  c. Virus protection
  d. Physical security
  e. Encryption
	This section focuses on users' relationships to systems management. It is important that all such responsibilities be designated to either the systems administrators or the users; otherwise, both parties may infer that the responsibility belongs to the other party.

5. Violations of policy
  a. Procedures for reporting violations
  b. Penalties for violations
	This section specifies the penalties for each category of violation as well as instructions on how individuals in the organization can report observed or suspected violations. Allowing anonymous submissions is often the only way to convince users to report the unauthorized activities of other, more influential employees.

6. Policy review and modification a. Scheduled review of policy and procedures for modification	Because a document is only useful if it is up to date, each policy should contain procedures and a timetable for periodic review. This section should specify a methodology for the review and modification of the policy, to ensure that users do not begin circumventing it as it grows obsolete.
7. Limitations of liability a. Statements of liability or disclaimers	If an employee is caught conducting illegal activities with organizational equipment or assets, management does not want the organization held liable. The policy should state that the organization will not protect employees who violate a company policy or any law using company technologies, and that the company is not liable for such actions.

Table 2-2 Components of an ISSP

Systems-Specific Policy (SysSP)

Whereas ISSPs are usually readily identifiable as policy, system-specific security policies (SysSPs) may sometimes look different from other kinds of policy. Whereas ISSPs will avoid detailed coverage of practices, SysSPs usually appear with the **managerial guidance** expected in a policy and may also include detailed **technical specifications** not usually found in other types of policy documents.

Managerial Guidance SysSPs A managerial guidance SysSP document is created by management to guide the implementation and configuration of a specific technology so as to direct the way a technology is to be used to control the behavior of people in the organization. For example, a firewall configuration must follow management guidelines in the way it is configured. If an organization didn't want its employees to have access to the Internet via the organization's network, the firewall configuration managerial guidance would say so and the firewall would have to be implemented accordingly.

Imagine that management fails to convey to the firewall technicians its intent with respect to the firewall's technical configuration. In the absence of such guidance, the technicians will rely on their own experiences and training to select rules they feel are appropriate. The organization will then experience numerous problems if and when business needs conflict with the technicians' perception of the security function of a firewall. If this were an organization with a need for ultra-high security, such as a Department of Defense contractor, and if the technicians developed a set of firewall rules with an intermediate degree of control, the organization might find itself underprotected, having a need for a high degree of control. On the other hand, with the same set of intermediate-level rules, an organization with an open environment, such as an academic institution, might find itself overly restricted, with the flow of information stifled. This wide range of possible needs is why it's necessary to carefully direct the development, implementation, and configuration of all technologies in the organization, especially security technologies.

Technical Specifications SysSPs While a manager can work with a systems administrator to create managerial policy, the systems administrator may in turn need to create a policy to implement the managerial policy and thus direct practices with a larger degree of detail than what is usually found in policy. Each technology may require its own set of technical specification policies to translate the managerial intent into an enforceable technical approach. For example, an ISSP may require that user passwords be changed quarterly; a systems administrator can implement a technical control within a specific application to enforce this policy. There are two general methods for implementing such technical controls: access control lists and configuration rules. Whereas access control lists link system objects (devices) to system subjects (users) with access rights in a matrix, configuration rules specify the procedural steps to be used in allowing access to system resources. Each of these approaches is now described.

An **access control list,** or ACL (also referred to as a user access list), is a set of specifications that identifies a piece of technology's authorized users and includes details on the rights and privileges those users have on that technology. ACLs can control access to file storage systems, software components, or network communications devices. A **capability table** specifies the subjects and objects that users or groups can access; in some systems, capability tables are called user profiles or user policies. These specifications frequently take the form of complex matrices, rather than simple lists or tables. The **access control matrix** combines capability tables and ACLs, so that organizational assets are listed along the vertical axis while users are listed along the horizontal axis. The resulting matrix contains ACLs in columns for a particular device or asset, while a row contains the capability table for a particular user.

Configuration rules are the specific instructions entered into a security system to regulate how it reacts to the data it receives. **Rule-based policies** are more specific to a system's operation than ACLs are, and they may or may not deal with users directly. Many security systems—firewalls, intrusion detection systems (IDSs), and proxy servers, for example—use specific configuration scripts to show how the systems handle each data element they process.

Frameworks and Industry Standards

To build a good security program and implement effective firewalls, an organization needs to follow an effective plan. The plan may be developed exclusively by the organization, or it may be based on the guidance of outside organizations with vastly more experience and resources. It is usually in the organization's best interest, however, to identify and adopt an external framework for security, and then apply that framework to the organization's blueprint for security implementation.

This **security blueprint** is the basis for the design, selection, and implementation of all security program elements, including policy implementation, ongoing policy management, risk management programs, education and training programs, technological controls, and maintenance of the security program. The security blueprint, built on top of the organization's information security policies, is a comprehensive plan that is able to grow and be changed so as to meet the organization's current and future information security needs. The blueprint specifies the tasks in the order in which they are to be accomplished.

To select a methodology by which to develop a security blueprint, you can adapt or adopt a published security model or framework. A **security framework** is an outline of the overall information security strategy and a roadmap for planned changes to the organization's information security environment. There are a number of published information security frameworks presented later in this chapter. Because each information security environment is unique, the security team may need to modify or adapt pieces from several frameworks; what works well for one organization may not precisely fit another.

The ISO 27000 Series

One of the most widely referenced security models is *Information Technology—Code of Practice for Information Security Management*, which was originally published as British Standard 7799 and widely referenced as BS7799. In 2000, the code was adopted as an international standard framework for information security by the International Standards Organization (ISO) and the International Electrotechnical Commission (IEC) as ISO/IEC 17799. The document was revised in 2005 (becoming ISO/IEC 17799:2005), and it was renamed ISO/IEC 27002 in 2007, to align it with the document ISO/IEC 27001, which is discussed later in this chapter. While the details of ISO/IEC 27002 are available only to those who purchase the standard, its structure and general organization are well known. For a summary description, see Table 2-3.

Sections of the ISO/IEC 27002
1. Risk Assessment and Treatment
2. Security Policy
3. Organization of Information Security
4. Asset Management
5. Human Resource Security
6. Physical and Environmental Security
7. Communications and Operations
8. Access Control
9. Information Systems Acquisition, Development, and Maintenance
10. Information Security Incident Management
11. Business Continuity Management
12. Compliance

Table 2-3 Sections of the ISO/IEC 27002[7]

Note that security technologies, such as firewalls and VPNs, don't have a dedicated section. This is because perimeter defense is a specific technical control. While technical controls are important to the organization, there are many controls, and each must be managed. There are specific items addressing the use of technical controls in various sections of ISO/IEC 27002. For example, under Communications and Operations Management, one item specifies that you must "control how your organization's service providers implement managed network security solutions such as firewalls and intrusion detection systems." Another item states that the organization must "monitor unauthorized access attempts by tracking notifications for network gateways and firewalls."[8] Although there is no section specifically dedicated to security technologies, these controls are a critical component of security management practices.

The stated purpose of ISO/IEC 27002 is to "give recommendations for information security management for use by those who are responsible for initiating, implementing, or maintaining security in their organization. It is intended to provide a common basis for developing organizational security standards and effective security management practice and to provide confidence in inter-organizational dealings."[9] Whereas ISO/IEC 27002 offers a broad overview of the various areas of security, providing information on 127 controls over 10 broad areas, ISO/IEC 27001 provides information on how to implement ISO/IEC 27002 and how to set up an information security management system (ISMS). The overall methodology for this process and its major steps are presented in Figure 2-2.

In 2007, the ISO announced plans for numbering current and forthcoming standards related to information security issues and topics, as shown in Table 2-4.

NIST Security Models

Another possible approach to designing a security framework is described in documents available from the Computer Security Resource Center (CSRC) of the National Institute of Standards and Technology (NIST) at *csrc.nist.gov*. Because the NIST documents are publicly

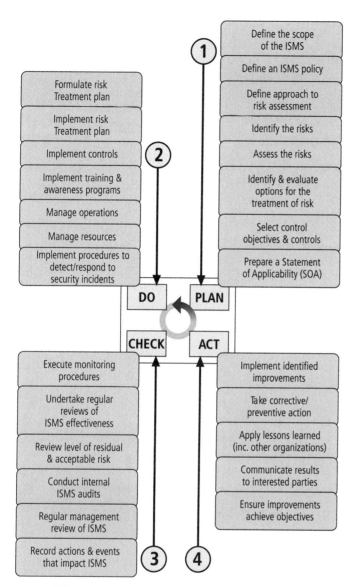

Figure 2-2 ISO 27001 Major Process Steps
© Cengage Learning 2012

available at no additional cost and have been available for some time, they have been broadly reviewed by government and industry professionals and were among the references cited by the federal government when it decided not to select the ISO/IEC 17799 standards. The following NIST documents can assist in the design of a security framework:

- SP 800-12: *An Introduction to Computer Security: The NIST Handbook*
- SP 800-14: *Generally Accepted Security Principles and Practices for Securing Information Technology Systems*
- SP 800-18 Rev. 1: *Guide for Developing Security Plans for Federal Information Systems*

Standard	Status	Title or Topic	Comment
27000	Published	Series Overview and Vocabulary	Typically, when ISO releases a series of standards, the first one defines the series' terminology.
27001	Published	Information Security Management System (ISMS) Specification	Drawn from BS 7799:2
27002	Published	Code of Practice for Information Security Management	Was renamed from ISO/IEC 17799, drawn from BS 7799:1
27003	Published	ISMS Implementation Guidelines	Provides guidance for implementing an ISMS
27004	Published	Information Security Measurements and Metrics	Helps organizations measure, report, and systematically improve the effectiveness of their ISMSs
27005	Published	ISMS Risk Management	Guidelines for InfoSec Risk Management—supporting requirement of ISO 27001
27006	Published	Requirements for Bodies Providing Audit and Certification of an ISMS	Largely intended to support the accreditation of ISMS certification bodies
27007	Planned	Guidelines for ISMS Auditing	Will provide guidance for those auditing ISMSs for various purposes other than certified compliance with ISO/IEC 27001
27008	Planned	Guideline for information security management auditing (focusing on the security controls)	
27011	Published	IT: InfoSec Management guidelines for Telecomm	Based on ISO/IEC 27002
27013	Planned	Guideline on the integrated implementation of ISO/IEC 20000-1 and ISO/IEC 27001	
27014	Planned	Information security governance framework	
27015	Planned	Information security management guidelines for the finance and insurance sectors	
27031	Planned	Guideline for ICT readiness for business continuity	
27032	Planned	Guideline for cybersecurity	Expected to target end users
27033	Planned	IT network security, a multipart standard based on ISO/IEC 18028:2006	
27034	Planned	Guideline for application security	

Table 2-4 ISO 27000 Series Standards (Published and Planned)

- SP 800-30: *Risk Management Guide for Information Technology Systems*
- SP 800-41 Rev. 1: *Guidelines on Firewalls and Firewall Policy*
- SP 800-53 Rev. 3: *Recommended Security Controls for Federal Information Systems and Organizations*

The more relevant documents are briefly discussed here. Additional details can be downloaded from *http://csrc.nist.gov/publications/PubsSPs.html*.

SP 800-14: Generally Accepted Principles and Practices for Securing Information Technology Systems

Special Publication 800-14 lists the principles and practices to be used in the development of a security blueprint, which is to say that, in addition to detailing the best practices across the whole spectrum of security areas, it provides the philosophical principles that the security team should integrate into the entire information security process. The document can guide the development of the security framework and should be combined with other NIST publications to provide the necessary structure to the entire security process.

SP 800-41 Rev. 1: Guidelines on Firewalls and Firewall Policy

Of particular interest for this text is Special Publication 800-41, Rev. 1, which provides an overview of the capabilities and technologies of firewalls and firewall policies. As stated in the document, SP 800-41 Rev. 1 "provides an overview of firewall technologies and discusses their security capabilities and relative advantages and disadvantages in detail. It also provides examples of where firewalls can be placed within networks and the implications of deploying firewalls in particular locations. The document also makes recommendations for establishing firewall policies and for selecting, configuring, testing, deploying, and managing firewall solutions."[10] The document provides several general recommendations toward building an effective firewall strategy:

- "Create a firewall policy that specifies how firewalls should handle inbound and outbound network traffic."
- "Identify all requirements that should be considered when determining which firewall to implement."
- "Create rule sets that implement the organization's firewall policy while supporting firewall performance."
- "Manage firewall architectures, policies, software, and other components throughout the life of the firewall solutions."[11]

These recommendations will be explored in detail in upcoming chapters.

SP 800-53 Rev. 3: Recommended Security Controls for Federal Information Systems and Organizations

This document describes the selection and implementation of security controls for information security to lower the possibility of successful attack from threats. It addresses the following questions:

- "What security controls are needed to adequately mitigate the risk incurred by the use of information and information systems in the execution of organizational missions and business functions?"

- "Have the selected security controls been implemented, or is there a realistic plan for their implementation?"
- "What is the desired or required level of assurance (i.e., grounds for confidence) that the selected security controls, as implemented, are effective in their application?"[12]

As shown in Table 2-5, the controls fall into 18 categories organized into three classes: Technical, Operational, and Management.

Identifier	Family	Class
AC	Access Control	Technical
AT	Awareness and Training	Operational
AU	Audit and Accountability	Technical
CA	Security Assessment and Authorization	Management
CM	Configuration Management	Operational
CP	Contingency Planning	Operational
IA	Identification and Authentication	Technical
IR	Incident Response	Operational
MA	Maintenance	Operational
MP	Media Protection	Operational
PE	Physical and Environmental Protection	Operational
PL	Planning	Management
PS	Personnel Security	Operational
RA	Risk Assessment	Management
SA	System and Services Acquisition	Management
SC	System and Communications Protection	Technical
SI	System and Information Integrity	Operational
PM	Program Management	Management

Table 2-5 Security Control Categories in NIST SP 800-53, Rev. 3

SP 800-53 A, Jul 2008: Guide for Assessing the Security Controls in Federal Information Systems: Building Effective Security Assessment Plans This

document is the successor to SP 800-26: Security Self-Assessment Guide for Information Technology Systems. SP 800-53A is designed to serve as a companion guide to SP 800-53 (currently in Revision 3): Recommended Security Controls for Federal Information Systems. The document provides a systems developmental lifecycle approach to security assessment of information systems.

Other NIST Special Publications Other publications that may be of interest in designing and implementing an effective perimeter defense are presented in Table 2-6.

Other NIST Special Publications of Interest for Perimeter Defense
SP 800-36: Guide to Selecting Information Technology Security Products
SP 800-40 Version 2.0: Creating a Patch and Vulnerability Management Program
SP 800-46 Rev. 1: Guide to Enterprise Telework and Remote Access Security
SP 800-47: Security Guide for Interconnecting Information Technology Systems
SP 800-48 Rev. 1: Guide to Securing Legacy IEEE 802.11 Wireless Networks
SP 800-51: Use of the Common Vulnerabilities and Exposures (CVE) Vulnerability Naming Scheme
SP 800-61 Rev. 1: Computer Security Incident Handling Guide
SP 800-77: Guide to IPsec VPNs
SP 800-83: Guide to Malware Incident Prevention and Handling
SP 800-92: Guide to Computer Security Log Management
SP 800-94: Guide to Intrusion Detection and Prevention Systems (IDPS)
SP 800-113: Guide to SSL VPNs
SP 800-114: User's Guide to Securing External Devices for Telework and Remote Access

Table 2-6 Other NIST Special Publications of Interest for Perimeter Defense

IETF Security Architecture

The Internet Society, the nongovernmental group that directs and controls the technology used by the Internet, created the Internet Engineering Task Force (IETF) to coordinate the technical issues involved in promulgating the Internet's technology standards. Within the IETF, the Security Area Working Group acts as an advisory board for security topics that affect the various Internet-related protocols. While the group endorses no specific information security architecture, it does prepare publications called requests for comment (RFCs), which are used to foster communication and reach consensus across many groups. One of these publications, *RFC 2196: Site Security Handbook* (available at *www.ietf.org/rfc/*), offers a good discussion of important security issues. It covers five basic areas of security, with detailed discussions on development and implementation. There are also chapters on such important topics as security policies, security technical architecture, security services, and security incident handling.

Benchmarking and Best Practices

To assess security practices, the IT industry also makes use of two approaches known as benchmarking and best practices. These approaches don't provide a complete methodology for the design and implementation of the practices needed by an organization; however, it is possible to put together the desired outcome of the security process and to work backward toward an effective design. The Federal Agency Security Practices (FASP) Web site, *http://csrc .nist.gov/groups/SMA/fasp/index.html*, is a popular place to look up best practices. Its best practices are designed for public agencies, but they can be easily adapted to private institutions. The documents found on this site include specific examples of key policies and planning documents, implementation strategies for key technologies, and position descriptions for key security personnel.

A number of other public and semipublic institutions provide information on best practices; one such group is the Computer Emergency Response Team Coordination Center (CERT/CC) at Carnegie Mellon University (*www.cert.org/certcc.html*). CERT/CC provides detailed assistance on how to implement a sound security methodology.

Spheres of Security Spheres of security, shown in Figure 2-3, are the generalized foundation of a good security framework and can be considered a type of best practice recommendation. Generally speaking, they illustrate how information is under attack from a variety of sources. The sphere of use, on the left side of Figure 2-3, illustrates the ways in which people access information. For example, systems users are intended to access information through systems. Information, the most important asset, is at the center of the sphere. It is always at risk from the people and computer systems that have access to it. Networks and the Internet represent indirect threats, because a person attempting to access information from the Internet must first go through the local networks and then access systems that contain the information. The sphere of protection, on the right side of Figure 2-3, shows that between each layer of the sphere of use there must exist a layer of protection to prevent the outer layer from accessing the inner layer. Each shaded band is a layer of protection and control. For example, the items labeled "Policy & law" and "Education & training" are located between people and the information.

Controls are also implemented between systems and the information, between networks and the computer systems, and between the Internet and internal networks. This reinforces the concept of defense in depth, which was discussed in Chapter 1. As illustrated in the sphere of protection, a variety of controls can be used to protect the information. The items of control shown in the figure are not intended to be comprehensive, but they illustrate individual safeguards that can protect the various systems that are located closer to the center of the

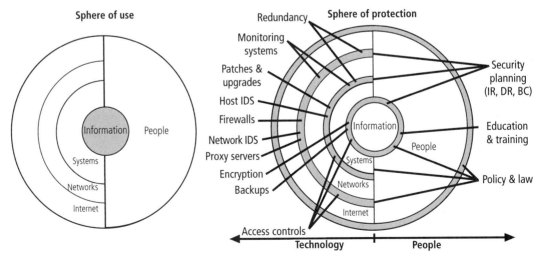

Figure 2-3 Spheres of Security

sphere. However, because people can directly access each ring as well as the information at the core of the model, the side of the sphere of protection that attempts to control access by relying on people requires a different approach to security than the side that uses technology. The members of the organization must become a safeguard, which is effectively trained, implemented, and maintained, or they, too, represent a threat to the information.

Information security is designed and implemented in three layers: policies, people (education, training, and awareness programs), and technology. While the design and implementation of the people layer and the technology layer overlap, both must follow the sound management policies discussed earlier in this chapter. Each of the layers contains controls and safeguards that protect the valuable information and information system assets. But before any technical controls or other safeguards are put into place, the policies defining the management philosophies that guide the security process must already be in place.

Security Education, Training, and Awareness Program

Once your organization has defined the polices that will guide its security program, and then selected an overall security model by creating or adapting a security framework and a corresponding detailed blueprint for implementation, it is time to implement a **security education, training, and awareness (SETA)** program. The SETA program is the responsibility of the CISO and is a control measure designed to reduce the incidences of accidental security breaches by employees. Employee errors are among the top threats to information assets, so it is worth expending the organization's resources to develop programs to combat this threat. SETA programs are designed to supplement the general education and training programs that many organizations have in place to educate staff on information security. For example, if an organization detects that many employees are opening e-mail attachments inappropriately, those employees must be retrained. As a matter of good practice, systems development life cycles must include user training during the implementation phase.

The SETA program consists of three elements: security education, security training, and security awareness. An organization may not be capable of or willing to undertake all three of these elements; in this case, it may outsource elements to local educational institutions. The purpose of SETA is to enhance security by:

- Improving awareness of the need to protect system resources
- Developing skills and knowledge so computer users can perform their jobs more securely
- Building in-depth knowledge, as needed, to design, implement, or operate security programs for organizations and systems[13]

Table 2-7 compares the features of security education, training, and awareness within the organization.

Security Education

Everyone in an organization needs to be trained in information security, but not every member of the organization needs a formal degree or certification in information security. When management agrees that formal education is appropriate, an employee can investigate

	Education	Training	Awareness
Attribute	Why	How	What
Level	Insight	Knowledge	Information
Objective	Understanding	Skill	Exposure
Teaching method	Theoretical instruction • Discussion seminar • Background reading • Hands-on practice	Practical instruction • Lecture • Case study workshop • Posters	Media • Videos • Newsletters
Test measure	Essay (interpret learning)	Problem solving (apply learning)	• True or false • Multiple choice (identify learning)
Impact timeframe	Long-term	Intermediate	Short-term

Table 2-7 Comparative Framework of SETA[14]

available courses from local institutions of higher learning or continuing education. A number of universities have formal coursework in information security. Those interested in researching formal information security programs that have been adopted by the U.S. National Security Agency and Department of Homeland Security can use resources such as the National Centers of Excellence in Information Assurance Education (*www.nsa.gov/ia/academic_outreach/nat_cae/index.shtml*). The Centers of Excellence program identifies outstanding universities that have both coursework in information security and an integrated view of information security in the institution itself. Other local resources can also provide security education information, such as Kennesaw State University's Center for Information Security Education (*http://infosec.kennesaw.edu*).

Security Training

Security training provides detailed information and hands-on instruction to employees to prepare them to perform their duties securely. Management of information security can develop customized in-house training or outsource the training program.

An alternative to formal training programs are industry training conferences and programs offered through professional agencies such as SANS (*www.sans.org*), ISC2 (*www.isc2.org*), ISSA (*www.issa.org*), and CSI (*www.gocsi.com*). Many of these programs are too technical for the average employee, but they may be perfect for the continuing education requirements of information security professionals. A number of SETA resources offer assistance in the form of sample topics and structures for security classes. The Computer Security Resource Center at NIST provides several useful documents free of charge in its special publications area.

Security Awareness

One of the least frequently implemented but most beneficial programs is the security awareness program. A security awareness program is designed to keep information security at the forefront of users' minds. These programs don't have to be complicated or expensive. Good programs can include newsletters, security posters, videos, bulletin boards, flyers, and trinkets. Trinkets can include security slogans printed on mouse pads, coffee cups, T-shirts, pens, or any object frequently used during the workday that reminds employees of security. In addition, a good security awareness program requires a dedicated individual willing to invest the time and effort into promoting the program, and a champion willing to provide the needed financial support.

The security newsletter is the most cost-effective method of disseminating security information and news to the employee. Newsletters can be distributed via hard copy, e-mail, or intranet. Newsletter topics can include information about new threats to the organization's information assets, the schedule for upcoming security classes, and security personnel updates. The goal is to keep the idea of information security in users' minds and to stimulate users to care about security. If a security awareness program is not actively implemented, employees may begin to neglect security matters, and the risk of employee accidents and failures is likely to increase.

Continuity Strategies

Managers in the IT and information security communities are usually called on to provide strategic planning to assure the continuous availability of information systems.[15] Unfortunately for managers, the probability that some form of attack will occur, whether from inside or outside, intentional or accidental, human or nonhuman, annoying or catastrophic, is very high. Thus, managers from each community of interest within the organization must be ready to act when a successful attack occurs.

There are various types of plans that can be used to prepare for an attack: business continuity (BC) plans, disaster recovery (DR) plans, incident response (IR) plans, and contingency plans. In some organizations, these might be handled as a single integrated plan. In large, complex organizations, each of these plans may cover separate but related functions that differ in scope, applicability, and design. In a small organization, the security administrator (or systems administrator) may have one simple plan that consists of a straightforward set of media backup and recovery strategies, along with a few service agreements from the company's service providers. But the sad reality is that many organizations have a level of planning that is woefully deficient.

Business continuity, incident response, and disaster recovery planning are components of a contingency plan, as shown in Figure 2-4. A **contingency plan** is prepared by the organization to anticipate, react to, and recover from events that threaten the security of information and information assets in the organization and, subsequently, to restore the organization to normal modes of business operations. The discussion of contingency planning begins with an explanation of the differences among its various components and an examination of the points at which each component is brought into play.

An **incident** is any clearly identified attack on the organization's information assets that would threaten the assets' confidentiality, integrity, or availability. An **incident response (IR) plan** addresses the identification, classification, response, and recovery from an incident. A **disaster recovery (DR) plan** addresses the preparation for and recovery from a disaster, whether natural or man-made. A **business continuity (BC) plan** ensures that critical business

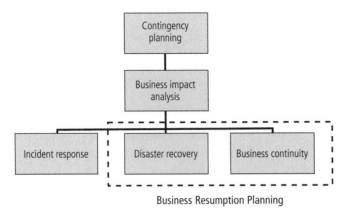

Figure 2-4 Components of Contingency Planning
© Cengage Learning 2012

functions continue if a catastrophic incident or disaster occurs. The primary functions of these three types of planning are as follows:

- The IR plan focuses on immediate response, but if the attack escalates or is disastrous (e.g., fire, flood, earthquake, or total blackout), the process moves on to the DR plan and BC plan.

- The DR plan typically focuses on restoring systems at the original site after disasters occur, and it is therefore closely associated with the BC plan.

- The BC plan occurs concurrently with the DR plan when the damage is major or long term, requiring more than simple restoration of information and information resources. The BC plan establishes critical business functions at an alternate site.

Some experts argue that DR plans and BC plans are so closely linked as to be indistinguishable. However, each has a distinct role and planning requirement. The following sections detail the tasks necessary for each of these three types of plans. You can also further distinguish the three types of planning by examining when each comes into play during the life of an incident. Figure 2-5 shows a sample sequence of events and the overlap between the various plans as they come into play. For example, disaster recovery activities typically continue even after the organization has resumed operations at the original site.

Contingency planning is similar to another process—one that you may have heard of and are likely to encounter in your education or future employment—called the risk management process, defined earlier in this text. The contingency plan is a microcosm of risk management activities, and it focuses on the specific steps that must be taken to restore all information assets to their pre-incident or disaster states. As a result, the planning process closely emulates the risk management process. Before any planning can begin, an assigned person or a planning team must begin the process. Typically, a contingency planning team is assembled for that purpose. A roster for this team may consist of the following members:

- Champion—As with any strategic function, the contingency planning project must have a high-level manager to support, promote, and endorse the findings of the project. In a contingency planning project, this could be the CIO or, ideally, the CEO.

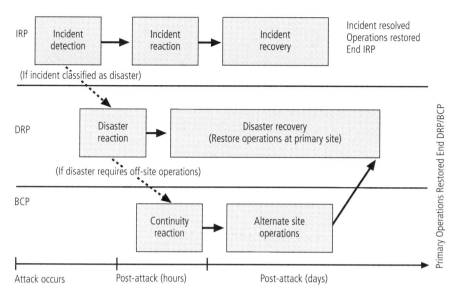

Figure 2-5 Contingency Planning Timeline
© Cengage Learning 2012

- Project manager—A project manager, possibly a mid-level manager or even the CISO, must lead the project and make sure a sound project planning process is used, a complete and useful project plan is developed, and project resources are prudently managed to reach the goals of the project.

- Team members—The team members for this project should be the managers or their representatives from the various communities of interest: business, information technology, and information security. Representative business managers, familiar with the operations of their respective functional areas, should supply details on their activities and provide insight into the criticality of their functions to the overall sustainability of the business. Information technology managers on the project team should be familiar with the systems that could be at risk and with the IR plans, DR plans, and BC plans that are needed to provide technical content within the planning process. Information security managers must oversee the security planning of the project and provide information on the threats, vulnerabilities, attacks, and recovery requirements needed in the planning process.

The major project work modules performed by the contingency planning project team are shown in Figure 2-6. As you read the remainder of this chapter, it may help you to return to this diagram, since many of the upcoming sections correspond to the steps depicted in the diagram.

Business Impact Analysis

The first phase in the development of the contingency planning process is the **business impact analysis (BIA)**. A BIA is an investigation and assessment of the impact that various attacks can have on the organization. BIA takes up where the risk assessment process leaves off. It begins with a prioritized list of threats and vulnerabilities and adds information about the

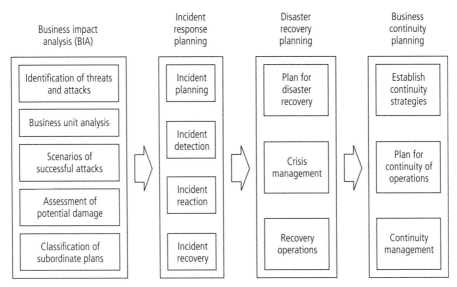

Figure 2-6 Major Steps in Contingency Planning

criticality of the systems involved and detailed assessments of the threats and vulnerabilities in the context in which the systems are used. The BIA is a crucial component of the initial planning stages, as it provides detailed analyses of the potential impact each attack could have on the organization. The BIA therefore adds insight into what the organization must do to respond to attack, minimize the damage from the attack, recover from the effects, and return to normal operations. One of the fundamental differences between a BIA and the risk management process is that the risk management process identifies the threats, vulnerabilities, and attacks to determine what controls can protect the information. The BIA assumes that these controls have been bypassed, have failed, or have proven otherwise ineffective—that is, that an attack has succeeded. It then attempts to answer the question: What do we do now?

The contingency planning team conducts the BIA in the following stages, which are shown in Figure 2-6 and described in the sections that follow.

Identification and Prioritization of Threats and Attacks

Organizations that have a well-established risk management process will not need to develop this aspect of the BIA. They will only need to update the threat list from their risk management process with new developments and add an additional piece of information, the attack profile. An **attack profile** is a detailed description of the activities that occur during an attack. The content items in a sample attack profile (created on June 21, 2008), shown in Table 2-8, include preliminary indications of an attack, as well as actions and outcomes. These profiles must be developed for every serious threat the organization faces, natural or man-made, deliberate or accidental. It is as important to know the typical hacker's profile as it is to know what kind of data entry mistakes employees make or the weather conditions that indicate an imminent tornado or hurricane. The attack profile is useful in later planning stages to provide indicators of attacks. It is used here to determine the extent of damage that could result to a business unit if a given attack were successful.

Attack Profile	
Attack name and description	Tojan.Mako (a.k.a Win32.Mako)—Malicious payload usually delivered by e-mail, but able to infect using multiple vectors; named for picture of a shark that sometimes is attached to the infecting message
Threat and probable threat agent	Malicious code via automated attack
Known or possible vulnerabilities	All desktop systems not updated with all latest patches
Likely precursor activities or indicators	Attachments to e-mails
Likely attack activities or indicators of attack in progress	Systems sending e-mails to entries from address book; activity on port 80 without browser being used
Information assets at risk from this attack	All desktop and server systems
Damage or loss to information assets likely from this attack	Business partners and others connected to our networks
Other assets at risk from this attack	None identified at this time
Damage or loss to other assets likely from this attack	Will vary depending on severity; minimum disruption will be needed to repair worm infection

Table 2-8 Attack Profile

Business Unit Analysis The second major task within the BIA is the analysis and prioritization of the business functions within the organization's departments, sections, divisions, groups, or other units to determine which are most vital to continued operations. Each unit must also be evaluated to determine how important its functions are to the organization as a whole. For example, recovery operations would probably focus on the IT department and network operation before addressing the personnel department and hiring activities. Likewise, it is more urgent to reinstate a manufacturing company's assembly line than to reinstate the maintenance tracking system for that assembly line. This is not to say that personnel functions and assembly line maintenance are not important to the business; but if the organization's main revenue-producing operations cannot be restored quickly, there may cease to be a need for other functions.

Scenarios of Successful Attacks Once the threat attack profiles have been developed and the business functions prioritized, the business impact analysis team must create a series of scenarios depicting the impact of a successful attack from each threat on each prioritized functional area. This can be a long and detailed process, as threats that succeed can affect many functions. Attack profiles should include scenarios depicting a typical attack, with details on the method, the indicators, and the broad consequences of the attack. Once the attack profiles are completed, the business function details can be integrated with the attack profiles, after which more details are added to the attack profile, including alternate outcomes. These alternate outcomes should describe a best, worst, and most likely case that could result from each type of attack on a particular business functional area. This level of detail allows planners to address each business function in turn.

Assessment of Potential Damage Using the attack success scenarios, the BIA planning team must estimate the cost of the best, worst, and most likely cases. At this stage, you are not determining how much to spend on the protection of information assets; rather, you are identifying what must be done to recover from each possible case. These costs include the actions of the response team(s), which are described in subsequent sections, as they attempt to recover quickly and effectively from an incident or disaster. These cost estimates can also inform management representatives from all the organization's communities of interest of the importance of the planning and recovery efforts. The final result of the assessment is referred to as an **attack scenario end case**.

Classification of Subordinate Plans   Once the potential damage has been assessed and each scenario and attack scenario end case has been evaluated, one or more subordinate plans must be developed or identified from among plans already in place. These subordinate plans take into account the identification of, reaction to, and recovery from each attack scenario. An attack scenario end case is categorized either as disastrous or not disastrous. Most attacks are not disastrous and therefore fall into the category of incident. Those scenarios that do qualify as disastrous are addressed in the disaster recovery plan. The qualifying difference is whether or not an organization is able to take effective action during the attack to combat its effects. Attack end cases that are disastrous find members of the organization waiting out the attack with hopes to recover effectively after it is over. In a typical disaster recovery operation, the lives and welfare of the employees are the most important priority while the attack is occurring, given that most disasters are fires, floods, hurricanes, and tornadoes. However, there are attacks that are not natural disasters that fit this category as well, including:

- Electrical blackouts
- Attacks on service providers that result in a loss of communications to the organization (either telephone or Internet)
- Massive, malicious code attacks that sweep through an organization before they can be contained

The objective of this process is that each scenario should be classified as a probable incident or a disaster, and then the corresponding actions required to respond to the scenario should be built into either the IR plan or DR plan.

Incident Response Planning

Incident response planning (IRP) includes the identification of, classification of, and response to an incident. The IR plan is made up of activities that are to be performed when an incident has been identified. Before developing such a plan, you should understand the philosophical approach to incident response planning.

What is an incident? What is incident response? As stated earlier, an incident is an attack against an information asset that poses a clear threat to the confidentiality, integrity, or availability of information resources. If an action that threatens information is confirmed, the action is classified as an incident. All of the threats identified in Chapter 1 could result in attacks that would be classified as information security incidents. For purposes of this discussion, however, attacks are only classified as incidents if they have the following characteristics:

- They are directed against information assets.
- They have a realistic chance of success.
- They could threaten the confidentiality, integrity, or availability of information resources.

Incident response (IR) is, therefore, the set of activities taken to plan for, detect, and correct the impact of an incident on information assets. Prevention is purposefully omitted, as this activity is more a function of information security in general than of incident response. In other words, IR is more reactive than proactive, with the exception of the planning that must occur to prepare the IR teams to be ready to react to an incident.

IR consists of the following four phases:

1. Planning—getting ready to handle incidents

2. Detection—identifying that an incident has occurred

3. Reaction—responding to the immediate threat of an incident and regaining control of information assets

4. Recovery—getting things "back to normal," resolving the damage done during the incident, and understanding what happened to prevent reoccurrence

Disaster Recovery Planning

An event can be categorized as a disaster when the following happens: (1) the organization is unable to mitigate the impact of an incident during the incident, and (2) the level of damage or destruction is so severe that the organization is unable to recover quickly. The difference between an incident and a disaster may be subtle; the contingency planning team must make the distinction, and it may not be possible to do so until an attack occurs. Often an event that is initially classified as an incident is later determined to be a disaster. When this happens, the organization must change how it is responding and take action to secure its most valuable assets to preserve value for the longer term even at the risk of more disruption in the short term.

Disaster recovery planning (DRP) is the process of preparing an organization to handle and recover from a disaster, whether natural or man-made. The key emphasis of a DR plan is to reestablish operations at the primary site, the location at which the organization performs its business. The goal is to make things whole, or as they were before the disaster.

The Disaster Recovery Plan Similar in structure to the IR plan, the DR plan provides detailed guidance in the event of a disaster. It is organized by the type or nature of the disaster and specifies recovery procedures during and after each type of disaster. It also provides details on the roles and responsibilities of the people involved in the disaster recovery effort, and identifies the personnel and agencies that must be notified. Just as the IR plan must be tested, so must the DR plan, using the same testing mechanisms. At a minimum, the DR plan must be reviewed during a walk-through or talk-through on a periodic basis.

Many of the same precepts of incident response apply to disaster recovery:

1. Priorities must be clearly established. The first priority is always the preservation of human life. The protection of data and systems immediately falls to the wayside if the disaster threatens the lives, health, or welfare of the employees of the organization or members of the community in which the organization operates. Only after all employees and neighbors have been safeguarded can the disaster recovery team attend to nonhuman asset protection.

2. Roles and responsibilities must be clearly delineated. Everyone assigned to the DR team should be aware of his or her expected actions during a disaster. Some people are

responsible for coordinating with local authorities, such as fire, police, and medical staff. Others are responsible for the evacuation of personnel, if required. Still others are tasked simply to pack up and leave.

3. Someone must initiate the alert roster and notify key personnel. Those to be notified may be the fire, police, or medical authorities mentioned earlier. They may also include insurance agencies, disaster teams like the Red Cross, and management teams.

4. Someone must be tasked with the documentation of the disaster. Just as in an IR reaction, someone must begin recording what happened to serve as a basis for later determination of why and how the event occurred.

5. If and only if it is possible, attempts must be made to mitigate the impact of the disaster on the operations of the organization. If everyone is safe, and if all the necessary authorities have been notified, some individuals can be tasked with the evacuation of physical assets. Some can be responsible for making sure all systems are securely shut down to prevent further loss of data.

Recovery Operations Reaction to a disaster can vary so widely that it is impossible to describe the process with any accuracy. Each organization must examine the scenarios developed at the start of contingency planning and determine how to respond.

If the physical facilities are spared, the disaster recovery team should begin the restoration of systems and data to reestablish full operational capability. If the organization's facilities do not survive, alternative actions must be taken until new facilities can be acquired. When disaster threatens the viability of the organization at the primary site, disaster recovery undergoes a transition into business continuity.

Business Continuity Planning

Business continuity planning prepares an organization to reestablish critical business operations during a disaster that affects operations at the primary site. If a disaster has rendered the current location unusable, there must be a plan to allow the business to continue to function. Not every business needs such a plan or such facilities. Small companies or fiscally sound organizations may have the latitude to cease operations until the physical facilities can be restored. But organizations such as those in manufacturing and retail may not have this option, because they depend on physical types of commerce and may not be able to relocate operations.

Developing Continuity Programs Once the incident response plans and disaster recovery plans are in place, the organization needs to consider finding temporary facilities to support the continued viability of the business in the event of a disaster. The development of the BC plan is somewhat simpler than that of the IR plan or DR plan, in that it consists primarily of selecting a continuity strategy and integrating the off-site data storage and recovery functions into this strategy. Some of the components of the BC plan could already be integral to the normal operations of the organization, such as an off-site backup service. Others require special consideration and negotiation. The first part of business continuity planning is performed when the joint DR/BC plan is developed. The identification of critical business functions and the resources needed to support them is the cornerstone of the BC plan. When a disaster strikes, these functions are the first to be reestablished at the alternate site. The contingency planning team needs to appoint a group of individuals to evaluate and compare the available alternatives and recommend which strategy should be selected and implemented. The strategy selected usually involves some form of off-site facility, which should be inspected, configured, secured, and tested on a periodic basis. The selection should be reviewed periodically to determine if a superior alternative has emerged or if the organization needs a different solution.

Crisis Management

Disasters are, of course, larger in scale and less manageable than incidents, but the planning processes are the same and in many cases are conducted simultaneously. What may truly distinguish an incident from a disaster are the actions of the response teams. An incident response team typically rushes to duty stations or to the office from home. The first act is to reach for the IR plan. A disaster recovery team may not have the luxury of flipping through a binder to see what must be done. Disaster recovery personnel must know their roles without any supporting documentation. This is a function of preparation, training, and rehearsal. You probably all remember the frequent emergency drills (fire, tornado, or hurricane) from your public school days. Fire or disaster is no less likely in the business world.

Human welfare actions taken during and after a disaster are referred to as **crisis management**. Crisis management differs dramatically from incident response, as it focuses first and foremost on the people involved. It also addresses the viability of the business. The disaster recovery team works closely with the crisis management team. The crisis management team is charged with managing the organization's response to an event. This includes several activities:

- Providing information and perhaps material support for employees and families and other stakeholders during the event

- Assessing the impact that the event has on routine business operations and, when needed, declaring the event an organizational disaster

- Informing stakeholders and, when appropriate, the public of the facts surrounding the event and the action being taken[16]

The crisis management team should establish a base of operations or command center to support communications until the disaster has ended. The team includes individuals from all functional areas of the organization. Key crisis management actions include:

- Verifying personnel head count—Everyone must be accounted for, including those on vacations, leaves of absence, and business trips.

- Checking the alert roster—Alert rosters and general personnel phone lists are used to notify individuals whose assistance may be needed, or simply to tell employees not to report to work until the disaster is over.

- Checking emergency information cards—It is important that each employee have two types of emergency information card. The first is personal emergency information that specifies whom to notify in case of an emergency, any medical conditions, and a photocopy of the employee's driver's license or other identification. The second is a set of instructions on what to do in the event of an emergency. This mini-snapshot of the disaster recovery plan should contain, at a minimum, a contact number or hot line, emergency services numbers (fire, police, medical), evacuation and assembly locations (storm shelters, for example), the name and number of the disaster recovery coordinator, and any other needed information.

Crisis management must balance the needs of the employees with the needs of the business in providing personnel with support for personal and family issues during disasters.

Running Case: For Business Use Only

Mike looked at Alex over the stack of policies Alex had been reading. "Very good start on these, Mr. Truman," he said.

"Thanks, Mike. I've spent a good deal of time on these and wanted them to be on target," Alex replied. "What else do I need to focus on?"

"Well, I think you're going to need a new ISSP called Employee Fair and Responsible Use of Data Mart Equipment *that meets with your CEO's and COO's new intent," Mike replied. "They've indicated that they want to restrict computer use to business only and only provide Web access to those users who really need it."*

"That's not going to go over well," Alex said. "We've traditionally been too relaxed in that area, letting employees use the technology as long as it doesn't interfere with business. Okay, I'll need help with that one. What else?"

"Well, it would help to go ahead and start on the corresponding Managerial SysSP," Mike replied. "That will tell the firewall administrator what rules should be incorporated into the new firewall, based on this ISSP. You won't be able to finish it until we cover exactly what firewall rules are and how they impact the firewall's performance, but you should be able to get started."

"What should go into that document?" Alex asked.

"Oh, allowing Internet access to certain workstations, or blocking external requests for access to remote services unless they are directed to those specific known servers, or no accessing of remote control applications, or prohibiting ICMP from outside—things of that nature," Mike replied.

Chapter Summary

- In order to most effectively secure its networks, an organization must establish a functional and well-designed information security program in the context of a well-planned and fully defined information policy and planning environment. The creation of an information security program requires information security policies, standards and practices, an information security architecture, and a detailed information security blueprint.

- Management must make policy the basis for all information security planning, design, and deployment in order to direct how issues are addressed and how technologies are used. Policy must never conflict with laws; they must stand up in court, if challenged; and they must be properly administered through dissemination and documented

2

acceptance. For a policy to be considered effective and legally enforceable, it must be disseminated, reviewed, understood, complied with, and uniformly enforced. Policy is implemented with an organization-wide information security policy and with as many issue-specific and system-specific policies as are needed.

- After the information security team identifies the vulnerabilities in the information technology systems, the security team develops a design blueprint used to implement the security program. The security blueprint is a detailed version of the security framework, an outline of steps to take to design and implement information security in the organization. There are a number of published information security frameworks, but since each information security environment is unique, the security team may need to modify or adapt pieces from several frameworks.

- Each organization should implement a security education, training, and awareness (SETA) program to supplement the general education and training programs that many organizations have in place to educate staff on information security. A SETA program consists of three elements: security education, security training, and security awareness. The purpose of SETA is to enhance security by improving awareness of the need to protect system resources, developing skills and knowledge so computer users can perform their jobs more securely, and building in-depth knowledge to design, implement, or operate security programs for organizations and systems.

- Managers in IT and information security must assure the continuous availability of information systems. This is achieved with various types of contingency planning, such as incident response, disaster recovery, and business continuity planning. An incident response (IR) plan addresses the identification, classification, response, and recovery from an incident. A disaster recovery (DR) plan addresses the preparation for and recovery from a disaster, whether natural or man-made. A business continuity (BC) plan ensures that critical business functions continue if a catastrophic incident or disaster occurs.

Review Questions

1. What is management's role with regard to information security policies and practices?

2. What are the differences between a policy, a standard, and a practice? What are the three types of security policies? Where would each be used? What type of policy would be needed to guide use of the Web? E-mail? Office equipment for personal use?

3. For a policy to be considered effective and legally enforceable, what must it accomplish?

4. What are the components of an effective EISP?

5. What are the components of an effective ISSP?

6. What is an ACL, and how does it fit into the discussion about policy? (*Hint*: Look at the SysSP.)

7. Who is ultimately responsible for managing a technology? Who is responsible for enforcing policy that affects the use of a technology?

8. What technical means can be established to enhance the probability of success when implementing security policies?

9. What is the difference between a security framework and a security blueprint?

10. How can a security framework assist in the design and implementation of a security infrastructure?

11. Where can a security administrator attain information on established security frameworks?

12. What is the ISO 27000 series of standards? What individual standards make up the series?

13. Briefly describe the history of the standard now known as ISO 27002. In which country did it originate? Has it had any other names?

14. What documents are available from the NIST Computer Resource Center, and how can they support the development of a security framework?

15. Define "benchmarking." What is it used for?

16. Briefly describe the spheres of security. Who could benefit from understanding this approach to security?

17. What is defense in depth? Why is it so often encountered in information security technical control settings?

18. What resources are available on the Web that can aid an organization in developing best practices as part of a security framework?

19. What is SETA? Which organizations should have a SETA program?

20. What is contingency planning? How is it different from routine management planning?

21. What are the components of contingency planning, and what are the major steps used for contingency planning?

22. When is IR planning used?

23. When is DR planning used?

24. When is BC planning used? How do you determine when to use IR planning, DR planning, or BC planning?

25. What are the elements of a business impact analysis?

Real World Exercises

1. Using a graphics program, design security awareness posters on the following themes: updating antivirus signatures, protecting sensitive information, watching out for e-mail viruses, prohibiting the personal use of company equipment, changing and protecting passwords, avoiding social engineering, and protecting software copyrights. What other areas can you come up with?

2. Search the Web for a listing of security education and training programs in your area. Make a list and determine which type of program (online, on-site at an employer's location, at a conference facility, at a training facility) has the most examples. Determine the costs associated with each example. Which do you feel would be more cost effective?

3. Search the Web for examples of issue-specific security policies. What types of policies can you find? Draft a simple issue-specific policy (using the format provided in the text) called "Fair and Responsible Use of College Computers." Does your school have a similar policy? Does it contain all the elements listed in the text?

4. Use your library or the Web to find a reported natural disaster that occurred at least 180 days ago. From the news accounts, determine if local or national officials had prepared disaster plans and if these plans were used. Determine how the plans helped the officials improve the response to the disaster. How did the plans help the recovery?

5. Classify each of the following occurrences as an incident or disaster. If an occurrence is a disaster, determine whether or not business continuity plans would be called into play.

   a. A hacker gets into the network and deletes files from a server.

   b. A fire breaks out in the storeroom and sets off sprinklers on that floor. Some computers are damaged, but the fire is contained.

   c. A tornado hits a local power company, and the company will be without power for three to five days.

   d. Employees go on strike, and the company could be without critical workers for weeks.

   e. A disgruntled employee takes a critical server home, sneaking it out after hours.

6. For each of the scenarios in question 5, describe the steps necessary to restore operations. Indicate whether or not law enforcement would be involved.

Hands-On Projects

Project 2-1: Identifying Local Computer Security Policies

As mentioned in this chapter, the term "policy" also describes the configurations of security devices and security software installed on computer systems. In this exercise, you look at the security policies configuration of a Windows computer. This exercise presumes you are using Windows XP (SP 2 or later) or Vista (SP 1 or later).

First, you will look at the various tools that are available to secure the Windows operating system, and then you will look at some policy templates that can be implemented for immediate improvements in system security. The security professional can choose to employ recommended settings provided in Microsoft's Security Guides. These guides, consisting of a combination of documents and .msi software kits, provide a quick way to get a predefined set of security standards implemented. Administrators can then make any custom changes they desire. The kits can be downloaded from the Microsoft Download Center (*www.microsoft.com/downloads/en/default.aspx*) by searching on Windows XP (or Vista) Security Guide.

1. If your instructor has not already downloaded the materials, do so at this time. After determining which type of system you have—an enterprise client (EC), a stand-alone system (SA), or a specialized security system with limited functions (SSLF), you can select the security template that best suits your situation. (*Note*: The Vista version does not have a stand-alone option.) The templates also differ for desktops and for laptop

computers. Most settings can be made manually based on recommendations in the guide, or they can be selected from an auto-installer.

2. Double-click the Microsoft Security Compliance Manager file and follow the instructions to install the kit.

3. Open the folder containing the installed files. If you have a computer that is part of an Active Directory domain, you should consult with your instructor on whether you should change the security settings. Chapter 1 in the XP Security Guide provides information on using the guide for clients in a domain. The remainder of this exercise will focus on installing the XP Default Security Template on a stand-alone system. It is recommended that the entire Security Guide be reviewed and the decision made on which template is best for the organization before installing templates in a corporate environment.

4. Open a new MMC console by clicking **Start, Run** and typing **mmc**. Click **OK**. Now, click **File, Add/Remove Snap-in**, and then click **Add**. Click **Group Policy Object Editor** and click **Add**. Ensure the Local Computer is listed in the Group Policy Object data field.

5. Click **Finish**, and then click **Close** on the Add Standalone Snap-in window. Click **OK**.

6. Click the **plus** [+] symbol beside Local Computer Policy, Computer Configuration and Windows Settings to expand the folders.

7. Select Security Settings.

8. Right-click the **Security Settings** folder, and then click **Import Policy**.

9. Browse to the location you installed the security templates to and select the default security template for Windows XP, and then click **Open**. The settings from the file will be imported into the Group Policy Editor. Disregard any error messages you may see. If a higher-level template has already been installed, the system may reject the lower-level template, in which case note the error message and move on.

10. You've updated the security policy on this system. In order to allow the next person to use this system without your changes interfering, close the console without saving.

Project 2-2: Incident Handling Form

You don't have to start from scratch when it comes to developing incident response materials. In fact, if you are hired to handle security at a company, when it comes time to discuss the development of an incident response program, you can produce a template and show it to management so they get an idea of what's required.

1. Open a Web browser and go to **www.sans.org/score/incidentforms/**.

2. Click the **Incident Identification** link.

3. Using the scenario below, print and complete the Incident form for submission to your instructor or for discussion in class.

4. Close all open applications when finished.

Scenario: The Data Mart help desk has just received an anonymous e-mail. A hacker has accessed one of the company's data servers and provided a screenshot of the root directory. You're manning the help desk and want to report the incident to your supervisor, but you don't have an established IR plan. You've done a lot of reading on the subject, however, and you know about the SANS site, so you take the initiative to use their template.

Running Case Projects

CASE PROJECTS

Now it's time to help Alex with some of his policy issues related to the firewall operations. For these exercises, you will create two policy documents that will guide you in building the firewall in future exercises.

2

Student Tasks

1. Create an ISSP for *Employee Fair and Responsible Use of Data Mart Equipment* using the outline specified in this chapter. If you're having problems visualizing what the completed document will look like, use a Web browser to look for sample policies. Look for examples of organizational computer use or Web use policies, starting with your own institution.

2. Begin a Managerial SysSP for the proposed firewall. You don't have all the information to complete the document, but get started by using the outline provided in this chapter and completing as much information as possible. Questions you'll need to make assumptions about include:

   • Does Data Mart have its own Web server for customer information? How about an e-commerce server?

   • Does Data Mart have its own e-mail server, or does it outsource this to its Internet Service Provider?

   • Does Data Mart have other servers or services that need to be accessed internally or externally? What are they and who needs to access them?

Endnotes

1. National Institute of Standards and Technology, *Executive Guide to the Protection of Information Resources*, SP 500–169, 1989. Accessed 15 April 2006 from *http://csrc .nist.gov/publications/PubsSPArch.html*.

2. Charles Cresson Wood, "Integrated Approach Includes Information Security." *Security* 37, no. 2 (February 2000): 43–44.

3. National Institute of Standards and Technology, *An Introduction to Computer Security: The NIST Handbook*, SP 800–12, Accessed 31 January, 2011 from *http://csrc .nist.gov/publications/nistpubs/800-12/handbook.pdf*.

4. Derived from a number of sources, the most notable of which is *www.wustl.edu/policies/ infosecurity.html*.

5. Robert J. Aalberts, Anthony M. Townsend, and Michael E. Whitman. "Considerations for an Effective Telecommunications Use Policy." *Communications of the ACM* 42, no. 6 (June 1999): 101–109.

6. National Institute of Standards and Technology. *An Introduction to Computer Security: The NIST Handbook*, SP 800–12.

7. National Institute of Standards and Technology. *Information Security Management, Code of Practice for Information Security Management*. ISO/IEC 17799. (6 December 2001).

8. Praxiom Title 37: ISO 17799: 2005 in Plain English.

9. National Institute of Standards and Technology. *Information Security Management, Code of Practice for Information Security Management,* ISO/IEC 17799. (6 December 2001).

10. National Institute of Standards and Technology. *Guidelines on Firewalls and Firewall Policy*, SP 800–41, Rev. 1 Accessed 11 November 2009 from *csrc.nist.gov/publications/ PubsSPs.html.*

11. National Institute of Standards and Technology. *Guidelines on Firewalls and Firewall Policy*, SP 800–41, Rev. 1 Accessed 11 November 2009 from *csrc.nist.gov/publications/PubsSPs. html.*

12. National Institute of Standards and Technology. *Recommended Security Controls for Federal Information Systems and Organizations*, SP 800–53, Rev. 3 Accessed 11 November 2009 from *csrc.nist.gov/publications/PubsSPs.html.*

13. National Institute of Standards and Technology, *An Introduction to Computer Security: The NIST Handbook*, SP 800–12, Accessed 31 January 2011 from *http://csrc .nist.gov/publications/nistpubs/800-12/handbook.pdf.*

14. National Institute of Standards and Technology, *An Introduction to Computer Security: The NIST Handbook*, SP 800–12, Accessed 31 January 2011 from *http://csrc.nist .gov/publications/nistpubs/800-12/handbook.pdf.*

15. William R. King and Paul Gray, *The Management of Information Systems* (Chicago: Dryden Press, 1989), 359.

16. Roberta Witty, "What is Crisis Management?" *Gartner Online* (19 September 2001) Accessed 30 April 2007 from *www.gartner.com/DisplayDocument?id=340971.*

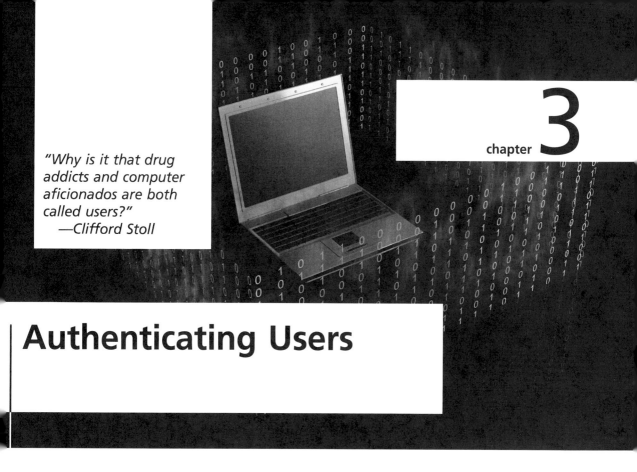

chapter 3

Authenticating Users

"Why is it that drug addicts and computer aficionados are both called users?"
—Clifford Stoll

After reading this chapter and completing the exercises, you will be able to:

- Explain why authentication is a critical aspect of perimeter defense
- Explain why firewalls authenticate and how they identify users
- Describe user, client, and session authentication
- List the advantages and disadvantages of popular centralized authentication systems
- Discuss the potential weaknesses of password security systems
- Describe the use of password security tools

Running Case: Getting Them to Drink

"You know, the more security you're advising us to add, the harder and harder it is for us to get any actual work done around here."

This was just one of several dozen comments that Rachel, the office manager at Onsite Security Services, had been reacting to all morning. Ever since she was asked by her manager to take over some of the information security tasks that were left undone in the company, she had been trying to build a consensus for action. Her meeting with representatives from Data Mart hadn't been going well. No matter how hard Rachel tried to convince them that increased security would give them the data protection they wanted, the users continued to balk.

"I certainly understand your concerns," she said to the group. "But strong authentication, for example, is crucial to making sure that only authorized individuals with a valid, business-justified need to know are accessing the information. And since that information doesn't belong to Data Mart, we have to be extra careful to protect it against unauthorized disclosure, modification, or destruction."

"Okay, but why are you insisting on this labeling scheme?" one of the Data Mart representatives asked. "Our customers' data isn't paper-based, it's all electronic."

You can lead a horse to water, Rachel thought to herself, but you can't make it drink. "Your customers' data may not be paper-based, but a lot of your internal infrastructure plans, your database schema, and your network architecture documents are. You say you need hard copies for planning purposes, and that's fine, but if those documents are unintentionally disclosed, unauthorized individuals could gain access to your networks, and then to your customers' data."

"So you're recommending token-based authentication, with key fobs that we have to keep on us at all times?" a member of the Data Mart group asked. "And all our critical data should be clearly labeled as such when printed out?"

"Exactly," Rachel replied. "It may seem onerous at first, but you'll quickly get used to it. The government and military have been operating with much higher security than this for a very long time. It becomes second nature. Now about your fax modems...."

"We don't have fax modems, those are obsolete!" A chuckle spread through the room, and then died quickly when Rachel fleshed out the issue.

"Our phone sweep identified 14 fax modems currently connected to computers on your internal network," Rachel said. "Most appear to be unused, but we were able to access several computers over them with minimal effort. Apparently, it was standard operating procedure several years ago to automatically connect phone lines to computers when installing."

"Oh, yeah," Dan Fielding, the tech support coordinator, said, looking around. "I completely forgot about that. I thought we disconnected all of those when we went to a fax service. The new service sends faxes as e-mail attachments, and we use scanners now to send outbound faxes. I bet every single secretary's computer is still hooked up."

"I guess we have something that needs to be done right away," Rachel replied. "Now about those tokens...."

Introduction

Firewall security strategies, such as packet filtering, are used to authenticate communications requests rather than individuals. Some firewalls can perform a stronger level of authentication—that is, they can reliably determine whether persons or entities are who or what they claim to be. This level of authentication is important because if an unauthorized user gains access to protected resources, the whole purpose of the firewall has been defeated. For this reason, many firewalls implement user authentication schemes to support their other security approaches. Authentication is a critical component in effective access control. Without authentication, it is impossible to control the flow of information so that only those with a need to access the information for legitimate business purposes have it.

In this chapter, you learn what access controls are and why they are important to perimeter defense in general. Then you learn how and why firewalls serve as access controls in providing authentication services. This chapter also introduces the main types of authentication performed by firewalls—client, user, and session—as well as the different types of centralized authentication methods that firewalls can use, including Kerberos, TACACS+, and RADIUS. Because passwords are a critical part of all the aforementioned authentication schemes, you'll explore password security issues and learn about special password security tools, including one-time passwords. The chapter ends with a section on the different authentication protocols used by full-featured, enterprise-level firewalls.

Access Controls

Access controls encompass four processes:

- **Identification**—obtaining the identity of the entity requesting access to a logical or physical area
- **Authentication**—confirming the identity of the entity seeking access to a logical or physical area
- **Authorization**—determining which actions that entity can perform in that physical or logical area
- **Accountability**—documenting the activities of the authorized individual and systems

Access controls specifically address the admission of users into a trusted area of the organization. These areas can include information systems, physically restricted areas such as computer rooms, and even the organization in its entirety. Access controls usually consist of a combination of policies, programs, and technologies. Physical and technological access controls will be discussed in more depth in later chapters.

Access controls integrate a number of key principles related to information security. These principles, which emphasize the need to restrict information to those with a real business need, include the following:

- **Least privilege**—This is the principle by which employees are provided access to the minimal amount of information for the least duration of time necessary to perform their duties. It presumes a need to know, but restricts the level of access within that principle. Also, individuals are only provided the degree of control needed—that is e.g., read-only access.

- **Need to know**—Similar to least privilege, this principle limits individuals' information access to what is required to perform their jobs. It is most frequently associated with data classification schemes, discussed later in this chapter.

- **Separation of duties**—This principle increases the security of information and other assets by requiring that more than one individual be responsible for a particular information asset, process, or task. It reduces the chance of an individual violating information security by increasing the scrutiny on any one user.

Access controls can be classified based on their function:

- Preventive—help the organization avoid an incident
- Deterrent—discourage or deter an incident from occurring
- Detective—detect or identify an incident or threat when it occurs
- Corrective—remedy a circumstance or mitigate the damage caused during an incident
- Recovery—restore operating conditions to normal
- Compensating—use alternate controls to resolve shortcomings[1]

A second approach to categorizing access controls involves the authority for the controls. They can be mandatory, nondiscretionary, or discretionary. Each category regulates access to a particular type or collection of information, as explained below.

Mandatory Access Control (MAC)

Mandatory Access Control (MAC) is a requirement in some settings. When used, it is structured and coordinated with both a data classification scheme and a personnel clearance scheme. Users and data owners have little or no control over access to the information resources being controlled by the MAC environment. A MAC will use a data classification scheme that assigns each collection or type of information to a sensitivity level. Each user is also rated with a sensitivity level called a clearance that will specify the level of information he or she may access.

One variation of MAC is called **lattice-based access control**, in which users are assigned a matrix of authorizations for various areas of access. The level of authorization may vary depending on the classification authorizations that individuals possess for each group of information assets or resources. The lattice structure contains subjects and objects, and the boundaries associated with each subject/object pair are clearly demarcated. Lattice-based access control specifies the level of access each subject has to each object, if any. With this type of control, the column of attributes associated with a particular object (such as a printer) is referred to as an **access control list (ACL)**. The row of attributes associated with a particular subject (such as a user) is referred to as a **capability table**, as described in Chapter 2.

Data Classification Model Corporate and military organizations use a variety of classification schemes. As you might expect, the **U.S. Department of Defense (DoD) classification scheme** relies on a more complex categorization system than the schemes of most corporations. The military is perhaps the best-known user of data classification schemes. It has invested heavily in information security (InfoSec), operations security (OpSec), and communications security (ComSec). In fact, many developments in data communications and information security are the result of military-sponsored research and development.

For most information, the U.S. military uses a five-level classification scheme, defined in Executive Order 12958 and presented here:

1. Unclassified data—information that is freely distributed to the public, given that it poses no threat to U.S. national interests.

2. Sensitive But Unclassified (SBU) data—information that, when misused, might have negative consequences for the U.S. national interest, the DoD, or the privacy of affected personnel; common designations include For Official Use Only, Not for Public Release, and For Internal Use Only.

3. Confidential data—information that, when misused, might cause damage to U.S. national security interests; examples include information that describes military forces or reveals technical details about national defense capabilities.

4. Secret data—information that, when misused, might cause serious damage to U.S. national security interests; examples include information that could cause a disruption of foreign relations or could reveal military plans or compromise scientific or technological issues relating to national security.

5. Top secret data—information the disclosure of which could cause grave damage to U.S. national security interests. This classification comes with the general expectation that individuals entrusted with top secret information are expected to honor the classification of the information even after they are no longer employed in the role that originally allowed them to access the information.

The military also has some specialty classification ratings, such as Personnel Information and Evaluation Reports, to protect some specialized areas of information. Federal agencies such as the FBI and CIA also use specialty classification schemes, such as Need-to-Know and Named Projects. Obviously, Need-to-Know authorization allows access to information by individuals who need the information to perform their work. Named Projects are clearance levels based on a scheme similar to Need-to-Know. When an operation, project, or set of classified data is created, it is assigned a code name. Next, a list of authorized individuals is created and assigned to either the Need-to-Know or the Named Projects category.

Most organizations do not need the detailed level of classification used by the military or federal agencies. Nevertheless, they may need to classify their data to provide protection. A simple scheme can allow an organization to protect sensitive information, such as marketing or research data, personnel data, customer data, and general internal communications. A scheme such as the following could be adopted:

- Public—for general public dissemination, such as an advertisement or press release

- For Official Use Only—not for public release, but not particularly sensitive, such as internal communications

- Sensitive—important information that could embarrass the organization or cause loss of market share if compromised

- Classified—essential and confidential information, disclosure of which could severely damage the well-being of the organization

Security Clearances Another thing to consider with respect to data classification schemes is the personnel security clearance structure, in which each user of an information asset is assigned an authorization level that indicates the level of information classification he or she can access. This is usually accomplished by assigning each employee a titular role, such as data entry clerk, development programmer, information security analyst, or even CIO. Most organizations have developed a set of roles and corresponding security clearances, so that individuals are assigned authorization levels that correlate with the classifications of the information assets.

Beyond a simple reliance on an individual's security clearance is the need-to-know principle, discussed earlier. In some organizations, regardless of your security clearance, you are not allowed to view data simply because it falls within your clearance level; you must also meet the need-to-know requirement. This extra requirement ensures that the confidentiality of information is properly maintained.

Nondiscretionary Access Controls

Nondiscretionary access controls are determined by a central authority in the organization. When they are based on roles, they are called **role-based access controls** or **RBAC**; when they are based on a specified set of tasks, they are called **task-based access controls**. Task-based controls can, in turn, be based on lists of tasks that are maintained on subjects or objects. Role-based controls are tied to the role that a particular user performs in an organization, whereas task-based controls are tied to a particular assignment or responsibility.

Task- and role-based controls make it easier to manage the complexity that is a natural part of these types of restrictions, especially if there are many assets being controlled, many personnel being controlled, and frequent personnel changes. Instead of constantly assigning and revoking privileges, the administrator simply assigns the associated access rights to the role or task. When individuals are subsequently assigned to that role or task, they automatically receive the corresponding access. The administrator can easily remove individuals' associations with roles and tasks, thereby revoking their access.

Discretionary Access Controls (DACs)

DACs are implemented at the discretion of the data user. The ability to share resources in a peer-to-peer configuration allows users to control and possibly provide access to information or resources at their disposal. The users can allow general, unrestricted access, or they can allow specific individuals or sets of individuals to access these resources. As an example, suppose a user has a hard drive containing information to be shared with office coworkers. This user can allow access to specific individuals by listing their names in the share control function. Most personal computer operating systems are designed based on the DAC model.

One discretionary model is **rule-based access controls**, where access is granted based on a set of rules specified by the central authority. This is a DAC model because the individual user is the one who creates the rules. Role-based models, described in the previous section, can also be implemented under DAC if an individual system owner desires to create the rules for other users of that system or its data.

Other DAC models include the following:

- Content-dependent access controls—Here, access to a specific set of information is dependent on the information's content. For example, the marketing department needs access to marketing data, the accounting department needs access to accounting data, etc.

- Constrained user interfaces—Some systems are designed specifically to restrict the information that an individual user can access. The most well-known example is a bank's Automated Teller Machine (ATM). While there is additional data that can be viewed by an authorized user, the interface restricts the user options to simple queries, transfers, deposits, and withdrawls.

- Temporal (time-based) isolation—Some information can only be accessed depending on what time of day it is. A physical example is a time-release safe, used in most convenience and fast-food establishments. The safe can only be opened during a specific time frame, even by an authorized user (e.g., the store manager).

3

Centralized vs. Decentralized Access Controls

When a discretionary form of access control is specified, it does not necessarily mean that the individual user will be responsible for making all decisions about access to the data. A collection of users with access to the same data will typically have a centralized access control authority, even using a discretionary access control model. The level of centralization as opposed to decentralization will vary by organization and type of information protected. The lower the level of information needed to be protected, the more decentralized the control will be. Centralized access control tools like RADIUS and Kerberos, described later in this chapter, are frequently employed.

The Authentication Process

Authentication is the act of confirming the identity of a potential user. Once the identity is confirmed as authentic, that user is authorized to perform specific actions on the system or network. Potential users (sometimes called supplicants) first propose an identity and then verify that identity by providing one or more of the following:

- Something you know—a piece of information known to the supplicant, such as a password or passphrase

- Something you have—proof of physical possession of something, such as a smart card (a plastic card with an embedded microchip that can store data about the owner) or a metal key

- Something you are—a piece of information regarding your physical nature; this can be subdivided into physical attributes (fingerprints or iris scans) or pattern evaluations and recognition (e.g., a voiceprint speech pattern)

- Something you do—an activity that only the user can perform, which is then measured or analyzed, such as a signature analysis or a keyboard typing pattern

If you have a bank card that enables you to withdraw cash from a debit account, you have made use of a smart card. Along with the card (something you have) you also need to enter a PIN (something you know) to authenticate yourself to the bank's network. After you are authenticated, the ATM gives you access to your account. When an authentication system uses two or more different forms of confirming the proposed identity, it is said to use **strong authentication**.

In the field of network computing, authentication takes one of two forms:

- Local authentication: A server maintains a local file of usernames and passwords that it refers to for matching the username-password pair being supplied by a client. This is the most common form of authentication, the weakness of which is that passwords can be forgotten, stolen, or accidentally revealed.

- Centralized authentication service: A centralized server handles identification, authentication, authorization, and accountability. Accountability means tracking who has done what and when. It is most commonly set up as a form of auditing and occurs when a system records the activities of each user and writes details about each activity to a log file.

Both types of authentication might require a user to enter a password at some point, which by itself is single-factor authentication: the user only needs to know one item (the password) to initiate the authentication process. Physical objects, such as smart cards or other tokens, provide two-factor authentication, a more stringent level in which users need to both have something (the token) and know something (the PIN or password) to gain access. Two-factor authentication can be used to strengthen either of the aforementioned systems, but it is most commonly used with a centralized authentication server.

There are two types of **tokens** shown in Figure 3-1: synchronous and asynchronous. **Synchronous tokens** use the present time, to which both the token and the server have been synchronized, to generate an authentication number entered during the user login. **Asynchronous tokens** use a challenge-response system. The server challenges the user with a number, the user enters the challenge number into the token, and the token calculates a response number. The user then enters the response number into the system to gain access. Only a person who has the correct token can calculate the correct response number and thus log into the system. This system does not require synchronization and does not suffer from timing issues.

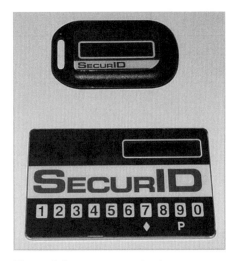

Figure 3-1 Access Control Tokens
© Cengage Learning 2012

The use of **biometrics** (retinal scans, fingerprints, and the like) for authentication is mainly done by large, security-minded entities such as banking institutions and credit card centers for regulating access to sensitive information, but it is also gaining ground in the rest of the corporate world.

How Firewalls Implement the Authentication Process

Most operating systems are equipped with access control schemes. Web servers can be configured to authenticate clients who want to access certain protected content. Firewalls, too, can perform user authentication. In fact, many organizations depend on firewalls to provide more secure authentication than conventional systems. Authentication is a key function because firewalls exist to give external users (such as mobile users and telecommuters) access to protected resources.

Authentication comes into play when a firewall is called upon to apply its set of rules to specific individuals or groups of users. For instance, if the IT staff has access to all the organization's computers, a higher level of security is needed to ensure that only the proper individuals are granted that level of access. On the other hand, the head of a corporate headquarters accounting department may need remote access to the subordinate division's bookkeeping system once a quarter or once a year—not frequently enough to warrant the establishment of a persistent VPN between the two locations' LANs.

A firewall uses authentication to identify individuals so that it can apply the rules that are associated with those individuals. Some firewalls use authentication to give employees access to common resources, such as the Web or a file transfer protocol (FTP). Some identify the user associated with a particular IP address; after the user is authorized, the IP address can then be used to send and receive information with hosts on the internal network.

The exact steps that firewalls follow to authenticate users may vary, but the general process is the same:

1. The client makes a request to access a resource.
2. The firewall intercepts the request and prompts the user for name and password.
3. The user submits the requested information to the firewall.
4. The user is authenticated.
5. The request is checked against the firewall's rule base.
6. If the request matches an existing allow rule, the user is granted access.
7. The user accesses the desired resources.

This exchange between external client and authenticating firewall is illustrated in Figure 3-2.

Firewall Authentication Methods

Some firewalls, such as Check Point's firewall architectures, provide a variety of authentication methods, including user, client, or session authentication.

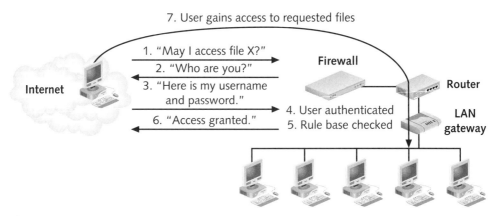

Figure 3-2 Basic User Authentication
© Cengage Learning 2012

User Authentication User authentication is the simplest type of authentication and the one with which you are most likely to be familiar. Upon receiving a request, a program prompts the user for a username and password. When the information is submitted, the software checks the information against a list of usernames and passwords in its database. If a match is made, the user is authenticated. An example of how a new user authentication setup looks for the program NetProxy is shown in Figure 3-3.

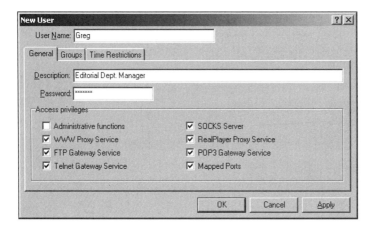

Figure 3-3 NetProxy Authentication
© Cengage Learning 2012

User authentication can enable the following users to access your internal servers:

- Employees who work remotely or who are traveling
- Contractors who work on-site
- Freelancers who work off-site
- Visitors who want to do some work or take a look at your system from your offices

- Employees in branch offices
- Interns
- Employees of partner companies
- Members of the public who may need to get into your internal network to make purchases, change contact information, or review account information

Authorized users should be added to your access control lists (ACLs). The ACLs can be organized by directory or even by individual files, but most often they're organized by groups of users, because this simplifies administration. How you organize the ACLs depends on how many users you have, how many resources you need to protect, and how much time you have to administer the ACL.

Client Authentication Of course, not every outside user should have access to every-thing on the network. **Client authentication** can help you establish limits to user access. It is similar to user authentication, but with the addition of usage limits. The firewall enables the authenticated user to access the desired resources for a specific period of time (for instance, one hour) or a specific number of times (for instance, three accesses). For example, NetProxy lets you assign time limits by double-clicking the name of a configured user group and then editing the settings in the Time Restrictions tab (see Figure 3-4).

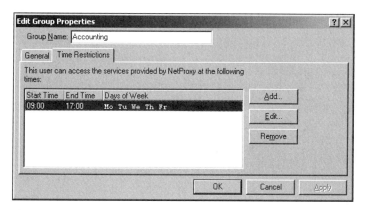

Figure 3-4 Example of Time-Limited Authentication
© Cengage Learning 2012

To configure client authentication, you need to set up one of two types of authentication systems:

- **Standard sign-on** system—clients, after being successfully authenticated, are allowed to access whatever resources they need or perform any desired functions, such as transferring files or viewing Web pages
- **Specific sign-on** system—clients must authenticate each time they access a server or use a service on the protected network

Session Authentication Session authentication requires authentication whenever a client system attempts to connect to a network resource and establish a session (a period when communications are exchanged). It can be used with any service. The client system wishing to be authenticated is usually equipped with a software agent that enables the authentication process; the server or firewall detects the agent when the connection request is made. When necessary, the firewall intercepts the connection request and contacts the agent. The agent performs the authentication, and the firewall allows the connection to the required resource.

Some advanced firewalls offer multiple authentication methods. Choosing one depends on the client operating system and the applications you need to authenticate. Choose user authentication if the protocols you want authorized users to use include FTP, HTTP, HTTPS, rlogin, or Telnet. Client authentication or session authentication should be used when only a single user is coming from a single IP address. Table 3-1 gives the reasons for using each service.

Method	Use When...
User Authentication	• You want to scan the content of IP packets. • The protocol in use is HTTP, HTTPS, FTP, rlogin, or Telnet. • You need to authenticate for each session.
Client Authentication	• The user to be authenticated will use a specific IP address. • The protocol in use is not HTTP, HTTPS, FTP, rlogin, or Telnet. • You want a user to be authenticated for a specific length of time.
Session Authentication	• The individual user to be authenticated will come from a specific IP address. • The protocol in use is not HTTP, HTTPS, FTP, rlogin, or Telnet. • You want a client to be authenticated for each session.

Table 3-1   Authentication Methods

Centralized Authentication

Large corporations can develop complex sets of security requirements that are difficult to maintain and require different types of authentication control for different purposes. Fortunately, deploying a centralized authentication server can greatly simplify such enterprise-wide authentication. This centralized server maintains all the authorizations for users regardless of where the user is located or how the user connects to the network.

In a centralized authentication setup, a server—sometimes referred to as an **authentication, authorization, and accounting (AAA) server**—alleviates the need to provide each server on the network with a separate database of usernames and passwords, each of which would have to be updated every time a password changed or a user was added. The centralized authentication process is illustrated in Figure 3-5. Here, a client on a local network requests access to a program held on an application server, but first the client has to be authenticated using the authentication server. Two levels of trust are involved: the client trusts that the authentication server holds the correct information, as indicated by number 2 in Figure 3-5, and the application server trusts that the authentication server can correctly identity and authorize the client, as indicated by number 3 in Figure 3-5. The scenario illustrated in Figure 3-5 has a substantial downside: the authentication server becomes a single point of

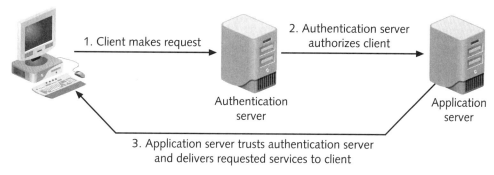

Figure 3-5 Centralized Authentication
© Cengage Learning 2012

failure. If that device fails or is compromised, the authentication process used for the entire organization will come to a standstill, and all information systems will become inoperable. This is a severe threat to the availability of these systems, when they are one glitch or one failed hard drive away from failure. An organization that uses this type of method must also have a contingency plan in place to get the server back online or provide alternative servers to limit the downtime a failure or compromise to this system would cause.

Centralized authentication can use a number of different authentication methods. The following sections examine some of the most common ones, including Kerberos, TACACS+, and RADIUS.

Kerberos

Kerberos was developed at the Massachusetts Institute of Technology (MIT) in the university's Athena Project. It is designed to provide authentication and encryption on standard clients and servers. Instead of a server having to trust a client over an untrusted network, both client and server place their trust in the Kerberos server. Kerberos provides an effective network authentication system that is used internally on many Windows systems. Although Kerberos is useful on internal networks, it is not recommended for authentication of outside users because it uses cleartext, or unencrypted, passwords.

Remote users should make use of encrypted transmissions or one-time passwords, which are discussed in Chapter 9.

The Kerberos system of granting access to a client that requests a service is quite involved (and thus quite secure). The steps are as follows:

1. The client requests a file or other service.

2. The client is prompted for a username and password.

3. The client submits a username and password. The request goes to an Authentication Server (AS) that is part of the Kerberos system. The AS creates an encrypted code called a **session key** that is based on the client's password plus a random number associated with the service being requested. The session key functions as a **Ticket-granting ticket (TGT)**.

4. AS grants the TGT.

5. The client presents the TGT to a **Ticket-granting server (TGS)**, which is also part of the Kerberos system and that may or may not be the same server as the AS.

6. The TGS grants a session ticket. The TGS forwards the session ticket to the server holding the requested file or service.

7. The client gains access.

The Kerberos authentication server is also known as a Key Distribution Center (KDC). In Windows 2003, 2008, XP, Vista, and 7, a Windows domain controller can also function as an authentication server. The Kerberos server must be highly secured because of the strong level of trust placed in it.

One great advantage of using the Kerberos ticket system is that passwords are not stored on the system and thus cannot be intercepted by hackers. The tickets issued are specific to the individual user who made the request and to the services the user is attempting to access. Tickets tend to have a time limit (typically, eight hours, though this can be configured by the security administrator). Before a ticket expires, the client may make additional requests using the same ticket without reauthenticating. Another advantage of Kerberos is that it is widely used in the UNIX environment, which enables authentication to take place across operating systems: a Windows client can be authenticated by a UNIX server, and vice versa. The authentication process is illustrated in Figure 3-6. You can download multiple versions of both the Kerberos client and server from the various releases of krb5 shown on the MIT Kerberos Distribution page at *http://web.mit.edu/Kerberos/*.

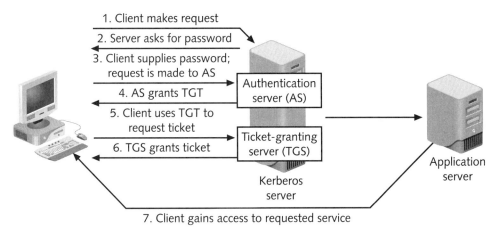

Figure 3-6 Kerberos Authentication
© Cengage Learning 2012

TACACS+

Terminal Access Controller Access Control System Plus (TACACS+)—commonly called "tac-plus"—is the latest and strongest version of a set of authentication protocols developed by Cisco Systems. TACACS+ replaced its less-secure predecessor protocols, TACACS and XTACACS. All of these protocols provide what Cisco has dubbed the **AAA services (authentication, authorization, accounting)**, which form an essential part of a dial-up environment.

TACACS+ and its predecessor protocols all provide authentication for dial-in users and are used primarily on UNIX-based networks. TACACS+ uses a hashing algorithm (MD5) to keep the password itself a secret while it is being authenticated over the network. It provides centralized authentication services so that a network access server such as a router or firewall doesn't have to handle dial-in user authentication. You might have to use TACACS+ or RADIUS (described in the following section) if your firewall doesn't support authentication or if your authentication needs are so extensive that they might slow down other tasks the firewall is called on to perform. For more information about the widely used Internet hashing algorithm MD5, read RFC 1321—The MD5 Message-Digest Algorithm at *www.rfc-editor .org/rfc/rfc1321.txt.*

3

RADIUS

Remote Authentication Dial-In User Service (RADIUS) is the other common protocol used to provide dial-in authentication. Note that RADIUS still transmits unencrypted authentication packets across the network, which means they are vulnerable to attacks from packet sniffers. RADIUS is generally considered to provide a lower level of security than TACACS+, even though it's more widely supported.

TACACS+ and RADIUS Compared

If you authenticate users who connect to your network from remote locations, chances are you'll use either TACACS+ or RADIUS. The following sections compare the two protocols' strength of security, filtering characteristics, proxy characteristics, and NAT characteristics.

Strength of Security Table 3-2 summarizes the characteristics of TACACS+ and RADIUS.

As Table 3-2 suggests, TACACS+ provides stronger security than RADIUS. For example, the Transmission Control Protocol (TCP) is considered more secure than User Datagram Protocol (UDP), an alternative network communications protocol, because when a host sends a TCP packet, it expects a packet to be sent in response with the ACK bit sent to show that a connection has been established. ACK (for "acknowledgement"), is one of the flags in the TCP header part of a packet, and it indicates that the destination computer has received the packets that were previously sent. UDP, in contrast, is considered "connectionless." If a UDP packet is sent, an acknowledgement packet is not sent. If the destination host doesn't receive the packet, it simply asks for the packet to be re-sent.

TACACS+	RADIUS
Uses TCP	Uses UDP
Full packet encryption between client and server	Encrypts only passwords—other information is unencrypted
Separate authentication, authorization, and accounting	Combined authentication and authorization
Passwords in the database may be encrypted	Passwords in the database are in clear text

Table 3-2 Security Characteristics of TACACS+ and RADIUS

TCP traffic can be selectively blocked by firewalls based on the presence of the ACK bit. TACACS+ also does full-packet encryption and handles accounting (that is, auditing or logging) as well as authentication and authorization; RADIUS stores passwords in clear text. Note, however, that if you use both a firewall and an authentication server, the encryption benefits of TACACS+ aren't as dramatic because the firewall receives communications directly from the Internet, and the firewall and authentication server communicate with one another over a trusted network. RADIUS can be a viable solution in this type of network configuration.

Filtering Characteristics TACACS+ uses TCP Port 49, so in order to use it, you need to set up rules that enable clients to exchange authorization packets with the TACACS+ or RADIUS server. RADIUS uses UDP Port 1812 for authentication and UDP Port 1813 for accounting. Table 3-3 shows a set of packet-filtering rules that enables users on an internal network protected by a firewall to be authenticated by a TACACS+ or RADIUS server.

Direction	Protocol	Source Port	Destination Port	Remarks
Inbound	TCP	All ports > 1023	49	Enables external client to connect to internal TACACS+ server
Outbound	TCP	49	All ports > 1023	Allows internal TACACS+ server to respond to external clients
Inbound	UDP	All ports > 1023	1812	Allows external client to connect to internal RADIUS server
Outbound	UDP	1812	All ports > 1023	Allows internal RADIUS server to respond to external client
Inbound	UDP	All ports > 1023	1813	Enables accounting when external client connects to RADIUS server
Outbound	UDP	1813	All ports > 1023	Enables accounting when internal RADIUS server responds to a client

Table 3-3 Filtering Rules for TACACS+ and RADIUS

Proxy Characteristics Note that RADIUS doesn't work with generic proxy systems. However, a RADIUS server can function as a proxy server, speaking to other RADIUS servers or other services that do authorization, such as Windows domain authentication. TACACS+ does work with generic proxy systems. Because some TACACS+ systems use the same IP address to generate the key, you may need a dedicated proxy that has its own encryption key.

NAT Characteristics RADIUS doesn't work with Network Address Translation (NAT). Addresses that are intended to go through NAT need to be static, not dynamic. TACACS+ should work with NAT systems, but because TACACS+ supports encryption using a secret key shared between server and client, there is no way for the server to know which key to use if different clients make use of different keys. Static IP address mappings work best because some TACACS+ systems use the source IP address to create the encryption key.

Password Security Issues

Many authentication systems depend in part or entirely on passwords. The simplest forms of authentication require typing a username and a reusable password. This method is truly secure only for controlling outbound Internet access, because password guessing and eavesdropping attacks are likely on inbound access attempts. The following sections discuss password security issues that you need to be aware of to prevent your network from being accessed by unauthorized users.

3

Preventing Passwords from Being Cracked

Systems that rely on passwords for authentication can be cracked—that is, deciphered by an unauthorized user—in a number of different ways. Passwords that are transmitted or stored in cleartext (plain, unencrypted text) are easy to crack because they are readable. Systems that exchange hashed passwords (passwords that have been encrypted) that a hacker can copy and reuse (that is, in their encrypted format) also create vulnerabilities. You can avoid both these vulnerabilities by ensuring that your network's authorized users protect their passwords effectively and observe some simple security habits. The risks introduced by poor password management can be offset by passwords that are generated for one-time use with each session and then discarded. In addition, Linux makes use of a "shadow password system" that also makes passwords difficult if not impossible to crack, as described in the following section. Additional discussions of password protection through encryption can be found in Chapter 9.

The Shadow Password System Linux stores passwords in the **/etc/passwd** file in encrypted format. As in most operating systems, the passwords are encrypted using a one-way hash function—this describes a computational algorithm that is relatively fast to calculate when hashing the passwords, but takes an extreme degree of effort or may even be impossible to reverse-calculate. The algorithm begins to hash the password after receiving the password and also using an assigned value called the **salt**. The salt has one of 4096 possible values that is chosen by the system owner and used for all systems and users that are sharing the same authentication process, such as within one organization. Hackers can possibly figure out passwords by compiling a database of words and common passwords and hashing each one, storing the hashed value and the original password. When salting is used, it becomes more complex for the attacker since the effort to store all hashed passwords would also have to be generated with all of the 4096 possible salt values. If this is done properly (or downloaded from the Internet) hackers can compare hashed passwords in your /etc/passwd file with their database; if they find a match, they can gain access to your computer or network.

The **shadow password system**, which is a feature of the Linux operating system that enables the secure storage of passwords, stores them in another file that has restricted access. In addition, passwords are stored only after being encrypted with the salt value and an encoding algorithm. The key is then stored along with the encrypted password. When a user enters a password, it is encrypted using the same formula and then compared to the stored password; if the passwords match, the user is granted access to the requested system resources.

One-Time Password Software

The many problems associated with passwords and the ease of cracking them are alleviated by a one-time password. Two types of one-time passwords are available:

- Challenge-response passwords—The authenticating computer or firewall generates a random number (the challenge) and sends it to the user, who enters a secret PIN or password (the response). If the code and PIN or password match the information stored on the authenticating server, the user gains access.

- Password list passwords—The user enters a seed phrase, and the password system generates a list of passwords that can be used. The user picks one from the list and submits it along with the seed phrase to gain access.

For inbound access, one-time passwords using a scheme, such as Telcordia Technologies' S/KEY, provide a higher level of security. Users type a different password each time they connect. An even higher level of security is realized by some firewalls that work with hardware devices called token generators, which automatically generate and display the next password the user types.

Other Authentication Systems

Most firewalls that handle authentication make use of one or more well-known systems. Check Point's firewall architectures, for instance, use the two centralized authentication protocols discussed earlier in this chapter, RADIUS and TACACS+. In addition, they can provide access control to other authentication systems, including those mentioned in the following sections.

Certificate-Based Authentication

Many modern firewalls support the use of digital certificates, rather than passwords, to authenticate users. An organization using this approach must set up a Public-Key Infrastructure (PKI) that generates keys for users. The user receives a code called a public key that is generated using the server's private key and uses the public key to send encrypted information to the server. The server receives the public key and can decrypt the information using its private key. PKI is discussed in more detail in Chapter 9.

802.1x Wi-Fi Authentication

IEEE 802.1x is one of the fastest growing standards being used in enterprise networks today. It's popular because it supports wireless Ethernet connections (sometimes called Wi-Fi). Wireless networks make it easy for users to connect to the network regardless of inside wiring. At the same time, they present the security administrator with a considerable challenge: without some kind of authentication, any hacker with a laptop computer equipped with a wireless network card who ventures within a few hundred feet of the wireless network can potentially connect to it. The 802.1x protocol provides for authentication of users on wireless networks. Windows clients can be configured to use such authentication, which also requires the use of a smart card or digital certificate (see Figure 3-7).

Figure 3-7 Wireless Authentication
© Cengage Learning 2012

Wi-Fi makes use of Extensible Authentication Protocol (EAP), which enables a system that uses Wi-Fi to authenticate users on other kinds of network operating systems. For instance, the EAP-MD5 type enables a Windows client user to authenticate with Ethernet LANs, and the EAP-TLS type works with 802.11b WLANs.

Running Case: Start at the Beginning

Alex looked at Rachel across a stack of documents.

"Okay, using stronger authentication makes sense, and I know we'll need a new firewall," Alex said, with more than a hint of despair in his voice. "We're already starting to think about those. And I know management wants much tighter access control on all our information assets, but where do we start?"

Rachel had become accustomed to Alex's frustrations by now. "It's really easy, Alex," she said. "You know that list of information assets I had you draft up?"

"Yeah," Alex hesitantly responded.

"Take that list and start with a sketch of your current network diagram, incorporating those assets," Rachel began. "Next, for each asset, create a list of users who need access, and then describe the level of access they need. To keep it simple, just describe them as a user, a power user, or an administrator."

"What's the difference?" Alex asked.

"Well, you ultimately get to decide that, but for now consider a user someone who just needs to be able to read the data, or access a server or service. Consider an administrator someone who has absolute control over the data or technology. And a power user is somewhere in between," Rachel explained.

"Okay, I see your point," Alex said. "Then we turn those lists into access control lists."

"Right!" Rachel exclaimed, pleased to see Alex was finally starting to catch on.

Chapter Summary

- Firewalls authenticate when they need to assign different levels of authorization to different users and groups. By determining that users or computers are really who or what they claim to be, the firewall can then grant access to the needed network resources.

- Firewalls can make use of many different authentication schemes, including user, client, and session authentication. In general, they require a user to supply either something they have (such as a smart card) or something they know (such as a password), or both. The latest authentication systems measure or evaluate a physical attribute, such as a fingerprint or voiceprint.

- In a centralized authentication system, the firewall works in tandem with an authentication server. The authentication server handles the maintenance (or generation) of usernames and passwords as well as login requests and auditing. Kerberos is a centralized authentication system used by Windows and UNIX, whereas TACACS+ and RADIUS are systems used to authenticate users who remotely connect to the network.

- Password systems are an important part of virtually every authentication system and take one of two general forms: single-word password systems and one-time password systems.

- Single-word, static password systems receive a password from a user, compare it against a database of passwords, and then grant access if a match is made. Such simple password security is vulnerable to hackers (who can determine passwords), user error, and bad security habits.

- One-time password systems generate a password each time the user attempts to log on to the network. A secret key is used to generate a single- or multiple-word password. Hardware devices might also generate one-time passwords that, when combined with PINs previously assigned to users, provide an authentication system that is especially difficult to crack.

Review Questions

1. What is authentication? What is a supplicant as the term is used in this chapter?

2. What characteristics distinguish user authentication from the other security approaches used by firewalls?

3. What are the factors on which authentication may be based?

4. Which authentication factor is being used by an authenticating server that responds to a login request by generating a random number or code, expecting to receive that code plus a secret password in return?

5. How is local authentication different from centralized authentication? How is it similar?

6. Identify and define the three elements associated with AAA services.

7. Which type of network environment is not suitable for Kerberos authentication services?

8. Why is Kerberos considered less secure than other authenticating methods?

9. Kerberos and RADIUS are more complex to set up and use than other systems, so what is the advantage of using them?

10. In addition to a password, what is often the second factor in a two-factor authentication system?

11. What is a token? How is a token different from a biometric measurement? How is it similar?

12. When should a firewall require authentication?

13. How are client and session authentication similar? How are they different?

14. What is Kerberos? Briefly describe how it works.

15. What is the name given to the service used within Kerberos to grant tokens?

16. What is the advantage of TACACS+ over RADIUS?

17. Why is a one-time password system considered more secure than a basic authentication system? Provide at least two reasons.

18. If TACACS+ provides a much stronger level of security than RADIUS, why would you consider using a RADIUS server to authenticate dial-in users?

19. Which authentication protocol creates one-time passwords that consist of multiple words?

20. Why is authentication important in wireless networks?

Real World Exercises

1. You need to restrict your company's rank-and-file employees to using the Internet only during regular working hours (9 a.m. to 5 p.m., five days a week). However, as network administrator, you want to be able to access the network at any time of the day or night, seven days a week. How could you meet the needs of the employees and yourself?

2. A group of freelance designers who work at home using DSL or cable modem connections needs to gain access to a set of your company's publication files to redesign them. How could you enable this?

3. Your network employs basic authentication that centers on usernames and passwords. However, you have two ongoing problems. The first is that usernames and passwords are frequently lost by negligent users. The second is that hackers, on occasion, have fooled employees into giving up their authentication information. Identify two things you could do to strengthen the use of username and password authentication.

4. You have configured your firewall to authenticate a group of 100 users who are in your company. You set up the database of users using your firewall's own user management software. As your network grows and security items are added, other network components need to access the same database of users. What strategies could you employ to provide the other network components with access to the database of users?

5. Using an Internet search engine, look up the term "one-time password." Access Web sites that define the term. After reading at least two definitions, write your own definition. Using an Internet search engine, look up the term "biometric user authentication." Access several Web sites that define the term. Write a paragraph expressing your opinion about if and when this will be the dominant way that users authenticate when using home computers.

Hands-On Projects

Project 3-1: The Microsoft Security Compliance Manager

Microsoft has issued security assessment tools to assist in the securing of Windows-based workstations. These include settings for improved security in user authentication. The current version is the Microsoft Security Compliance Manager. (*Note:* According to Microsoft, the current version works for XP as well as Vista and Windows 7; however, this functionality has not been tested.)

How does one use this tool? It allows you to create a baseline configuration on one system and then apply this baseline to other systems. The idea is that you successfully configure one computer the way you want it, and then all you have to do is create a baseline, export the baseline, and apply it to other computers, which duplicates the security and user configuration settings.

This lab walks you through setting up and running the current version. Note that this lab was adapted from the instructions provided within the Security Compliance Manager:

Download and Install the Microsoft Security Compliance Manager

1. Using a Web browser, visit the Microsoft Download Center and search on the term "Microsoft Security Compliance Manager."

2. Scroll down the page and click the **Download** button next to the file Microsoft_Security_Compliance_Manager.Setup.exe. Download to a file location you can access in the next step.

3. Use Windows Explorer to access the location the file was downloaded to and double-click the filename. Click **Run** at the first prompt.

4. Click **Next** at the Welcome screen.

5. Select the "**I accept the terms of the license agreement.**" option and click **Next**.

6. In the Publisher Name: Field, type your institution's name, a space, and your name (e.g., KSU-Whitman), and then click **Next**.

7. In the SQL Server Express setup window, select the **Download and install** option, and then click **Next**.

8. Select the "**I accept the terms of the license agreement.**" option, click **Next**, and then click **Install**. The software will download and install the SQL Server Express, and then the Microsoft Security Compliance Manager. When the installation is complete, select **Finish**.

9. To start the program, click the **Start** button, point to **All Programs**, point to the **Microsoft Security Compliance Manager** folder, and then click **Security Compliance Manager**. The SCM opens as shown in Figure 3-8.

Figure 3-8 Microsoft Security Compliance Manager
© Cengage Learning 2012

10. In the menu on the right, under Actions, select **Quick Start Video**. This opens up a Web browser to a Microsoft Web page. Scroll down and click and view the following videos/ Webcasts, closing the Quick Start Video window after viewing:

a. **Solution Accelerators Team Presents Security Compliance Manager**—Run time: 4:03

b. **Introducing the Security Compliance Toolkit Series (Part 1 of 3)**: Vlad Pigin, Senior Program Manager, and Shruti Kala, Product Manager—Run time: 6:37

c. **Security Baselines and Compliance Demo (Part 3 of 3)**: Vlad Pigin, Senior Program Manager, and Michael Tan, Senior Program Manager—Run time: 15:06

Download and Install the Microsoft Baseline Templates

11. The first thing you need to do is download and import some of the baseline templates created by Microsoft. Open the Tools menu and select **Check for Baselines**. When the Download Baselines window opens, select all of the files presented except the Windows Server files, as shown in Figure 3-9. Click **Download**, and then specify a location to save the download files to.

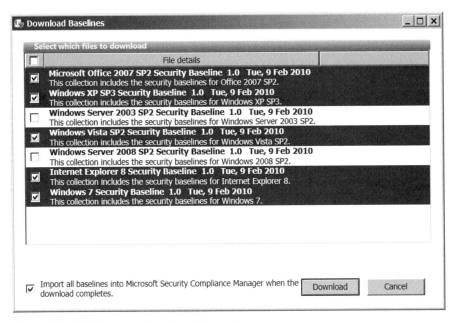

Figure 3-9 SCM Download Baseline File Details
© Cengage Learning 2012

12. The Import Baselines Wizard appears.

13. Click the **Add** button, and then browse to the location you downloaded the files to. Select the .cab files you downloaded and click **Open**. If you see a message warning that the publisher cannot be verified, click **Run** to continue with the import process. Repeat until all appropriate files are added. Appropriate files should include IE8 and Office 2007 (if installed on your local system), as well as your current operating system (XP, Vista, or Windows 7).

14. Click **Next** to import the selected files.

15. The Baseline page appears, as shown in Figure 3-10; it provides information about the baseline configuration. Check the **Create modifiable copies of each baseline to be imported** check box at the bottom of the page to be able to make copies of each baseline that you are importing. You will have the opportunity to modify and adapt these baselines later if you choose.

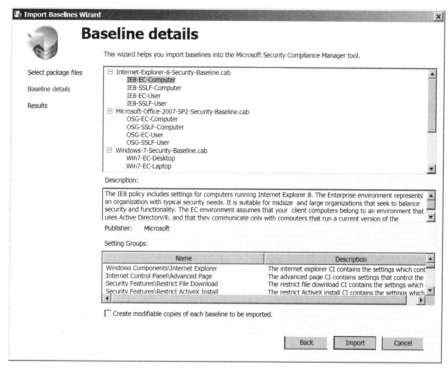

3

Figure 3-10 SCM Import Baselines Wizard
© Cengage Learning 2012

16. Click **Import** to continue the import, and then click **Finish** to finish the wizard.

Modify and Apply a Baseline Template

17. Next, we adapt and apply a security baseline from the list of copies in the Baselines Library pane of the tool. Microsoft baselines are available for two different types of security environments:

   a. Enterprise Client (EC) baselines, which are intended for most organizations

   b. Specialized Security—Limited Functionality (SSLF) baselines, which are intended for environments in which some loss of functionality is acceptable because the concern for security is more important than functionality

18. You can accept the existing baselines without making any modification; however, it is recommended that you customize the template to your particular preference or your organization's policies. You cannot modify the Microsoft baselines that are included

with the Microsoft SCM tool, but you can use the modifiable copies you made when you installed the baseline templates.

19. To modify an existing custom baseline, simply right-click the baseline in the Baselines Library pane on the left, select **Customize**, and then select **Properties**. Rename the baseline from "copy of xyz" to "yourlastname xyz," as in "Whitman IE8-EC-Computer."

20. To create a new copy of an existing baseline, right-click the baseline in the Baselines Library pane, select **Customize**, and then select **Duplicate**. When the Duplicate Baseline dialog box appears, rename the baseline and give it a new description, or enter comments.

21. Baselines can include numerous settings. The Microsoft SCM tool simplifies viewing them by categorizing settings within setting groups, such as Account Lockout Policy or User Rights Assignment. To view a baseline and its contents, navigate to the desired baseline in the Baselines Library pane and select it in the Baseline Information Pane.

22. Select a settings group in the Settings Group(s) list, and then select a setting in the Setting(s) list. Use the tabs in the lower portion of the Baseline Information Pane to choose which setting details to view.

23. Export the baseline from the master copy you create, and then import it and apply it on the new system, which is outside the scope of this exercise.

Project 3-2: Microsoft Baseline Security Analyzer

Another security assessment tool for Microsoft systems is the Microsoft Baseline Security Analyzer, which is described as follows on Microsoft's Web site:

"To easily assess the security state of Windows machines, Microsoft offers the free Microsoft Baseline Security Analyzer (MBSA) scan tool. MBSA includes a graphical and command line interface that can perform local or remote scans of Microsoft Windows systems.

MBSA 2.1.1 runs on Windows Server 2008 R2, Windows 7, Windows Server 2008, Windows Vista, Windows Server 2003, Windows XP, and Windows 2000 systems and will scan for missing security updates, rollups, and service packs using Microsoft Update technologies. MBSA will also scan for common security misconfigurations (also called Vulnerability Assessment checks) using a known list of less secure settings and configurations for all versions of Windows, Internet Information Server (IIS) 5.0, 6.0, and 6.1, SQL Server 2000 and 2005, Internet Explorer (IE) 5.01 and later, and Office 2000, 2002, and 2003 only.

To assess missing security updates, MBSA will only scan for missing security updates, update rollups, and service packs available from Microsoft Update. MBSA will not scan or report missing non-security updates, tools, or drivers."[2]

1. Using a Web browser, visit the Microsoft Download Center and search on the term "Microsoft Baseline Security Analyzer." Click the appropriate link to the MBSA page.

2. Scroll down the page and click the **Download** button next to the file MBSASetup-x86-EN.msi. That is for 32-bit systems. (Substitute the file MBSASetup-x64-EN.msi for 64-bit systems.) Download to a file location you can access in the next step.

3. Use Windows Explorer to access the location the file was downloaded to and double-click the filename. Click **Run** at the first prompt. Click **Next** on the Welcome screen, select **I accept the license agreement**, click **Next** twice, and then click **Install**.

4. Click **Start, All Programs,** and then click **Microsoft Baseline Security Analyzer.** Your window should appear similar to Figure 3-11.

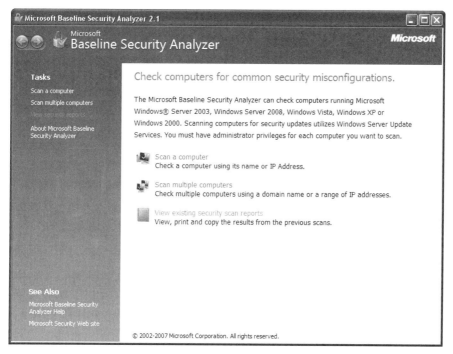

3-11 Microsoft Baseline Security Analyzer
© Cengage Learning 2012

5. This tool is capable of scanning remote machines in a network, but you will only be scanning the local machine for this lab. Click **Scan a computer**.

6. You are presented with several options pertaining to the computer that you would like to scan. The name of your computer should appear in the box labeled Computer name.

7. Click **Start scan**. The scan finishes more quickly if no other applications are running at the same time. When the scan has finished, you should see results similar to those seen in Figure 3-12.

8. Click **Result details** below any of the listed vulnerabilities. A new window opens with any details about the listed issue. This can provide very helpful information for systems administrators. The "How to correct this" link for each vulnerability is also handy.

9. In a Word document, discuss several of the most important items (severe risk) and how fixing them could harden your system.

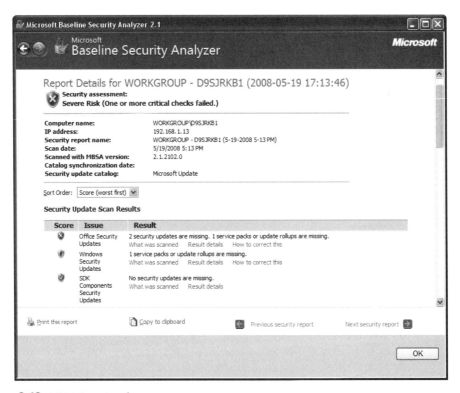

3-12 MSBA Scan Results

© Cengage Learning 2012

Running Case Projects

For each of the tasks below, create the corresponding diagram, list, or explanation to help Alex complete the tasks before him having to do with authenticating users.

Student Tasks

1. Create a network diagram for Data Mart's current network configuration. Then create a second diagram incorporating the proposed firewall architectures. Be sure to include the information assets identified in Chapter 2's Running Case Project. A simple network diagram is provided in Figure 3-13 to show the basics of how network diagramming is performed. You may use any graphical program you choose, including Microsoft Powerpoint or Microsoft Visio.

2. Create a table for each asset listed, including the firewall. In this table, list the users who need access as well as their corresponding level of access based on the simple three-layered scheme discussed by Rachel and Alex (user, power user, and administrator). Then explain which privileges are needed for the roles of user, power user, and administrator with regard to each device, dataset, or service.

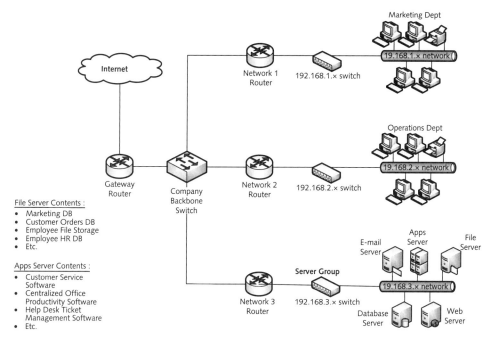

Figure 3-13 Sample (Simple) Network Diagram
© Cengage Learning 2012

Endnotes

1. Tiller, J. S. Access Control in Official (ISC) 2 Guide to the CISSP CBK, Tipton, H. & Henry, K. (eds), Auerbach Publishers, Boca Raton, FL, 2007.

2. Microsoft Baseline Security Analyzer 2.1.1 (for IT Professionals). Accessed 10 May 2010 from *www.microsoft.com/downloads/details.aspx?familyid=B1E76BBE-71DF-41E8-8B52-C871D012BA78&displaylang=en.*

chapter 4

Introduction to Firewalls

**After reading this chapter and completing
the exercises, you will be able to:**

- Identify common misconceptions about firewalls
- Explain why a firewall is dependent on an effective security policy
- Understand what a firewall does
- Describe the types of firewall protection
- Recognize the limitations of firewalls

"Technology makes it
possible for people to
gain control over
everything, except over
technology."
—John Tudor

Running Case: A $50 Router

"And that is why a residential-grade firewall really isn't capable of handling the bandwidth or traffic analysis you need for this facility."

Jason Robertson took a deep breath and sat down. Over the past two hours, he'd made what he hoped was an effective argument for Data Mart to significantly upgrade its perimeter defense, specifically the puny firewall that was currently "protecting" the company's information assets. Throughout the presentation, Data Mart's IT Director, Alex Truman, had sat stone-faced while the company's owner and president, Ann Lee, periodically cast a telling glance in his direction. It was clear she was not happy with what she was hearing. Apparently, Alex's naive approach to his job had flown under the radar for some time.

"So all this time, over a million dollars' worth of hardware and software was being protected by a $50 router that I wouldn't trust to protect my home network?" Lee asked.

"Well, I really can't comment on the decisions made before Onsite Security Systems was brought in," Jason replied, "but we strongly advise you not to continue with the current perimeter defense configuration. We recommend a complete overhaul of the network security architecture, with special emphasis on a new commercial-grade firewall." While saying this, Jason was careful not to look directly at Alex. "Exactly what type of firewall and how much should be spent on it are decisions that must be made based on your business needs and budgetary constraints," he continued.

"Oh, I think you'll find I'm quite willing to follow your recommendations regarding the firewall issue," Ann replied coldly. "Work with Alex to draw up a business case and new technology specification, and I'll sign off on it."

Introduction

Any information security effort is going to be a balancing act between costs and benefits. Organizations cannot afford to spend an unlimited amount of time or money on any one security solution. They have to balance the needs of the organization against the available resources. Achieving effective network security is a process that imposes controls on an organization's network resources, with the goal of balancing the risks and rewards that come from network usage. The controls are a continually evolving set of policies, programs, and technologies. Networks that connect to the Internet for communications or commerce are particularly vulnerable; attacks that get lots of publicity are usually accomplished by network-based hackers who gain access from remote network locations. In this light, firewalls and related technical controls have become a fundamental security tool. They are now a required component of virtually every network, and serve as part of the defense in depth strategy by protecting many individual computers.

No security system can guarantee it will protect all of an organization's information all of the time. But firewalls, if used in conjunction with other technical controls and security policies and programs, deployed according to the needs of the businesses they protect, and maintained and upgraded on a regular basis, are one of the most effective security tools a network administrator has. This chapter provides an overview of the issues involved in planning and designing firewalls. First, you learn what a firewall is not, so that you can begin to understand what it is. Then you learn about security policies and the rules and procedures that govern how a firewall works. Then you learn about types of firewall protection, the limitations of firewalls, and hardware firewall implementations. This chapter finishes with evaluations of firewall software packages.

Throughout this book, the term "firewall" is used in the singular, but a firewall is not necessarily a single device, whether a router, appliance, VPN gateway, or software program. Each individual firewall is a combination of software and hardware components. At this point in your preparation, you should have a working knowledge of TCP/IP, the basics of network infrastructures, IP addressing and the domain system, and Internet and Web-based software. If you're a bit rusty on the basics of TCP/IP or other aspects of network infrastructure, visit *www.cengage.com/coursetechnology* or another source to refresh your skills.

Firewalls Explained

In general, a **firewall** is anything—hardware, software, or a combination of the two—that can filter the transmission of packets of digital information as they attempt to pass through an interface between networks.

Firewalls perform two basic security functions:

- Packet filtering—Determining whether to allow or deny the passage of packets of digital information, based on established security policy rules.
- Application proxy—Providing network services to users while shielding individual host computers. This is done by breaking the IP flow (i.e., the traffic into and out of the network).

Firewalls can be complex, but if you thoroughly understand each of these two functions, you'll be able to choose the right firewall and configure it to protect a computer or network. Figure 4-1 illustrates the basic nature of a firewall stationed at a network perimeter.

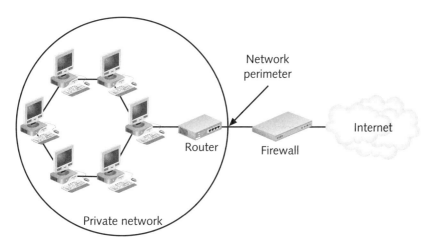

Figure 4-1 Firewall at the Perimeter
© Cengage Learning 2012

Misconceptions about Firewalls

Most people have heard of the term *firewall*, but not in connection with the Internet. They may know about the fireproof barrier between the engine of a car and its interior, or may have heard the term used to describe a brick wall or other fireproof barrier in building construction. Such firewalls are intended to slow the movement of a dangerous element—specifically, fire—from one location to another. While they may not prevent every disaster, they can provide to those who are affected ample time to react.

Comparisons with structural firewalls have led to the false notion that a firewall is designed to prevent all attackers, viruses, and would-be intruders from entering a computer or computer network. In fact, software firewalls are designed simply to permit authorized traffic to pass through while blocking unauthorized and unwanted traffic. If unwanted traffic is disguised well enough to fool the firewall, it will be able to get past the barrier.

Some managers may also think that once you deploy a firewall, you're done. You can just set it up and it will function on its own. Actually, firewalls aren't perfect, and they are not permanent. They are, after all, designed and configured by people, who can be fallible. Firewalls need constant maintenance to keep up with the latest security threats. They work best when they are part of a multilayered approach to network security. This layered strategy is called defense in depth, which encompasses multiple types and levels of control and might include a security policy, the firewall, intrusion detection software, virus scanners, and encryption.

An Analogy: Office Tower Security Guard

A firewall is like a security guard at a guardhouse or checkpoint. Suppose you have taken a job as a security guard at a big, modern office tower. Thousands of people pass into and out of the building's security checkpoint every day. (For reasons of control, there's only one or just a few security checkpoints.) How do you know who's an authorized employee and who's an intruder? To enable you to make decisions about who gets in and who does not, the security department has set up these rules:

- All personnel must enter and leave through designated entrances.
- Individuals wearing a green ID card can go through the checkpoint without signing in.
- Individuals wearing blue ID cards must sign in when entering and sign out when leaving.
- Everyone must pass through the metal detector and surrender weapons or other potentially harmful devices.
- If someone passes through the checkpoint without being checked, push the red security button to alert the response team.

A firewall performs the same types of functions as does a security guard at a checkpoint. In addition, it may perform a few more advanced functions that a security guard would never perform, like filtering unacceptable content or **caching** data (storing it on disk). Nevertheless, the security rules we created for our imaginary security checkpoint have equivalents in the digital realm of the firewall:

- Entry and exit points (called ports in the TCP/IP network) are specified for different types of content. For example, Web-page content typically travels through port 80.
- Information that meets specified security criteria (such as coming from or going to a specific IP address) is allowed to pass, while other data is stopped.

- Data, in some cases, must pass through firewall software that functions as a sort of electronic metal detector, scanning for viruses and repairing infected files before they invade the network.

- Firewalls can be configured to send out alert messages and notify staff of break-ins if viruses are detected.

Firewall Security Features

As firewalls become more widely used, their manufacturers compete more fiercely to make their products stand out from the competition. Some companies have added a number of advanced security functions, such as the following:

- Logging unauthorized (as well as authorized) accesses into and out of a network

- Providing a virtual private network (VPN) link, which can make two separated networks appear to be connected to one another

- Authenticating users who provide usernames and passwords so they can be identified and given access to the services they need

- Shielding hosts inside the network so that attackers cannot identify them and use them as staging areas for sustained attacks

- Caching data so that files that are repeatedly requested can be called from cache to reduce server load and improve Web-site performance

- Filtering content that is considered inappropriate (such as video streams) or dangerous (such as executable e-mail attachments)

For a home user who uses the Internet for routine activities like surfing the Web, sending e-mail, social networking, watching an occasional video, and instant messaging, a firewall's primary job is to isolate the local network from remote attackers. It may also help prevent some Trojan horses from leveraging the local network through hidden openings called **back doors**. Some home firewall software products, such as Norton Internet Security, also have an antivirus program that alerts users when an e-mail attachment or file containing a known virus is found.

Firewall Network Perimeter Security

A perimeter is a boundary between two zones of trust. For example, an organization's internal network is more trusted than the Internet, and it is common to install a firewall at this boundary to inspect and control the traffic that flows across it. There are additional zones of trust within the organization's network, such as among the Web, application, and database tiers of a three-tiered application.

If you have an extranet—an extended network that shares part of an organization's network with a third party (for example, a business partner)—the location of the "perimeter" becomes a bit more murky. If the extranet operates over a VPN, it should have its own perimeter firewall because your network boundary technically extends to the end of the VPN. To be really secure, you should install a firewall on the partner's VPN host (as shown in Figure 4-2).

Mobile devices such as laptops, PDAs, and smartphones blur the perimeter boundary even more as these mobile endpoints may extend the organization's network into Internet cafes, coffee shops, etc.

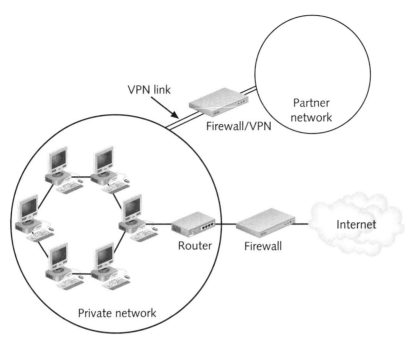

Figure 4-2 VPN Perimeter
© Cengage Learning 2012

Locating the firewall at the perimeter has one obvious benefit: it enables you to set up a checkpoint where you can block viruses and infected e-mail messages before they get inside. However, it has less obvious benefits, too. A perimeter firewall enables you to log passing traffic, protecting the whole network at one time. If an attack does occur, by having defined network boundaries, especially those that include firewalls, damage can be minimized.

The firewall is positioned at the border of the network (zone of trust), providing security for all the computers within it, so each individual server or workstation need not completely provide for its own security.

Firewall Components

A firewall can contain many components, including a packet filter, a proxy server, an authentication system, and software that perform Network or Port Address Translation (NAT or PAT). Some firewalls can encrypt traffic, and some help establish VPNs. Some firewalls are packaged in a hardware device that also functions as a router. Firewalls themselves are often part of multiple-component security setups. The most effective protection systems used by large corporate networks employ not just one but several firewalls. They combine the firewalls with routers and other components to delineate zones of trust such as a screened subnet, also known as a demilitarized zone (DMZ), which is positioned between the internal network and the outside world.

Many firewalls make use of a bastion host, a machine that has no unnecessary services, only the bare essentials. A network that needs to connect to the Internet might have a bastion host and a service network (another term for screened subnet). Together, they are the only part of the organization exposed to the Internet. Figure 4-3 shows such a configuration.

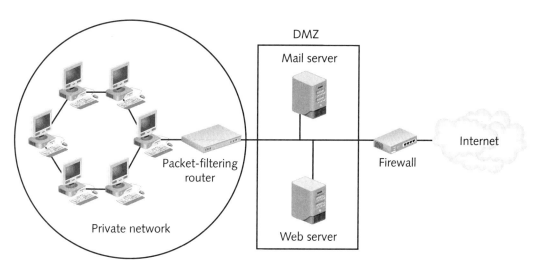

Figure 4-3 DMZ Networks
© Cengage Learning 2012

Firewall Security Tasks

To understand how a firewall works, you need to have a general idea of the range of threats against which you need to protect your network, and which security tasks the firewall can perform.

Restricting Access from Outside the Network The most obvious goal of a firewall is to regulate which packets of information can enter the network. To do so, a firewall examines each packet to determine whether it meets the necessary "authorized" criteria. The criteria might be protocols or IP addresses on an "approved" list. Anything not on the list is excluded. Such packet filtering is discussed in more detail later in this chapter.

A firewall that does packet filtering (and virtually all do) protects networks from port scanning attacks. A port is a network subaddress (assigned a number between 0 and 65,535) through which a particular type of data is allowed to pass. In a port scanning attack, special software scans a series of network addresses, attempting to connect to each one. If a connection is made, it gives the attacker a target. A properly configured firewall only allows authorized connection attempts to the ports on the network it protects.

Restricting Unauthorized Access from Inside the Network It is sometimes easier to protect a network from the Internet than from an inside attack. Whether they are disgruntled, dishonest, or just ignorant of the proper security procedures, employees can be a major source of trouble. Be aware of the following:

- Employees who bring to the office mobile media (memory sticks, CD/DVDs, etc.) that contain virus-infected files

- Employees who access office computers from home using remote-access software that bypasses the perimeter firewall

- Attackers who obtain confidential information by contacting employees and deceiving them into giving up passwords, IP addresses, server names, and so on—that is, social engineering

Technical Details
Ports

Ports work like apartment numbers in that they allow many network services to share a single network address. Just as Bob, Alice, and Eve each have their own apartment numbers in the building at 324 Evergreen Terrace, network services all have their own port numbers.

To send a letter to Bob, the sender would add the street address to the envelope, and then add the apartment number. The sender would then add his own address to the envelope, including the apartment number of his own building. This combination of a sender's full address (network address plus port) and receiver's address (network address plus port) makes up a **socket**. To initiate a connection to a network service, the user specifies both the IP address and the port number.

Port numbers come in two flavors: well-known ports (those with the number 1023 or below) and ephemeral ports (those with a number from 1024 to 65535). Well-known ports are defined for most common services, such as the Web (port 80), SSH (port 22), Simple Mail Transport Protocol (port 25), POP Mail (port 110), and many others. So, for example, when a user requests a connection to a Web server running at address 192.168.5.203, the Web browser knows to attempt the connection at port 80. Ephemeral port numbers are dynamically assigned as needed and have no special meaning outside the connection using them.

Some organizations find that they unintentionally activate network services. This can occur when network services are turned on without adequate planning—such as an unplanned mail server that starts by default when the company starts a Web server. This type of event is one of the biggest vulnerabilities that firewalls can protect against. A firewall can block external access to such unplanned services, so that, for example, mail server connection requests are always routed to the actual mail server and not any other systems that may have inadvertently set up a mail server.

- Poorly trained firewall administrators who might, for example, configure the firewall to filter out certain IP packets while passing along packets that arrive in fragments

- Employees who receive e-mail messages with executable attachments, which, if the employee downloads and executes the attachment, may launch a program that could spread to other computers using the recipient's e-mail address book

Firewalls cannot prevent all internal threats. You can configure a firewall to recognize packets or to prevent access to protected files from internal as well as external hosts. Note, however, that remote access and social engineering attacks can be prevented only through training and by raising awareness about security procedures.

Limiting Employee Access to External Hosts Along with restricting external traffic from outside the network, firewalls can selectively permit traffic to go from inside the network to the Internet or another network as a way of providing more precise control of how employees inside the network use external resources. In other words, the firewall can act as a **proxy server** that makes high-level application connections on behalf of internal hosts and other machines. A single firewall product can provide both outbound packet filtering (shown in Figure 4-4) and outbound proxy services.

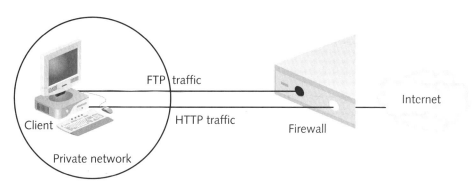

Figure 4-4 Outbound Packet Filtering
© Cengage Learning 2012

Application proxies can restrict internal users who want to gain unrestricted access to the Internet. Some technically sophisticated users might be able to circumvent the security measures you set up. They might, for instance, dial into the office using remote access, thus opening a security hole. They might use a remote-access program like *www.gotomypc.com*, which provides client software they install on both their home and work computers. The software is configured so that every 15 or 20 seconds, the work computer sends out the query "Does anyone want to connect to me?" (The target port used is TCP port 80, the commonly used HTTP port.) Such traffic may well go through the firewall unchecked, and it presents an obvious security risk since home networks are seldom as well defended as corporate networks and attackers may be able to first attack a user's home network and thus gain access to the more valuable corporate network.

Protecting Critical Resources Attacks on critical resources are becoming all too common. These attacks are many and varied and can cause many kinds of losses. Implementing minimal, reasonable, and prudent levels of firewall protection is necessary to secure these critical resources.

Protecting against Hacking Hacking, in general, is the practice of infiltrating computers or networks to steal data, cause harm, or simply claim bragging rights. Such attacks can also have tangible organization-wide impact, including the following:

- Loss of data—Many organizations now use the Internet to run their businesses. They calculate payroll, record health insurance information, and maintain staff directories online; most perform common accounting tasks online. Personnel and financial information is among a company's most valuable assets and can, if compromised, have a big impact on its bottom line.

- Loss of time—The time spent recovering files, rebuilding servers, and otherwise dealing with security breaches can be extensive, far outweighing the time spent preventing trouble.

- Staff resources—In response to a security incident, many staff members may need to take time away from their regular business activities to recover data.

- Confidentiality—E-business customer data, such as contact information and credit card numbers, is a valuable asset that must be kept secure. Such information has been obtained by hackers, even published online.

Providing Centralization A firewall centralizes security for the organization it protects. It simplifies the security-related activities of the network administrator, who typically has many other responsibilities. Having a firewall on the perimeter gives the network administrator a single location from which to configure security policies and monitor arriving and departing traffic.

Enabling Documentation Every firewall should be configured to provide information to the network administrator in the form of log files. Log files record attempted intrusions and other suspicious activity, as well as mundane events like legitimate file accesses, unsuccessful connection attempts, and the like. Looking through log files is tedious, but it can help a network administrator identify weak points in the security system so they can be strengthened.

Log files can also identify intruders so they can be apprehended in case theft or damage actually occur. Regular review and analysis of log file data are what make firewalls effective because methods of attack change all the time. The firewall rules must be evaluated and adjusted to account for the many new and emerging threats.

Providing for Authentication You are probably familiar with authentication—the process of logging in to a server with a username and a password before being allowed access to protected information. Only users who have registered their usernames and passwords are recognized by the server and allowed to enter. The authentication process can also be performed at the firewall and make use of encryption to protect the usernames and passwords transmitted from client to server (or client to firewall).

Contributing to a VPN A firewall is an ideal endpoint for VPN, which connects two companies' networks over the Internet. A VPN is one of the safest ways to exchange information online. You find out more about VPNs later in this chapter.

Types of Firewall Protection

Firewalls work in different ways, and some firewalls work using multiple approaches, which is one reason they're so effective. One way we can discuss how firewalls work is to use the seven-layer OSI networking model. It is assumed that you are familiar with the OSI model from your prerequisite courses in networking. If not, you should take some time to look up the OSI model online, where there are many good resources. Figure 4-5 gives some examples of firewall functions and the corresponding OSI model layers at which they operate.

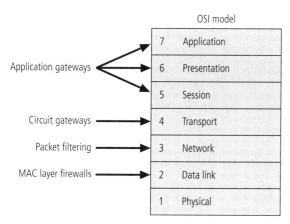

Figure 4-5 Firewalls in the OSI Model
© Cengage Learning 2012

Packet Filtering

Packet filtering is a key function of any firewall. In fact, packet filters were one of the first types of firewalls. They are an effective element in any perimeter security setup.

A packet (sometimes called a **datagram**) is the basic element of network data. It contains two types of information:

- The **header**, which consists of general information about the size of the packet, the protocol that was used to send it, and the IP address of both the source computer and the destination

- The data, which is the information you view and use—that is, the text of an e-mail message, the contents of a Web page, a piece of a file being transferred, or the bits of a digital photograph

A packet-filtering firewall installed on a TCP/IP-based network typically functions at the IP level and determines whether to drop a packet (deny) or forward it to the next network connection (allow) based on the rules programmed into the firewall. Packet-filtering firewalls examine every incoming packet header and can selectively filter packets based on header information such as destination address, source address, packet type, and other key information. Figure 4-6 shows the structure of an IPv4 packet.

Bit offset	0–3	4–7	8–13	14–15	16–18	19–31
0	Version	Header Length	Differentiated Services Code Point	Explicit Congestion Notification	Total Length	
32	Identification			Flags	Fragment Offset	
64	Time to Live		Protocol		Header Checksum	
96	Source IP Address					
128	Destination IP Address					
160	Options (if Header Length > 5)					
160 or 192+	Data					

Figure 4-6 IPv4 Packet Structure
© Cengage Learning 2012

Packet-filtering firewalls scan network data packets looking for compliance with or violation of the rules of the firewall's database. Filtering firewalls inspect packets at the network layer (Layer 3) of the OSI model. If the device finds a packet that violates a rule, it stops the packet from traveling from one network to another. The restrictions most commonly implemented in packet-filtering firewalls are based on a combination of the following:

- IP source and destination address
- Direction (inbound or outbound)
- TCP or UDP (User Datagram Protocol) source and destination port (These protocols are discussed in the following pages.)

Packet structure varies, depending on the nature of the packet. The server that receives the packet makes use of the details of its packet structure when it processes the packet. The two primary service types are TCP and UDP (as noted earlier). Figures 4-7 and 4-8 show the structures of these two major elements of the combined protocol known as TCP/IP.

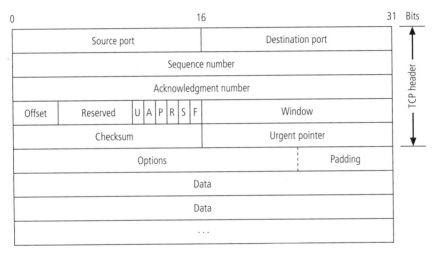

Figure 4-7 TCP Packet Structure
© Cengage Learning 2012

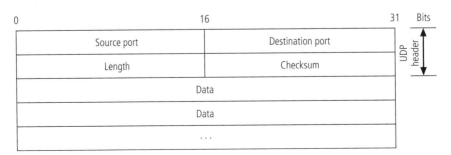

Figure 4-8 UDP Packet Structure
© Cengage Learning 2012

Simple firewall models examine two components of the packet header: the destination and the source address. They enforce address restrictions—rules designed to prohibit packets with specific addresses or incomplete addresses from passing through the device. These restrictions are defined in access control lists (ACLs), which are created and modified by the firewall administrators. Figure 4-9 shows how a packet-filtering router can be used as a simple firewall to filter data packets from inbound connections and allow outbound connections unrestricted access to the public network.

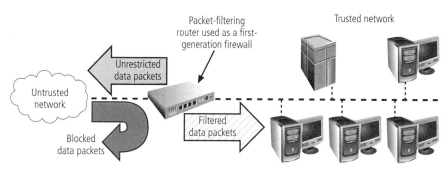

Figure 4-9 Packet Filtering Router
© Cengage Learning 2012

The ability to restrict a specific service is now standard in most routers and is invisible to the user. Unfortunately, such routers are unable to detect whether packet headers have been modified, which occurs in some advanced attack methods, including IP spoofing attacks. IP spoofing is the falsification of the source IP address in a packet's header, so that it appears to have come from a trusted or legitimate sender. In some cases, attackers spoof using a source IP address that belongs to the target, to make it look as though the file is coming from a computer within the organization.

Stateless Packet-Filtering Firewalls Stateless inspection, also called stateless packet filtering, is firewall packet inspection that ignores the state of the connection between the internal computer and the external computer. A firewall that conducts stateless packet filtering simply blocks or allows a packet based on the information in the header.

Stateful Packet-Filtering Firewalls Stateful inspection, also called stateful packet filtering, is an examination of the data contained in a packet as well as the state of the connection between the internal and the external computer. This information, known as the state table, is kept in a memory location called the cache. Stateful inspection is superior to stateless inspection because it uses the connection state to make decisions on whether to allow the traffic.

A state table tracks the state and context of each packet in the conversation by recording which station sent what packet and when. Whereas simple packet-filtering firewalls allow or deny certain packets based only on their addresses, a stateful packet-filtering firewall can allow incoming packets that have been sent in response to internal requests. If the stateful firewall receives an incoming packet that it cannot match in its state table, it defaults to its ACL to determine whether to allow the packet to pass. The primary disadvantage of this type of firewall is the additional processing required to manage and verify packets against the state table, which can leave the system vulnerable to a DoS or DDoS attack. In such an attack, the system receives a large number of external packets, which slows the firewall because it attempts to compare all of the incoming packets first to the state table and then to the ACL. On the positive side, these firewalls can track connectionless packet traffic, such as UDP and remote procedure calls (RPC) traffic. Dynamic stateful filtering firewalls maintain a dynamic state table, making changes (within predefined limits) to the filtering rules based on events as they happen.

A sample state table is shown in Table 4-1. It contains the source's IP and port as well as the destination's IP and port, and it also provides information on the total time in seconds, the time remaining in seconds, and the protocol used (UDP or TCP). Many state table implementations allow a connection to remain in place for up to 60 minutes without any activity before the state entry is deleted. Table 4-1 shows this in the column labeled Total time. The time-remaining column shows a countdown of the time that is left until the entry is deleted.

Source Address	Source Port	Destination Address	Destination Port	Time Remaining (in seconds)	Total Time (in seconds)	Protocol
192.168.2.5	1028	10.10.10.7	80	2725	3600	TCP

Table 4-1 State Table

Stateful inspection also blocks packets that are sent from an external computer that does not have a currently active connection to an internal computer.

Here's an example of how stateful inspection works. Suppose you have set up a firewall for a company and an employee attempts to connect to the Web site for the White House. When the employee's request packet arrives at the stateful firewall, the following events occur:

1. The firewall checks a list of active connections—the state table—to see whether an active connection to the White House's Web site already exists.

2. Because a connection does not yet exist, the firewall checks its list of rules (called a **rule base**). The firewall is configured so that users inside the network are allowed to access the Internet on TCP port 80 and are allowed to access any host on the Internet. The packet is allowed to go on its way after the firewall makes an entry to the state table recording the connection attempt.

3. When the packet is received by the White House server (probably after passing through one or more firewalls), a reply packet is generated and returned to the source company's firewall.

4. At the company's firewall, the state table is checked, and the inbound packet's header is inspected. The header conveys the following information:
   - Source IP: *www.whitehouse.gov*
   - Source port: 80
   - Destination IP: the originating user's computer address
   - Protocol: TCP

5. Because there's nothing suspicious about this packet, the firewall sends it to the computer that made the request.

Now, imagine a very different scenario. Here, an attacker with the IP address *hack.yourcomputer.net* tries to access your system through port 80. The packet header contains the following information:

- Source IP: *hack.yourcomputer.net*
- Source port: 80
- Destination IP: The address of a computer on your system that the attacker has previously uncovered through address or port scanning
- Destination port: 2400

The firewall's stateful packet inspector first checks its state table to see if such a request matches a previous entry. Because no such previous entry exists, the firewall consults its rule base. Because the only rule specified is that only internal users can connect to port 80, the packet is blocked.

Packet-Filtering Rules Packet filtering depends on the establishment of rules. Among the most general rules are the following:

- Any outbound packet must have a source address that is in your internal network.
- Any outbound packet must not have a destination address that is in your internal network.
- Any inbound packet must not have a source address that is in your internal network.
- Any inbound packet must have a destination address that is in your internal network.
- Any packet that enters or leaves your network must have a source or destination address that falls within the range of addresses in your network. Your network may use (but does not have to use) private addresses or addresses listed in RFC1918 reserved space. These include 10.x.x.x/8, 172.16.x.x/12, and 192.168.x.x/16. Remember that we always also include the loopback network 127.0.0.0/8.

To better understand an address restriction scheme, consider Table 4-2. If an administrator were to configure a simple rule based on the content of Table 4-2, any attempt to connect that was made by an external computer or network device in the 192.168.x.x address range (192.168.0.0–192.168.255.255) would be allowed. The ability to restrict a specific service rather than just a range of IP addresses is available in a more advanced version of this first-generation firewall. Additional details on firewall rules and configuration are presented in a later section of this chapter.

Source Address	Destination Address	Service (HTTP, SMTP, FTP, Telnet)	Action (allow or deny)
172.16.x.x	10.10.x.x	Any	Deny
192.168.x.x	10.10.10.25	HTTP	Allow
192.168.0.1	10.10.10.10	FTP	Allow

Table 4-2 Sample Firewall Rule and Format

Filter rules affect the transmission of packets. These rules require that you have a basic understanding of how some of the various protocols that make up the Internet function:

- Internet Control Message Protocol (ICMP)—IP, by itself, has no way of letting the host that originated a request know whether a packet was received at its destination in its entirety. It can, however, use ICMP to report any errors that occurred in the transmission. Utilities like Ping and Traceroute use ICMP. The danger is that ICMP packets can be filled with false information that can trick your hosts into redirecting or stopping communications.

- User Datagram Protocol (UDP)—This protocol is similar to TCP in that it handles the addressing of a message. UDP breaks a message into numbered segments so that it can be transmitted. It then reassembles the message when it reaches the destination computer. Unlike TCP, UDP is connectionless: it simply sends segments of messages without performing error-checking or waiting for an acknowledgment that the message has been received. Such a protocol is useful for video and audio broadcasts on the Internet. TCP and UDP are often mentioned together in discussions of firewalls because both transmit data through ports and thus open up vulnerabilities. It's useful to set up rules to block UDP traffic on all ports 21 and below so as to block traffic on ports that control hardware and are not part of the routed network environment.

- TCP filtering—The rules used to control filtering of TCP packets are similar to those used for UDP packets. For example, you should block packets that use ports below 20, and you can block specific protocols—for example, Telnet connections on port 23.

- IP filtering—The rules used for all parts of the IP protocol control the overall flow of IP traffic through your network. If you have identified a computer or network that you want to block from your company's network, you would specify Source IP or Destination IP rule criteria. These rules will affect the entire TCP/IP suite of protocols (ICMP, UDP, or TCP).

Packet filtering has limitations. Filtering does not hide the IP addresses of the hosts on the inside of a network perimeter that appear to be behind the filter from an outsider's perspective. These IP addresses are contained in outbound traffic, which makes it easy for attackers to target individual hosts that are behind the filter. Packet-filtering firewalls don't check to make sure the protocols inside packets are legitimate, either. Packet filtering can only limit addresses based on the source IP address listed in the packet's header, and thus it does not protect against IP spoofing. For these reasons, firewalls that perform only packet filtering do not provide adequate network protection.

Larger organizations use multiple packet filters in a DMZ perimeter security setup. They might use a router that functions as a static packet filter, a stateful packet filter that has been set up in a bastion host, and firewall software (as shown in Figure 4-10).

PAT and NAT

Each computer on a network is assigned an IP address. One approach to assigning these numbers is to use static, routable IP addresses for all computers, where each computer is configured to use one IP address and that address can be reached by outside computers to make a connection directly to it. A computer with a static IP address that can be accessed via the Internet is an easy target for an attacker, who might also use it as a staging area for launching long, sustained attacks.

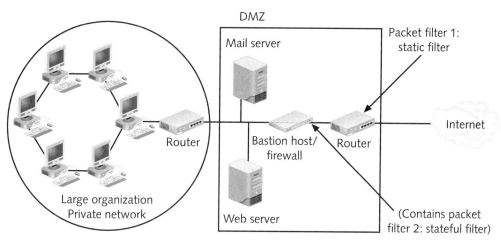

Figure 4-10 Multiple Packet Filters
© Cengage Learning 2012

Port Address Translation (PAT) and Network Address Translation (NAT) are addressing methods that make internal network addresses invisible to outside computers. They hide the TCP/IP information of hosts in the network so that attackers are unable to get the addresses, thereby rendering the attackers unable to send malformed packets or virus-laden messages to those machines.

PAT and NAT function as an outbound network-level proxy, acting as a single host that makes requests on behalf of all the internal hosts on the network. PAT uses one external address for all other systems, assigning random and high-order port numbers to each internal computer. In Figure 4-11, the port number was randomly chosen as 24001. NAT uses a pool of valid external IP addresses, assigning one to each internal computer requesting an outside connection. Both techniques convert the IP addresses of internal hosts to the IP address assigned by the firewall. To someone on the Internet or another outside network, it appears that all information is coming from a single computer when PAT is used, or from a small number of computers (IP numbers that do not change) when NAT is used. This is sometimes called IP masquerading, because the individual machines can be assigned IP addresses in a private address range—for example, 10.0.0.1, 10.0.0.2, 10.0.0.2, and so on. But when the PAT/NAT-equipped firewall receives a request from one of these computers, it replaces the real IP address with its own address (for PAT) or one from the outbound pool (for NAT). The computer outside the network that receives the request gets a packet whose header includes a source IP address of, say, 24.33.9.100, not 10.0.0.3, as shown in Figure 4-11.

The internal network addresses assigned by PAT or NAT are drawn from three different ranges (specified by the IETF, as published in RFC1918). Organizations that need large numbers of internally assigned addresses use the Class A address range of 10.x.x.x, which has over 16.5 million addresses. Organizations that need smaller numbers of internally assigned addresses can select from the reserved group of 16 Class B address blocks found in the 172.16.x.x to 172.31.x.x range, which has a combined total of about 1.05 million addresses. Those with smaller needs can use Class C addresses in the 192.168.x.x range, each of which has approximately 65,500 addresses. See Table 4-3 for the IP address ranges reserved for non-public networks (the information in the table about network masks will be explained

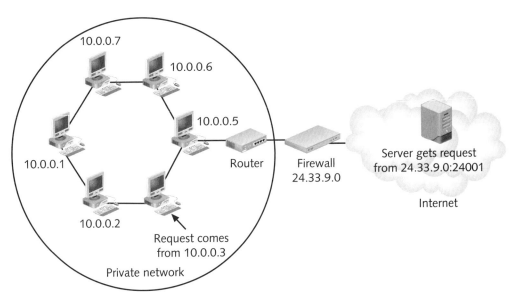

Figure 4-11 Port Address Translation (PAT)
© Cengage Learning 2012

later in the text). Messages sent with internal addresses within these three reserved ranges cannot be routed externally, so if a computer with one of these internal-use addresses is directly connected to the external network and avoids the PAT/NAT server, its traffic cannot be routed on the public network. Therefore, PAT/NAT prevents external attacks from reaching internal machines with addresses in specified ranges.

Class	From	To	CIDR Mask	Decimal Mask
Class "A" (or 24 bit)	10.0.0.0	10.255.255.255	/8	255.0.0.0
Class B (20 bit)	172.16.0.0	172.31.255.255	/12 or /16	255.240.0.0 or 255.255.0.0
Class C (16 bit)	192.168.0.0	192.168.255.255	/16 or /24	255.255.0.0 or 255.255.255.0

Table 4-3   Reserved Nonroutable Address Ranges

Application Layer Gateways

Another type of firewall protection is the application layer gateway, also known as a proxy server. The **application-layer gateway** works at the Application layer, the top layer of the OSI model of network communications.

Application-layer gateways can control the way applications inside the network access external networks by setting up proxy services. This service acts as a substitute (i.e., a proxy) for the client, making requests for Web pages or sending and receiving e-mail on behalf of individual users, who are thus shielded from directly connecting with the Internet. This shielding minimizes the effect of viruses, worms, Trojan horses, and other malware.

The letter "x" occasionally gets used in a network address. What does it mean? It gets used in two ways. When an organization is assigned a network address range, it is given a set of values it can use for its addresses—10.10.0.1–10.10.254.254, for example. The shorthand notation for this range of values would be 10.10.x.x, where the "x" indicates a value in the range of 0 to 254 that can be assigned by the user organization.

The other way "x" gets used is to represent "any" value—also used in shorthand notation, but in a different location. If you see it used in a firewall or VPN rule, it refers to any address that meets the defined portion of the address. For example, if the firewall should deny (drop) any packets from the 192.168 address range, such as 192.168.2.54 or 192.168.34.127, then the rule could state:

Source Add: 192.168.x.x   Destination Add: any   Service: any   Action: drop

Thus, any packet with an address starting with 192.168 would have that rule applied to it—that is, drop the packet.

The application-layer gateway runs special software that enables it to act as a proxy for a specific service request. For example, an organization that runs a Web server can avoid exposing the server to direct user traffic by installing such a proxy server, configured with the registered domain's URL. This proxy server receives requests for Web pages, accesses the Web server on behalf of the external client, and returns the requested pages to the users. These servers can store the most recently accessed pages in their internal caches, and are therefore also called cache servers. The benefits of this type of implementation are significant. For one, the proxy server is placed in an unsecured area of the network or in the demilitarized zone (DMZ)—an intermediate area between a trusted network and an untrusted network—so that it, rather than the Web server, is exposed to the higher levels of risk from the less trusted networks. Additional filtering routers can be implemented behind the proxy server, limiting access to the more secure internal system, and thereby further protecting internal systems.

One common example of a proxy server implementation is a firewall that blocks all requests for and responses to requests for Web pages and services from the organization's internal computers and instead makes all such requests and responses go to intermediate computers (or proxies) in the less protected areas of the organization's network. This technique is still widely used to implement electronic commerce functions, although most users of this technology have upgraded to take advantage of the DMZ approach discussed later.

The primary disadvantage of application-level firewalls is that they are designed for a specific protocol and cannot easily be reconfigured to protect against attacks on other protocols. Since application firewalls work at the application layer (hence the name), they are typically restricted to a single application (e.g., FTP, Telnet, HTTP, SMTP, SNMP). The processing

Technical Details
Fresh Hot CIDR

In Table 4-3, notice a column called CIDR Mask. "CIDR" stands for Classless Inter-Domain Routing, and a CIDR Mask is designed to mitigate the inefficiencies in the way IP addresses used to be organized and assigned. A nongovernmental organization called the Internet Corporation for Assigned Names and Numbers is currently responsible for this task. Prior to CIDR, addresses were issued based on the location in the overall range of numbers used in the addressing scheme, with some numbers in the Class A range, some in Class B, and so on. If the organization was assigned a Class A address, the first octet (that would be the first 8 bits of the address as represented by the first number in the Dotted Decimal Notation) was the network address, and the remainder represented the host address.

Organizations assign host addresses to various computers. For example, in the Class A address 10.11.12.13, 10 is the organization's network address and cannot be changed; the rest of the numbers after the 10 can be assigned by the organization and used for hosts. Class B addresses reserve the first 16 bits (two octets in Dotted Decimal Notation) for the network address. For example, the Class B address 172.16.14.15 uses 172.16 to identify the organization's network, and the 14.15 is assigned to a specific host computer. Class C addresses reserve the first 24 bits (three octets) for the network address and only 8 bits (one octet) for host assignment.

The simple assignment of these large blocks of addresses became problematic as organizations that planned ahead were assigned numbers of addresses far beyond what they could quickly use. For example, a Class B address—not an uncommon assignment for a large organization or university—would have over 65,500 usable addresses. But the number of addresses under IP version 4 is finite, and the availability of open addresses is rapidly dwindling.

Enter CIDR, which ignores the old Dotted Decimal Notation and simply assigns addresses using the demarcation between network address and host address. The slash (/) and the number following the slash indicate where the boundary between network address and host address is located. In other words, /8 means that the first 8 bits are part of the network address, and the remaining bits are part of the host address. The CIDR Masks /8, /16, and /24 correspond to the Class A, B, and C of the old system, as shown in Table 4-3. Today, however, addresses are assigned in such a way that only the ones that are actually needed get assigned. Once an organization is assigned a range of addresses (e.g., 10.10.x.x/12), it can manage the addresses within its CIDR-based address range more easily (e.g., 10.10.0.1–10.10.15.254).

time and resources necessary to read each packet down to the application layer diminish the ability of these firewalls to handle multiple types of applications.

An application-layer gateway provides you with one especially valuable security benefit, however. Unlike a packet filter, which decides whether to allow or deny a request based on the information contained in the packet header, the gateway understands the contents of the requested data. It can be configured to allow or deny (both actions can be taken as a result of filtering) specific content, such as viruses and executables.

Content filtering is only one of the complex tasks that application-layer gateways can perform, enabling them to go far beyond merely blocking specified IP addresses. Here are some of the other tasks they can perform:

4

- Load balancing—When a network has more than one entry address, the number of connections assigned to each can be managed to assure an even workload. Large organizations commonly install more than one firewall and divide the traffic load between them.

- IP address mapping—This is a type of NAT or PAT in which a static IP address assigned by an ISP is mapped to the private IP address of a computer on the local network; it is sometimes called address vectoring or static IP mapping. The benefit of this to an internal network is to shield actual internal IP addresses from the prying eyes of unauthorized external clients.

- Filtering content—An application proxy server can be set up to filter on some detailed criteria. You can block files that have a certain filename or part of a filename, a keyword, an e-mail attachment, or a type of content.

- URL filtering—You can also block a site's Domain Name System (DNS) name, such as *www.criminalactivity.com*.

Most of these application-level security techniques are discussed in more detail in later parts of this book.

Firewall Categories

Firewalls can be categorized by processing mode, generation, or structure. "Processing mode" is how the firewall examines the network traffic that it is trying to filter. "Generation" refers to the level of technology a firewall has, later generations being more complex and more recently developed. "Structure" refers to the kind of structure the firewalls are intended for, including such categories as residential-grade or commercial-grade firewalls, hardware-based or software-based firewalls, and firewalls for appliance-based devices.

Processing Mode

There are five major processing-mode categories for firewalls: (1) packet-filtering firewalls, (2) application gateways, (3) circuit gateways, (4) MAC layer firewalls, and (5) hybrids.[1] Hybrid firewalls use a combination of the other four methods; and, in practice, most firewalls fall into this category, since most use multiple approaches within the same device. This section recaps the types of firewalls that have already been described and provides a short overview of the other variants.

Packet-Filtering Firewalls There are three kinds of packet-filtering firewalls: static filtering, dynamic filtering, and stateful inspection. Static filtering requires that the filtering rules be developed and installed with the firewall. The rules are created and sequenced either by a person directly editing the rule set or by a person using a programmable interface to specify the rules and the sequence. Any changes to the rules require human intervention. This type of filtering is common in network routers and gateways.

Dynamic filtering reacts to an emergent event and updates or creates rules to deal with that event. This reaction can be positive, as in allowing an internal user to engage in a specific activity upon request, or it can be negative, as in dropping all packets from a particular address when an increase in the presence of a particular type of malformed packet is detected. While static filtering allows entire sets of one type of packet to enter in response to authorized requests, dynamic filtering allows only a particular packet with a particular source, destination, and port address to enter through the firewall. It does this by opening and closing "doors" in the firewall based on the information contained in the packet header, which makes dynamic packet filters an intermediate form, between traditional static packet filters and application proxies.

Stateful inspection firewalls (also called stateful firewalls), as described earlier in this chapter, keep track of each network connection between internal and external systems using a state table.

Application Gateways The application gateway, described earlier, is also known as an application-level firewall, proxy server, or application firewall. It is frequently installed on a dedicated computer, separate from the filtering router, but it is commonly used in conjunction with a filtering router.

Circuit Gateways A circuit gateway operates at the transport layer. Connections are authorized based on addresses. Like filtering firewalls, circuit gateway firewalls do not usually examine traffic flowing between one network and another, but they do prevent direct connections between one network and another. They accomplish this by creating tunnels connecting specific processes or systems on each side of the firewall, and then allowing only authorized traffic through these tunnels, such as a specific type of TCP connection. Circuit gateways are often included in the application gateway category, but they are, in fact, a separate type of firewall. Writing for NIST in SP 800-10, John Wack describes the operation of a circuit gateway as follows:

> "A circuit-level gateway relays TCP connections but does no extra processing or filtering of the protocol. For example, if an organization has a static VPN defined between a remote site and a VPN device inside its network, a firewall that receives that traffic would simply pass it to the assigned internal VPN concentrator since it is already anticipated. This could be considered an example of a circuit-level gateway, since once the connection between the source and destination is established, the firewall simply passes bytes between the systems. Another example of a circuit-level gateway would be for NNTP, in which the NNTP server would connect to the firewall, and then the internal system's NNTP clients would connect to the firewall. The firewall would, again, simply pass bytes."

MAC Layer Firewalls While not as well known or widely referenced as the processing-mode firewalls just discussed, MAC layer firewalls are designed to operate at the media access control sublayer of the data link layer (Layer 2) of the OSI network model. This enables these firewalls to consider, in their filtering decisions, the specific host computer's identity, as represented by its MAC or Network Interface Card (NIC) address. Using this approach, the MAC addresses of specific host computers are linked to ACL entries that identify the specific types of packets that can be sent to each host; all other traffic is blocked.

Hybrid Firewalls Hybrid firewalls combine the elements of various types of firewalls—that is, the elements of packet filtering and proxy services, or of packet filtering and circuit gateways. A hybrid firewall system may consist of two separate firewall devices; each is a separate firewall system, but they work in tandem. For example, a hybrid firewall system might include a packet-filtering firewall that is set up to screen all acceptable requests, and then pass the requests to a proxy server, which, in turn, requests services from a Web server deep inside the organization's networks. An advantage to the hybrid firewall approach is that it enables an organization to make security improvements without completely replacing its existing firewalls.

Firewall Generations

Firewalls are frequently categorized by their position on a developmental continuum—that is, by generation. The first generation of firewall devices consists of routers that perform only simple packet-filtering operations. More recent generations of firewalls offer increasingly complex capabilities, including the increased security and convenience of creating a DMZ—"demilitarized zone." At present, there are five generally recognized generations of firewalls, which can be implemented in a wide variety of architectures:

- First-generation firewalls are static packet-filtering firewalls—that is, simple networking devices that filter packets according to their headers as the packets travel to and from the organization's networks.

- Second-generation firewalls are application-level firewalls or proxy servers—that is, dedicated systems that are separate from the filtering router and that provide intermediate services for requesters.

- Third-generation firewalls are stateful inspection firewalls, which, as described previously, monitor network connections between internal and external systems using state tables.

- Fourth-generation firewalls, also known as dynamic packet-filtering firewalls, allow only a particular packet with a particular source, destination, and port address to enter.

- Fifth-generation firewalls are kernel proxies, a specialized form that works under Windows NT Executive, which is the kernel of Windows NT. Kernel proxies evaluate packets at multiple layers of the protocol stack by checking security in the kernel as data is passed up and down the stack. Cisco implemented this technology in the security kernel of its Centri Firewall, which is no longer in production.

Firewall Structures

Firewalls can also be categorized by the structures used to implement them. Most commercial-grade firewalls are dedicated appliances. That is, they are stand-alone units running on fully customized computing platforms that provide both the physical network connection and firmware programming necessary to perform their function, whatever that function (static packet filtering, application proxy, etc.) may be. Some firewall appliances use highly customized, sometimes-proprietary hardware systems that are developed exclusively as firewall devices. Other commercial firewall systems are actually off-the-shelf general-purpose computer systems that use custom application software running either over standard operating systems like Windows or Linux/UNIX or on specialized variants of these operating systems. Most small office or residential-grade firewalls are either simplified dedicated appliances running on computing devices or application software installed directly on the user's computer.

Commercial-Grade Firewall Appliances Firewall appliances are stand-alone, self-contained combinations of computing hardware and software. These devices frequently have many of the features of a general-purpose computer, with the addition of firmware-based instructions that increase their reliability and performance and minimize the likelihood of their being compromised. The customized software operating system that drives the device can be periodically upgraded but can only be modified using a direct physical connection or using extensive authentication and authorization protocols. The firewall rule sets are stored in nonvolatile memory and can thus be changed by technical staff when necessary and are available each time the device is restarted.

These appliances may be manufactured from stripped-down, general-purpose computer systems, and/or they may be designed to run on a customized version of a general-purpose operating system. These variant operating systems are tuned to meet the type of firewall activity built into the application software that provides the firewall functionality.

Commercial-Grade Firewall Systems A commercial-grade firewall system consists of application software that is configured for the firewall application and runs on a general-purpose computer. Organizations can install firewall software on an existing general-purpose computer system, or they can purchase hardware that has been configured to specifications that yield optimal firewall performance. These systems exploit the fact that firewalls are essentially application software packages that use common general-purpose network connections to move data from one network to another. Full-featured, commercial-grade firewall packages include:

- Check Point Power-1—Power-1, by Check Point Software Technologies Ltd., is considered by many security experts to be the product of choice when it comes to software firewalls. The product is notable for being among the first to use stateful packet inspection to monitor network traffic.

  Incorporating the Check Point's original FireWall-1, Power-1 includes a full array of security tools, including authentication, virus checking (via a third-party application that is integrated into the firewall package), intrusion detection, and packet filtering. In its day, FireWall-1 was the only firewall that was compliant with the Open Platform for SECurity (OPSEC) security standard. OPSEC is an industry standards group that defines how firewalls should interoperate. A high-availability feature enables a corporate network to run multiple parallel installations of Power-1 in tandem. If one firewall goes down, the others remain functioning, keeping the network connected and maintaining current connections, thus making Power-1 especially good for large-scale networks.

  Check Point's firewall software has been incorporated into a number of firewall appliances, including virtualized security gateways (VSX-1), intrusion detection and prevention systems (IPS-1), and a unified threat management appliance (UTM-1). Recently, Check Point acquired the Nokia line and has incorporated their technologies into the Check Point product suite.

- Cisco ASA—The Adaptive Security Appliance (ASA) is not a single product but a name given to a series of secure, self-contained hardware devices that contain full-featured firewalls. The line ranges from the ASA 5505, which can handle 10,000 concurrent connections operating at 150 Megabits per second for small office/home office (SOHO) environments, to the ASA 5580-40, which is able to handle up to 2 million concurrent connections operating at 10 Gigabits per second.

  The Cisco ASA firewalls are notable for competitive pricing, extensive online documentation, and excellent customer support. Cisco's firewall products have been available for several years and are reliable and rich in features, including high availability, an intrusion detection system, and protection against DoS attacks. Recently, the ASA line replaced the Cisco PIX line as its primary firewall architecture. The PIX line has been retired or End-Of-Life (EOL).

- Microsoft Internet Security & Acceleration Server—The Internet Security & Acceleration Server (ISA) 2000 series is an application-level firewall from Microsoft Corporation, the features of which include authentication through integration with Active Directory, virus scanning (through integrated third-party products), data-aware filtering capabilities, and IP packet-filtering functionality. ISA also supports the Cache Array Routing Protocol (CARP) so that the product can be scaled to fit larger traffic requirements.

- McAfee Firewall Enterprise (Sidewinder)—Sidewinder is McAfee's product offering in the commercial firewall industry, representing technology purchased from Secure Computing (which in turn was purchased from NAI). It is a flexible product, supporting application proxies, stateful inspection packet filtering, and IPSec VPNs.

Small Office/Home Office (SOHO) Firewall Appliances

As more and more small businesses and residences obtain fast Internet connections with digital subscriber lines (DSL) or cable modem connections, they become more and more vulnerable to attacks. What many small business and work-from-home users don't realize is that these high-speed services are always on, and thus the computers connected to them are much more likely to be visible to the scans performed by attackers than those connected only for the duration of a dial-up session. Even with the improved security capabilities of home computing operating systems like Windows XP, Vista, and 7, most of these systems are still susceptible to outside intrusion. Even modern home computing operating systems with secure capabilities are rarely configured securely by their users. Users can still benefit from having solid SOHO networking security in place. Just as organizations must protect their information, residential users must implement some form of firewall to prevent loss, damage, or disclosure of personal information.

One of the most effective methods of improving computing security in the SOHO setting is by means of a SOHO or residential-grade firewall. These devices, also known as broadband gateways or DSL/cable modem routers, connect the user's local area network or a specific computer system to the Internetworking device—in this case, the cable modem or DSL router provided by the Internet service provider (ISP). The SOHO firewall serves first as a stateful firewall to enable inside-to-outside access and can be configured to allow limited

TCP/IP port forwarding and/or screened subnet capabilities (see the later sections of this chapter for definitions of these terms).

In recent years, the broadband router devices that can function as packet-filtering firewalls have been enhanced to combine the features of wireless access points (WAPs) as well as small stackable LAN switches in a single device. These convenient combination devices give the SOHO user the strong protection that comes from the use of NAT services. NAT assigns nonrouting local addresses to the computer systems in the local area network and uses the single ISP-assigned address to communicate with the Internet. Since the internal computers are not visible to the public network, they are much less likely to be scanned or compromised. Many users implement these devices primarily to allow multiple internal users to share a single external Internet connection. Figure 4-12 shows a few examples of the SOHO firewall devices currently available on the market.

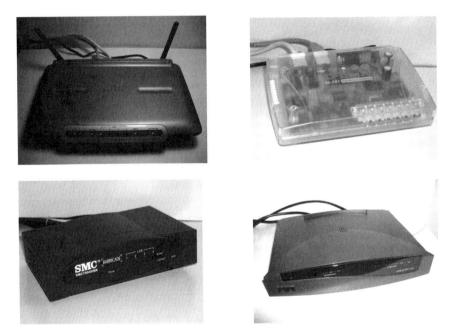

Figure 4-12 Example SOHO Firewalls
© Cengage Learning 2012

Many of these firewalls provide more than simple NAT services. As illustrated with the sample screen shots in Figures 4-13 through 4-16, some SOHO firewalls include packet filtering, port filtering, and simple intrusion detection systems, and some can even restrict access to specific MAC addresses. Users may be able to configure port forwarding and enable outside users to access specific TCP or UDP ports on specific computers on the protected network.

Figure 4-13 shows the MAC Address Filter setup screen from the SMC Barricade residential broadband router, which can be used to identify which computers inside the trusted network may access the Internet.

Some firewall devices provide a limited intrusion detection capability. Figure 4-14 shows the configuration screen from an SMC Barricade residential broadband router that enables the

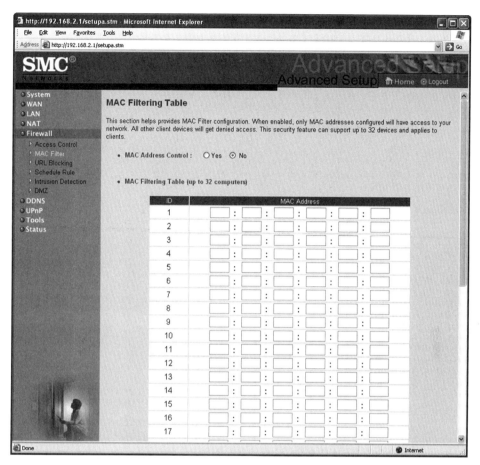

Figure 4-13 Filtering MAC Addresses
© Cengage Learning 2012

intrusion detection feature. When enabled, this feature detects specific intrusion attempts that are defined in the currently installed detection library—that is, attempts to compromise the protected network that are known to the device manufacturer and are detectable based on the nature of the attack. In addition to recording intrusion attempts, the router can be configured to use the contact information to notify the firewall administrator when an intrusion attempt has occurred.

Figure 4-15 shows a continuation of the configuration screen for the intrusion detection feature. Note that the intrusion criteria are limited in number, but the actual threshold levels of the various activities detected can be customized by the administrator.

Figure 4-16 illustrates that even simple residential firewalls can be used to create a logical screened subnetwork (often called a demilitarized zone, or DMZ) that can provide Web services. This screen shows how the Barricade router can be configured to allow port forwarding to be established so that Internet users can be allowed access to servers inside the trusted network for services at specific port numbers. The network administrator is expected to ensure that the exposed servers are sufficiently secured for this type of exposure.

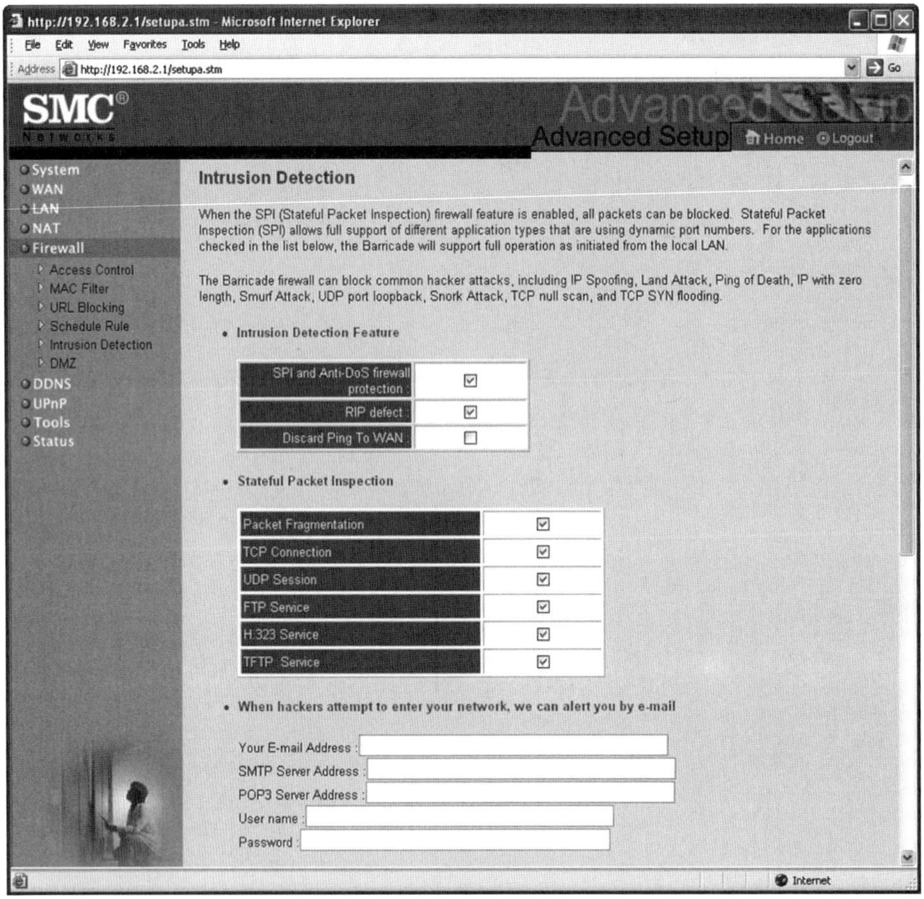

Figure 4-14 Configuring Intrusion Detection
© Cengage Learning 2012

Software Firewalls Many people have installed software-based firewalls (some of which also provide antivirus or intrusion detection capabilities); but, unfortunately, these people may not be as protected as they think they are. The most commonly used residential-grade software-based firewalls are listed in Table 4-4 along with a rating given by *CNET* magazine's editors. *CNET* magazine is a widely recognized source for technology industry reporting and product evaluations. These firewalls claim to detect and prevent intrusion into the user's system without affecting usability. However, many of the firewalls in Table 4-4 provide free versions of their software that are not fully functional, and the old adage "you get what you pay for" certainly applies to software in this category. Users who implement this free, less-capable software often find that it delivers less-than-complete protection.

Note that there are several additional firewalls available for download. Only those posted since 2007 were included.

Free Firewall Tools on the Internet Most of the free firewall software on the Internet, including the packet filter IPChains and TIS Firewall Toolkit, also run on a free operating system, such as Linux, the Berkeley Software Design variety of UNIX (BSD), or DOS.

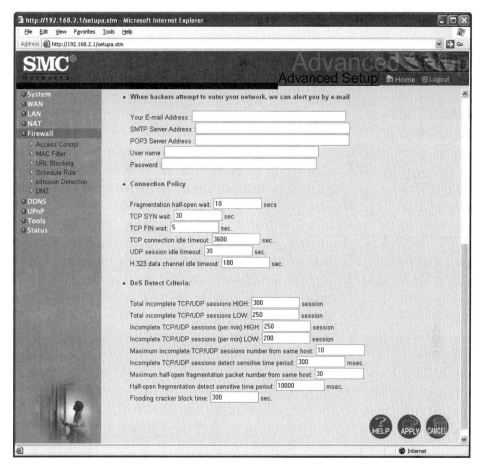

Figure 4-15 Configuring Intrusion Detection (Cont.)
© Cengage Learning 2012

Free firewall programs aren't perfect. Their logging capabilities aren't as robust as those of some commercial products, they can be difficult to configure, and they usually don't include a way to monitor the firewall in real time. Nonetheless, they have a place in networking because of their convenience, simplicity, and unbeatable price.

Of particular note is Netfilter. Netfilter is the firewall software that comes with the Linux 2.4 kernel, and it is a powerful (and available for free) solution for stateless and stateful packet filtering, NAT, and packet processing.

There are limits to the level of configurability and protection that software firewalls can provide. Many of the applications in Table 4-4 have very limited configuration capability. They offer their users a range of capabilities from practically no security up to fairly high levels of security. With only three or four levels of configuration, they may be difficult to use in everyday situations. Users find themselves sacrificing security for usability, because at higher levels of security the application constantly asks for instruction on whether to allow a particular application, packet, or service to connect internally or externally. The Microsoft Windows XP, Vista, and 7 versions of Internet Explorer have similar configuration settings that allow users to choose from a list of preconfigured options or choose a custom setting with a more detailed security configuration.

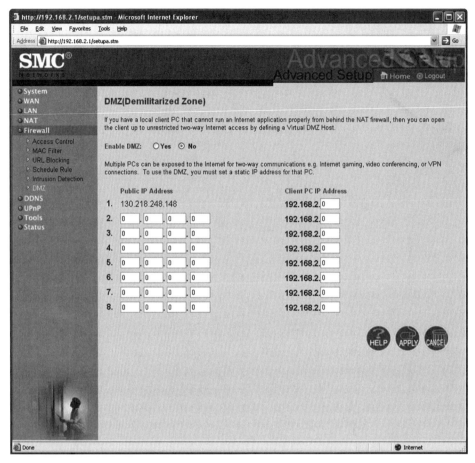

Figure 4-16 Configuring Port Forwarding
© Cengage Learning 2012

Software vs. Hardware: The SOHO Firewall Debate

Which type of firewall should the residential user implement? Ask yourself this question: Where would you rather defend against an attacker? When you use software only, the attacker is inside your computer, battling a piece of software (free software, in many cases) that may not have been correctly installed, configured, patched, upgraded, or designed. If the software happens to have a known vulnerability, the attacker could gain unrestricted access to your system. When you use the hardware device, even if the attacker manages to crash the firewall system, your computer and information are still safely behind the now-disabled connection, which is assigned a nonroutable IP address, making it virtually impossible to reach from the outside.

A former student of one of the authors of this book responded to this debate by installing a hardware firewall, and then visiting an attacker chat room. He challenged the group to penetrate his system. A few days later, he received an e-mail from an attacker claiming to have accessed his system. The attacker included a graphic of a screen showing a C:\ prompt, which he claimed was from the student's system. After doing a bit of research, the student found out that the firewall had an image stored in firmware that was designed to distract attackers. It was an image of a command window with a DOS prompt. The hardware (NAT) solution had withstood the challenge.

Firewall	*CNET* Editor's Rating (out of five stars)
Norton 360	4
ZoneAlarm Extreme Security 2010	3
Trend Micro Internet Security 2009	3.5
Panda Internet Security 2009	3.5
McAfee Internet Security 2009	3.5
PC Tools Firewall Plus (2009)	4
Agnitum Outpost Firewall Pro 2009	4
Sygate Personal Firewall 5.6.2808 (2007)	4
AVG Anti-Virus plus Firewall 9.0.700 (2009)	unrated
Comodo Internet Security 3.12 (2009)	5
Ashampoo FireWall Free 1.2 (2007)	5
Webroot AV with AntiSpyware and Firewall 6.1 (2007)	unrated
VisNetic Firewall 3.0 (2007)	unrated
Kerio WinRoute Firewall 6.7 (2009)	unrated
Microsoft Windows Firewall (integral to Windows XP and Vista systems)	unrated
CA Internet Security Suite Plus 2009	2.5
In addition, many commercial products have desktop endpoint security systems (IBM Proventia, Checkpoint, etc.)	unrated

Table 4-4 Common Software Firewalls As Rated by CNET (*www.cnet.com*)

Firewall Architectures

Each of the firewall devices described earlier can be configured in a number of network connection architectures. These approaches are sometimes mutually exclusive, but sometimes can be combined.

The configuration that works best for a particular organization depends on three factors: the objectives of the network, the organization's ability to develop and implement the architectures, and the budget available for the function. Although literally hundreds of variations exist, there are four common architectural implementations for firewalls: packet-filtering routers, screened host firewalls, dual-homed firewalls, and screened subnet firewalls. Each of these is examined in more detail in the following sections.

Packet-Filtering Routers Most organizations with an Internet connection have some form of router at the perimeter, between the organization's internal networks and the external service provider. Many of these routers can be configured to reject packets that the organization does not allow into the network. This is a simple but effective way to lower the organization's risk from external attack. The drawbacks to this type of system include a lack of auditing and strong authentication. Also, the complexity of the access control lists used to filter the packets can degrade network performance.

Screened Host Firewalls Screened host firewalls combine the packet-filtering router with a separate, dedicated firewall, such as an application proxy server. This approach allows the router to prescreen packets to minimize the network traffic and load on the internal proxy. The application proxy examines an application layer protocol, such as HTTP, and performs the proxy services. This separate host is often referred to as a bastion host; it can be a rich target for external attacks, and should be very thoroughly secured. Even though the bastion host/application proxy actually contains only cached copies of the internal Web documents, it can still present a promising target, because compromising the bastion host can disclose the configuration of internal networks and possibly provide external sources with internal information. Since the bastion host stands as a sole defender on the network perimeter, it is also commonly referred to as the sacrificial host. To its advantage, this configuration requires the external attack to compromise two separate systems before the attack can access internal data. In this way, the bastion host protects the data more fully than the router alone. Figure 4-17 shows a typical configuration of a screened host architecture.

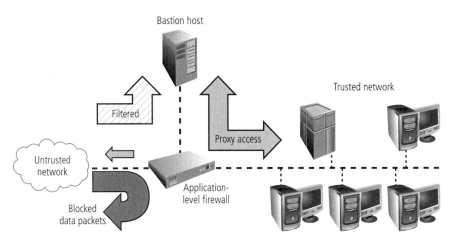

Figure 4-17 Screened Host Architecture
© Cengage Learning 2012

Dual-Homed Host Firewalls The next step up in firewall architectural complexity is the dual-homed host. When this architectural approach is used, the bastion host contains two NICs (network interface cards) rather than one, as in the bastion host configuration. One NIC is connected to the external network, and one is connected to the internal network, providing an additional layer of protection. With two NICs, all traffic must physically go through the firewall to move between the internal and external networks. This architecture often makes use of NAT—mapping real, valid, external IP addresses to special ranges of nonroutable internal IP addresses—thereby creating yet another barrier to intrusion from external attackers. If the NAT server is a multihomed bastion host, it translates between the true, external IP addresses assigned to the organization by public network naming authorities and the internally assigned, nonroutable IP addresses. NAT translates by dynamically assigning addresses to internal communications and tracking the conversations with sessions to determine which incoming message is a response to which outgoing traffic. Figure 4-18 shows a typical configuration of a dual-homed host firewall that uses NAT and proxy access to protect the internal network.

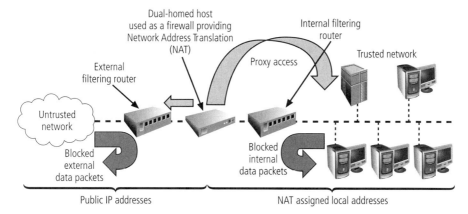

Figure 4-18 Dual-Homed Host
© Cengage Learning 2012

A benefit of a dual-homed host is its ability to translate many different protocols at their respective data link layers, including Ethernet, Token Ring, Fiber Distributed Data Interface (FDDI), and Asynchronous Transfer Method (ATM). On the downside, if a dual-homed host is compromised, that compromise will likely disable the connection to the external network. In addition, as traffic volume increases, a dual-homed host firewall may become overloaded with a corresponding reduction in throughput of filtered traffic. Compared to more complex solutions, however, this architecture provides strong overall protection with minimal expense.

Screened Subnet Firewalls (with DMZ) The dominant architecture used today is the screened subnet firewall. The architecture of a screened subnet firewall provides a DMZ. The DMZ can be a dedicated port on the firewall device linking a single bastion host, or it can be connected to a screened subnet, as shown in Figure 4-19. Until recently, servers providing services through an untrusted network were commonly placed in the DMZ. Examples of these include Web servers, file transfer protocol (FTP) servers, and certain database servers. More recent strategies using proxy servers have provided much more secure solutions.

A common arrangement is a subnet firewall consisting of two or more internal bastion hosts behind a packet-filtering router, with each host protecting the trusted network. There are many variants of the screened subnet architecture. The first general model consists of two filtering routers, with one or more dual-homed bastion hosts between them. In the second general model, the connections are routed as follows:

- Connections from the outside or untrusted network are routed through an external filtering router.
- Connections from the outside or untrusted network are routed into—and then out of—a routing firewall to the separate network segment known as the DMZ.
- Connections into the trusted internal network are allowed only from the DMZ bastion host servers.

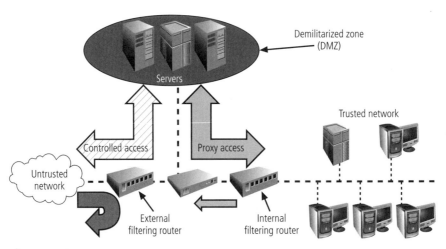

Figure 4-19 Screened Subnet
© Cengage Learning 2012

The screened subnet is an entire network segment that performs two functions: it protects the DMZ systems and information from outside threats by providing a network of intermediate security (more secure than the general public networks, but less secure than the internal network), and it protects the internal networks by limiting how external connections can gain access to them. Although extremely secure, the screened subnet can be expensive to implement and complex to configure and manage. The value of the information it protects must justify the cost.

Another facet of the DMZ is the creation of an area known as an extranet. An extranet is a segment of the DMZ where additional authentication and authorization controls are put into place to provide services that are not available to the general public. An example is an online retailer that allows anyone to browse the product catalog and place items into a shopping cart, but requires extra authentication and authorization when the customer is ready to check out and place an order.

Limitations Of Firewalls

Firewalls can do a lot, but they can't be expected to do everything. Therefore, they should not be the only form of protection for a network. Instead, they should be part of an overall security plan and used in conjunction with other forms of protection, including ID cards, passwords, and employee rules of conduct. Even the most elaborate firewall can't protect against an employee who brings a floppy disk to work containing files that have been infected with a virus, or employees who use a host inside the firewall to gain unauthorized access to sensitive information.

Running Case: Apology Accepted

"You okay, Alex?" Mike asked, looking at Data Mart's IT manager across the table.

Alex looked like someone had stolen his car—embarrassed and angry at the same time. "Yeah, Mike, I've been kicking myself since I realized how big the screw-up I made was," he said. "When I bought that thing, I really thought I was making an improvement in our security, not putting everything at risk."

"What did you have before you installed the residential firewall?" Mike asked.

"That's just it! Nothing!" Alex said. "And I thought I was helping!"

"Well, what's important now is to start improving what you started, regardless of whether it was a good decision or not," Mike said. "Let's fix that problem so we can move on to problems you may not have known about."

1. What are Mike and Alex's options with regard to commercial firewalls?
2. Based on the firewall architectures discussed in this chapter, what would you recommend?

4

Chapter Summary

- Achieving network security is a process that imposes controls on an organization's network resources in order to balance the risks and rewards that come from network usage. The controls are a continually evolving set of policies, programs, and technologies.

- A firewall is anything, whether hardware or software (or a combination of the two), that can filter the transmission of packets of digital information as they attempt to pass through a network boundary. They perform two basic security functions: packet filtering and application proxying.

- A firewall can contain many components, including a packet filter, a proxy server, an authentication system, and software that performs Network Address Translation (NAT) or Port Address Transaction (PAT). Some firewalls can encrypt traffic, and some help establish VPNs.

- Packet filtering is a key function of any firewall. In fact, packet filters were one of the first types of firewalls. Packet filters are an effective element in any perimeter security setup. A packet-filtering firewall may be stateless or stateful. Stateless packet filtering ignores the state of the connection between the internal computer and the external computer. Stateful packet filtering is an examination of the data contained in a packet with a memory of the state of the connection between client and internal and external computers.

- Port Address Translation (PAT) and Network Address Translation (NAT) are addressing methods that make internal network addresses invisible to outside computers while still providing access to the Internet. PAT uses one assigned address from an ISP for each internal user connecting to the Internet (one to one), and PAT uses one assigned address to allow multiple internal users to access the Internet (one to many).

- Application layer gateways, also known as proxy servers, control the way applications inside the network access external networks. They work by having the gateway device act as a substitute (i.e., a proxy) for the client, making requests for Web pages or sending and receiving e-mail on behalf of individual users, who are thus shielded from directly connecting with the Internet.

- Firewalls can be categorized by processing mode, generation, or structure. "Processing mode" is how the firewall examines the network traffic that it is trying to filter.

"Generation" refers to the level of technology a firewall has, later generations being more complex and more recently developed. "Structure" refers to the kind of structure the firewalls are intended for, including such categories as residential-grade or commercial-grade firewalls, hardware-based or software-based firewalls, and firewalls for appliance-based devices.

■ Each of the firewall devices described earlier can be configured in a number of network connection architectures. The configuration that works best for a particular organization depends on three factors: the objectives of the network, the organization's ability to develop and implement the architectures, and the budget available for the function. There are four common architectural implementations of firewalls: packet-filtering routers, screened host firewalls, dual-homed firewalls, and screened subnet firewalls.

Review Questions

1. Why is it important that a firewall provide a centralized security checkpoint for a network?

2. What are the two basic functions of a firewall?

3. What advanced security features can be incorporated into a firewall?

4. What technology was used in the earliest firewalls?

5. What components are found in many firewalls?

6. Why is packet filtering by itself inadequate for security purposes?

7. When does packet filtering offer an advantage over other security methods, such as proxy services?

8. What actions are taken by a firewall when a request from a user is received?

9. Web site requests are routed to which TCP port by default?

10. What can TCP do that UDP cannot do?

11. How is a firewall configured to allow Web access to a Web server?

12. At how many ports can a computer offer services?

13. What is a stateless firewall?

14. What is a stateful firewall?

15. List the benefits of locating your firewall on the perimeter of a network.

16. What network information do attackers initially try to find?

17. Name two reasons a hardware firewall solution is a good choice compared with software-only solutions.

18. Which protocol is connectionless?

19. For what kinds of communications is a connectionless protocol useful?

20. What is a proxy server and what can it do?

Real World Exercises

1. Your company's owner just got back from a conference. He says he thinks your small business, with only 23 employees, needs a firewall for better network security. He wants you to prepare a report on how a firewall would affect your business. Create a presentation (using PowerPoint or another software tool) with no more than five slides that explains what a firewall is, how it works, and what it would do for your business.

2. You have been asked to explain the difference between NAT and PAT. Do so in a few paragraphs. When is it appropriate to use one instead of the other?

3. Your company wants to make sure no internal computer is allowed to make a direct connection from the inside network to an outside network. You heard from someone that this means you need a proxy server. But someone else said it calls for a reverse-proxy server. Which is the correct tool for this need and why?

4. Your local network needs to be set up with an IP address range that cannot be routed over the Internet. What are the nonroutable IPv4 address ranges you can use? If you have fewer than 25 computers to network, pick one of the classes and create an IP address range that will be suitable. What if you have 2500 computers? Which range will you use?

5. What is the Media Access Control (MAC) or hardware address of your computer's network connector? You can use the Internet to find out, based on what operating system you are using. If you work on a Mac, use a search engine with the phrase "finding MAC on Macintosh." If you have a Windows system, search with the phrase "finding MAC on Windows." If you have a Linux system, search with the phrase "finding MAC on Linux."

Hands-On Projects

Project 4-1: View Active Connections

The Netstat application is useful when you need to isolate problems with a computer's Internet or local network connection. You can use it not only to show active network connections, but also for statistics related to a specific protocol, such as TCP, UDP, IP, or ICMP.

To do this project, you will need a computer running Windows XP or Vista that is configured with TCP/IP on a network with other properly configured TCP/IP computers.

1. If your computer is not powered up, power it up now.

2. Click **Start**, point to **Programs** (or **All Programs** on Windows XP), point to **Accessories**, and then click **Command Prompt** to open a command prompt window.

3. Type **netstat**.

4. Press **Enter** to view the computer's current active connections.

5. Type **netstat –a**.

6. Press **Enter** to view not only the currently established connections, but also the ports on which your computer is listening for new connections.

7. Type **netstat –p TCP** and press **Enter** to view information about TCP connections.

8. Type **netstat –p UDP** and press **Enter** to view information about UDP connections.

9. To get a summary of all of Netstat's switches, type **netstat /?** and press **Enter**.

10. Type **exit** and press **Enter** to close the window.

Project 4-2: Do Your Own Manual "Port Scanning" at the Internet Assigned Numbers Authority (IANA) Web Site

Any networked computer has access to as many as 65,535 ports through which it can exchange information. When configuring firewalls, it's often important to record port numbers on which you want to block traffic. Certain port numbers are frequently used by attackers, and you should be aware of what they are. You can research these and many other ports online at the IANA Web site.

1. In a Web browser, go to this address: *www.iana.org/assignments/port-numbers*.

2. From the PORT NUMBERS document that appears, write down port numbers that are considered Well Known Ports, Registered Ports, Dynamic Ports, and/or Private Ports in a lab book or a word-processing document.

3. Scroll down the page. Find which port number is assigned to Whois, which is presented in the list as Who Is. Because the list is very long, you can save time by using the Find (on This Page) function of your Web browser.

4. In the Find What text box in the Find dialog box, type **Who Is**, and then click **Find Next**.

5. Repeat the previous steps to look up the port numbers used by other common applications that need to be monitored by a firewall. These applications include HTTP, FTP, SMTP, POP3, Telnet, and DNS. Write down the answers in a lab book or word-processing document.

6. Exit the site and close your browser.

Project 4-3: Determine Your Computer's IP Address

Every computer that is connected to the Internet is assigned an IP address. Often the address is dynamically generated; that is, it changes from session to session. With some DSL connections and many T-1 or other connections, a static IP address is obtained. To determine the IP address of one of the computers to which you have access, follow these steps:

1. Click **Start, All Programs, Accessories**, and then click **Command Prompt** to open a command prompt window (or you can click **Start Run** and type **cmd** in the text window).

2. Type **ipconfig** and press **Enter**. The display that comes up will show you your IP address. This will be four numbers separated by periods. In some cases, you might have several addresses. The IP address assigned to your Ethernet adapter is the external address. Write down the address in a lab book or word-processing document.

3. Type **ipconfig /all** and press **Enter**. What information is different on this screen?

4. To view other options for the ipconfig command, type **ipconfig /**.

5. Type **exit** and press **Enter** to close the command prompt window.

Running Case Projects

In this exercise, the students will prep the new hardware host and begin the initial install and configure for a firewall application to support Data Mart's needs.

Student Tasks

For the case exercises in this textbook, use the Vyatta software firewall application, version 6.0 or 6.1. Run Vyatta as a virtual machine on your system, using Sun's Virtual-Box 3.2.6 for Windows hosts. To get started, follow the steps below to install both applications.

1. Download and install VirtualBox 3.2.6 for Windows hosts from the VirtualBox Web site, *www.virtualbox.org/wiki/Downloads*. Accept all default values during installation unless your instructor gives alternative information. You may get warnings during installation that the software has not passed Windows Logo testing. If this happens, select **Continue Anyway** to continue with the installation. After installation is complete, uncheck the option to start VirtualBox and click **Finish**.

2. Download the Vyatta VC6.0 – Virtualization ISO from the Vyatta Web Site, *www.vyatta. org/downloads*. Make a note of the download location for use in the next few steps.

3. Start VirtualBox by double-clicking the icon that was created on your desktop during installation.

4. Select **Virtual Media Manager** from the File menu.

5. Select the **CD/DVD Images** tab, and then select the **Add** button.

6. Navigate to the location where you downloaded the Vyatta ISO, and then select it, as shown in Figure 4-20. When you are returned to the CD/DVD Images tab, select **OK** to return to the main menu.

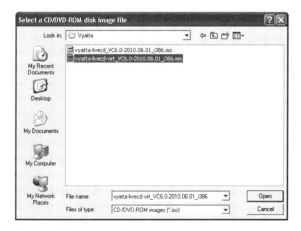

Figure 4-20 Vyatta ISO Location
© Cengage Learning 2012

7. Click the **New** button to begin the VM creation process, and then click the **Next** button to move through the introduction.

8. Give your VM a name by typing it in the input box, select **Linux** as the operating system, and then select your specific Linux version, as shown in Figure 4-21. If your version is not shown, choose **Other Linux** as the version, and then select **Next**.

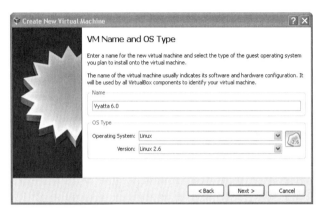

Figure 4-21 VM Name and OS type
© Cengage Learning 2012

9. Select **Next** to accept the default memory value of 256 MB.

10. Make sure the **Boot Hard Disk** and the **Create new hard disk** options are selected, and then select **Next**.

11. Select **Next** to move through the Welcome screen.

12. Select **Fixed-size storage**, and then select **Next**.

13. Enter the location for the virtual disk, set the size to 4 GB, select **Next**, and then select **Finish** to complete the disk creation process. VirtualBox will now create your virtual disk, which may take a few minutes to complete. After the disk is created, select **Finish** to complete the VM creation process and return to the main menu.

14. Click the **Settings** button from the main menu to begin editing some of the VM details.

15. Select **System** in the menu on the left, and then select the **Processor** tab. Activate the Enable PAE/NX feature, as shown in Figure 4-22.

16. Select **Storage** in the menu on the left, and then select the **Empty** CD-ROM drive under the IDE controller in the Storage Tree. In the Attributes section, select the Vyatta ISO from the pulldown menu next to CD/DVD Device:.

17. Select **Audio** in the menu on the left, and then disable the Enable Audio feature.

18. Select **Network** in the menu on the left. On the Adapter 1 tab, make sure the Enable Network Adapter option is enabled and is attached to the bridged adapter. Then, select the name of the external-facing NIC in your system.

19. Select the **Adapter 2** tab. Select the **Enable Network Adapter** option, and then attach it to the bridged adapter. Then, select the name of the internal-facing NIC in your system.

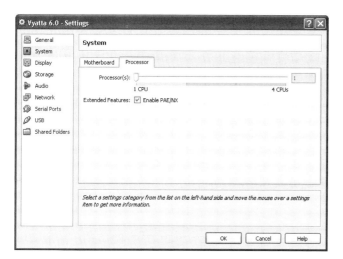

Figure 4-22 Vyatta Processor Settings
© Cengage Learning 2012

20. Select **OK** to complete the VM modification process and return to the main menu.

21. Power on your VM by clicking the green start arrow icon. Select **OK** when presented with various informational messages.

22. After the bootup process is complete, log in using **vyatta** for both username and password. After logging in, enter **install-system** at the prompt to begin the installation process for Vyatta inside the virtual machine, as shown in Figure 4-23.

```
Welcome to Vyatta - vyatta tty1

vyatta login: vyatta
Password:
Last login: Fri Jun 25 04:33:27 GMT 2010 on tty1
Linux vyatta 2.6.31-1-586-vyatta-virt #1 SMP Fri Mar 19 12:46:35 PDT 2010 i686
Welcome to Vyatta.
This system is open-source software. The exact distribution terms for
each module comprising the full system are described in the individual
files in /usr/share/doc/*/copyright.
vyatta@vyatta:~$ install-system_
```

Figure 4-23 Installing Vyatta
© Cengage Learning 2012

23. Press **Enter** to continue the installation.

24. The installation process will now scan for available disk drives and Vyatta installations. After this scan is complete, you will be prompted to select an installation partition. Press **Enter** to accept the default value of Auto.

25. Next, you will be asked on which partition to install. Press **Enter** to select the default value of sda.

26. When prompted, enter **y** and press **Enter** to acknowledge the loss of all data on the /dev/sda partition.

27. Press **Enter** to accept the default value for the root partition, as shown in Figure 4-24.

```
Would you like to continue? (Yes/No) [Yes]:
Probing drives: OK
Looking for pre-existing RAID groups...none found.
The Vyatta image will require a minimum 1000MB root.
Would you like me to try to partition a drive automatically
or would you rather partition it manually with parted?  If
you have already setup your partitions, you may skip this step.

Partition (Auto/Union/Parted/Skip) [Auto]:

I found the following drives on your system:
  sda    16000MB


Install the image on? [sda]:

This will destroy all data on /dev/sda.
Continue? (Yes/No) [No]: yes

How big of a root partition should I create? (1000MB - 16000MB) [16000]MB:

Creating filesystem on /dev/sda1: -_
```

Figure 4-24 Vyatta Installation Options
© Cengage Learning 2012

28. Press **Enter** to accept the default config.boot file installation.

29. Enter the password for the administrator account, and then press **Enter**. Retype the password and press **Enter**.

30. Press **Enter** to accept the default partition to install the GRUB boot loader.

31. After the GRUB boot loader install completes, the installation process is complete. Type **shutdown** at the command prompt and press **Enter** to shut the VM down and return to the VirtualBox main menu.

32. Right-click anywhere on the name of your Vyatta virtual machine and select **Settings**, as shown in Figure 4-25.

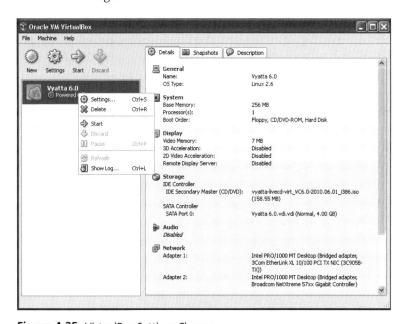

Figure 4-25 VirtualBox Settings Change
© Cengage Learning 2012

33. Select **Storage** in the menu on the left, and then select the CD-ROM drive under the IDE controller in the Storage Tree. In the Attributes section, select the **Host Drive** option from the pull-down menu, as shown in Figure 4-26. Select **OK** to return to the main menu.

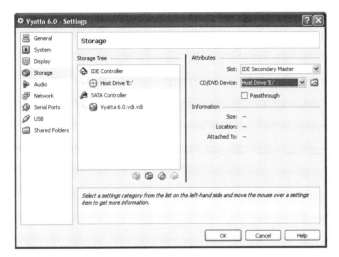

Figure 4-26 CD-ROM Drive Change
© Cengage Learning 2012

34. Restart the virtual machine and login using "vyatta" as the user and the admin password entered during installation.

35. At the command prompt, enter **show version,** and then press **Enter** to verify system status. Verify the Boot via value is "disk," as shown in Figure 4-27.

```
vyatta@vyatta:~$ show version
Version    :   VC6.0-2010.06.01
Description:   Vyatta Core 6.0 2010.06.01
Copyright:    2006-2010 Vyatta, Inc.
Built by :    autobuild@vyatta.com
Built on :    Tue Jun  1 18:38:58 UTC 2010
Build ID :    1006011903-edff915
Boot via :    disk
Uptime   :    05:09:08 up 8 min,  1 user,  load average: 0.00, 0.06, 0.06

vyatta@vyatta:~$ _
```

Figure 4-27 "show version" Output
© Cengage Learning 2012

36. At the command prompt, enter **configure,** and then press **Enter** to configure the external interface. The command prompt will change to reflect a pound sign (#) to show you are in configuration mode. *192.168.201.122/24*

37. Enter **set interfaces ethernet eth0 address** xxx.xxx.xxx.xxx/xx, using the IP address and CIDR mask given to you by the instructor for use, and then press **Enter.** *10.1.22.1/24*

38. Enter **set interfaces ethernet eth1 address** xxx.xxx.xxx.xxx/xx, using the IP address and CIDR mask given to you by the instructor for use, and then press **Enter.**

39. Enter **commit**, and then press **Enter**.

Start here 40. To test system connectivity, have another student on the same network segment as you ping the IP address used above for eth0.

41. To enable the Web GUI, enter **set service https**, and then press **Enter**.

42. After some setup dialogue appears, enter **commit**, and then press **Enter**.

43. To verify GUI setup, open a Web browser on any client within the internal network and point it to https://<external-facing IP address>, logging in using "vyatta" and the admin password created earlier. After successful verification, select the **Log out** option in the upper-right corner of the GUI, and then close the browser window.

10.1.1.1 #50 cyan 44. Now, we will add DNS server information using the command line in the virtual machine. At the Vyatta command prompt, enter **set system name-server <IP address of DNS server>**, and then press **Enter**.

45. Enter **commit**, and then press **Enter**.

192.168.201.253 46. Now, we will configure the default gateway. At the command prompt, enter **set system gateway-address <IP address of default gateway>**, and then press **Enter**.

47. Enter **commit**, and then press **Enter**.

Now, we will enable the DHCP server for our internal network with a series of commands.

10.1.22.0/24 48. Enter **set service dhcp-server shared-network-name DHCP_INTERNAL_POOL subnet <internal IP address range/mask>start <first IP address in pool>stop <last IP address in pool>**, and then press **Enter**.

10.1.22.2 *10.1.22.200* 49. Enter **set service dhcp-server shared-network-name DHCP_INTERNAL_POOL subnet <internal IP address range/mask>default-router <IP address of internal-facing NIC>**, and then press **Enter**.   *10.1.22.1*

10.1.22.0 50. Enter **set service dhcp-server shared-network-name DHCP_INTERNAL_POOL subnet <internal IP address range/mask>dns-server <IP address of DNS server>**, and then press **Enter**.

51. Enter **commit**, and then press **Enter** to commit the changes, as shown in Figure 4-28.

Now, we will enable Network Address Translation (NAT) for our internal network with a series of commands.

```
vyatta@vyatta# set service dhcp-server shared-network-name DHCP_INTERNAL_POOL su
bnet 10.10.10.0/24 start 10.10.10.100 stop 10.10.10.250
[edit]
vyatta@vyatta# set service dhcp-server shared-network-name DHCP_INTERNAL_POOL su

[edit]
vyatta@vyatta# set service dhcp-server shared-network-name DHCP_INTERNAL_POOL su
bnet 10.10.10.0/24 dns-server 10.10.10.1
[edit]
vyatta@vyatta# commit
[edit]
vyatta@vyatta# _
```

Figure 4-28 DHCP Server Settings

52. Enter **set service nat rule 1 source address** **<internal IP address range/mask>**, and then press **Enter**.

53. Enter **set service nat rule 1 outbound-interface eth0**, and then press **Enter**.

54. Enter **set service nat rule 1 type masquerade**, and then press **Enter**.

55. Enter **commit**, and then press **Enter** to commit the changes, as shown in Figure 4-29.

```
vyatta@vyatta# set service nat rule 1 source address 10.10.10.0/24
[edit]
vyatta@vyatta# set service nat rule 1 outbound-interface eth0
[edit]
vyatta@vyatta# set service nat rule 1 type masquerade
[edit]
vyatta@vyatta# commit
[edit]
vyatta@vyatta# _
```

Figure 4-29 NAT Rule Settings
© Cengage Learning 2012

56. Enter **save** to write our changes permanently, and then enter **exit** to leave configuration mode.

Endnotes

1. Avolio, Frederic. Firewalls and Internet Security, the Second Hundred (Internet) Years. Accessed 6 May 2007 from *www.cisco.com/web/about/ac123/ac147/ac174/ac200/about_cisco_ipj_archive_article09186a00800c85ae.html*.

"Once we are in the
habit of filtering what
we want to believe
through a sieve, disbelief
splashes back in our
face."
—Anonymous

chapter 5

Packet Filtering

After reading this chapter and completing the exercises, you will be able to:

- Describe packets and packet filtering
- Explain the approaches to packet filtering
- Configure specific filtering rules based on business needs

Running Case: Not My Job

"So who will be installing and configuring the new firewall?" Rachel asked. She looked around the room at the Data Mart employees.

"We thought you would be," Tom said. "I don't mean to sound rude, but that's what we were told you were hired for."

Rachel tried to smile. "My task is to facilitate the selection, implementation, and configuration of a security solution, including an effective perimeter defense with sustainable network technology. This includes a firewall architecture solution. But it wouldn't help you for long if one of my technicians set up the firewall and then left. Pretty soon, the firewall would need updating, reconfiguring, or simply auditing, and you'd have to keep calling us in. It's really more efficient and effective if you have a firewall technician yourself. You can either train one of your existing employees, or once you select a firewall you could hire a qualified new employee. It's really up to you."

"But what requires so much management?" The question came from the back of the conference room. "I know our server administrators are busy with patches and updates, but that's not a constant job. We batch them up for planned maintenance periods."

"Well, the rule base needs management, for one thing," Rachel answered, flipping through her PowerPoint slide deck presentation, and then bringing up a rather complex table. "Each of these rules represents an organizational policy you want enforced. For example, you only want incoming e-mail traffic to go to the e-mail server. You also want to screen out known attacks. Firewalls use complicated sets of rules like these to enforce your security intent."

"Well, I'm no networking engineer," the person in the back of the room continued, "but won't all this screening slow down our network throughput?"

Rachel nodded. "It can if the rules aren't carefully created, organized, and managed. A firewall is really just another computer with a very specific task. It's only as good as its hardware and software. Let's start talking about firewall functions, and you'll see my point." She browsed through her laptop's directory and selected a slide show. "Now, this is what I mean by screening or, in firewall terms, filtering...."

Introduction

To understand how firewalls work, you must first understand packets. Packets, as described in previous chapters, are discrete blocks of data and the basic unit of data handled by a network. All network traffic is broken down into packets for network transmission, and then reassembled into its original form at its destination. A **packet filter** is hardware or software that blocks or allows transmission of information packets based on criteria such as port, IP address, and protocol.

Packet filters not only help you learn about firewalls, they provide a basis for understanding TCP/IP network communications. To figure out how to control the movement of traffic through the network perimeter, you should know how packets are structured and what goes into packet headers. In this chapter, you learn how packet header criteria can be used to filter traffic, as well as various approaches to packet filtering and the configuration of specific packet-filtering rules.

Understanding Packets and Packet Filtering

A packet filter acts like a doorman in a very popular night club. The doorman's task is to admit only those with the right credentials—for example, VIPs on a list or a certain quota of attractive partygoers. Those not on the list or not meeting the quota specifications are turned away. Similarly, a packet filter reviews the packet **header** before sending it on its way to a specific location within the network.

Packet-Filtering Devices

There are a variety of hardware devices and software programs that perform packet filtering. Here are a few examples:

- Routers: These are probably the most common packet filters. Most modern routers are capable of rudimentary packet filtering, but with drawbacks that will be explained later in this chapter.

- Operating systems: Some systems, like Windows and Linux, have built-in utilities that can filter packets on the TCP/IP stack of the server software. Linux has a kernel-level packet filter called IPtables; Windows has TCP/IP Filtering.

- Software firewalls: Most enterprise-level programs, such as Check Point FireWall-1, filter packets, as do personal firewalls like ZoneAlarm and Sygate Personal Firewall, although, in general, personal firewalls use less sophisticated methods than enterprise-level ones.

- Firewall appliances: These are the most recognizable firewalls. Appliances are stand-alone hardware and software devices that have self-contained components. When customers purchase firewall appliances, they receive a device that is connected to the network, configured, and then set into operation. They receive all of the hardware, software, and networking components they need in one package.

Anatomy of a Packet

Packets are part of Transport Control Protocol/Internet Protocol (TCP/IP), the collection of protocols that computers use to communicate with one another on the network and, increasingly, in local area networks. Most modern client operating systems use TCP/IP as the basis for file sharing and communications. TCP/IP provides for the transmission of data in small, manageable chunks called **packets**. Packets start as messages developed by the higher-level protocols that take the user data and format it into usable data sets. Once TCP/IP has formulated the packets, the lower-networking protocols, like Ethernet, take those packets and break them into frames, which are eventually coded as electronic pulses on the media.

Each packet (also called a **datagram**) consists of two parts: the header and the data. The header contains information that is normally only read by computers, such as where the packet is coming from and its destination. The data is the part that end users actually see— the body of an e-mail message or a Web page. Understanding exactly what goes in a packet header is important because it can help you configure packet filters against possible attacks. Some firewall programs can give you a glimpse of the contents of a packet. For instance, when a personal firewall program (like Sygate) detects a packet for which a rule has not been established, it presents you with an alert box asking whether it should allow the packet to pass. When you click the Details button, you can view the header contents, as shown in Figure 5-1, to decide if anything is suspicious.

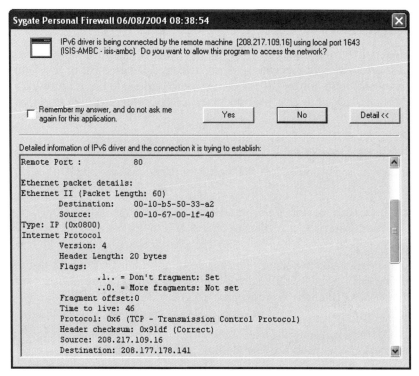

Figure 5-1 Firewall View of Packet Data
© Cengage Learning 2012

To find out more about headers and their contents, go to the original Internet Protocol specification at *www.ietf.org*, click RFC Pages, and search for RFC 791.

The header of an IP packet is commonly illustrated according to the layers of information within it, as in Figure 5-2.

Here are descriptions of the packet elements shown in this figure:

- Version: This identifies the version of IP that was used to generate the packet. As this book was being written (early in 2011), TCP/IP version 4 was still in common use. However, some larger organizations and ISPs have begun to deploy IPv6 on their internal networks.

- Internet Header Length: This describes the length of the header in 32-bit words and is a 4-bit value. The default value is 20.

- Type of Service: This indicates which of four service options is used to transmit the packet: minimize delay, maximize throughput, maximize reliability, and minimize cost. This field is of limited value, however, because most IP network setups don't enable an application to set this value.

- Total Length: This 16-bit field gives the total length of the packet, to a maximum of 165,535 bytes.

- Identification: This 16-bit value aids in the division of the data stream into packets of information. The receiving computer (possibly a firewall) uses each packet's identification number to reassemble, in the correct order, the packets that make up the data stream.

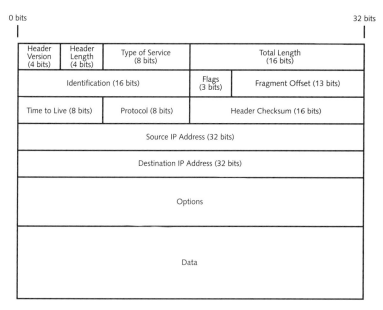

Figure 5-2 IP Packet Header
© Cengage Learning 2012

- Flags: This 3-bit value tells whether this packet is a **fragment** (i.e., is fragmented or subdivided) of a whole packet and, more specifically, whether it's the last fragment or more fragments are to follow.

- Fragment Offset: If the data received is a fragment, this value indicates where the fragment belongs in the sequence of fragments so that a packet can be reassembled.

- Time to Live (TTL): This 8-bit value identifies the maximum time the packet can remain in the system before it is dropped. Each router or device through which the packet passes reduces the TTL by a value of one. Having a TTL prevents a packet from getting caught in loops because it is undeliverable. When the value reaches zero, the packet is destroyed and an ICMP message is transmitted to the sender.

- Protocol: This identifies the IP protocol that was used in the data portion of the packet and should receive the data at its destination (e.g., TCP, UDP, or ICMP).

- Header Checksum: This is a summing up of all the 16-bit values in the packet header in a single value.

- Source IP Address: This is the address of the computer or device that sent the IP packet.

- Destination IP Address: This is the address of the computer or device that is to receive the IP packet.

- Options: This element can contain a security field, which enables the sender to assign a classification level to the packet (such as Secret, Top Secret, and so on), as well as several source routing fields by which the sender can supply routing information that gateways can use to send the packet to its destination.

- Data: This is the part that the end user actually sees, such as the body of an e-mail message.

Technical Details
The Binary Connection

The actual packets sent and received across the Internet are encoded into binary—just 1s and 0s. It's important to understand the relationship between this binary code and the configurations used in networking. For example, the Time to Live (TTL) was just described as an 8-bit value. In binary, that means the packet's life can be between 00000001 and 11111111, or between 1 and 255 hops (also referred to as device transfers), where the packet is sent from router to router to server, etc.

For those not familiar with binary-to-decimal conversion, consider the following:

Binary 8-bit value:	0	0	0	0	0	0	0	0
Decimal equivalent:	128s	64s	32s	16s	8s	4s	2s	1s

Therefore, a binary number is the addition of the number of values in each place:

	1	0	1	1	0	0	1	0

We have a 128, no 64s, a 32, a 16, no 8s, no 4s, a 2, and no 1s. Add these all together and the result is 178—the decimal equivalent. These conversions are important once you get into networking and subnet calculations.

- Trailer or footer: Some packets have an additional segmented section at the end that is called either a trailer or footer, which contains data that indicates the end of the packet. The data needed to support an error-checking procedure called a Cyclical Redundancy Check (CRC) might also be added.

Packet-Filtering Rules

Packet-filtering devices evaluate information in packet headers and compare it to one or more sets of rules that have been established to conform to network usage policy. If a packet appears to satisfy one of the "Allow" rules, the packet is allowed to pass. On the other hand, if the information matches one of the "Deny" rules, the packet is dropped. Note that packet filters only examine packet headers, in contrast to application proxies, which examine packet data and then forward the packet to its destination on behalf of the originating host.

Some of the more common rules for packet filtering are as follows:

- Drop all inbound connections except connection requests for configured servers—that is, on Port 80 (HTTP) for Web servers, Port 25 (SMTP) for e-mail servers, and Port 21 (FTP) for file transfer servers. If you don't have these types of servers set up, don't allow inbound traffic for them.

- Eliminate packets bound for all ports that should not be available to the Internet, such as NetBIOS, but allow Internet-related traffic, such as SMTP, to pass.

- Filter out any ICMP redirect or echo (ping) messages, which may be used by attackers attempting to locate open ports or host IP addresses.

- Drop all packets that use the IP header **source routing** feature. In IP source routing, the originator of a packet can attempt to partially or completely control the path through the network to the destination. Source routing is widely considered a suspect activity from a security standpoint since it is a favorite technique of network attackers and there are few legitimate uses for it.

Although small-scale, software-only personal firewall programs can protect one computer, they can cause problems in a network situation. Often, they block traffic between networked computers unless rules are set up to enable communications. Thus, you need to set up an access list that includes all of the computers in your local network by name or IP address so communications can flow between them.

Many software-based firewall applications, like Norton Internet Security, have an easy way to identify computers on the local network: they put them in a list of machines in a trusted zone. The software can detect how much it should trust other networked machines that have IP addresses in one of the private ranges (10.0.0.1 and so on), or you can add IP addresses of networked machines yourself, as shown in Figure 5-3.

Other firewall programs require you to set up rules yourself. Typically, you start with a protocol, such as ICMP, UDP, or HTTP. A good practice is to block all the traffic that

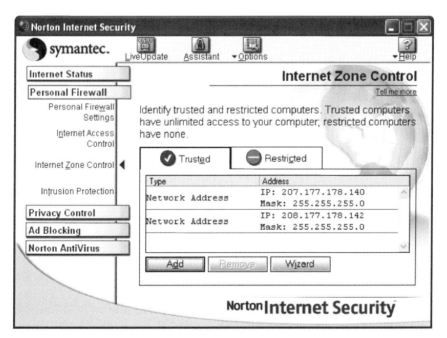

Figure 5-3 Trust Rules
© Cengage Learning 2012

uses that protocol on all ports and then add specific ports or programs that enable only the functionality that is needed. The subsequent rules identify the specific types of communication you want to permit. The allowances may be based on a specific program being executed, a precise time of day, a specific port, a known IP address, or other specific criteria. Sygate Personal Firewall, for example, lets you identify hosts yourself and set up the filtering criteria that the program uses to block or allow packets (see Figure 5-4).

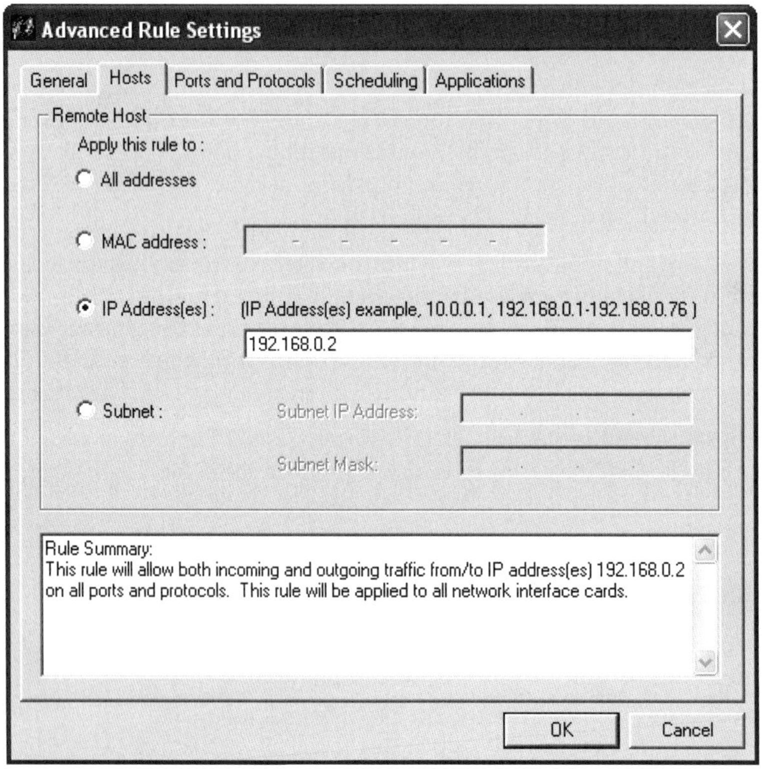

Figure 5-4 Adding Rules
© Cengage Learning 2012

Packet-Filtering Methods

The simplest packet-filtering method, **stateless packet filtering** (also called static packet filtering), reviews packet header content and makes decisions on whether to allow or drop the packets based on whether a connection has actually been established between an external host and an internal one. A more sophisticated and secure method, **stateful packet filtering**, maintains a record of the state of a connection and can thus make informed decisions—for example, allowing traffic that is a genuine reply to an established connection. A third method performs packet filtering based on the contents of the data part of a packet and the header.

Stateless Packet Filtering

It's easy to jump to the conclusion that stateless packet filtering is of no value at all because, unlike stateful packet filtering, it doesn't pay attention to the state of the connection when making decisions about blocking or allowing packets. However, stateless packet filters are useful for completely blocking traffic from a subnet or other network.

Some of the most common criteria that a stateless filter can be configured to use are IP header information, the TCP or UDP port number being used, the ICMP message type, fragmentation flags such as ACK and SYN, and suspect inbound IP addresses (an external packet that contains an internal address).

Filtering on IP Header Criteria A stateless filter looks at each packet's header individually. It compares the header data against its **rule base** and forwards each packet as a rule is found to match the specifics of that packet. For instance, if the filter has a rule stating that all connections from outside the network are to be blocked and it receives a request from an external host, it drops the packet(s) associated with that request. Or, if it has a rule that all incoming HTTP traffic needs to be routed to the public Web server at IP address 192.168.100.2, it sends any HTTP packets to 192.168.100.2. Suppose you set up a filter to allow TCP packets to pass through for a session that has already been established. Such sessions make use of one or more identifiers called flags. Flags that identify the status of a session are found in the TCP header section of a packet. Figure 5-5 shows detailed packet information from the packet log of Sygate Personal Firewall. The upper part of the log shows attributes of the packet, such as source IP, destination IP, and so on. The TCP header information is shown in the box in the lower-left corner. The Flags

5

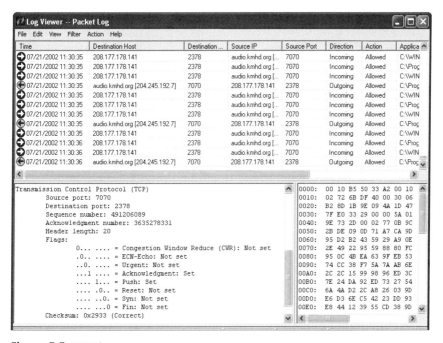

Figure 5-5 TCP Flags
© Cengage Learning 2012

section shows that the **Acknowledgement (ACK) flag** has been set, signifying that the destination computer has received the packets that were previously sent.

However, an attacker can craft a false TCP header that contains an ACK flag (and, presumably, a Trojan horse or other harmful software). The stateless packet filter would allow such a packet to pass through even though no connection has actually been established.

One of the first IP header criteria you can filter on is the packet's source IP address. If someone tries to access your database server from IP address 62.10.100.6, however, it doesn't do any good to simply set up a single rule blocking all access from 62.10.100.6. If this is a hack attempt, the attacker will make another attempt from a different host. In addition, so many attackers will attempt to come at you from so many different addresses that it will be impossible to keep up with all of them. A much more effective approach is to allow only certain source IP addresses to access your resources; denying all hosts except a group of trusted IP addresses is the most effective security approach for a stateless packet filter. You can use a stateless filter to block all access from untrusted networks or subnets.

You can also set up filter rules based on the destination or target IP address. The most obvious example is to enable external hosts to connect to your public servers in the DMZ, but not to hosts in the internal LAN. You can go a step further and specify which protocols are available. For instance, you could set up a rule that allows all external hosts to access your Web server at TCP Port 80, but that limits internal addresses to TCP Port 23 (Telnet). Table 5-1 shows the filtering rules that combine IP addresses and port numbers to control how hosts gain access to your internal network.

Protocol	Transport Protocol	Source IP	Source Port	Destination IP	Destination Port	Action
HTTP	TCP	Any	Any	192.168.0.1	80	Allow
HTTPS	TCP	Any	Any	192.168.0.1	443	Allow
Telnet	TCP	10.0.0.1/24	Any	192.168.0.5	223	Allow

Table 5-1   Filtering by Destination IP and Port Number

Packets can also be filtered based on the IP protocol ID field in the header. The filter can use the data to allow or deny traffic attempting to connect to a particular service, including the following:

- TCP (Protocol number 6)
- UDP (Protocol number 17)
- IGMP (Protocol number 2)
- ICMP (Protocol number 1)

Internet Group Management Protocol (IGMP) enables a computer to identify its multicast group membership to routers so that it can receive a multicast (a broadcast of streaming media, newsletters, or other content) from another computer. You can find a complete list of protocol numbers at *www.iana.org/assignments/protocol-numbers*.

Most simple packet filters cannot store lists of hosts that are permitted access to a particular protocol. They can only block or allow traffic for an entire designated protocol. Filtering by protocol might work if you can block all traffic for one protocol—all UDP traffic on a public FTP server, for instance. The Options field in an IP header can be set by both hosts and routers. Options, though, are rarely used. Source routing, for instance, is not required by any protocol or ISP. Yet, source routing is a tempting tool to attackers, who only need to enter their own IP addresses in the destination to have the packet returned to them, using this method to gain valuable intelligence about the internal network they would otherwise be unable to gain.

Filtering by TCP or UDP Port Number Filtering by TCP or UDP port number is commonly called port filtering or protocol filtering. Using TCP or UDP port numbers can help you filter a wide variety of information, including SMTP and POP e-mail messages, NetBIOS sessions, DNS requests, and Network News Transfer Protocol (NNTP) newsgroup sessions. For instance, you can block everything but TCP Port 80 for Web, TCP Port 25 for e-mail, and TCP Port 21 for FTP.

Filtering by ICMP Message Type Internet Control Message Protocol (ICMP) is a general management protocol for TCP/IP, helping networked systems and administrators diagnose various communication problems and communicate certain status information. From a security standpoint, ICMP packets have a downside: they may be used in some situations by attackers to crash computers on your network. Because ICMP packets cannot be verified as to the recipient of a packet, attackers may attempt to engineer man-in-the-middle attacks, in which they redirect network traffic using the ICMP Redirect message. This might trick users into believing a rogue network server is a trusted server by directing traffic to a computer the attacker controls that is outside the protected network. The users think they are using a known and trusted computer.

A firewall/packet filter must be able to determine, based on message type, whether an ICMP packet should be allowed to pass. Some of the more common ICMP message types are shown in Table 5-2.

ICMP Type	Name	Possible Cause
0	Echo reply	Normal response to a ping
3	Destination unreachable	Destination unreachable
3 code 6	Destination network unknown	Destination network unknown
3 code 7	Destination host unknown	Destination host unknown
4	Source quench	Router receiving too much traffic
5	Redirect	Faster route located
8	Echo request	Normal ping request
11	Time exceeded	Too many hops to destination
12	Parameter problem	Problem with a parameter

Table 5-2 ICMP Message Types

You'll find a complete list of ICMP message types at *www.iana.org/assignments/icmp-parameters*.

One type of network protocol attack takes advantage of the ICMP Echo Request message type by flooding a target computer with ICMP echo requests. The receiving machine is so busy fielding requests that it can't process any other network traffic. If the computer that goes down is providing important services, such as DNS, then an ICMP Redirect packet can take advantage of that unavailability and step in to misdirect targeted computers to the attacker's computer, where the attacker can attempt to intercept confidential information such as passwords.

Firewall logs indicate whether a large number of echo messages are being received. You can configure your firewall to drop ICMP packets that change network behavior (e.g., that do ICMP Redirect) and that have come from sources outside your own network.

Filtering by Fragmentation Flags Fragmentation of IP packets isn't bad in theory. Fragmentation was originally developed as a means of enabling large packets to pass through early routers that had frame size limitations. Routers were able to divide packets into multiple fragments and send them along the network, where receiving routers would reassemble them in the correct order and pass them to their destination.

The problem with fragmentation is that because the TCP or UDP port number is provided only at the beginning of a packet, it appears only in fragments numbered 0. Fragments numbered 1 or higher pass through the filter because they don't contain any port information. All an attacker has to do is modify the IP header to start all fragment numbers of a packet at 1 or higher.

To be safe, you should have the firewall reassemble fragmented packets before making the admit/drop decision.

Filtering by ACK Flag A single bit of information in a TCP packet—the ACK bit or ACK flag—indicates if a packet is requesting a connection or a connection has already been established. Packets requesting a connection have the ACK bit set to 0; those that are part of an ongoing connection have the ACK bit set to 1. An attacker can insert a false ACK bit of 1 into a packet to fool a host into thinking a connection is ongoing. You should configure the firewall to allow packets with the ACK bit set to 1 to access only the ports you specify and only in the direction you want.

Filtering Suspicious Inbound Packets If a packet arrives at the firewall from the external network but contains an IP address that is inside the network, the firewall should send an alert message. In Figure 5-6, Tiny Personal Firewall has encountered a request from an external host to access the protected host's SQL server.

This firewall, like others, lets users graphically decide whether to permit or deny the packet on a case-by-case basis or automatically by setting up a rule to cover all future instances of such connection attempts.

Most firewalls customize rules to work with all ports or all protocols, if you wish. If you receive an alert message like the one shown in Figure 5-6, click the Customize rule button at the bottom of the alert window. You can then customize the rule to apply to specific ports or addresses, as shown in Figure 5-7.

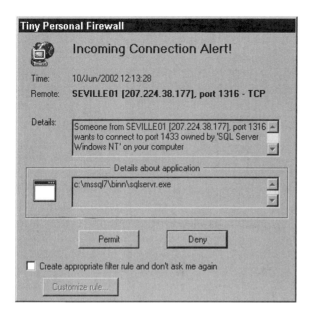

Figure 5-6 Firewall Alert
© Cengage Learning 2012

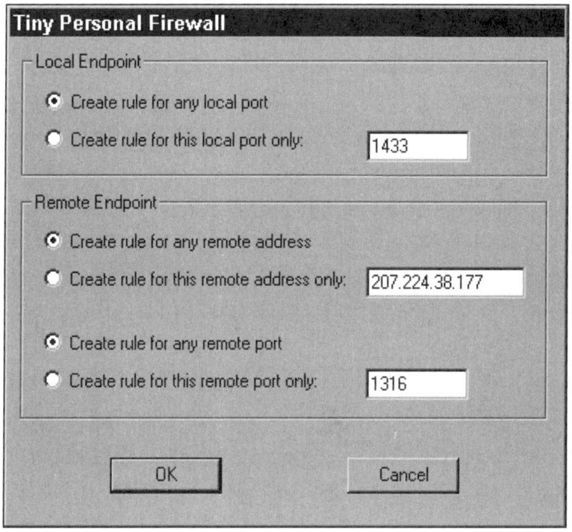

Figure 5-7 Customizing Rules
© Cengage Learning 2012

You can set up other common rules for inbound packets, such as:

- Dropping all inbound packets that have a source IP address that is within your internal network

- Dropping all inbound traffic that has the loopback address 127.0.0.1 as the source IP address

- Dropping traffic that has a source IP address that has not yet been allocated to any network, such as 0.x.x.x, 1.x.x.x, or 2.x.x.x

You may encounter repeated alerts if you block packets individually rather than setting up rules so that the firewall can handle them automatically. However, it can also be enlightening to track how many connection attempts are made, what ports and services are being accessed, and where the attempts are originating—provided you have the time to review them.

Stateful Packet Filtering

Stateful packet filtering takes the concept of packet filtering a step further than stateless filtering. A stateful filter can do everything a stateless filter can, but with one significant addition: the ability to maintain a record of the state of a connection. By "remembering" which packets are part of an active connection and which are not, the stateful filter can make "intelligent" decisions to allow traffic that is a true reply to an established connection and to deny packets that contain false information. The more powerful enterprise firewalls, such as those in the Cisco PIX series or Check Point FireWall-1, do stateful packet filtering. However, versions 1 and 2 of FireWall-1 do stateful filtering only on UDP. More recent versions handle UDP, TCP, and some ICMP packets.

In addition to a rule base, a stateful filter has a state table, which is a list of current connections. The stateful packet filter compares the packet with the state table as well as the rule base. Entries that match criteria in both the state table and rule base are allowed to pass; all others are dropped. Figure 5-8 illustrates steps involved in processing a single request from a computer within your network to access the Web site *www.cengage.com/coursetechnology*.

A stateful packet filter has to consult its state table and its rule base when a packet is encountered. However, it's worth noting that when the packet shown in Figure 5-8 arrives at the router, the state table is consulted, but the rule base is not. It is not consulted because the rule base was consulted, when the state table entry for the session was created. Also, stateful packet filters don't require a rule that allows reply packets to pass, but a stateless filter does.

If an attacker tries to craft a packet with a false ACK bit set to 1, the stateful filter passes it to the rule base because no entry exists in the state table, and the rule base drops the packet since there would be no rule in place to allow it to pass. There's no need to create a special rule for packets that have the ACK bit set to 1.

Two of the flags that are part of a packet's TCP header information, and that indicate whether a session is beginning or ending, are RST (Reset), which tells a host to immediately terminate a connection, and FIN (Finished), which tells a host to gracefully end a connection. If a session ends abnormally (if one system goes offline or a computer crashes) and neither RST nor FIN flag is received, the filter uses a timer to determine when to remove state table entries. The timer can be set to remove entries as soon as 60 seconds or as late as several days after a session ends.

Note that stateful packet filtering has limitations. It inspects only header information and doesn't verify the packet data. It works by controlling the type of transport and the port number being used. If one of your servers is set up to listen for inbound communications on a nonstandard but well-known port, such as TCP/25 for SMTP, the filter might let in traffic that is bound for the well-known port but block traffic bound for other ports.

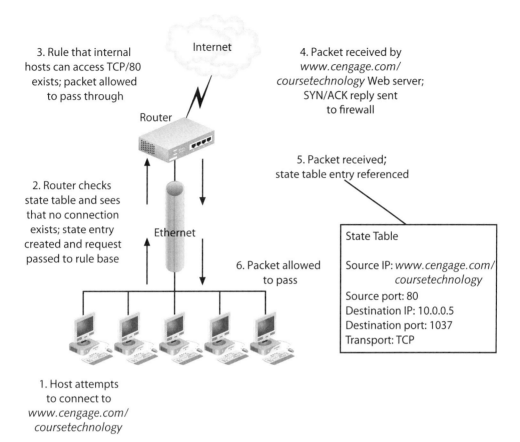

3. Rule that internal hosts can access TCP/80 exists; packet allowed to pass through

Internet

4. Packet received by *www.cengage.com/ coursetechnology* Web server; SYN/ACK reply sent to firewall

Router

5. Packet received; state table entry referenced

2. Router checks state table and sees that no connection exists; state entry created and request passed to rule base

Ethernet

6. Packet allowed to pass

State Table

Source IP: *www.cengage.com/ coursetechnology*
Source port: 80
Destination IP: 10.0.0.5
Destination port: 1037
Transport: TCP

1. Host attempts to connect to *www.cengage.com/ coursetechnology*

Figure 5-8 Stateful Packet Filtering
© Cengage Learning 2012

Filtering Based on Packet Content

As mentioned, both stateless and stateful packet filters examine the header of a packet. Some traffic, such as ICMP traffic, uses packets that are difficult to filter reliably for various reasons, including that ICMP packets don't always originate from the same source and destination IP addresses. If a server has become unreachable, for example, a status message is created by an intermediary device instead. Because this message comes from a different source IP address than was recorded in the original state table entry, the message would be dropped by a stateful filter even though it's part of a legitimate session.

To handle such cases, some stateful firewalls examine both the contents of packets and the headers for signs that they are legitimate. Such content filtering is sometimes called stateful inspection. For example, active FTP might use ports that are determined as a session is initiated. A stateless or stateful packet filter that supports active FTP must allow all traffic coming from TCP Port 20 as well as outbound traffic coming from ports above 1023. However, a stateful inspection looks at the data part of the FTP command packets to determine which ports are to be used for this session; instead of opening all possible FTP ports, the packet filter opens ports as needed. After the session is done, the ports are again closed.

There are two other types of firewall-related programs that examine packet content. One type is the proxy gateway. It looks at the data within a packet and decides which application should handle it. The other type is the specialty firewall, like a spam or content filter, which looks at the body of e-mail messages or Web pages for profanities or other content identified as offensive. It then blocks the transmission of such information based on the presence of such terms. Such specialty firewalls are primarily designed to prevent employees within an organization from visiting inappropriate Web sites and from sending or receiving inappropriate e-mail messages.

Setting Specific Packet Filter Rules

Once you have a general idea of how packet filtering works, you can establish the actual packet-filter rules that control traffic to various resources. The following sections describe the types of rules that can block potentially harmful packets, as well as rules that pass packets that contain legitimate traffic.

Best Practices for Firewall Rules

In practice, configuring firewall rule sets can be something of a nightmare. Logic errors in the preparation of the rules can cause unintended behavior, such as allowing access instead of denying it, specifying the wrong port or service type, or causing the network to misroute traffic. These and a myriad of other mistakes can turn a device designed to protect communications into a choke point. For example, a novice firewall administrator might improperly configure a virus-screening e-mail gateway (think of it as a type of e-mail firewall), thus blocking all incoming e-mail instead of only e-mail that contains malicious code. Each firewall rule must be carefully crafted, placed into the list in the proper sequence, debugged, and tested. The proper rule sequence ensures that the most resource-intensive actions are performed after the most restrictive ones, thereby reducing the number of packets that undergo intense scrutiny.

Here are some of the best practices for firewall use:

- The firewall device is never accessible directly from the public network. Almost all access to the firewall device is denied to internal users as well. Only authorized firewall administrators can access the device via secure authentication mechanisms, with preference for a method based on cryptographically strong authentication using two-factor access control techniques.

- Simple Mail Transport Protocol (SMTP) data is allowed to pass through the firewall, but all of it is routed to a well-configured SMTP gateway to securely filter and route messaging traffic.

- All Internet Control Message Protocol (ICMP) data is denied. Known as the ping service, this is a common method for attacker reconnaissance and should be turned off to prevent snooping.

- Telnet (a program for terminal emulation) access to all internal servers from the public networks is blocked. At the very least, Telnet access to the organization's Domain Name Service (DNS) server should be blocked to prevent illegal zone transfers and to prevent attackers from taking down the organization's entire network. If internal users need to reach an organization's network from outside the firewall, a virtual private network (VPN) client or other secure authentication system is used to allow this kind of access.

- When Web services are offered outside the firewall, HTTP traffic is prevented from reaching the internal networks via the implementation of some form of proxy access or DMZ architecture. That way, any Web servers running on employees' desktops for internal use are invisible to the Internet. If the Web server is located behind the firewall, HTTP or HTTPS (SHTTP) data has to be allowed through for the Internet at large to view it. The best solution is to place the Web servers containing critical data inside the network and use proxy services from a DMZ (the shorthand name for a screened network segment). It is also advisable to restrict incoming HTTP traffic to internal network addresses so that the traffic must be responding to requests originating at internal addresses. This restriction can be accomplished through NAT or firewalls that can support stateful inspection or are directed at the proxy server itself. All other incoming HTTP traffic should be blocked. If the Web servers contain only advertising, they should be placed in the DMZ and rebuilt when (not if) they are compromised.

- Test all firewall rules before they are placed into production use. Testing should include what is called regression testing, when all rules are tested with a representative set of traffic. The practice of testing just the new rules should be avoided since it is necessary to test all of the rules together in order to ferret out any unexpected interactions. Tools such as the Open Source tool ftester (*http://dev.inversepath.com/trac/ftester*) are available for this purpose.

Rules That Cover Multiple Variations

Packet-filter rules must account for all possible ports that a type of communication might use or for all variations within a particular protocol—for example, passive and active FTP, or standard HTTP and secure HTTP. This is a tricky process; rules are often created and modified as a result of trial and error. For example, an employee might complain that he or she can't communicate with someone using MSN Messenger, and you will have to adjust the packet filter's rule base accordingly (after consulting the security policy, of course).

Consider the network shown in Figure 5-9, which will serve as a basis for the discussion in this section.

Figure 5-9 illustrates a typical LAN that is protected by a firewall and two routers. A DMZ connected to the firewall provides services that the public network can access, such as a Web server, FTP server, and e-mail server. Accordingly, packet-filter rules need to be set up to allow Web, FTP, e-mail, and other services while blocking potentially harmful packets from getting to the internal LAN.

Rules for ICMP Packets

ICMP rules are especially important because ICMP packets can be easily forged and used to redirect other communications.

The most common ICMP command is Packet Internet Groper (commonly called ping). The command determines if a host is unreachable on the network. You send a packet to a host you're trying to reach, and the host responds with an ICMP response packet that tells you

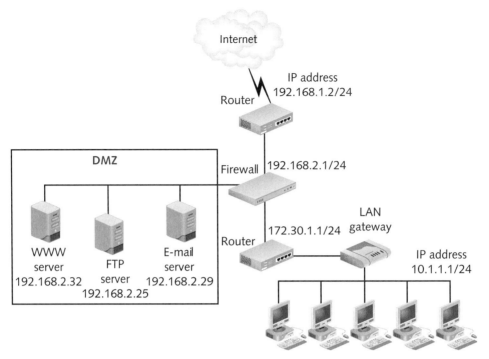

Figure 5-9 Sample Network
© Cengage Learning 2012

the host is "alive." Many attackers begin attacks by using ping to see whether a host is reachable by them as well. If all of your hosts respond to the ping command, you could be opening up your network to an attack.

To prevent attackers from using the ping command to identify some of your resources, you need to establish specific ICMP commands that cover common ICMP messages. Table 5-3 gives some rules that enable you to send and receive the ICMP packets you need while blocking those that open your internal hosts to intruders.

The rules shown in Table 5-3 serve the following purposes:

- Rule 1 (Source Quench): Lets external hosts tell your internal hosts if the network is saturated

- Rule 2 (Echo Request): Gives your computers the ability to ping external computers

- Rule 3 (Echo Reply): Enables your computers to receive ping replies from external hosts

- Rule 4 (Destination Unreachable): Lets your hosts receive packets stating that an external resource is unreachable

- Rule 5 (Service Unavailable): Lets your hosts receive packets stating that an external resource is unavailable

- Rule 6 (Time to Live Exceeded): Lets your hosts know that an exterior resource is too many hops away

Rule	Protocol	Transport IP	Source IP	Destination Message	ICMP	Action
1	ICMP	ICMP	Any	Any	Source Quench	Allow Inbound
2	ICMP	ICMP	192.168.2.1/24	Any	Echo Request	Allow Outbound
3	ICMP	ICMP	Any	192.168.2.1/24	Echo Reply	Allow Inbound
4	ICMP	ICMP	Any	192.168.2.1/24	Destination Unreachable	Allow Inbound
5	ICMP	ICMP	Any	192.168.2.1/24	Service Unavailable	Allow Inbound
6	ICMP	ICMP	Any	192.168.2.1/24	Time to Live (TTL) Exceeded	Allow Inbound
7	ICMP	ICMP	Any	192.168.2.1/24	Echo Request	Drop Inbound
8	ICMP	ICMP	Any	192.168.2.1/24	Redirect	Drop Inbound
9	ICMP	ICMP	192.168.2.1/24	Any	Echo Reply	Drop Outbound
10	ICMP	ICMP	192.168.2. 1/24	Any	TTL Exceeded	Drop Outbound
11	ICMP Block	ICMP	Any	Any	All	Drop

Table 5-3 ICMP Packet Filter Rules

- Rule 7 (Echo Request): Blocks ping packets that might be used to locate internal hosts
- Rule 8 (Redirect): Prevents attackers or others from changing your **routing tables,** which are data stored in the router about network routes that this device uses or knows about that it keeps handy for ready reference as it makes routing decisions
- Rule 9 (Echo Reply): Prevents attackers from receiving replies to ping requests
- Rule 10 (Time to Live Exceeded): Prevents attackers from determining the number of hops inside your network
- Rule 11 (ICMP Block): After setting your rules, drops all other ICMP packets for extra security; that is, all ICMP packets not listed in the preceding rules will be dropped at the firewall

Rules That Enable Web Access

The first priority of employees in a protected network is to be able to surf the Web and exchange e-mail messages. The rules for accessing the Web need to cover both standard HTTP traffic on TCP Port 80 as well as Secure HTTP (HTTPS) traffic on TCP Port 443. The rules for the Internet-accessible Web server in our test network would look like those shown in Table 5-4. These assume that the firewall uses a deny-all policy. All packets are denied except for those that meet the rules listed in the rule base.

Rule	Protocol	Transport IP	Source Port	Source IP	Destination Port	Destination	Action
12	HTTP Inbound	TCP	Any	Any	192.168.2.32	80	Allow
13	HTTPS Inbound	TCP	Any	Any	192.168.2.32	443	Allow
14	HTTP Outbound	TCP	192.168.1.2/24	Any	Any	80	Allow
15	HTTPS Outbound	TCP	192.168.2.32	Any	Any	443	Allow

Table 5-4   **HTTP Access Rules**

Rules That Enable DNS

To connect to Web sites, the employees in our sample organization need to be able to resolve the fully qualified domain names (FQDNs) they enter, such as *www.cengage.com/coursetechnology*, to their corresponding IP addresses using the Domain Name System (DNS). Internal users connect to external hosts using a DNS server located in the DMZ of the security perimeter. DNS uses either UDP Port 53 or TCP Port 53 for connection attempts. In addition, you need to set up rules that enable external clients to access computers in your own network using the same TCP and UDP ports, as shown in Table 5-5.

Rule	Protocol	Transport Protocol	Source IP	Source Port	Destination IP	Destination Port	Action
16	DNS	TCP	192.168. 2.31	Any	Any	53	Allow
17	DNS	UDP	192.168. 2.31	Any	Any	53	Allow
18	DNS	TCP	Any	Any	192.168. 2.31	53	Allow
19	DNS	UDP	Any	Any	192.168. 2.31	53	Allow

Table 5-5   **Rules That Enable DNS Resolution**

If your network uses DNS forwarding to an ISP's DNS server, enter the IP address of the ISP's DNS server as the destination IP and your own DNS server as the source IP. Some security administrators believe that allowing their company's DNS server to communicate with any DNS server is a security risk, and thus they direct all DNS traffic to a single DNS server operated by an ISP.

Rules That Enable FTP

As stated, FTP transactions can be either active or passive. The rules you set up for FTP need to support two separate connections: TCP Port 21, which is the FTP control port, and TCP 20, which is the FTP data port. If some clients in your network support active FTP, you can't specify a particular port because the client can establish a connection with the FTP server at any port above 1023. Instead, you specify the IP address of your FTP server, as shown in Table 5-6.

Technical Details
DNS

You've heard the term "DNS" by now, but may not quite understand what DNS is or what role it plays in network security. The Domain Name System (DNS) is a structure for organizing Internet names associated with IP addresses—most commonly for Web services. Since it's not easy for human beings to remember long numbers like IP addresses, DNS was developed to facilitate easy remembrance of site locations for HTTP, FTP, and other services. Instead of having to remember 10.10.10.15 as the server site, a customer could simply remember *www.cengage.com/coursetechnology*. The DNS system works through a set of servers, beginning with the root servers—13 servers that store the base address, also referred to as a top-level domain (TLD): .com, .net, .org, etc., including country codes: .uk, .au, .mx. The root server also knows what secondary addresses fall under these TLDs—for example, *www.cengage.com/coursetechnology*, kennesaw.edu, and microsoft.com. When a user types a domain name, the Web browser contacts a root server to determine which subordinate name server contains the rest of the address. The root DNS server provides the IP address of the primary name server for the organization registered with that domain name (e.g., *www.cengage.com/coursetechnology*) The primary name server is a server owned or leased by the organization (or its Internet service provider) to handle these requests. The organization must also maintain a secondary name server just in case the primary goes down. These name servers also know the location of any specific devices associated with the tertiary name service, such as www for Web services, ftp for file transfer services, or third-level names like infosec.kennesaw.edu for subordinate services. The entire process is seamless to the user.

Rule	Protocol	Transport Protocol	Source IP	Source Port	Destination IP	Destination Port	Action
20	FTP control	TCP	Any	Any	192.168.1.25	21	Allow inbound
21	FTP data	TCP	192.168.1.25	20	Any	Any	Allow inbound
22	FTP PASV	TCP	Any	Any	192.168.1.25	Any	Allow
23	FTP control	TCP	192.168.1.25	Any	Any	21	Allow outbound
24	FTP data	TCP	Any	20	192.168.1.25	Any	Allow outbound

Table 5-6 Rules to Enable Active and Passive FTP

Some administrators prefer to drop incoming active FTP connections because of the danger of FTP port scanning. They allow only passive connections to go through.

Rules That Enable E-Mail

Setting up firewall rules that filter e-mail messages can be difficult. One reason is the sheer variety of e-mail protocols that might be used, including the following:

- Post Office Protocol 3 (POP3) and Internet Message Access Protocol version 4 (IMAP4) for inbound mail transport
- Simple Mail Transfer Protocol (SMTP) for outbound mail transport
- Lightweight Directory Access Protocol (LDAP) for looking up e-mail addresses
- Hypertext Transfer Protocol (HTTP) and/or TLS (HTTPS) for Web-based mail service

To keep things simple, our sample configuration only uses POP3 and SMTP for inbound and outbound e-mail, respectively. However, SSL encryption is used for additional security. Some sample rules are found in Table 5-7.

Rule	Protocol	Transport Protocol	Source IP	Source Port	Destination IP	Destination Port	Action
25	POP3	TCP	192.168.2.1/24	Any	Any	110	Allow outbound
26	POP3/S	TCP	192.168.2.1/24	Any	Any	995	Allow outbound
27	POP3	TCP	Any	Any	192.168.2.1/24	110	Allow inbound
28	POP3/S	TCP	Any	Any	192.168.2.1/24	995	Allow inbound
29	SMTP	TCP	192.168. 2.29	Any	Any	25	Allow outbound
30	SMTP/S	TCP	192.168. 2.29	Any	Any	465	Allow outbound
31	SMTP	TCP	Any	Any	192.168.2.29	25	Allow inbound
32	SMTP/S	TCP	Any	Any	192.168.2.29	465	Allow inbound

Table 5-7   POP3 and SMTP E-mail Rules

To set up your own configuration rules, you need to assess whether your organization needs to accept incoming e-mail messages at all, whether internal users can access mail services outside your company (such as Hotmail), and what e-mail clients are supported by your company. By identifying the e-mail clients your company will support, you can provide the highest level of security without blocking e-mail access.

Running Case: Unauthorized Personnel

Kiara was applying for a job at Data Mart. She had gone to the Human Resources Department and completed an application. While she was there, the receptionist got up from her desk and left the room. Kiara walked over to the receptionist's desk and saw a sticky note with a user ID and a password. Kiara jotted them down on a slip of paper and stuck them in her pocket. She also saw a sticker on the computer with an IP address.

Later, at home, Kiara connected to the Data Mart network and was able to connect to the IP address of the computer that was on the receptionist's desk. With the user ID and password, she connected to the hiring application and was able to monitor her application in the Data Mart system.

5

Chapter Summary

- Packets are the basic unit of data handled by a network. The dominant form of firewall is some form of packet filter that is designed to block or allow transmission of packets of information based on criteria such as port, IP address, and protocol.

- A packet filter acts like a ticket taker in a multiplex movie theater, admitting only those with valid tickets, reserving the option of rejecting patrons that do not meet the requirement. Packet filtering can be done by a variety of hardware devices and software programs, such as routers, operating systems, or software firewalls.

- Packet-filtering devices evaluate information in packet headers and compare it to one or more sets of rules that have been established to conform to network usage policy.

- The simplest packet-filtering method, stateless packet filtering, reviews packet header content and makes decisions on whether to allow or drop the packets. A more sophisticated and secure method, stateful packet filtering, maintains a record of the state of a connection.

Review Questions

1. What is the primary difference between router packet handling and application proxy packet handling?

2. How do content-based filtering programs decide whether to allow packets into the protected network?

3. Describe how a firewall reassembles a data stream that has been divided into packets.

4. Why is it important to be familiar with the structure of the fields in an IP packet header?

5. What does stateful packet filtering do that stateless packet filtering does not do?

6. What are the functions of an IP packet footer?

7. What purposes do stateless packet filters serve best?

8. What type of data can an attacker insert into a TCP header to fool a stateless packet filter?

9. What is the most effective security approach to use with a stateless packet filter?

10. Why isn't it practical to filter by the protocol ID field in an IP header?

11. How can ICMP packets be misused by an attacker to gain access to internal network resources?

12. What is the primary weakness in the ICMP protocol that makes it subject to attack?

13. How would you configure a firewall/packet filter to prevent ICMP attacks?

14. Which fragment numbers could be security risks because a packet filter might let them through?

15. What kinds of packets can cause problems for even a stateful packet filter?

16. State the reasons internal clients need to be able to send outbound ICMP packets to hosts on the Internet.

17. Where should a packet be directed when it doesn't match any host in the interior LAN?

18. Which types of ICMP messages are directly involved in blocking hack attempts?

19. What is the difference between active and passive FTP that makes stateful packet filtering a good choice?

20. What is the purpose of blocking all ICMP packets after specifying a group of ICMP rules?

Real World Exercises

1. Your employer asks you to block traffic from the Web site *www.offensivecontent.com*, which a group of employees has been caught visiting. You open a command prompt window and type ping *www.offensivecontent.com* to determine the IP address of the site. After a few minutes, the IP address 197.34.5.56 comes back, but you get several messages stating that the request has timed out, and no packets are exchanged. Based on what you've read in this chapter, what does this tell you about the security measures at the *www.offensivecontent.com* Web site? What rule would you add to the rule base to block access to this site?

2. When you install a personal firewall, it doesn't work. You suddenly lose the ability to share files with other computers in your lab. You open a command prompt, ping your default gateway router, and get a successful response. You try to ping another computer on your network and get a series of "Request Timed Out" messages. You are sure the problem has to do with the firewall blocking communications with the "trusted" computer. What would you do to restore communications with the other local machine?

3. Employees complain that it's taking longer than usual to access the Web, receive e-mail messages, and otherwise communicate with external hosts. In reviewing your firewall

logs, you notice a large number of ICMP echo requests coming from external host 63.10.100.4. You suspect an attempted ICMP flooding attack. How would you respond?

4. Employees in your organization are complaining about the amount of spam e-mail messages they are receiving. You are asked to attempt to "filter out" such messages. Come up with two different ways to help reduce such messages.

Hands-On Projects

Project 5-1: Explore and Configure Windows Firewall (Vista or XP SP3)

To enable Windows Firewall (if it's not already on), perform the following tasks:

1. Click **Start**, click **Run**, type **Firewall.cpl**, and then click **OK**. You should see the Microsoft Windows Firewall.

2. On the **General** tab, click **On (recommended)**, and then click **OK**.

3. Next, we will access the Windows Firewall through the Windows Security Center. Click **Start**, click **Run**, type **wscui.cpl**, and then click **OK**. The Windows Security Center opens.

4. Click **Windows Firewall** at the bottom of the Security Center.

5. In the Windows Firewall window, look at the General tab. We've already used On and Off in previous steps. If you select Don't allow exceptions, Windows Firewall blocks all requests to connect to your computer, including requests from programs or services that are listed on the Exceptions tab. The firewall also blocks discovery of network devices, file sharing, and printer sharing. This is very useful when on insecure networks like public wireless networks or hotel networks.

6. Click the **Exceptions** tab. Here, you will see a list of programs that have "permission" for a remote component to connect to the system.

7. You may find file and print sharing checked, as well as remote desktop, Windows Messenger, etc. If any programs are checked that you are not comfortable having access to your computer, deselect them. If you wish to add a program to the list, click **Add Program** and select the program.

8. If you wish to add a specific port to the list that is not directly associated with a program, click **Add Port**. In the corresponding dialog boxes, type the Name and Port Number.

9. Click **Add Port** and enter the following information in these dialog boxes: Name: **HTTPS**, Port: **443**. (Leave TCP selected.) Click **OK**. If you were hosting a secure HTTP server, you would now be able to service requests for Web pages. If you activated the XP Web Server, the application would automatically do this for you.

10. If you wanted to set up these services for an intranet only, you could click **Change scope for this entry** and specify **My network (subnet) only**.

11. This setting will only allow computers on your subnet (e.g., 192.168.X.X) to access the services.

12. Click the **Advanced** tab. Here, you can specify network settings for the Firewall, Manage Firewall logging, specify the use of ICMP, or reset the firewall to default settings.

13. Click the **Settings** button in the Network Connections Settings section. Here, you can specify what services the user can access.

14. Select **FTP Server** by checking the box to the left of the title. Click the **Edit** button at the bottom of the window. If you were using a service on a nonstandard port, you could specify that here. If you click the ICMP tab at the top, it will bring you to the same screen you get by clicking the Settings button on the Windows Firewall Advanced tab. Click **Cancel** twice.

15. Click the **Settings** button in the Security Logging area. Select both the **Log dropped packets** and **Log successful connections** boxes.

16. Record the location of the firewall log.

17. Leave the size limit at the default and click **OK**.

18. Open an Internet browser and surf the Web for a few minutes. Look at a number of different sites. After a few minutes, open the log file you identified earlier in a Notepad window. What do you see? Record a summary.

19. Go back to the Windows Firewall window. If you closed it previously, reopen it: Click **Start**, click **Run**, type **Firewall.cpl**, and then click **OK**. Back on the Advanced tab, click the **Settings** button in the ICMP window. ICMP can be used to conduct attacks on your systems, so ensure none of the options are checked.

20. Click **OK** to close the window.

21. From a partner's computer, attempt to ping your workstation. Did it work? Record your results.

22. Click **OK** to close Windows Firewall, and then close the Windows Security Center. Once you've completed the earlier steps in this exercise, you may need to disable the firewall. If so, perform the following tasks.

23. Click **Start**, click **Run**, type **Firewall.cpl**, and then click **OK**.

24. On the **General** tab, click **Off** (**not recommended**), and then click **OK**.

Project 5-2: Set Up Windows Packet Filtering

Windows XP has a variety of TCP/IP packet-filtering options that can be applied to a local area connection. This isn't a very sophisticated form of packet filtering, but it can prove useful if you have a specific port or protocol you want to block. The steps shown are for Windows XP. This lab is not possible under Windows Vista or 7.

1. On the Windows XP desktop, click **Start**, click **Control Panel**, select **Network and Internet Connections**, and then double-click **Network Connections**. The Local Area Connection Status dialog box opens.

2. Click **Properties**. The Local Area Connection Properties dialog box opens.

3. Click **Internet Protocol (TCP/IP)** (or **Internet Protocol Version 4 (TCP/IPv4)**), and then click **Properties**. The Internet Protocol (TCP/IP) Properties dialog box opens.

4. Click **Advanced**.

5. In the Advanced TCP/IP Settings dialog box, click **Options**, click **TCP/IP filtering**, and then click **Properties**. The TCP/IP Filtering dialog box opens.

6. In the TCP/IP Filtering dialog box, make sure the Enable TCP/IP Filtering (All adapters) check box is checked. Click the **Permit Only** radio button above TCP Ports. The TCP Ports option becomes active.

7. Click **Add**. The Add Filter dialog box opens.

8. In the TCP Port text box, type the port number usually associated with the DNS service, **53**, then click **OK**.

9. Repeat Steps 6, 7, and 8 for the UDP Ports section. Use Port 53.

10. Repeat Steps 6, 7, and 8 for the IP Protocols section. Enter protocol number **45** for Inter-Domain Routing Protocol.

11. Close all open windows.

Project 5-3: Use Windows IPSec Packet Filtering

You can set up an IPSec filter to block or permit traffic without regard to encryption. This exercise gives you a chance to do some rudimentary packet filtering. For this exercise, you need a Windows XP workstation that has IPSec enabled.

1. Click **Start** and click **Control Panel**.

2. In the Control Panel window, double-click **Administrative Tools**. (*Note*: Administrative tools will only be available if the Control Panel is set to Classic View.)

3. In the Administrative Tools dialog box, double-click **Local Security Policy**.

4. In the Local Security Settings management console, click **IP Security Policies on Local Computer** in the left pane.

5. In the right pane, right-click **Secure Server** (**Require Security**), and then click **Properties**.

6. If the Add Standalone Snap-in dialog box appears, click **Close**, and then click **OK** to close the Add/Remove Snap-in.

7. In the Rules tab of the Secure Server (Require Security) Properties dialog box, make sure the check box next to **Use Add Wizard** is checked, and then click **Add**.

8. Click **Next** four times until you get to the screen in the Security Rule Wizard entitled "IP Filter List." (If you receive a dialog box stating that your computer is not a member of a domain, click **Yes** to continue.)

9. Click the **All IP Traffic** button, and then click **Add**.

10. For the purposes of this exercise, let's assume you want to enable Port 80 communications between your computer and one with the IP address 192.168.1.1. In the name text box, delete the default name New IP Filter List and replace it with **Project 5-5 Rule**.

11. In the Description text box, type **Enables IPSec secure communication with one computer**.

12. Uncheck the **Use Add Wizard** check box, and then click **Add**.

13. In the Filter Properties dialog box, leave My IP Address in the Source address box. Click the **Destination address list** arrow and click **A specific IP Address**. The IP address and Subnet mask boxes appear.

14. Type **192.168.1.1** in the IP address box, and then click the **Protocol** tab.

15. Click the **Select a protocol type list** arrow, and then click **TCP** on the drop-down list.

16. Under Set the IP protocol port, click the **From this port** button, and then type **80** in the text box beneath it.

17. Click the **To this port** button, and then type **80** in the text box beneath it.

18. Click **OK**.

19. Because this is a very restrictive filtering policy with a fictitious computer, if asked, you should click **Cancel** to close Filter Properties and return to IP Filter List. If you were setting up actual security policies, you would click **Add in IP Filter List** and enter information for protocols and ports to be used by the computers in your local network.

20. Click **Cancel** to return to the Security Rule Wizard, click **Cancel**, and then click **Cancel** again to close the Secure Server (Require Security) Properties dialog box.

Project 5-4: Install and Configure ZoneAlarm Basic Firewall

This section will walk you through some common configuration, attack detection, and blocking with the free version of ZoneAlarm Basic.

1. If ZoneAlarm is not already installed, ask your instructor for the location of the ZoneAlarm install package and record it.

2. Using a Windows file browser, browse to the location of the file specified in the previous step. Double-click the file **ZaSetup_92_102_000_en.exe**. When the initial installation window opens, click **Next**, and then click **Run**.

3. Enter the required information in the text boxes on the form, and then make sure the check box at the bottom of the page is unchecked. Click **Next** to proceed. You see the software's License Agreement. Check the check box at the bottom of the page, and then click **Install**.

4. Select **Default quick installation (recommended)**, and then click **Next**.

5. Continue to click **Next** to proceed through the setup windows and click **Restart** when instructed.

6. After the computer restarts, you will choose to keep the new network in the Internet Zone and then close the dialog box that appears. You should then see the primary ZoneAlarm Interface.

7. In the Overview tab, you should see several statistics showing the performance of the system.

8. By now, you may have noticed the frequent pop-ups labeled ZoneAlarm Security Alerts.

9. Until you have configured ZoneAlarm and operated it for some time, you will get these on a constant basis, as basic system functions attempt to communicate with internal and external systems. Click the **Find out how** option under SmartDefense Advisor. ZoneAlarm will ask you to grant Internet access rights to your default browser. Click **Yes**. Unfortunately, this brings you to a marketing Web page promoting the Pro version of ZoneAlarm. So, until you complete this lab and/or uninstall the application, you will have to keep clicking **Allow** on the pop-ups. You can reduce the frequency somewhat by selecting the **Remember this setting** check box before doing so. Close the Web browser.

10. Click the **Firewall** option to the left. Much like the Internet Explorer Zone security feature, here you can adjust the slider bars to tweak the level of security for the Internet and your local network.

11. Click the **Advanced** button to determine additional options to filter unwanted traffic. Click the **Cancel** button to exit the Advanced Settings window.

12. Click the **Program Control** option to the left. Here, you can adjust the program options (and reduce the bothersome pop-ups).

13. Click the slider under Program control and adjust it until it reads **Low**. This puts program control in "learning mode" and should reduce the frequency of pop-ups. Click the **Custom** button inside the Automatic Lock area. This window presents options to lock your Internet access under defined conditions. These options require you to lock the Auto Lock in the previous window. Close this window for now. In the Program Control window, select **On** in the Automatic Lock window. Now click the **Custom** button again. Click the **Lock after _ minutes of inactivity** option and change the number of minutes to **1**. In the second box, select **Block all Internet access**. Click **OK**. Look at your watch and then wait two minutes.

14. After two minutes, what happens? Record your findings.

15. Open a Web browser. What happens?

16. Change the Automatic Lock back to **off**, and then retry the Web browser. What happens?

17. Look in the icon tray at the bottom right of the screen. Once the lock is enabled, you must right-click the ZoneAlarm lock icon and deselect **Engage Internet lock**. This will automatically disable the Stop All Internet Access option.

18. Retry your Web browser. Can you access the Internet now?

19. The next two tabs work like Windows Security Center and monitor the status of antivirus and e-mail protection. Advanced versions of ZoneAlarm are bundled with CheckPoint antivirus and e-mail protection software.

20. Click the **Alerts & Logs** option to the left. Here, you can specify whether or not non-program alerts will be displayed.

21. Program-based alerts will still be shown. Click the **Advanced** button. Here, you can manage the log file associated with ZoneAlarm.

22. Record the location of the log file.

23. Using a Windows File browser, go to the location recorded. Open the log file with Notepad. What do you see? Record a summary of your log file.

24. To observe ZoneAlarm in action, have a neighbor use his or her computer to ping your system to determine if ZoneAlarm picks up the traffic. Alternatively, have your neighbor scan your computer using a tool like NMap to see the result. Refer to the earlier exercises where you learned how to use NMap (or any other scanning tool) to generate scanning activity on a computer that is running ZoneAlarm. Depending on how you configure ZoneAlarm, you will see alerts or log entries of the scanning activity.

25. Close all open windows.

Running Case Projects

CASE PROJECTS

In this project, the student takes the SysSP from Chapter 2 and updates it to more accurately reflect the rules that should be included in the firewall and to prevent a hacking event like Kiara's. The student then begins configuring the firewall rules.

Student Tasks

In this exercise, we will create rule sets that allow inbound and outbound traffic for HTTP, HTTPS, and DNS protocols.

Vyatta requires a two-step process for firewall implementation. First, the rule set has to be created. After that, Vyatta has to be told which interface(s) to apply the rule set to. Vyatta has an implicit "deny all" entry once a firewall rule set is defined, so we will not need to create this entry in any of our rule sets. As a practical matter, it is recommended you use a rule set name that is descriptive of the interface being configured in the rule set.

1. Log in to the Vyatta interface via the command line, using "vyatta" as the username and the password you created in Chapter 4. First, we will configure the inbound and outbound rule sets for the internal NIC(eth1):

   Inbound rule set for eth1:

2. Enter **configure** and press **Enter** to enter configuration mode.

3. Enter **set firewall conntrack-tcp-loose disable** and press **Enter**.

4. Enter **set firewall name eth1_in rule 10 action accept** and press **Enter**.

5. Enter **set firewall name eth1_in rule 10 protocol tcp** and press **Enter**.

6. Enter **set firewall name eth1_in rule 10 source address** *Internal NIC IP address/range* and press **Enter**.

7. Enter **set firewall name eth1_in rule 10 destination port 80,443** and press **Enter**.

8. Enter **set firewall name eth1_in rule 10 state new enable** and press **Enter**.

9. Enter **set firewall name eth1_in rule 10 state established enable** and press **Enter**.

10. Enter **set firewall name eth1_in rule 10 state related enable** and press **Enter**.

    When you're through, the screen should look like Figure 5-10.

```
vyatta@vyatta# set firewall conntrack-tcp-loose disable
[edit]
vyatta@vyatta# set firewall name eth1_in rule 10 action accept
[edit]
vyatta@vyatta# set firewall name eth1_in rule 10 protocol tcp
[edit]
vyatta@vyatta# set firewall name eth1_in rule 10 source address 10.10.10.0/24
[edit]
vyatta@vyatta# set firewall name eth1_in rule 10 destination port 80,443
[edit]
vyatta@vyatta# set firewall name eth1_in rule 10 state new enable
[edit]
vyatta@vyatta# set firewall name eth1_in rule 10 state established enable
[edit]
vyatta@vyatta# set firewall name eth1_in rule 10 state related enable
[edit]
vyatta@vyatta# _
```

Figure 5-10 HTTP eth1 Inbound Rules
© Cengage Learning 2012

Outbound rule set for eth1:

11. Enter **set firewall name eth1_out rule 10 action accept** and press **Enter**.

12. Enter **set firewall name eth1_out rule 10 protocol tcp** and press **Enter**.

13. Enter **set firewall name eth1_out rule 10 destination address** *Internal NIC IP address/ range* and press **Enter**.

14. Enter **set firewall name eth1_out rule 10 source port 80,443** and press **Enter**.

15. Enter **set firewall name eth1_out rule 10 state established enable** and press **Enter**.

16. Enter **set firewall name eth1_out rule 10 state related enable** and press **Enter**.

When you're through, the screen should look like Figure 5-11.

```
vyatta@vyatta# set firewall name eth1_out rule 10 action accept
[edit]
vyatta@vyatta# set firewall name eth1_out rule 10 protocol tcp
[edit]
vyatta@vyatta# set firewall name eth1_out rule 10 destination address 10.10.10.0
/24
[edit]
vyatta@vyatta# set firewall name eth1_out rule 10 source port 80,443
[edit]
vyatta@vyatta# set firewall name eth1_out rule 10 state established enable
[edit]
vyatta@vyatta# set firewall name eth1_out rule 10 state related enable
[edit]
vyatta@vyatta# _
```

Figure 5-11 HTTP eth1 Outbound Rules
© Cengage Learning 2012

5

Now, we will configure the inbound and outbound rule sets for the external NIC(eth0). Inbound rule set for eth0:

17. Enter **set firewall name eth0_in rule 10 action accept** and press **Enter**.

18. Enter **set firewall name eth0_in rule 10 protocol tcp** and press **Enter**.

19. Enter **set firewall name eth0_in rule 10 destination address** *Internal NIC IP address/range* and press **Enter**.

20. Enter **set firewall name eth0_in rule 10 source port 80,443** and press **Enter**.

21. Enter **set firewall name eth0_in rule 10 state established enable** and press **Enter**.

22. Enter **set firewall name eth0_in rule 10 state related enable** and press **Enter**.

When you're through, the screen should look like Figure 5-12.

```
vyatta@vyatta# set firewall name eth0_in rule 10 action accept
[edit]
vyatta@vyatta# set firewall name eth0_in rule 10 protocol tcp
[edit]
vyatta@vyatta# set firewall name eth0_in rule 10 destination address 10.10.10.0/
24
[edit]
vyatta@vyatta# set firewall name eth0_in rule 10 source port 80,443
[edit]
vyatta@vyatta# set firewall name eth0_in rule 10 state established enable
[edit]
vyatta@vyatta# set firewall name eth0_in rule 10 state related enable
[edit]
vyatta@vyatta# _
```

Figure 5-12 HTTP eth0 Inbound Rules
© Cengage Learning 2012

Outbound rule set for eth0:

23. Enter **set firewall name eth0_out rule 10 action accept** and press **Enter**.

24. Enter **set firewall name eth0_out rule 10 protocol tcp** and press **Enter**.

25. Enter **set firewall name eth0_out rule 10 source address** *Internal NIC IP address/range* and press **Enter**.

26. Enter **set firewall name eth0_out rule 10 destination port 80,443** and press **Enter**.

27. Enter **set firewall name eth0_out rule 10 state new enable** and press **Enter**.

28. Enter **set firewall name eth0_out rule 10 state established enable** and press **Enter**.

29. Enter **set firewall name eth0_out rule 10 state related enable** and press **Enter**.

When you're through, the screen should look like Figure 5-13.

```
vyatta@vyatta# set firewall name eth0_out rule 10 action accept
[edit]
vyatta@vyatta# set firewall name eth0_out rule 10 protocol tcp
[edit]
vyatta@vyatta# set firewall name eth0_out rule 10 source address 10.10.10.0/24
[edit]
vyatta@vyatta# set firewall name eth0_out rule 10 destination 80,443
The specified configuration node is not valid
Set failed
[edit]
vyatta@vyatta# set firewall name eth0_out rule 10 destination port 80,443
[edit]
vyatta@vyatta# set firewall name eth0_out rule 10 state new enable
[edit]
vyatta@vyatta# delete firewall name eth0_out rule 10
action        destination protocol     source        state
[edit]
vyatta@vyatta# delete firewall name eth0_out rule 10 state new enable
[edit]
vyatta@vyatta# set firewall name eth0_out rule 10 state established enable
[edit]
vyatta@vyatta# set firewall name eth0_out rule 10 state related enable
[edit]
vyatta@vyatta# _
```

Figure 5-13 HTTP eth0 Outbound Rules
© Cengage Learning 2012

Now, we will assign the rule sets to the appropriate interfaces:

30. Enter **set interfaces ethernet eth1 firewall in name eth1_in** and press **Enter**.

31. Enter **set interfaces ethernet eth1 firewall out name eth1_out** and press **Enter**.

32. Enter **set interfaces ethernet eth0 firewall in name eth0_in** and press **Enter**.

33. Enter**set interfaces ethernet eth0 firewall out name eth0_out** and press **Enter**.

Now, we will apply the rule sets and save them permanently:

34. Enter **commit** and press **Enter**.

35. Enter **save** and press **Enter**.

When you're through, the screen should look like Figure 5-14.

```
vyatta@vyatta# set interfaces ethernet eth1 firewall in name HTTP_ETH1_IN
[edit]
vyatta@vyatta# set interfaces ethernet eth1 firewall out name HTTP_ETH1_OUT
[edit]
vyatta@vyatta# set interfaces ethernet eth0 firewall in name HTTP_ETH0_IN
[edit]
vyatta@vyatta# set interfaces ethernet eth0 firewall out name HTTP_ETH0_OUT
[edit]
vyatta@vyatta# commit
[edit]
vyatta@vyatta# save
Saving configuration to '/opt/vyatta/etc/config/config.boot'...
Done
[edit]
vyatta@vyatta# _
```

Figure 5-14 Commit Rules to Interfaces
© Cengage Learning 2012

To verify that the rule set is functioning as desired, do the following:

36. Open a Web browser and enter the IP address **130.218.100.94**. You should see the home page of the Web site for Kennesaw State University.

37. In the same browser window, replace the IP address with the domain *www.kennesaw.edu*. This should fail, as we have yet to enter a rule set to allow DNS requests.

Now, we will create a rule set to manage DNS requests.

Inbound rule set for eth1:

38. Enter **set firewall name eth1_in rule 20 action accept** and press **Enter**.

39. Enter **set firewall name eth1_in rule 20 protocol udp** and press **Enter**.

40. Enter **set firewall name eth1_in rule 20 source address** *Internal NIC IP address/range* and press **Enter**.

41. Enter **set firewall name eth1_in rule 20 destination port 53** and press **Enter**.

42. Enter **set firewall name eth1_in rule 20 destination address** *IP address of DNS server* and press **Enter**.

43. Enter **set firewall name eth1_in rule 20 state new enable** and press **Enter**.

44. Enter **set firewall name eth1_in rule 20 state established enable** and press **Enter**.

45. Enter **set firewall name eth1_in rule 20 state related enable** and press **Enter**.

When you're through, the screen should look like Figure 5-15.

```
vyatta@vyatta# set firewall name eth1_in rule 20 action accept
[edit]
vyatta@vyatta# set firewall name eth1_in rule 20 protocol udp
[edit]
vyatta@vyatta# set firewall name eth1_in rule 20 source address 10.10.10.0/24
[edit]
vyatta@vyatta# set firewall name eth1_in rule 20 destination port 53
[edit]
vyatta@vyatta# set firewall name eth1_in rule 20 destination address 192.168.1.1
[edit]
vyatta@vyatta# set firewall name eth1_in rule 20 state established enable
[edit]
vyatta@vyatta# set firewall name eth1_in rule 20 state related enable
[edit]
vyatta@vyatta# _
```

Figure 5-15 DNS eth1 Inbound Rules
© Cengage Learning 2012

Outbound rule set for eth1:

46. Enter **set firewall name eth1_out rule 20 action accept** and press **Enter**.

47. Enter **set firewall name eth1_out rule 20 protocol udp** and press **Enter**.

48. Enter **set firewall name eth1_out rule 20 destination address** *Internal NIC IP address/ range* and press **Enter**.

49. Enter **set firewall name eth1_out rule 20 source port 53** and press **Enter**.

50. Enter **set firewall name eth1_out rule 20 source address** *IP address of DNS server* and press **Enter**.

51. Enter **set firewall name eth1_out rule 20 state established enable** and press **Enter**.

52. Enter **set firewall name eth1_out rule 20 state related enable** and press **Enter**.

53. Enter **set firewall name eth1_out rule 20 state new enable** and press **Enter**.

When you're through, the screen should look like Figure 5-16.

```
vyatta@vyatta# set firewall name eth1_out rule 20 action accept
[edit]
vyatta@vyatta# set firewall name eth1_out rule 20 protocol udp
[edit]
vyatta@vyatta# set firewall name eth1_out rule 20 destination address 10.10.10.0
/24
[edit]
vyatta@vyatta# set firewall name eth1_out rule 20 source port 53
[edit]
vyatta@vyatta# set firewall name eth1_out rule 20 source address 192.168.1.1
[edit]
vyatta@vyatta# set firewall name eth1_out rule 20 state established enable
[edit]
vyatta@vyatta# set firewall name eth1_out rule 20 state related enable
[edit]
vyatta@vyatta# set firewall name eth1_out rule 20 state new enable
[edit]
vyatta@vyatta# _
```

Figure 5-16 DNS eth1 Outbound Rules
© Cengage Learning 2012

Inbound rule set for eth0:

54. Enter **set firewall name eth0_in rule 20 action accept** and press **Enter**.

55. Enter **set firewall name eth0_in rule 20 protocol udp** and press **Enter**.

56. Enter **set firewall name eth0_in rule 20 source address** *IP address of DNS server* and press **Enter**.

57. Enter **set firewall name eth0_in rule 20 source port 53** and press **Enter**.

58. Enter **set firewall name eth0_in rule 20 destination address** *Internal NIC IP address/range* and press **Enter**.

59. Enter **set firewall name eth0_in rule 20 state established enable** and press **Enter**.

60. Enter **set firewall name eth0_in rule 20 state related enable** and press **Enter**.

When you're through, the screen should look like Figure 5-17.

Outbound rule set for eth0:

```
vyatta@vyatta# set firewall name eth0_in rule 20 action accept
[edit]
vyatta@vyatta# set firewall name eth0_in rule 20 protocol udp
[edit]
vyatta@vyatta# set firewall name eth0_in rule 20 source address 192.168.1.1
[edit]
vyatta@vyatta# set firewall name eth0_in rule 20 source port 53
[edit]
vyatta@vyatta# set firewall name eth0_in rule 20 destination address 10.10.10.0/
24
[edit]
vyatta@vyatta# set firewall name eth0_in rule 20 state established enable
[edit]
vyatta@vyatta# set firewall name eth0_in rule 20 state related enable
[edit]
vyatta@vyatta# _
```

Figure 5-17 DNS eth0 Inbound Rules
© Cengage Learning 2012

61. Enter **set firewall name eth0_out rule 20 action accept** and press **Enter**.

62. Enter **set firewall name eth0_out rule 20 protocol udp** and press **Enter**.

63. Enter **set firewall name eth0_out rule 20 source address** *Internal NIC IP address/range* and press **Enter**.

64. Enter **set firewall name eth0_out rule 20 destination port 53** and press **Enter**.

65. Enter **set firewall name eth0_out rule 20 destination address** *IP address of DNS server* and press **Enter**.

66. Enter **set firewall name eth0_out rule 20 state new enable** and press **Enter**.

67. Enter **set firewall name eth0_out rule 20 state established enable** and press **Enter**.

68. Enter **set firewall name eth0_out rule 20 state related enable** and press **Enter**.

When you're through, the screen should look like Figure 5-18.

```
vyatta@vyatta# set firewall name eth0_out rule 20 action accept
[edit]
vyatta@vyatta# set firewall name eth0_out rule 20 protocol udp
[edit]
vyatta@vyatta# set firewall name eth0_out rule 20 source address 10.10.10.0/24
[edit]
vyatta@vyatta# set firewall name eth0_out rule 20 destination port 53
[edit]
vyatta@vyatta# set firewall name eth0_out rule 20 destination address 192.168.1.
1
[edit]
vyatta@vyatta# set firewall name eth0_out rule 20 state new enable
[edit]
vyatta@vyatta# set firewall name eth0_out rule 20 state established enable
[edit]
vyatta@vyatta# set firewall name eth0_out rule 20 state related enable
[edit]
vyatta@vyatta# _
```

Figure 5-18 DNS eth0 Outbound Rules
© Cengage Learning 2012

Now, we will assign the rule sets to the appropriate interfaces:

69. Enter **set interfaces ethernet eth1 firewall in name eth1_in** and press **Enter**.

70. Enter **set interfaces ethernet eth1 firewall out name eth1_out** and press **Enter**.

71. Enter **set interfaces ethernet eth0 firewall in name eth0_in** and press **Enter**.

72. Enter **set interfaces ethernet eth0 firewall out name eth0_out** and press **Enter**.

Now, we will commit the rule sets and save them permanently:

73. Enter **commit** and press **Enter**.

74. Enter **save** and press **Enter**.

When you're through, the screen should look like Figure 5-19.

```
vyatta@vyatta# set interfaces ethernet eth1 firewall in name eth1_in
[edit]
vyatta@vyatta# set interfaces ethernet eth1 firewall out name eth1_out
[edit]
vyatta@vyatta# set interfaces ethernet eth1 firewall in name eth0_in
[edit]
vyatta@vyatta# set interfaces ethernet eth1 firewall out name eth0_out
[edit]
vyatta@vyatta# commit
[edit]
vyatta@vyatta# save
Saving configuration to '/opt/vyatta/etc/config/config.boot'...
Done
[edit]
vyatta@vyatta# _
```

Figure 5-19 Commit Rules to Interfaces
© Cengage Learning 2012

To verify that the rule set is functioning as desired, do the following from a computer on the internal network:

75. Open a Web browser and enter the URL **www.kennesaw.edu**. You should see the home page of the Web site for Kennesaw State University.

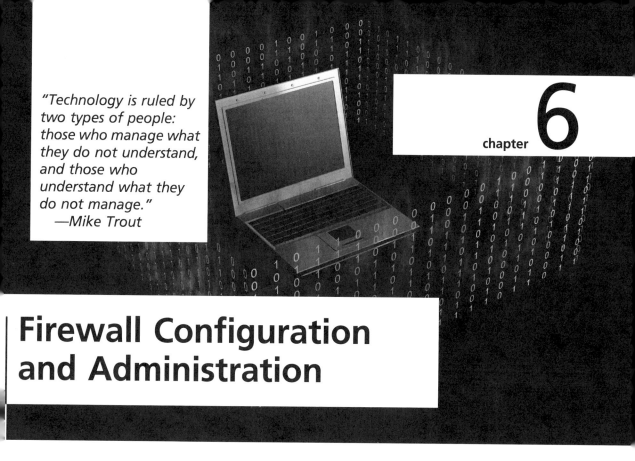

> "Technology is ruled by two types of people: those who manage what they do not understand, and those who understand what they do not manage."
> —Mike Trout

chapter 6

Firewall Configuration and Administration

After reading this chapter and completing the exercises, you will be able to:

- Identify and implement different firewall configuration strategies
- Update a firewall to meet new needs and threats
- Adhere to proven security principles to help the firewall protect network resources
- Use a remote management interface
- Track firewall log files and follow the basic initial steps in responding to security incidents
- Understand the nature of advanced firewall functions

Running Case: The Prohibition Era

"Okay," Rachel said, "now that you understand the purpose of the rule base, let's talk about configuration and other management issues with the new firewall. The first decision you need to make is whether your organization's philosophy will be 'That which is not prohibited is permitted' or 'That which is not permitted is prohibited'."

"That's easy!" a Data Mart employee chimed in, "We'll definitely want to be a 'permitted' kind of organization!"

Julie Matford, VP of Operations, spoke up from the rear of the room. "Actually," she said, "management has already discussed this issue. We feel that it is in the best interest of the organization to become more of a 'What is not permitted is prohibited' type of organization. We feel this will be more conducive to the type of business we want to show our customers—that is, a more business-focused organization. After the online gambling issues we've had in the past, we want to make sure we have a more professional demeanor in the workplace. So, we plan to crack down on non-business-related system use."

Rachel could feel the dissatisfaction growing in the room. She tried to move on with the meeting. "Okay," she said, "we'll need to make sure we develop some policy documents that reflect that decision, to ensure compliance. The next item we should discuss is the physical parameters for the firewall—things like scalability, productivity, capacity, and so forth. There are a number of approaches you could take to calculate these. We recommend the best practices model—in particular, a model based on similar implementations at organizations that use similar data."

"That's fine," Meghan said. "We'll accept your recommendations at face value, as long as we understand the financial impacts of the firewall. Just work with Alex on a set of specifications." "Great!" Rachel exclaimed. "Lastly, we should identify what auxiliary tasks, if any, your firewall should perform. These will impact the specifications, since the more auxiliary tasks it performs the more capacity it needs to have."

"What type of auxiliary tasks?" someone asked.

"Things like Virtual Private Networks, address translation, and data caching," Rachel replied.

"Uh, the only one of those I understood was data caching," the same person said.

Rachel sighed. It was going to be another long meeting.

Introduction

In this chapter, you learn how to design perimeter security for a network that integrates firewalls with other software and hardware components. Firewalls aren't intended to do just one thing or to block just one type of threat. By using one or more firewalls in conjunction with routers, gateways, hubs, and switches, you can block many common attacks while permitting hosts inside the network to access the Internet. But setting up a firewall is only the start of an effective perimeter security effort. Ongoing firewall administration ensures that the network is actually protected and that intrusions are detected and thwarted. Without routine log reviews, firewall performance evaluation, and regular hardware and software upgrades, the best firewall configuration in the world can quickly become useless.

Establishing Firewall Rules and Restrictions

After you have established a security policy, as described in Chapter 2, you can begin to implement the strategies that policy specifies. The cornerstone of most firewalls is the rule set, a set of instructions based on organizational policy, configured by the administrator. Rules give the firewall specific criteria for deciding whether to allow packets through or drop them. In the absence of effective policy, the administrator may not accurately represent the will of the organization in configuring these devices. For example, a firewall administrator who has left the defense industry and is now working in a university setting may configure a new firewall the way he was taught to configure them at his previous, ultra-secure facility. This configuration would be completely inappropriate to the open exchange of information that an academic institution requires. With effective guidance from management, however, the administrator will create rules suitable for allowing the information to be used while the organization is protected.

Firewall rules tell the firewall what types of traffic to let in and out of your network. Virtually all firewalls have a rule set; it is the most important firewall configuration file. In residential or small office/home office (SOHO) systems, the rule sets may be hidden from the user, behind a set of simple configuration questions or graphical user interfaces (GUIs).

The Importance of the Rule Set

The specific packet-filtering rules that are used to set up a firewall will implement the security approach specified in the organization's security policy. A restrictive approach is reflected in a set of rules that blocks all access by default, and then permits only specific types of traffic to pass through. A permissive or connectivity-based approach has fewer rules because its primary intent is to let all traffic through and then block specific types of traffic.

The rules implemented by the firewall not only block traffic coming from outside the protected network, they enable internal traffic to get outside the network. Rules that permit traffic to your DNS server, for instance, are essential if your internal users are going to access other computers on the Internet using domain name resolution.

Finally, the rules are important because they establish an execution order that the firewall should follow. Firewalls typically process rules in top-to-bottom order, so the first rules cover the most basic types of traffic, such as ICMP messages that computers use to establish basic communications. Rules are almost always processed in sequential order to avoid confusion about which is most important.

Restrictive Firewalls

If the primary goal of a firewall is to block unauthorized access, the emphasis needs to be on restricting rather than enabling connectivity. In such a Deny-All approach, the firewall blocks everything by default and only allows those services you need on a case-by-case basis. In other words, "that which is not permitted is prohibited." Deny-All and other primarily restrictive approaches are described in Table 6-1.

If you decide to first restrict all transmissions through the gateway except a specific set of services, you are following the principle of **least privilege**, which refers to the practice of designing the operational aspects of a system so that there are minimum system privileges. Least privilege means that a security design attempts to reduce the use of escalated authorization

Approach	What It Does	Advantage	Disadvantage
Deny-All	Blocks all packets except those specifically permitted	More secure; requires fewer rules	May result in user complaints
In Order (sometimes called "First Fit")	Processes firewall rules in top-to-bottom order	Good security	Incorrect order can cause chaos
Best Fit	The firewall determines the order in which the rules are processed; it usually starts with the most specific rules and goes to the most general	Easy to manage; reduces risk of operator error	Lack of control

Table 6-1   Restrictive Firewall Approaches

levels for the performance of some actions and also attempts to decrease the chance that a process or user with high privileges will perform unauthorized activity. These combine to reduce the probability of a privileged user inadvertently causing a security breach.

There are other ways to implement approaches to security as it is described in an organization's security policy. Specific elements of a policy can be implemented by a firewall when following strategies such as these:

- Spell out which services employees cannot use. On the firewall, you can block services such as FTP or Telnet. You can use authentication to enable such services to be used only by a network administrator.

- Use and maintain passwords. Enable authentication on the firewall so users can only surf the Web or use e-mail after they successfully authenticate themselves. This forces employees to keep track of passwords and to remember them.

- Follow an *open* approach to security. Set the firewall to allow all traffic to pass through by default, but block specific Web sites or specific services as needed.

- Follow an *optimistic* approach to security. Set up a stateful packet filter configured to let most packets pass, but to block traffic from troublesome or questionable IP addresses, or deny access to specific database servers on the internal network.

- Follow a *cautious* approach to security. Set up a stateful instead of (or in addition to) a stateless packet filter.

- Follow a *strict* approach to security. Set up application proxy gateways that forward requests on behalf of internal users.

- Follow a *paranoid* approach to security. Set up one or more packet filters to protect a pool of workstations that have been set aside to allow access to the Web and e-mail only, and that are not connected to the internal network, which has no connection at all to any external networks.

Connectivity-Based Firewalls

If the primary orientation of your firewall is permissive—that is, it allows connectivity through the gateway—the burden is on the security administrator to educate coworkers on how to use the network responsibly. Most employees don't want to put the company's assets at risk, but they do want to access data and be productive. It's the security administrator's job to help them understand how to get their work done in a secure manner.

Table 6-2 lists the advantages and disadvantages of firewalls that emphasize connectivity.

Approach	What It Does	Advantage	Disadvantage
Allow-All	Allows all packets to pass through except those specified to be blocked	Easy to implement	Provides minimal security; requires complex rules
Port 80/Except Video	Allows Web surfing without restrictions, except for video files	Lets users surf Web	Opens network to Web vulnerabilities

Table 6-2 **Connectivity-Based Firewall Approaches**

6

In almost all instances, permissiveness is not an either/or question. Most firewalls are partly restrictive and partly permissive (connective). The firewall administrator's job is to strike a balance between the two.

The rules on a firewall must be placed in a very specific order or they will not work properly. Some firewalls order the rules automatically, but this feature should not be used unless the administrator has a high degree of confidence that it will work as expected. If the algorithms and code used to make the order-independent rule-setting decisions are not completely bug free, using this feature could open up security holes in your network. In a perfect world, automatic order-independent rule setting is a great feature, because if there are a lot of firewall rules, it can help order the rules properly. However, there is no substitute for human knowledge and experience in setting up firewall rules.

Firewall Configuration Strategies: A High-Level Overview

A firewall must be **scalable** so it can grow with the network it protects. It needs to take into account the communication needs of individual employees, who see Web surfing and e-mail as must-haves to be productive. Because TCP/IP is the protocol of choice for internal networks as well as the Internet itself, the firewall also needs to deal with the IP address needs of the organization—to enable port forwarding or NAT/PAT, for instance.

Scalability

A firewall needs to adapt to the changing needs of the organization whose network it protects. More Internet business and a growing staff are likely to increase the need for firewall resources. Be sure to provide for the firewall's growth by recommending a periodic review and upgrading software and hardware as needed.

Productivity

The stronger and more elaborate your firewall, the slower your data transmissions are likely to be. Productivity is definitely a concern if you use a proxy server, which tends to slow down communications for users inside the company who are trying to access the Internet.

Two important features of the firewall are the processing and memory resources available to the bastion host. The term **bastion host**, which refers to a stand-alone firewall, is generally attributed to Marcus Ranum, who wrote an article called "Thinking about Firewalls." In the article, Ranum defined a bastion host as "a system identified by the firewall administrator as a critical strong point in the network's security." Then he added: "Generally, bastion hosts will have some degree of extra attention paid to their security, may undergo regular audits, and may have modified software."[1]

The bastion host, although it may not be the only hardware component in a firewall architecture, is of central importance to the operation of the firewall software that it hosts. If the host machine runs too slowly or doesn't have enough memory to handle the large number of packet-filtering decisions, proxy service requests, and other traffic, the entire organization's productivity can be adversely affected. That's because the bastion host resides on the perimeter of the network and, unless other bastion hosts and firewalls have been set up to provide load balancing, is the only gateway through which inbound and outbound traffic can pass. Scalability and security are important not only to the firewall, but to its bastion host machine as well. The bastion host needs sufficient memory to support every instance of every program necessary to service the load placed on the machine.

A **critical resource** is defined as a software- or hardware-related item that is indispensable to the operation of a device or program. Critical resources for a firewall's successful operation are essentially the same that are needed for any high-throughput server, and they include the following:

- System memory
- Hard drive capacity
- Hard drive I/O throughput
- System CPU capacity
- Interface (Network card) data rate
- Host OS socket performance

Some services use more resources than others and, as such, should be controlled to prevent their use from impacting the base systems. Among the most resource-intensive services are e-mail and media services, such as video streaming. These two services will threaten to consume most of the system resources of both their native servers and the bastion host unless carefully managed.

Dealing with IP Address Issues

The more complex a network becomes, the more IP-addressing complications that arise. It's important to plan out the installation, including IP addressing, before the organization starts purchasing or installing firewalls. Both a demilitarized zone (DMZ) and a service network need IP addresses. If the service network needs to be privately rather than publicly accessible, which DNS will its component systems use? The organization can ask its ISP if more addresses are available. If they aren't, it may need to consider Network Address Translation (NAT) or Port Address Translation (PAT) and convert the internal network to private addressing. However, when an organization implements private addresses, new challenges arise. Developing a network to work with NAT and PAT requires specialized knowledge to configure the address translation to ensure that servers can communicate. Be sure to resolve any issues before the hardware goes online.

IP forwarding enables a packet to get from one network's OSI stack of interfaces to another. Most operating systems are set up to perform IP forwarding, as are routers. Proxy servers that handle the movement of data from one external network to another perform the same function; however, if a proxy server is in service, IP forwarding should be disabled on routers and other devices that lie between the networks. It's better to let the proxy server do the forwarding because it's the security device; having routers do the IP forwarding will defeat the purpose of using the proxy and make communications less secure.

The need for advance planning applies not only to firewalls but to servers and other hardware. There may be specific aspects of your design that influence your hardware selection. For example, suppose you want your firewall to include a proxy server function. You have to make sure you have the hardware to support a proxy server that provides services for the Web, e-mail, FTP, chat, instant messaging, and other means of network communication. Assess the hardware that will host the firewall or proxy server. If you expect high traffic volume—for example, if you run a busy e-commerce Web server—you may be better off avoiding a proxy server and sticking with packet filters, which don't require as much memory and processor speed. Proxy servers quickly consume memory and processor time, so if you plan to run them, buy a machine that has as much of these resources as you can afford.

Approaches That Add Functionality to the Firewall

Network security setups can become incrementally more complex when specific functions are added. Each function is discussed separately in the following sections; however, you should assume that any or all of the following can be part of a perimeter security system that includes a firewall.

NAT/PAT

As mentioned earlier, a router or firewall that performs NAT or PAT converts publicly accessible IP addresses to private ones and vice versa, thus shielding the IP addresses of computers on the protected network from those on the outside. For more on NAT and PAT, review the relevant section in Chapter 5. The ranges of commonly used private addresses are presented in Table 6-3.

Range	Number of Usable Addresses
10.x.x.x (10.0.0.0–10.255.255.255)	Approximately 16.5 million addresses
172.16.x.x–172.31.x.x (172.16.0.0–172.31.255.255)	Approximately 1.05 million addresses
192.168.x.x (192.168.0.0–192.168.255.255)	Approximately 65,500 addresses

Table 6-3 **Ranges of Available Private Addresses (IPv4)**

Encryption

A firewall or router that can do Secure Sockets Layer (SSL) or some other type of encryption takes a request, encrypts it using a private key, and exchanges the public key with the recipient firewall or router. The recipient then decrypts the message and presents it to the end user in readable form (see Figure 6-1). Encryption is covered in much greater detail in Chapter 9.

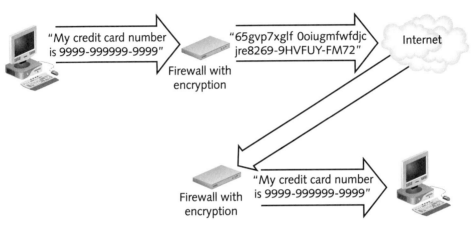

Figure 6-1 Using Encryption
© Cengage Learning 2012

Application Proxies

As discussed in Chapter 4, an application proxy (also known as an application gateway or proxy server) is a service that acts on behalf of a client, receiving requests, rebuilding them from scratch, and forwarding them to the intended location as though the request originated with it (the proxy). It can be set up with either a dual-homed host or a screened-host system. In a dual-homed host setup, the host that contains the firewall or proxy server software has two interfaces, one to the Internet and one to the internal network being protected (see Figure 6-2). Application proxies are discussed in Chapter 7.

Because the dual-homed host lies between the internal LAN and the Internet, the hosts on the internal network never access the Internet directly. (At least, they shouldn't; some employees may get frustrated with the slower functioning of the proxy system and try to establish their own Internet connections, and you should be on the alert for this.) The proxy server software on the dual-homed host makes requests on the hosts' behalf and forwards packets from the Internet to them. In a screened subnet system, the host that runs the proxy server software has a single network interface; packet filters on either side of the host filter out all traffic except that which is destined for the proxy server software.

VPNs

Many companies use the Internet to enable a virtual private network (VPN) that connects internal hosts with specific clients in other organizations. The advantage of a VPN over a conventional Internet-based connection is that VPN connections are encrypted

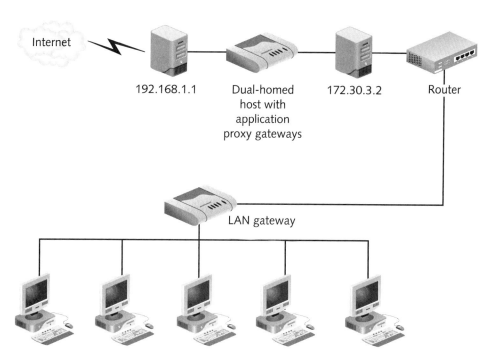

Figure 6-2 Using Application Proxies
© Cengage Learning 2012

and limited to machines with specific IP addresses. The VPN gateway can go in a screened sub-net (sometimes called a DMZ), or the gateway can bypass the firewall and connect directly to the internal LAN, as shown in Figure 6-3. VPNs are discussed in greater detail in Chapters 9 and 10.

Intrusion Detection and Prevention Systems

An intrusion detection and prevention system (IDPS)—software that can detect intrusion attempts and notify administrators when they occur, or react dynamically to the intrusion—can be installed in the external and/or the internal router at the perimeter of a network (see Figure 6-4). IDPS capability is also built into many popular software firewall packages, including Sidewinder, by Secure Computing.

Why install IDPS on both routers? An external router with IDPS can notify you of intrusion attempts from the Internet. An internal router with IDPS can notify you when a host on the internal network attempts to access the Internet via a suspicious port or using an unusual ser-vice, which may be a sign that a Trojan horse has entered the system. An IDPS might also be configured to look for a large number of TCP connection requests (SYN) to many different ports on a target machine, thus discovering if someone is attempting a TCP port scan. The IDPS sends the alert so an administrator can either prevent the attack or stop it before too much damage occurs.

Many IDPSs have sensors that can be placed in various locations to provide information on the attacks that are coming into or are already in a network. Figure 6-5 shows a number of locations at which IDPS sensors could be placed.

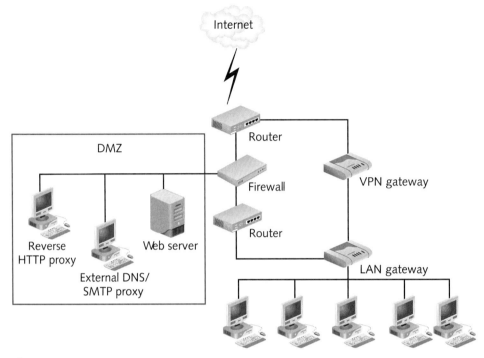

Figure 6-3 Virtual Private Networking
© Cengage Learning 2012

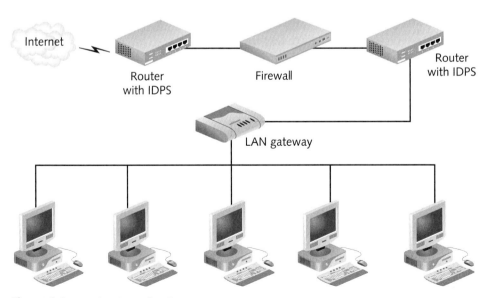

Figure 6-4 Intrusion Detection Systems
© Cengage Learning 2012

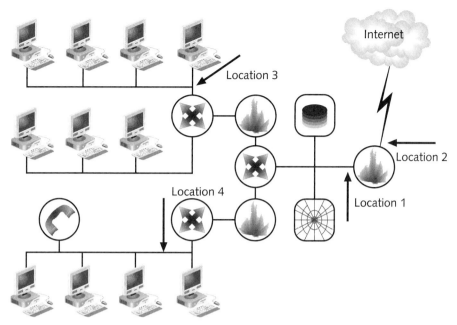

Figure 6-5 Example IDPS Placement
© Cengage Learning 2012

Enabling a Firewall to Meet New Needs

It is important that the organization consistently upgrade and patch its firewall architecture and add new components to keep the perimeter protected and traffic running smoothly. Overall, the organization should consider the following constraints on a firewall:

- Throughput—Because the firewall is the point through which all traffic flows, the organization should make sure traffic flows through it quickly and it is not slowing down the network.

- Scalability—Very few networks get smaller. It's almost inevitable that the network will grow, either in terms of the number of hosts that need to be protected or the amount of traffic received from the external Internet. The firewall and other security systems need to be able to grow along with your needs.

- Security—The firewall needs to effectively block traffic that has been identified as unacceptable based on its rule base and—if the firewall is also full featured enough to provide some intrusion detection functions—must detect and provide notifications of intrusion attempts.

- Recoverability—The firewall is critical not only to the network's security but to the network's connection with outside networks. If the firewall crashes, it needs to be restarted, have its original security configuration recovered, and be placed back online quickly.

- Manageability—The firewall should be easy to manage, either from within the organization or from a remote location.

To achieve these goals, the organization might need to upgrade the security software, hardware, or even add new layers of security to the overall firewall perimeter. The process the organization will go through as it makes these decisions is described in the following sections.

Verifying Resources Needed by the Firewall

The firewall administrator should test the firewall and evaluate its performance to ensure that the network traffic is moving efficiently. With software-only firewalls, something that can be easily evaluated is memory and CPU usage. Memory needs can be checked in one of three ways. The first way is to make use of vendor recommendations, such as the following formula provided for Check Point's FW-1 NG firewall[2]:

$$MemoryUsage = (ConcurrentConnections)/(AverageLifetime)*(AverageLifetime + 50 \ seconds)*120$$

In this formula, the memory usage needed by the firewall is calculated this way:

1. Divide the number of **concurrent connections** (ones that are made to hosts in the internal network at any one time) by the **average lifetime** of a typical connection (how long, in seconds, a connection to a host lasts, from handshake to termination) as indicated by log files.

2. Take the average lifetime (in seconds), add 50 seconds, and multiply by 120.

3. Multiply the number resulting from Step 1 by the number resulting from Step 2.

For example, if there are 1000 connections and the average lifetime of a connection is 10 minutes (120 seconds), the memory needed to run a firewall is (1000)/(120)*(120+50)*120 = 170,000, or 170 MB of RAM. While this value seems small considering the gigabyte range of modern memory, note that this function may not be the only service performed by the device and, therefore, should be considered a lower limit or minimum requirement to the system.

A second way to keep track of the memory and system resources being consumed is to use the vendor's software-monitoring feature. As an example, Figure 6-6 illustrates the Status Manager module in Check Point NG (renamed the SmartView Monitor in later models). If firewall administrators open the module and select their own networks, they will get data that reports how much memory is being consumed and how much of the available system resources are being used by the firewall. For a small network, the memory and system resources being used may be relatively small. But on a large enterprise in which hundreds or even thousands of users may send traffic through the firewall at any one time, such data can be invaluable to the network administrator attempting to track down network bottlenecks. CPU usage that climbs to a high level (perhaps as much as 60 percent, though this depends on the operating system being used) should be a warning to the administrator that some kind of load balancing is needed, which might require adding another firewall to the network.

A third way to keep track of the memory and system resources being consumed is simply to follow a best practice approach in which systems are purchased and equipped with the recommended amounts of memory—typically, 2 GB–4 GB of RAM currently, and ensure the system has the space to allow additional memory upgrades. This is accomplished by ensuring that there are RAM slots available and by buying memory in the largest feasible size (e.g., 2 GB or 4 GB RAM modules rather than multiple 1 GB RAM modules).

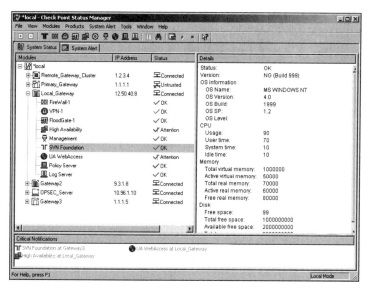

Figure 6-6 Check Point Status Manager
© Cengage Learning 2012

Identifying New Risks

A firewall needs regular care and attention to keep up with the new threats that are constantly appearing. It's a good idea, after the firewall is up and running, to monitor its activities on an ongoing basis and store, in the form of log files, all the data that accumulates. The administrator should periodically review the logs and analyze the traffic that passes through the firewall, paying particular attention to suspicious activity.

To keep informed of the latest dangers, so that patches and updates can be installed as they become available, administrators can check out the following Web sites:

- SecurityFocus (*www.securityfocus.com*)—This is the location of Bugtraq and the SecureFocus Vulnerability Database. It is the hub for a large mailing list that features frequent announcements about security flaws. The Web site hosts discussions and enables information sharing among the broader information security community. It is widely regarded as an essential tool for security professionals.[3]

- The National Vulnerability Database (*nvd.nist.gov*)—A jointly sponsored project of the Department of Homeland Security and US-CERT, this is a central repository for standards-based vulnerability management data as it is documented with the Security Content Automation Protocol (SCAP). "This data enables automation of vulnerability management, security measurement, and compliance. NVD includes databases of security checklists, security-related software flaws, misconfigurations, product names, and impact metrics."[4]

- CERT Coordination Center—United States Computer Emergency Readiness Team (US-CERT) (*http://www.us-cert.gov*)—"US-CERT is charged with providing response support and defense against cyber-attacks for the Federal Civil Executive Branch (.gov) and information sharing and collaboration with state and local government, industry, and international partners. US-CERT interacts with federal agencies, industry, the research community, state and local governments, and others to disseminate reasoned and actionable cyber security information to the public."[5]

- Common Vulnerabilities and Exposures Database hosted at the Mitre Corporation (*http://cve.mitre.org*)—International in scope and free for public use, CVE is a dictionary of publicly known information security vulnerabilities and exposures. CVE's common identifiers enable data exchange between security products and provide a baseline index point for evaluating coverage of tools and services."[6]
- The Open Source Vulnerability Database (*http://osvdb.org/*)—"OSVDB is an independent and open source database created by and for the community. Our goal is to provide accurate, detailed, current, and unbiased technical information."[7]
- Numerous vendor and security management sites, like *xforce.iss.net,* are also available for research and informational purposes.

Adding Software Updates and Patches

The best way to combat the constant stream of new viruses and security threats is to install updated software that is specifically designed to meet those threats. A change-management program that evaluates, schedules, and installs updates can help make sure that new software does not slow down systems, cause applications to crash, or lead to other problems. Vendors will typically provide information on available updates and security patches as they become available. You can also check the manufacturer's Web site for security patches and software updates. Develop a maintenance window—a period of two or three hours that is set aside every month for performing improvements such as software upgrades. It's a good way for organizations—even small ones—to manage changes to the network environment while minimizing the impact on production applications. It's also a good idea to participate in firewall-related mailing lists, not just to share ideas and ask questions of colleagues, but to learn about new security threats as they occur and news about patches as they become available.

Some software-only firewalls provide a module that automatically updates the software you have installed. The module enables licensed users of the software to remotely install and update software by connecting to the vendor's download center (see Figure 6-7 for an example of a Check Point NG SecureUpdate). Be cautious when using automatic update options, since the organization won't know how a new update or patch will affect the operations of its equipment. Most prudent organizations delay updates until they have been tested on off-line equipment.

Adding Hardware

Whenever a piece of hardware is added to the network, it should be identified in some way so the firewall can include it in its routing and protection services. Different firewalls require you to identify network hardware in different ways. Microsoft Internet Security and Acceleration Server (ISA), which functions as a proxy server, requires that you record the IP addresses of hosts or gateways on a Local Address Table. Check Point FireWall-1 requires you to "define" an object by giving it a name and recording its IP address and other information.

The need to list hardware as part of a protected network applies not only to workstations and the network, but to the routers, VPN appliances, and other gateways added as the network grows. It particularly applies to proxy servers such as ISA, which function as the default gateway for a network and need to know exactly how to route traffic through your different hardware devices.

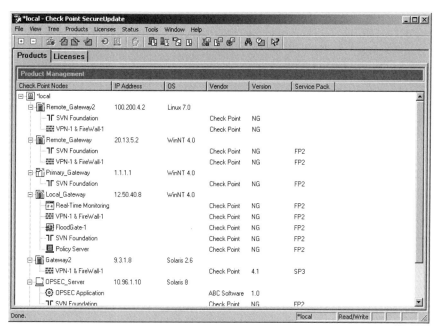

Figure 6-7 Check Point Update Manager
© Cengage Learning 2012

6

Different types of hardware can be secured in different ways, but one of the most important ways is to simply choose good passwords that you then guard closely. Some network hubs require the administrator to enter two separate passwords to manage or update those devices. One password gives the administrator read access, and the other gives the administrator write permission so he or she can change configuration files on the router if needed.

It's considered a mandatory security practice, with routers and other hardware or software, to change the write password from the default value to a strong, secure value. Switches and routers have their own passwords as well; some switches also have timeout periods that can be configured so the switches disconnect themselves from the network automatically via a management console if they are idle for a period of time.

Dealing with Complexity on the Network

Firewall configurations can take many forms, and they can grow in complexity as a network grows. One level of complexity you may need to manage comes from **distributed firewalls**, which are installed at all endpoints of the network, including the remote computers that connect to the network through VPNs. They add complexity because they require you to install and maintain a variety of firewalls that are located not only in your own corporate network but in remote locations. However, distributed firewalls also add security because they protect your network from viruses or other attacks that can originate from remote laptops or other machines that use VPNs to connect.

A firewall that is deployed on the desktop of a VPN client needs to adopt the security policy of the network to which it connects. It also needs to use Internet Protocol Security (IPSec), which, as will be explained in Chapter 9, provides for encryption, encapsulation, and authentication.

If you need to configure remote users to access your network via a VPN, determine what level of firewall security (if any) they already have. If they don't have a firewall already (or if they already installed their own firewall software and you find it to be weak or improperly configured), install a more effective desktop firewall along with the VPN client software. For example, one of Check Point's two VPN clients, Secure Desktop, includes desktop firewall support along with its VPN client software (see Figure 6-8). If you have a team of administrators involved in maintaining a security system, you need to keep strict records of any changes made to the system so that everyone on the team can be informed. You should hold regular meetings and report on any changes that have been made or problems that have been identified.

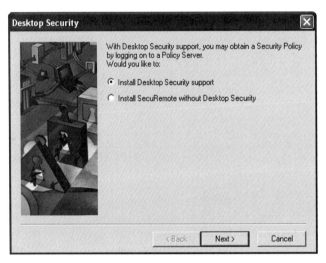

Figure 6-8 Check Point Secure Desktop
© Cengage Learning 2012

Adhering to Proven Security Principles

Part of firewall management—and network management in general—is adherence to principles that have been put forth by reputable organizations to ensure that you are maintaining your firewall and network security configuration correctly. The Generally Accepted System Security Principles (GASSP) is a set of security and information management practices put forth by the International Information Security Foundation (I2SF). In 2003, GASSP was succeeded by the **Generally Accepted Information Security Principles (GAISP)**, put forth by the Information Systems Security Association (ISSA). The latest version of the document, 3.0 (2004), can be viewed at *http://all.net/books/standards/GAISP-v30.pdf*. It appears that the project has stalled, although the last version still provides value as a guideline. GAISP begins with nine Pervasive Principles:

- Accountability—Define and acknowledge accountability and responsibility.
- Awareness—All stakeholders with a need to know have access to security principles as well as standards and practices and are informed of threats.
- Ethics—Information use and protection is performed in an ethical manner.

- Multidisciplinary—Security principles as well as standards and practices serve the perspectives of all relevant stakeholders.

- Proportionality—Controls are balanced against risk.

- Integration—Security principles are integrated and coordinated with standards and practices, and both are integrated and coordinated with other organizational principles, standards and practices, and policies, and procedures.

- Timeliness—Stakeholders act in a timely fashion to prevent and react to threats.

- Assessment—Risks are assessed regularly.

- Equity—Management acts respectfully to stakeholders in developing and implementing security measures and policies.

GAISP then derives 14 broad functional principles from these Pervasive Principles.

The following sections focus on the aspects of GAISP that apply to ongoing firewall management: securing the physical environment in which the firewall-related equipment is housed and securing software so that unauthorized users cannot access it.

6

Environmental Management

GAISP recommends the **environmental management** of IT assets and resources—that is, measures taken to reduce risks to the physical environment where the resources are stored. At the most basic level, this means you need to secure the building where your network resources are located in case of natural disasters such as earthquakes, floods, hurricanes, or tornadoes.

Such disasters might seem unlikely, but many businesses have run up huge losses due to hurricanes or other weather-related problems. Computer systems have failed when critical computers were placed on the top floor of buildings that were poorly air conditioned. Likewise, some firms have experienced water damage after placing critical systems in basement locations that are later flooded.

To prepare for environmental problems, an organization should consider installing the following:

- Power-conditioning systems to manage the quality of power being provided as well as provide back-up power when needed

- Back-up hardware and software to help recover network data and services in case of equipment failure

- Sprinkler and fire alarm systems

- Locks to guard against theft

BIOS, Boot, and Screen Locks and Passwords

Laptop computers that are used to connect to the main network should be secured not only by desktop firewalls, but also by more low-level types of security. Basic features you should look for in a laptop include boot-up and supervisor passwords, which protect the machine while it is booting up. A screen password should also be assigned.

GAISP includes the suggestion that a public notice be included in the company's logon screen that lets anyone who uses the network know that the organization has a security policy. Such a notice might read as follows: "Notice: Those who log on to the [Company Name] network are hereby notified that the files and databases you are about to access are valued assets and include much proprietary information that is protected by copyright. Unauthorized access to such resources is prohibited, and violators will be prosecuted."

Most computers give you the chance to set a **boot-up password**, which must be entered to complete the process of starting up a computer. Boot-up passwords (which are often called BIOS passwords or CMOS passwords) aren't perfect: they won't work when your computer is already on and is left unattended, for instance. In addition, a thief who can't crack your BIOS password can remove the hard drive and attach it to a computer that does not have a BIOS password, or remove the lithium battery from the computer's motherboard, thus erasing the BIOS password from memory.

Nevertheless, requiring people to enter a BIOS password on startup does add another level of defense to a computer. The BIOS password alone may discourage many thieves from making the effort to crack it. In addition, having a BIOS password in place prevents someone from starting up your computer and accessing your hard disk files with a floppy disk called a boot disk.

Supervisor Passwords   Some systems only use a BIOS password to enable the computer to complete booting up. On others (such as Windows NT and 2000), a second, higher-level password called a **supervisor password** is also used. In a case where a supervisor password and a BIOS password are used, the supervisor password is used to gain access to the BIOS set-up program or to change the BIOS password. Take care when assigning a supervisor password. Because of its importance, it should only be assigned to an administrator. Make every effort not to lose this password: if you do, you'll have to replace the system motherboard to access the BIOS.

Screen Saver Passwords   A screen saver is an image or design that appears on a computer monitor when the machine is idle. A screen saver password is a password you need to enter to make your screen saver vanish so you can return to your desktop and resume working. Configuring a screen saver password protects your computer while you're not working on it. It's thus a good complement to a BIOS password, which protects your computer during startup but not when the machine, though running, has been idle for a time. A screen saver password can be easily circumvented by rebooting the computer, but a BIOS password will be needed during the reboot.

Remote Management Interface

A remote management interface is software that enables you to configure and monitor one or more firewalls that are located at different network locations. You use it to start and stop the firewall or change the rule base from locations other than your primary computer. Without it, most administrators would spend hours moving from room to room or building to building, making the same changes on each of a company's firewalls.

Why Remote Management Tools Are Important

A remote management system is important because it saves many hours and makes the security administrator's job much easier. For instance, the Global Enterprise Management System (GEMS) for the McAfee Gauntlet firewall enables the administrator to use the same

Graphical User Interface (GUI) as a stand-alone firewall, but also allows the administrator to establish rules for as many as 500 separate firewalls. Although it's unlikely that any one administrator would have to manage that many firewalls, it's not uncommon for dozens of firewall devices to be deployed on a large-scale network.

Besides reducing time for the administrator, a remote management system reduces the chance of configuration errors that might result if the same changes have to be made manually for each firewall in the network. Many remote management programs come with a graphical interface in which network components are highlighted with colored icons to make it easier for administrators to evaluate their activities and determine the need for load balancing.

Security Concerns

Most firewall vendors offer GUI utilities that can be used to remotely manage a firewall or set of related firewalls. Because a GUI program has access to all of the firewalls on your network, it needs to be as secure as possible to prevent unauthorized users from circumventing your security systems. The remote management interface offers strong security controls, such as multifactor authentication and encryption. The interface should also be equipped with auditing features that keep track of who uses the software and when. The best remote management tools use tunneling to connect to the firewall or certificates for authentication rather than establishing an insecure connection like a Telnet interface. Once the management software is installed, be sure to evaluate the software to ensure that it does not introduce any new security vulnerabilities into the environment. A remote management interface should provide the administrator with a consistent appearance and operation across multiple platforms.

Basic Features of Remote Management Tools

Any remote management program should enable you to monitor and configure firewalls from a single centralized location. They should also enable you to start and stop firewalls as needed. Starting and stopping a firewall is a drastic step because it can affect network communications (unless you have a hot standby or load-sharing system set up, as described later in this chapter), but it's one you need to have at your disposal in case you detect an intrusion.

Remote management tools should help you perform such remote management tasks as the following:

- View and change firewall status
- View the firewall's current activity
- View any firewall event or alert messages
- Stop or start firewall services as needed

As a general rule, firewall administrators should not allow others to administer the firewall. Most administrators will not even allow the performance management consoles of firewalls to be publically viewable.

Automating Security Checks

A number of organizations and private security consultants provide security management services to handle ongoing checking and administration of firewalls. This is not simply passing the buck: if the network administrator's time is taken up with making sure the network is up and running and adding or removing users as needed, it may be more efficient to outsource the firewall administration. Be aware, though, that if firewall management is outsourced, there must be a high level of trust in the outside company to maintain network security. Outside companies may not devote the same level of attention to your systems that in-house employees would.

The best way to find an outside company to handle your firewall management responsibilities is to ask network administrators in other organizations for their personal recommendations, or scan security-related sites such as SANS (*www.sans.org*) for recommendations. Members of professional security associations such as ISSA (*www.issa.org*) can also help identify reliable security management services.

Configuring Advanced Firewall Functions

The ultimate goal for many organizations is the development of a high-performance firewall configuration that has **high availability** (i.e., it operates on a 24/7 basis or close to it) and that can be **scaled** (i.e., it can grow while maintaining its effectiveness) as the organization grows. This section briefly discusses some advanced firewall functions that can keep the firewall running effectively on a day-to-day basis: data caching, redundancy, load balancing, and content filtering.

Data Caching

Caching—the practice of storing data in a part of disk storage space so it can be retrieved as needed—is one of the primary functions of proxy servers. Firewalls can be configured to work with external servers to cache data, too. Caching of frequently accessed resources, such as Web page text and image files, can dramatically speed up the performance of your network because it reduces the load on your Web servers. The load is reduced because end users are able to call pages from disk cache rather than having to send a request to the Web server itself.

Usually, firewalls give you a variety of options for how data is cached. First, you need to set up a server that receives requests for URLs and that filters those requests against different criteria you set up. Those criteria include whether the Web page requested can be viewed by the public as per the organization's security policy; whether the Web page requested is part of a site that has been identified as containing harmful or inappropriate content and that should not be viewed by employees; and whether the site already exists in disk cache because it has been previously viewed and its contents have not changed since the last time it was viewed. The server returns the URL to the requesting host only if a set of caching criteria is met.

Typically, you choose one of four options with respect to caching data:

- No caching—With this option, caching is turned off and every request has to go to the originating Web server. This produces a heavier load on Web servers, but you might still choose this option if your server configuration changes frequently and you want to filter each request using the most up-to-date criteria.

- UFP server—Here, you specify the use of a **URI Filtering Protocol server**, which filters and processes requests for URIs and can work in conjunction with firewalls to call up Web pages from cache if needed. The UFP server reviews the requests, checks the URI against the contents of disk cache and returns documents from cache if they are present.

- VPN & Firewall (one request)—Here, the VPN and firewall servers control caching instead of the UFP server. When a Web page is requested by an end user for the first time, it is immediately sent to the UFP server after that one request and added to disk cache, which considerably improves network performance.

- VPN & Firewall (two requests)—Here, URIs are sent to the UFP server two times before they are added to disk cache. Performance isn't as good as with a one-request system, but security is improved because each URI is checked by the firewall twice before being sent to cache.

Hot Standby Redundancy

One way to balance the load placed on a firewall is to set up a **hot standby** system in which one or more auxiliary (or failover) firewalls are configured to take over all traffic if the primary firewall fails. Usually, hot standby only involves two firewalls, the primary and the secondary systems. Only one firewall operates at any given time. The two firewalls need to be connected in what is sometimes called a **heartbeat network**, which monitors the operation of the primary firewall and synchronizes the state table connections so the two firewalls have the same information at any given time.

Figure 6-9 shows a simplified diagram of a hot standby setup (simplified because in reality there would be more routers joining the various networks and probably more servers in the DMZs). The heartbeat network is made up of the two firewalls. The dashed line indicates the paths through which network traffic would flow if the primary firewall fails. The advantage

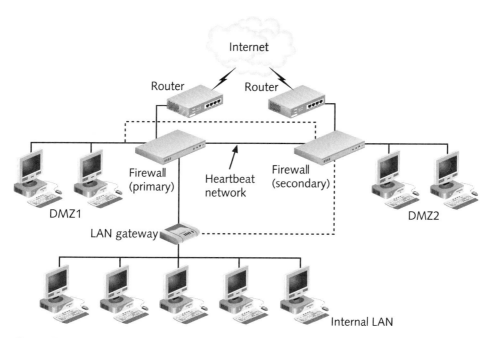

Figure 6-9 Hot Standby Example
© Cengage Learning 2012

of a hot standby system is the ease and economy with which it can be set up and the quick backup system it provides for the network. Another advantage is that one firewall can be stopped for maintenance purposes without stopping traffic to and from the network. On the downside, hot standby by itself doesn't improve network performance, and VPN connections may or may not be included in the failover system, depending on whether the firewall supports failover for VPN connections. Hot standby systems are just one aspect of incident response.

Load Balancing

As discussed in the early chapters of this book, the simplest firewalls function as gateways, monitoring all traffic as it passes into and out of a network. As organizations grow and Web, e-mail, and e-commerce services grow, it can be a liability to have a single firewall gateway that can become a single point of failure. When the firewall becomes **mission-critical**—an integral, key part of the company's core operations—everything possible must be done to maximize the firewall's uptime and smooth operation. One way to accomplish this goal is **load balancing,** the practice of distributing the work placed on the firewall so that it is handled by two or more firewall systems.

Load balancing can be accomplished with **load sharing,** the practice of configuring two or more firewalls to share the total traffic load. Each firewall in a load-sharing setup is active at the same time. Traffic between the firewalls is distributed by routers using special routing protocols such as:

- Open Shortest Path First (OSPF)—This protocol can route traffic based on its IP type. It can also divide traffic equally between two routers that are equally far apart or that have an equal load already.
- Border Gateway Protocol (BGP)—This protocol uses TCP as its transport protocol to divide traffic among available routers.

A load-sharing setup has many advantages. Total network performance is improved because the load is balanced among multiple firewalls, and the routing protocols needed to distribute traffic are present in virtually all routers. A big advantage is that maintenance can be performed on one firewall without disrupting total network traffic to the other firewall(s). On the downside, the load is usually distributed unevenly, and the configuration can be complex to administer. The connections between load-sharing firewalls may or may not include failover functions. This depends on whether the firewalls involved support failover connections. A load-sharing setup is illustrated in Figure 6-10.

The even distribution of traffic among two or more load-sharing firewalls can be achieved through the use of **layer four switches,** which are network devices with the intelligence to make routing decisions based on source and destination IP address or port numbers as specified in Layer 4 of the OSI reference model.

Filtering Content

One of the most malicious and difficult-to-filter network attacks is the inclusion of harmful code in e-mail messages. Firewalls, by themselves, don't scan for viruses, but their manufacturers enable them to work with third-party applications to scan for viruses or other related functions. ZoneAlarm and Check Point NG, for instance, have an **Open Platform**

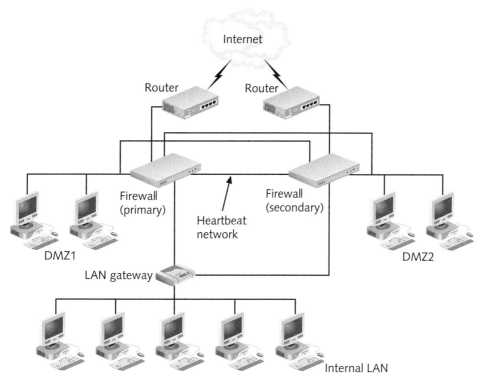

Figure 6-10 Load-Sharing Example
© Cengage Learning 2012

for Security (OPSEC) model that lets you extend their functionality and integrate virus scanning into their set of abilities.

Many advanced firewalls support the **Content Vectoring Protocol (CVP)**, which enables firewalls to work with virus-scanning applications so that such content can be filtered out. For instance, you can define a network object, such as a server that contains antivirus software, and have the firewall send SMTP traffic to that server using CVP. Once you define the server as a network object, you set the application properties for that server.

In Figure 6-11, the antivirus server is identified as an OPSEC Server in the Host list, CVP is identified as a Server Entity, and an OPSEC-compliant vendor intended for use on the antivirus server is chosen from the Vendor list. You then set options in the CVP Options tab to identify the server as a CVP object and identify the types of data you want to send to that server. CVP and OPSEC are two important tools you can use to help your firewall grow along with your organization's security needs.

Antivirus protection is fast becoming one of the most important aspects of network security due to the proliferation of viruses borne by e-mail messages. For this reason, consider installing antivirus software on your SMTP gateway in addition to providing desktop antivirus protection for each of your computers. Be sure to choose an antivirus gateway product that provides for content filtering, can be updated regularly to account for recent viruses, can scan the system in real time, and has detailed logging capabilities.

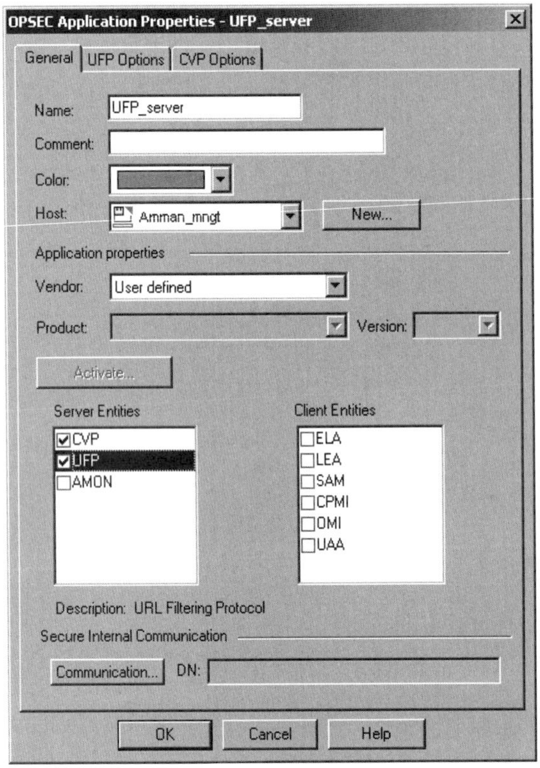

Figure 6-11 Content Filtering Example
© Cengage Learning 2012

Running Case: Actually, We Have Had a Problem

"And for these reasons, among others, I feel you should not add ancillary functions to the firewall," Rachel said to the group of Data Mart employees. *"The loss in CPU cycle for other tasks may result in adverse conditions should you experience high traffic levels. The addition of dedicated VPN appliances will still provide the needed functionality without reducing the effectiveness of the firewall."*

Rachel took a deep breath. Two hours of explaining the auxiliary functions of the proposed firewall had taken more out of her than she anticipated.

"So we're going to need a separate VPN appliance," Julie Matford asked. *"Are those expensive?"*

"No more so than any dedicated server we've recommended so far, but that's the subject of another meeting," Rachel answered. *"What we need to focus on now is the configuration of the firewall and its log management."*

"Why should log management for this device be any different than that for any other server or appliance?" Alex asked. *"We really haven't had a problem with those before, have we?"*

"Actually," Julie said, *"we have."*

Rachel looked at her watch. Well, another two hours wouldn't kill her.

Chapter Summary

- After establishing a security policy, you need to implement the strategies that the policy specifies. This is often done by setting rules for one or more firewalls. Rules give the firewall specific criteria to check before deciding whether to allow packets through or drop them; they also inform the firewall about what types of traffic to let in and out of your network.

- If the primary goal of your planned firewall is to block unauthorized access, you must emphasize restricting rather than enabling connectivity. In a Deny-All approach, the firewall blocks everything by default and only specifically allows those services you need on a case-by-case basis. Alternatively, if the primary orientation of your firewall is permissive, the rules should only block specific items, and the burden is shifted to education, training, and awareness.

- A firewall must be scalable so that it can grow with the network it protects. It needs to take into account the communication needs of individual employees. Because TCP/IP is the protocol of choice for internal networks as well as the Internet, the firewall also has to deal with the IP address needs of the organization.

- The stronger and more elaborate your firewall, the slower your data transmissions are likely to be. The productivity needs of users inside the company who are trying to access the Internet must be addressed.

- The more complex a network becomes, the more IP-addressing complications will arise. It's important to anticipate how firewalls will affect this facet of network operations.

- Network security setups can become incrementally more complex when specific functions are added. Any or all of the following can be part of a perimeter security system that includes a firewall: NAT/PAT, use of encryption, an application proxy, a virtual private network, and/or an intrusion detection and prevention system.

- Firewalls must be maintained regularly to assure that critical measures of success are kept within acceptable levels of performance. The firewall architecture and implementation must be maintained to assure throughput, scalability, security, recoverability, and manageability.

- Successful firewall management requires adherence to principles that have been put forth by reputable organizations to ensure that firewalls and network security configurations are maintained correctly. The Generally Accepted Information Security Principles (GAISP) is one such set of security and information management. GAISP provides guidelines that can help you manage a firewall as well as the information that passes through it. These guidelines encompass the following areas: environmental management, BIOS, boot and screen locks, and others.

- Remote management allows configuration and monitoring of one or more firewalls that are located at different network locations. These capabilities require security controls to enable their safe operation.

- The ultimate goal for many organizations is the development of a high-performance firewall configuration that has high availability and can be scaled as the organization grows. This is often accomplished by using data caching, redundancy, load balancing, and content filtering.

Review Questions

1. Give three reasons a set of packet-filtering rules is important to a firewall.

2. Describe how a firewall could be configured to implement a *strict* approach to security.

3. What is a potential concern with the firewall practice of processing all rules in top-to-bottom order?

4. What is the advantage of adding a second router between a firewall and the LAN it protects, in addition to a router outside the firewall?

5. Consider the following scenario: Your company operates a Web server and is promoting a new line of products. The server experiences a large number of visits from users on the Internet who want to place orders. The server needs to provide protection from viruses and harmful programs for users in the company; however, for business reasons, you are instructed that commerce and revenue should take priority over security. Under these circumstances, where should the Web server be positioned?

6. Proxy servers, routers, and operating systems are all designed to perform IP forwarding. If your security configuration includes a proxy server, why should IP forwarding be disabled on routers and other devices that lie between the networks?

7. What is the most important configuration file in a firewall?

8. A Deny-All approach would work best in which circumstances?

9. What is the principle of least privilege?

10. If a firewall is primarily permissive, how does this affect the work factor of the network administrator?

11. What are the potential problems of a Deny-All policy?

12. What is the primary difference between a screened host and a dual-homed gateway?

13. Describe how using multiple layers of protection can add security benefits to a network.

14. Describe how placing two routers with IDS at the perimeter of the network rather than one can improve the security of the network.

15. What are the primary goals you need to keep in mind when upgrading your firewall architecture?

16. A network administrator should be concerned when a firewall's CPU consumption climbs above what percentage of total CPU usage?

17. What circumstances indicate that data caching should be disabled?

18. When should a company hire an outside firm to handle the ongoing administration of a firewall?

19. What features are important for a remote network management program?

20. What is the primary advantage of using a hot standby setup to achieve load balancing?

Real World Exercises

1. Consider a user named Ken, who's a work-study student in a university department protected by a firewall and a member of the Work-Study user group in the Windows domain. Ken wants to access a Web site on the Internet from within the firewall. When Ken launches his Web browser and attempts to connect, the request is received by the firewall. The firewall has been configured with the rules pertaining to HTTP Web access shown in Table 6-4. What happens to the request if the firewall processes its rules using (a) In Order, (b) Deny-All, (c) Allow-All, and (d) Best Fit?

Rule	Port	Users	Action
1	80 (HTTP)	All	Allow
2	80 (HTTP)	Work-Study	Deny
3	80 (HTTP)	Ken	Allow

Table 6-4 Sample HTTP Firewall Rules

2. You are instructed to take a restrictive approach to firewall rules—"as close to Deny-All as is practically possible." However, the staff needs to look at training videos online during regular business hours. People should be allowed to use the Web and exchange e-mail at all times. However, access to multimedia should be prohibited at night. What rules would you set up for this?

3. Sterling Silver Widgets, a manufacturer of luxury office supplies for high-powered executives, sells its products on a Web site that receives an average of one 1000 visits per day. The company regularly receives shipments from Silver Supply, Inc., a supplier that wants to access its own shipping and receiving information in the office network as well as transmit invoices to the Sterling Silver Widgets accounting department. Sterling Silver Widgets has had problems in the past with DoS attacks. Design a perimeter setup that includes stateful packet filtering, public Web server access, a firewall-protected internal network, and VPN access to the accounting department server.

4. You need to monitor different types of traffic at different times of day using your firewall-protected network. You primarily want to monitor e-mail, Web, and videoconferencing activity during the day. But during the night, branch offices around the world might be connecting to your network for FTP, TCP, and UDP traffic. How would you specify different monitoring parameters for different times of the day?

5. You have set up a load-sharing configuration in which three firewalls provide separate gateways for an internal network. You are alarmed to yield only a slight improvement in network traffic performance, despite the fact that you purchased and configured two new bastion hosts and firewall products. What might be the cause of the continued poor network performance? What could you do to improve the situation?

6. Despite the fact that you have installed an enterprise-class firewall, your company's employees have reported receiving e-mail messages that contain potentially harmful executable code

attachments. Such attachments have been identified and isolated by the virus-protection software installed on each workstation. You know, however, that the number of such harmful attachments is growing all the time, and you are worried that one will slip through for which the virus-protection software isn't yet configured to handle. What can you do to keep such harmful e-mail messages from entering the protected network in the first place?

7. You congratulate yourself on configuring your firewall. The next morning, you check the log files. You discover a number of unsuccessful attempts to log on to the FTP server. You turn on your firewall's real-time monitoring program and you immediately notice that 15 MB worth of files is in the process of being transferred to an external user. You realize an attack is probably in progress. What should you do?

Hands-On Projects

Project 6-1: Draw a Simple Packet-Filtering Design

The following project gives you experience designing a basic firewall setup by asking you to draw a simple network that is protected from the Internet by a single stateful packet-filtering router. Although the configuration is simple, it can serve as the foundation for more complex designs.

1. Get a pencil and paper, or start a drawing program on your computer.

2. At the top of the drawing area, draw a large circle and label it *Internet*.

3. Draw a line leading from the circle to a packet-filtering router.

4. Identify the external and internal router interfaces.

5. Assign IP addresses to the interfaces and to the computers being protected.

6. Draw a line leading from the router to a group of computers on an internal network.

7. Draw a line joining the computers on the internal network to indicate that they are networked. Show one computer on the network that will not receive packets from the Internet.

Project 6-2: Drawing a DMZ

Now that you've drawn a simple network/router setup, you can draw a similar one that's a little more involved: a DMZ screened subnet connected to a firewall that has a router on either side of it.

1. Get a pencil and paper, or start a drawing program on your computer.

2. At the top of the drawing area, draw a large circle and label it *Internet*.

3. Draw a line leading from the circle to a packet-filtering router.

4. Draw a line leading from the Internet to a rectangle and label this the firewall.

5. Draw a short line leading from the firewall to a second router.

6. Draw a line leading from the second router to a network of computers. Label this group of computers the *internal LAN*.

7. Draw a line leading in another direction from the firewall to a DMZ. The DMZ should contain one or two computers. Label one computer *Web server* and the other *FTP server*. Label these computers (the ones in the DMZ) the *screened subnet*.

Running Case Projects

In this exercise, you add additional features to your firewall (logs, log management, remote management, and whatever bonus features are available, but no proxy features) and add additional (more complex) firewall rules.

Student Tasks

In this exercise, we perform the following tasks to further configure the Vyatta firewall:

- Enable SSH access to the Vyatta firewall.
- Restrict access to the Vyatta firewall to a specific IP address on the internal network.

To enable SSH access to the Vyatta firewall:

1. Log in to the Vyatta interface via the command line, using **vyatta** as the username and the password you created in Chapter 4.

2. Enter **configure**, and then press **Enter** to enter configuration mode.

3. Enter **set service ssh**, and then press **Enter**.

4. Enter **commit**, and then press **Enter**.

5. Enter **save**, and then press **Enter**.

When complete, your screen should look similar to Figure 6-12.

```
vyatta@vyatta:/var/log$ configure
[edit]
vyatta@vyatta# set service ssh
[edit]
vyatta@vyatta# commit
Restarting OpenBSD Secure Shell server: sshd.
[edit]
vyatta@vyatta# save
Saving configuration to '/opt/vyatta/etc/config/config.boot'...
Done
[edit]
vyatta@vyatta# _
```

Figure 6-12 Vyatta SSH Server Setup
© Cengage Learning 2012

Now, we will restrict GUI access to SSH, and then restrict HTTP management to occur only from a specific IP address on the internal network. This is a two-step process: completely denying access from the untrusted network, and then restricting access on the trusted network to the specific IP address.

6. Enter **set firewall name eth0_local default-action drop**, and then press **Enter**. This step blocks all access to the Vyatta firewall from the untrusted network.

7. Enter **set interfaces ethernet eth0 firewall local name eth0_local**, and then press **Enter** to assign the rule set to the interface.

8. Enter **commit**, and then press **Enter**.

Now, try to view the management GUI in a Web browser from the untrusted network. Do this by opening a browser and then typing the assigned IP address of the appliance in the

Address box. The browser will time out and tell you the Web site is not available, similar to what is shown in Figure 6-13.

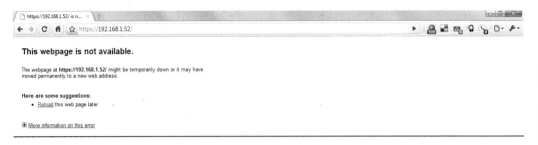

Figure 6-13 HTTP GUI Timeout
© Cengage Learning 2012

Do the same from the trusted network, and you will be able to view the management GUI. Now, we will take steps to limit this access to a single IP address.

9. Enter **set firewall name eth1_local default-action drop,** and then press **Enter**. This step blocks all access to the Vyatta firewall from the trusted network.

10. Enter **set interfaces ethernet eth1 firewall local name eth1_local,** and then press **Enter** to assign the rule set to the interface.

Now, we will create an exception to allow traffic to the Vyatta firewall from a specific IP address.

11. Enter **set firewall name eth1_local rule 10 action accept,** and then press **Enter**.

12. Enter **set firewall name eth1_local rule 10 source address** *trusted network IP address to be used,* and then press **Enter**.

13. Enter **save,** then press **Enter** to make the changes permanent.

Endnotes

1. Ranum, M. Thinking about Firewalls. Accessed 15 January 2010 from *www.vtcif.telstra. com.au/pub/docs/security/ThinkingFirewalls/ThinkingFirewalls.html*.

2. Tobkin, C. and Kligerman, D. *Check Point Next Generation with Application Intelligence Security Administration.* Rockland, MA: Syngress, 2004.

3. SecurityFocus. Accessed 15 January 2010 from *www.securityfocus.com/about*.

4. National Vulnerability Database. Accessed 15 January 2010 from *http://nvd.nist.gov/*.

5. US-CERT. Accessed 15 January 2010 from *www.us-cert.gov/aboutus.html*.

6. CVE. Accessed 15 January 2010 from *http://cve.mitre.org*.

7. OSVDB. Accessed 15 January 2010 from *http://osvdb.org*.

chapter 7

"Never do that by proxy
which you can do
yourself."
  —Italian proverb

Working with Proxy Servers
and Application-Level
Firewalls

After reading this chapter and completing
the exercises, you will be able to:

- Describe proxy servers and their function
- Identify the goals your organization can achieve using a proxy server
- Discuss critical issues in proxy server configurations
- Evaluate the most popular proxy-based firewall products
- Explain how to deploy and use reverse proxy
- Determine when a proxy server is not the correct choice

Running Case: Gambling with the Company's Future

Steve Verdi was furious. He'd just returned from Data Mart's most recent information security program briefing. While he knew that the new security procedures would help protect the information at Data Mart, he really didn't care about that. And having these new policies shoved down his throat by those consultants was just too much. For seven years, Steve had worked hard in the accounting department at Data Mart, climbing his way up from an entry-level clerk to head bookkeeper. He felt the company owed him a little respect. The most recent policy, which was going into effect immediately, indicated that employees would not be allowed to use the Web unless specifically required to do so for their work, and that a new proxy server would regulate access. Steve's job was among the dozens that were specifically listed as not needing Web access. He could still use e-mail, but only for work.

Steve sat at his desk, still fuming while absentmindedly moving the mouse back and forth, the cursor sliding across the screen. For the umpteenth time, he tried to open Firefox; yet again, he received an error message indicating that his access was restricted and that he needed to contact the network administrator if he felt he'd reached the message in error. Steve glanced at his watch. He could probably go to a nearby Internet cafe during his lunch break, but that was hours away. He wanted to be online now. He needed to be online now. He glanced across his cubicle at his filing cabinet, where he kept his company laptop. An idea popped into his head. Maybe they hadn't implemented the new controls on the wireless network yet! While it wasn't technically part of Data Mart's network infrastructure, several employees had set up a wireless network when the company had renovated the building to expand its infrastructure capacity. Maybe it was still up.

Steve's heart pounded as he opened his laptop. Boot-up seemed to take forever. Finally, he was logged into the computer and opened a Web browser. Success! He quickly typed in the address he'd wanted to visit since he came in to work: www.pokeraddix .com. The screen flickered, and then....Yes! It brought up a login screen. Steve entered his account information and clicked Join New Game! And for the next few minutes, he happily played his game. In fact, he was just about to pull off the largest win he'd had in weeks when suddenly the screen flickered and the Web browser flashed an all-too-familiar message.

"Noooooooooooooo!!!!" Steve yelled.

Introduction

Proxy servers were originally developed as a way to speed up communications on the Web by storing a site's most popular pages in a cache. Since then, they have become a formidable security solution. Proxies can conceal the end users in a network, filter out undesirable Web sites, and block harmful content in much the same manner as packet filters. Today, most proxy servers function as firewalls at the boundaries of networks, performing packet filtering, Network Address Translation (NAT), and other services. In this chapter, you will learn what proxy servers are, how they work, and in what ways they are vulnerable. You will also learn about the different kinds of proxy servers you can install so that you can make an informed decision about the one that's right for you.

Overview of Proxy Servers

Proxy servers—also called **proxy services, application-level gateways,** or **application proxies**—are specialized firewall software applications that run on a network device or appliance, or on a dedicated general-purpose computer. Proxy servers evaluate the application-layer data buried in the data portion of an IP packet (unlike packet filters, which examine only the IP header of the packet) to determine whether to allow the packet to pass into or out of the network. It is precisely because these devices examine the application data involved, as shown in Figure 7-1, that they are also referred to as application-level gateways or proxies. Since the proxy must "drill down" to the application-layer data, it is most common to dedicate a device to a single application—HTTP for Web traffic, SMTP for e-mail, etc. This prevents the device from being overwhelmed when dealing with multiple protocols.

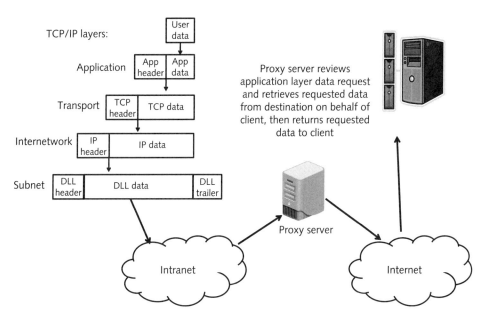

Figure 7-1   Application Layer of an IP Packet
© Cengage Learning 2012

How Proxy Servers Work

Proxies function as a software go-between, forwarding data among internal users and external hosts or among external users and internal hosts. They screen all traffic into and out of the relevant ports and decide whether to block or allow traffic based on rules set up by the proxy server administrator.

In a typical transaction, a proxy server intercepts a request from a user on the internal network and passes it along to a destination computer on the Internet. This might seem like a complex and time-consuming process, but it takes only milliseconds for the following steps to occur:

1. An internal host makes a request to access a Web site.

2. The request goes to the proxy server, which examines the header and data of the packet against rules configured by the firewall administrator.

3. The proxy server re-creates the packet in its entirety, with a different source IP address.

4. The proxy server sends the packet to its destination; the packet appears to be coming from the proxy server, not the original end user who made the request.

5. The returned packet is sent to the proxy server, which inspects it again and compares it against its rule base.

6. The returned packet is rebuilt by the proxy server and sent to the originating computer; when received, the packet appears to have come from the external host, not the proxy server.

Figure 7-2 illustrates these steps, which describe an inside-to-out transaction. Proxy servers are also used for outside-to-in transactions.

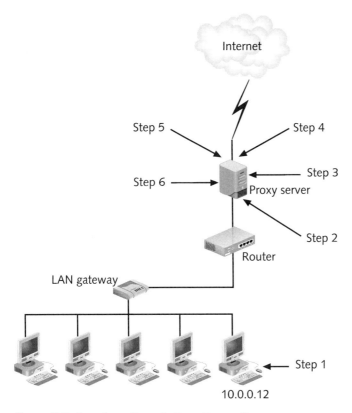

Figure 7-2 Steps in an Example Proxy Transaction
© Cengage Learning 2012

The main complaint about proxy servers is the time they take to inspect, compare, and rebuild packets and process client requests. However, in return, they conceal clients, translate network addresses, and filter content, among other tasks.

How Proxy Servers Differ from Packet Filters

Proxy servers and packet filters are used together in firewalls to provide multiple layers and different varieties of security. Each inspects different parts of IP packets and acts on them in different ways. Here are some of the specific differences between the two:

- Because proxy servers scan the entire data portion of IP packets, they create much more detailed log file listings than packet filters.

- If a packet matches one of the packet filter's rules, the filter simply acts as directed by the rule for that packet, allowing it to pass or blocking it from entering the destination network. A proxy server also rebuilds the packet with new source IP information, which shields internal users from those on the outside.

- Because a proxy server rebuilds all packets that pass between the Internet and the internal host, attacks that can start with mangled packet data never reach the internal host.

- Proxy servers are far more critical to network communications than packet filters. If a packet filter fails, all packets might be allowed into the internal network. If a proxy server gateway or firewall were to crash, all network communications would cease. Of course, if a failover or backup firewall is in place, it keeps network communications up and running while the primary device is being serviced.

Sample Proxy Server Configurations

A proxy server is positioned between the hosts in the internal LAN and the outside network to provide services on behalf of both internal and external users. A proxy server has two interfaces: one between itself and the external network, the other between itself and the internal network. The dual-interface nature of a proxy server suggests that a dual-homed host computer—that is, a computer that has two separate network interfaces, one to the external Internet and one to the internal LAN—provides an ideal setup for hosting (see Figure 7-3).

You can also configure a proxy server on a screened host and install routers that function as packet filters on either side.

In Figure 7-4, the packet filter that has an interface on the Internet is configured so that external traffic is allowed to pass only if it is destined for a service provided on the proxy server, which sits on the protected side of the perimeter.

Note that although the screened host/proxy server in Figure 7-4 has a direct interface on the Internet, it's far better in practice to use a proxy server behind a firewall or at least some form of router. As a rule, it is better for a firewall to have the direct interface to the Internet and to protect the proxy server by placing it behind the firewall, because if the proxy is compromised, hackers can disguise themselves as internal clients, and the results can be disastrous for the organization being protected. The only reason you should place a proxy server directly on the Internet is if the proxy is intended to serve as a reverse proxy, which is described later in this chapter. If you use proxy servers in conjunction with stateful or stateless packet filters, make sure you disable IP forwarding so that the proxy server handles packet delivery from one network to another.

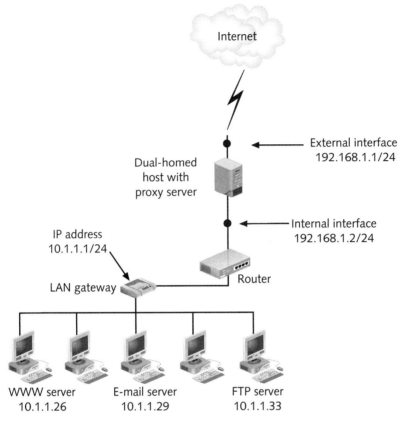

Figure 7-3 Proxy Using a Dual-Homed Host
© Cengage Learning 2012

Benefits of Proxy Servers

When you consider setting up a proxy system to protect a network, you should under-stand the benefits that proxy systems can provide. These are described in the following sections.

Concealing Internal Clients

Perhaps the most important benefit of a proxy server is its ability to conceal internal clients from external clients who try to gain access to the internal network. Rather than connecting directly to internal hosts, external clients see a single machine—the one that hosts the proxy server software (see Figure 7-5). This concealment of the internal network is useful to you because if external users cannot detect hosts on your internal network, they cannot initiate direct attacks against those hosts.

The concealment that proxy servers perform resembles NAT and PAT; however, proxy servers don't simply insert a new source IP into the headers of the packets they send out

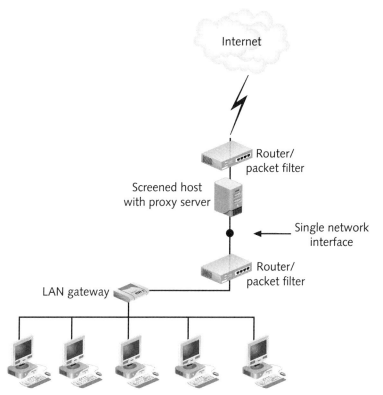

Figure 7-4 Proxy Using a Screened Host
© Cengage Learning 2012

in response to a request. Rather, the proxy server receives requests as though it was the destination server, and then generates a new request, which is sent to its destination.

Because proxy servers route all client requests through a single gateway, they are commonly used to share Internet connections. Simple proxy servers such as WinGate (for Windows) or Squid (for UNIX or Windows) are used to provide Internet-connection sharing in small office or home environments. More complex proxy servers, such as Microsoft Internet Security and Acceleration (ISA) Server and Sun's Java System Web Proxy Server, are designed to handle larger commercial operations.

Blocking URLs

Network administrators and managers like the fact that they can block users from certain URLs. This feature is frequently used to keep employees from visiting Web sites that offer content that management regards as unsuitable. URLs can be specified as either IP addresses or DNS names.

However, in practice, blocking URLs is unreliable, mainly because URLs are typically blocked by proxy servers as full-text URLs. The simple proxy server 1st Up Net Server (formerly NetProxy), for example, lets you enter the URLs of sites that you want to block from passing through the WWW proxy gateway (see Figure 7-6). However, if you only enter the

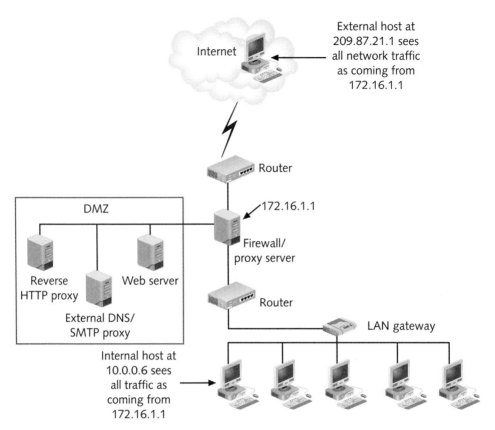

Figure 7-5 Concealing the Local Network
© Cengage Learning 2012

domain name of the site, users can still access the site using the IP address that corresponds to the URL. Security policy is a more effective method of preventing employees from visiting certain Web sites, because URLs could easily be changed.

Blocking and Filtering Content

Proxy servers can be configured to scan packets for questionable content. The proxy can be set up to not only block but remove Java applets or ActiveX controls if you don't want them to enter the internal network. In addition, you should certainly have the proxy delete executable files attached to e-mail messages. When an organization must send file attachments via e-mail, the organization should take specific steps to allow this without enabling the free flow of executables or even large attachments via uncontrolled e-mail. The approach could include using specific compression or encryption as well as appropriate levels of authentication and/or approval. Proxy servers, like packet filters, can filter out content based on rules that contain a variety of **parameters** (defined pieces of packet or system data), including time, IP address, and port number. Virtually all proxy server products scan the payload of a packet and provide some sort of content-filtering system. Typically, this is used to block children (in a home environment) or employees (in a work environment) from viewing Web sites that are considered unsuitable.

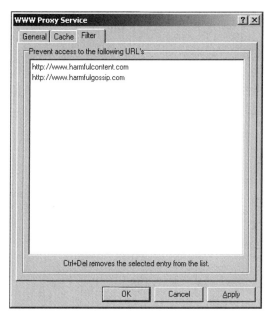

WWW Proxy Service

General | Cache | Filter

Prevent access to the following URL's

http://www.harmfulcontent.com
http://www.harmfulgossip.com

Ctrl+Del removes the selected entry from the list.

OK   Cancel   Apply

Figure 7-6 NetProxy Domain Name Blocking
© Cengage Learning 2012

E-Mail Proxy Protection

Casual users often assume that a proxy server exists primarily to protect users who are surfing the Web or to limit outside Web users' access to internal Web servers. However, proxy servers can be used to support and protect other network services, including e-mail. Figure 7-7 shows a configuration that provides e-mail protection for a network with a proxy Simple Mail Transfer Protocol (SMTP) server.

In Figure 7-7, a sendmail server has been placed in the DMZ, where it receives e-mail from the Internet. It passes requests on to the real mail server, which is the exchange server located on the internal network. Mail that originates on an internal host is sent from the exchange server to the sendmail server, which strips out the IP source address information when it rebuilds the packets and sends them on to the Internet. External e-mail users never interact directly with internal hosts, which is the great advantage of this configuration.

Improving Performance

Although proxy servers can slow down some requests for information, they can also speed up access to documents that have been requested repeatedly. For instance, they can be configured to store Web pages in a disk **cache**—a predefined temporary data storage location. When someone requests a previously accessed Web page, the proxy server can retrieve it from the cache. This lightens the load on the Web server, which doesn't have to serve up the same documents repeatedly.

Ensuring Security

Log files, which maintain records of events such as logon attempts and accesses to files, might be tedious and time consuming to review, but they can serve several different functions to help ensure the effectiveness of a firewall, including the following:

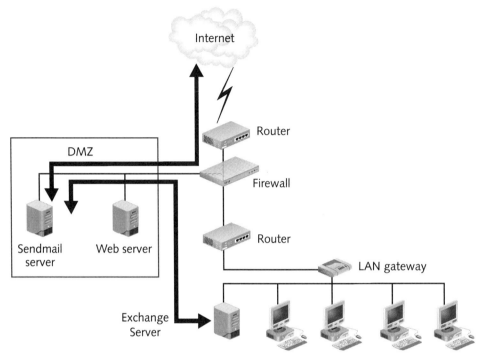

Figure 7-7 E-Mail Proxy Protection
© Cengage Learning 2012

- Detecting intrusions—By reviewing the firewall logs in detail, you can determine whether an unauthorized user has accessed resources that should be protected.

- Uncovering weaknesses—Log files can point to ports, machines, or other vulnerable computers through which hackers can gain entry. These entry points are known as **holes**.

- Providing documentation—If intrusions occur, log files record when the attack occurred and provide indications of the method that was used.

As stated, proxy servers provide very complete log files. The fact that proxies require all communications to flow through a single gateway means you have a reliable checkpoint from which to monitor network activity. To keep log files from getting unwieldy and eating up an inordinate amount of disk space, you should log only the services and events you view as most critical. (An event is an unusual occurrence that warrants additional attention; in this case, an event is something you want to log, like unauthorized connection attempts.)

1ˢᵗ Up Net Server, like other proxy servers, lets you log critical events (see Figure 7-8). Note that the applications and events you are going to log should be spelled out in your organiza- tion's security policy, as described in Chapter 2.

Some proxy servers have an alerting feature; they can notify you when a possible attack is in progress. An example of a possible attack is an attempted connection at the external interface of the proxy server.

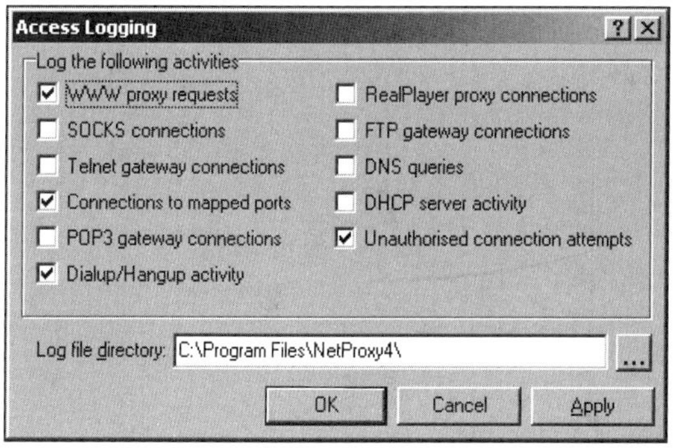

Figure 7-8 NetProxy Logging Services
© Cengage Learning 2012

Providing User Authentication

If user authentication is used in combination with a proxy server, you enhance security even more. Most proxy server products can prompt users who connect to the server for a username and password, which the server then checks against a database in your system. Authentication is discussed in more detail in later chapters.

Redirecting URLs

Some proxies can scan specific parts of the data portion of an HTTP packet and redirect it to a specific location (this is known as **URL redirection**). The proxy can be configured to recognize two types of content.

- Files or directories requested by the client
- The name of the host with which the client wants to communicate

The second method, which involves scanning the HTTP host field, is the most popular. It enables you to direct clients to a different Web server based on the host being requested. Suppose you have a single machine with a static IP address that hosts half a dozen or more virtual Web servers. Requests for the host *www.widgets.org* can be directed to one server, requests for *www.knicknacks.org* can be directed to another, and so on. Many Web servers, such as the popular freeware programs Apache and Microsoft Internet Information Server, have URL redirection built in, thus alleviating the need for a proxy server to do redirection.

Configuring Proxy Servers

Proxy servers offer many security-related benefits, but they also require special handling. First, you will have to make sure your proxy server has enough capacity because if it gets overloaded, client performance will suffer. Also, you must configure the environment properly. This will certainly involve the configuration of the proxy server itself and may also require that each piece of client software that uses the proxy server be configured across the organization. It may be necessary to maintain a separate proxy service for each network protocol as well as customize packet filter rules. In addition, proxy servers have potential security vulnerabilities, particularly because they present a single point of failure for the network and are also susceptible to various forms of attack.

Providing for Scalability

As the number of users on the network grows, the machine that hosts the proxy server should be upgraded. The capacity of the server that hosts the proxy service must match the amount of traffic that has to flow through each gateway. One way to cope with the issue of proxy server slowdown is to add multiple proxy servers to the same network connection. The servers can be configured in such a way that they share the total network traffic load. One server can handle traffic for one network service or from one subnet of users, one to another, and so on. Before building out a complex of multiple proxy servers, make sure your Internet connection throughput is robust enough to handle the amount of traffic your network is expected to process.

Working with Client Configurations

You have to configure each client program to work with the proxy server. For example, you must configure a Web browser to support the connection when you set up a proxy server. A typical setup for Internet Explorer is shown in Figure 7-9. No proxy server is specified for FTP and Gopher connections because the browser can use the **SOCKS** standard—a set of protocols that enable proxy server access to applications without an assigned proxy server—to make connections via the proxy server's gateway.

Figure 7-9 Internet Explorer Configuration Example
© Cengage Learning 2012

Such configurations are easy to perform once or twice, but when multiplied across dozens or even hundreds of client computers, the time and effort involved can be substantial. Most proxy servers will let you access a configuration file from which the browsers on your network can automatically retrieve the proxy settings. The file shown in Figure 7-10 contains some example scripts from the Microsoft Technet library used for autoconfiguring proxy servers based on the autoproxy format; you can edit the JavaScript to include the static IP address (if you have one) of the server that hosts the proxy server(s).

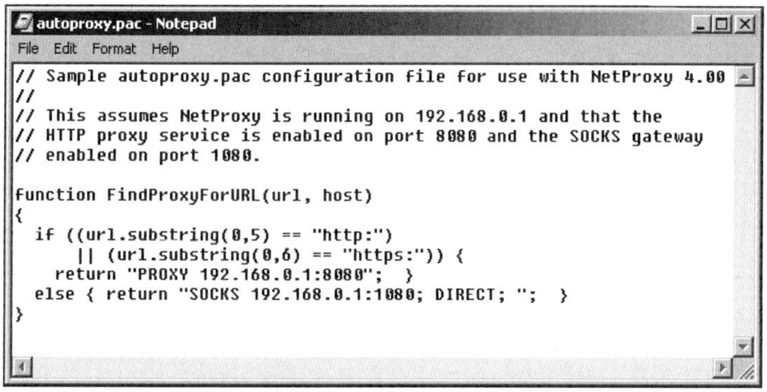

```
autoproxy.pac - Notepad
File  Edit  Format  Help
// Sample autoproxy.pac configuration file for use with NetProxy 4.00
//
// This assumes NetProxy is running on 192.168.0.1 and that the
// HTTP proxy service is enabled on port 8080 and the SOCKS gateway
// enabled on port 1080.

function FindProxyForURL(url, host)
{
  if ((url.substring(0,5) == "http:")
     || (url.substring(0,6) == "https:")) {
    return "PROXY 192.168.0.1:8080";  }
  else { return "SOCKS 192.168.0.1:1080; DIRECT; ";  }
}
```

Figure 7-10 NetProxy Configuration Script Example
© Cengage Learning 2012

Working with Service Configurations

A network must have one or more proxy servers available for each service protocol proxied on the network. The exact mixture of servers will depend on the needs of the configuration. For instance, a dedicated proxy can handle one type of traffic that is especially vulnerable to attack, such as SMTP. Services that receive an especially heavy load, such as HTTP, might also run more efficiently if given a dedicated proxy server (such as Squid) designed to work especially with HTTP.

More commonly, though, organizations use a general-purpose firewall that includes a proxy server that monitors all inbound and outbound traffic. You should certainly configure HTTP and DNS, as well as SMTP and POP3, for e-mail. The range of service options available with 1st Up Net Server is shown in Figure 7-11. Services for which no proxy server is available can make use of the SOCKS generic proxy. An example of proxy server configuration options in the Internet Explorer browser is presented in Figure 7-12.

Creating Filter Rules

Firewall rules should be established to optimize the performance of the proxy environment. While the details of how such rules should be created and managed are very complex, consider that rules can be established to enable known hosts to bypass the proxy. Also, it is possible to filter out specific URLs as well as set up rules that enable internal users to send outbound requests only at certain times. In an organization that only works during daylight hours, cutting off communications (except e-mail messages that might come in overnight) can be an important security level in the evening and overnight hours. During those hours, the protection prevents any Trojan horses that may have found their way into a system from connecting to the Internet. You can also set up rules governing the length of time a session can last. Cutting off a session after a lengthy period, such as an hour, can stall hackers who manage to get into your system and attempt to run executables from one of your host machines.

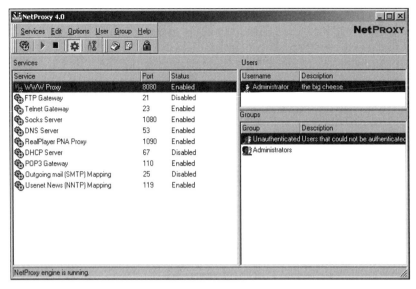

Figure 7-11 NetProxy Configuration Options
© Cengage Learning 2012

Figure 7-12 Example Nontransparent Proxy Configuration
© Cengage Learning 2012

Recognizing the Single Point of Failure

A proxy server that routes all traffic into and out of a network is a single point of ingress and egress and thus has the potential to be a single point of failure for the network. If the proxy server crashes due to a hardware failure or a hacker's efforts, your network could be totally cut off from the Internet.

This problem isn't unique to proxies, of course. Routers and firewalls that lie between your internal network and the Internet can provide the same failure point. Most network architectures include alternate means of enabling traffic to flow with a limited amount of protection in the event the primary protection controls have failed. This might mean that the network falls back to simple packet filtering if the proxy servers go offline. You can also use load-balancing systems, such as the Network Load Balancing feature in Windows Server, to create multiple proxies that are in use simultaneously and thus make your system less vulnerable—if one proxy ceases to function, the others will still work. **Network load balancing** (NLB) is a method of using multiple systems to take turns handling requests, to prevent any one system from getting overloaded.

Recognizing Buffer Overflow Vulnerabilities

Proxy servers can be subject to a number of problems that result from misconfiguration or other vulnerabilities. The most common problem is a buffer overflow, which occurs when a program (in this case, a proxy server) attempts to store more data in a temporary storage area (a buffer) than that area can hold. The resulting overflow of data (some of which might even contain executable code intended to cause harm to a network) renders the program nonfunctional.

Some proxy servers have been known to fall victim to buffer overflow problems, which might cause the proxy server to crash or allow an attacker to assume administrative rights for the server. The only way to combat such vulnerabilities is to check the Web site of the proxy server's manufacturer and install all available security patches.

7

Choosing a Proxy Server

Proxy servers come in different varieties. Some, like WinGate, are commercial products primarily used by home and small business users. Others, like Squid, are designed to protect one type of service (Web or FTP) and to serve cached Web pages. Most proxy systems are part of a **hybrid firewall**—a firewall that combines several different security technologies, such as packet filtering, application-level gateways, and VPNs. Others, like 1st Up Net Server, are true stand-alone proxy servers.

The following sections provide an overview of the different types of proxy servers you should be familiar with: transparent, nontransparent, and SOCKS-based.

Transparent Proxies

Transparent proxies can be configured so that they are totally invisible to end users. A transparent proxy sits between two networks like a router. The firewall intercepts outgoing traffic and directs it to a specific computer, such as a proxy server. The individual host does not know its traffic is being intercepted; in addition, the client software doesn't have to be configured, which makes network administrators very happy.

Nontransparent Proxies

Nontransparent proxies, also called explicit proxies, require that the client software be configured to use them. Every FTP client, chat program, browser, or e-mail software you use must be able to house a proxy server. All target traffic is forwarded to the proxy at a single target port, typically by means of the SOCKS protocol.

Nontransparent proxies require more labor to configure than transparent proxies because each client program must be set up to route all requests to a single port. However, nontransparent proxies provide greater security. Clients can have their routing entries removed so that only the proxy server knows how to reach the Internet. If you have a local network that does not need to go through the proxy, such as a branch of your own company, you should list it as shown. All traffic from that network will access resources directly.

SOCKS-Based Proxies

SOCKS is a protocol that enables the establishment of generic proxy applications—applications designed to act on behalf of many different services, such as FTP, NetMeeting, and other programs. SOCKS is known for its flexibility; it can help developers set up firewalls and virtual private networks (VPNs) as well as proxies. The term "SOCKS" is derived from sockets, a TCP/IP protocol used to establish a communication session. A socket is also an identifier consisting of an IP address and port number, such as 172.16.0.1:80. WinSock, for instance, is the name of a DLL that implements Sockets for Windows.

SOCKS Features SOCKS is typically used to direct all traffic from the client to the proxy using a target port of TCP/1080. (TCP 8080 may be used as well.) SOCKS acts as a transparent proxy. SOCKS is important because it provides a number of security-related advantages, including the following:

- It functions as a **circuit-level gateway** at the Session layer of the OSI model, filtering internal traffic that leaves the network being protected. Because it functions at the Session layer, it can work with virtually any TCP/IP application.
- It can encrypt data passing between client and proxy.
- It uses a single protocol to both transfer data via TCP and UDP and authenticate users.

SOCKS has one disadvantage, and it's a big one: it does not examine the data part of a packet. It does hide IP addresses of internal clients, however, and it does re-create packets before passing them on. Thus, it does provide some protection against malformed packets.

SocksCap

SocksCap, a free (for noncommercial use) SOCKS application available from Permeo Technologies (the originators of the SOCKS protocol), has a graphical interface that enables you to quickly configure applications to use SOCKS. In Figure 7-13, a chat application has been configured, and Microsoft Messenger is about to be added. (*Note*: Permeo Technologies was acquired by Blue Coat Systems in 2006; SOCKS was last updated in 2007, but version 2.40 is still available for download.)

Proxy Server-Based Firewalls Compared

You can choose from a number of firewalls that are based on proxy servers—that is, proxy servers either play an important role in their makeup or are their primary function. Your choice depends on the platform you are running and the number of hosts and services you need to protect.

Figure 7-13 SocksCap Configuration Example
© Cengage Learning 2012

7

Squid

Squid (*www.squid-cache.org/*) is a high-performance and free open-source application that is specially designed to act as a proxy server and cache files for Web and FTP servers. Squid isn't a full-featured firewall. It performs access control and filtering, and it is especially good at quickly serving cached files.

Squid runs on all UNIX-based systems. One nice feature is that the program is popular and well known enough that developers have come up with plug-in applications that enhance its functionality. Add-on applications include a banner ad filter created by the privacy organization Junkbusters and a log analyzer called Calamaris (*http://cord.de/tools/squid/calamaris/*). Squid is an excellent choice if you want to protect a UNIX-based (or Windows-based) network and you are on a budget.

WinGate

WinGate (*www.wingate.com*), by QBIK, is a very popular proxy server for home and small business environments. Currently, WinGate installs with the following:

- WinGate—the basic Internet gateway and proxy server
- WinGate VPN—an IP-tunnel remote access application
- PurSight—a Web content classification plug-in for WinGate
- Kaspersky AV—an antivirus plug-in for WinGate
- NetPatrol—an intrusion detection and prevention system that can be integrated with WinGate.

Norton from Symantec

After the discontinuation of its enterprise firewall suites (Raptor and Symantec Enterprise Firewall), Symantec shifted its firewall efforts to the residential, SOHO market. Currently, Norton, a Symantec product (*www.symantec.com/norton/*), offers a number of residential firewall and security applications that also provide various degrees of content filtering and proxy services. These applications, like Norton 360 or Internet Security, often combine anti-virus functions with network and system protection.

Microsoft Internet Security & Acceleration Server

Microsoft Internet Security & Acceleration Server (ISA) is the Microsoft proxy server product (*www.microsoft.com/forefront/edgesecurity/isaserver/en/us/*); it replaces the earlier Microsoft Proxy Server. It's a complex, full-featured firewall that includes stateful packet filtering as well as proxy services, NAT, and intrusion detection. ISA is designed to compete with Check Point's FireWall-1 and other high-performance firewall/proxy server products.

ISA does more than cache files and provide an application proxy gateway. It comes in two editions: Standard Edition and Enterprise Edition. The Standard Edition is a stand-alone product that supports up to four processors; the Enterprise Edition is a multiserver product with centralized management and no limit on the number of processors supported. However, both versions can be installed on a stand-alone basis for networks that don't use Active Directory.

Reverse Proxies

One form of proxy acts primarily on behalf of internal hosts—receiving, rebuilding, and forwarding outbound requests. However, you can improve security as well as enhance performance by setting up another form, the **reverse proxy**, which is a service that acts as a proxy for inbound connections. It can be used outside the firewall as a secure content server to outside clients, preventing direct, unmonitored access to your server's data from outside your company. A reverse proxy setup is shown in Figure 7-14.

Why use a reverse proxy when the primary clients you want to protect are those on the internal network rather than those on the external Internet? Performance, for one thing: reverse proxies cut down on unnecessary requests, which reduces the load on the company's Web server. Another reason is privacy, which can be critical to a company's bottom line if that company sells to the public and receives sensitive information such as credit card numbers. A reverse proxy that is set up outside the firewall as a stand-in for a Web server can protect sensitive information stored on that Web server that must remain secure, such as a database of credit card numbers. In practice, a company that does retail sales online should store customer data on a computer that has no direct connection to the Internet (i.e., not a Web server) for maximum security.

How do reverse proxy servers work? When someone on the Internet makes a request to connect to your company's Web server, the request goes first to the reverse proxy server. The proxy server then forwards the request through a specific port to the Web server over the trusted network. The Web server relays the reply back over the trusted, internal network to the reverse proxy server. The proxy, in turn, rebuilds the data packets from scratch (as proxies do) and sends the retrieved information to the client as if the proxy were the actual Web server. If the content server returns an error message, the proxy server can intercept the message and change any URLs listed in the headers before sending the message to the client. This prevents external clients from getting a glimpse of the redirection path of any URLs that point to the internal content server.

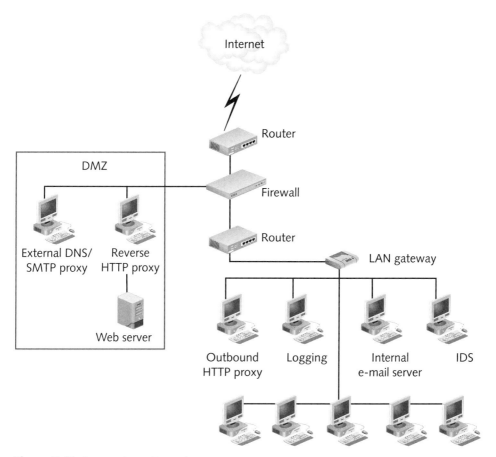

Figure 7-14 Reverse Proxy Example
© Cengage Learning 2012

By standing in for the public Web server, the reverse proxy server provides an additional barrier for the internal network. In the event of a successful attack, the hacker is more likely to be restricted to only the information involved in a single transaction, as opposed to having access to the entire data stores of the organization. The unauthorized user is unable to connect to the actual Web or database server because only the reverse proxy server is allowed such access.

When a Proxy Server Isn't the Correct Choice

Some organizations find that a proxy server slows down traffic excessively. Sometimes users who need to communicate using a messaging system find that the need to authenticate via the proxy server makes connection impossible; you can have external users connect to the firewall directly using Secure Sockets Layer (SSL) encryption, but only if the firewall has a static IP address, which may or may not be the case.

Another alternative to installing a proxy server is to use the proxy server of an Internet Service Provider (ISP). However, there's a downside: you have to depend on how well the ISP has configured the server. In fact, it may not be configured correctly and may actually slow down some Web sites unnecessarily. You can find publicly accessible proxy servers online, but they won't give you any improvement in security. They can speed performance by accessing cached Web pages, but since most Web pages these days are dynamic rather than static—that is, they generate their contents on the fly—caching is not all that valuable. You're better off installing and configuring your own proxy server, even if you have only a small home or business network to protect. A list of publicly accessible proxy servers is available at *http://tools.rosinstrument.com/proxy/*.

Running Case: Busted

"What's wrong, Steve?" a coworker named Karen asked from across the room. A cold shiver ran down Steve's spine. He knew that if his boss found out he was goofing off while on the clock he would be in trouble. And if he was caught gambling, he could be fired—right after a policy briefing on the new proxy setup.

"Oh, this stupid laptop's on the fritz again, and I just lost a document," Steve said, lying through his teeth. Steve turned around just as both Karen and his boss, Tina, were walking up. Tina smiled. "Sorry about that Steve," she said. "I'll see if we can get you a new laptop next fiscal cycle." Steve smiled, too. It looked like the day wouldn't be a waste after all. He turned back to his laptop.

"Uh, Steve?" Tina asked.

Steve turned back around. "Yeah, Tina?" His smile vanished as he saw Tina looking at a printout she had just been handed by one of the firewall consultants. The consultant then pointed to another document Tina was holding, after which Tina pointed to Steve while asking the consultant a question. The consultant nodded, and then frowned at Steve.

"Steve, we need to talk in my office...now," Tina said, her displeasure apparent. Steve felt the blood rush to his face. Maybe it won't be such a good day after all, he thought.

Questions

1. *Does the Data Mart policy on Web usage seem harsh to you? Why or why not?*

2. *What type of proxy services do you think were implemented?*

3. *How should Tina react to this situation if Steve is known to be a reliable and a diligent employee? What if she was already "on to him"?*

Chapter Summary

- Proxy servers are a formidable security solution that can conceal the end users in a network, filter out undesirable Web sites, and block harmful content. Most proxy servers function as firewalls at the boundary of a network, performing packet filtering, Network Address Translation (NAT), and other services.

- Proxy servers consist of software that runs on a network device or appliance or on a dedicated general-purpose computer. Proxy servers evaluate the data portion of an IP packet (unlike packet filters, which examine only the header of an IP packet) to determine whether to allow the packet to pass into or out of the network.

■ Proxies function as a software go-between, forwarding data between internal users and external hosts or external users and internal hosts, screening all traffic into and out of the relevant ports to decide whether to block or allow traffic based on rules set up by the proxy server administrator. In a typical transaction, a proxy server intercepts a request from a user on the internal network and passes it along to a destination computer on the Internet.

■ When establishing a proxy system to protect a network, you need to understand the benefits that proxy systems provide: concealing internal clients, blocking URLs, blocking and filtering content, e-mail proxy protection, improving performance, ensuring security, providing user authentication, and redirecting URLs.

■ Proxy servers require the performance of several special tasks: configuring each piece of client software that uses the proxy server, maintaining a separate proxy service for each network protocol, creating packet filter rules. In addition, proxy servers carry the risk of being a single point of failure for the network.

■ Proxy servers come in different varieties, some being enterprise solutions and others being oriented to the smaller business. Some are designed to protect one type of service while most are part of a hybrid firewall—a firewall that combines several different security technologies, such as packet filtering, application-level gateways, and VPNs.

■ Most proxies act primarily on behalf of their internal hosts, but some are reverse proxies that act as proxies for inbound connections.

Review Questions

1. Why were application-level proxies originally developed?

2. What proxy server functions are similar to packet-filtering firewall functions?

3. What can proxy servers do better than packet filters?

4. Why do proxy servers reassemble packets before sending them on their way?

5. Which is the most effective way proxy servers conceal internal clients?

6. What are the disadvantages or complications of using a proxy server gateway?

7. Why would load balancing be used in conjunction with a proxy server gateway?

8. What type of proxy server receives traffic from all services at a single port, such as a SOCKS proxy server?

9. When would you want to dedicate a proxy server to a single service?

10. What is a nontransparent proxy?

11. When a proxy server focuses on an HTTP header to redirect a request to a specific URL, what will it use as its most critical determinant?

12. Consider the following: You run an external Web site that lists catalog items for sale. The overwhelming number of requests your company receives from the Internet are HTTP

requests. You need to distribute the traffic load more evenly, and you need to protect sensitive client information contained on your Web server. What two proxy server approaches could help you achieve these goals?

13. Should a proxy server be located so that it has a direct interface to the Internet? If so, under what circumstances?

14. What functions are performed at the Session layer of the OSI model?

15. What are the disadvantages of using a reverse proxy?

16. What are the disadvantages of using SOCKS?

17. Why is authentication required when a proxy server completely separates internal clients from the Internet?

18. How might you protect an internal network overnight, when no employees are present?

19. Within application-level firewalls, what is the purpose of parameters such as time, IP address, or port number?

20. When is a proxy server the wrong protection mechanism for a network?

Real World Exercises

1. **Use Private IP Addresses and Share a Connection** You are hired as the network administrator of a small startup company with a limited budget. You are instructed to configure the LAN so that the company makes use of a single dynamic IP address it has obtained from its ISP as part of its low-cost Internet access account, but that gives three other computers Internet access as well. How would you do this? Using a Web browser, identify a number of options and compare the features of each.

2. **Repair a Default Configuration** You are called in by a small business that is experiencing performance problems with one of its network computers. The five workstations in the company share a connection to the Internet using the WinGate proxy server. The complaint is that the computer that hosts WinGate is running slowly and that the Internet connection is slower than normal. What would you look for as the cause of the problem, and how would you remedy it? Use a Web search tool to identify at least one solution to this problem.

3. **Troubleshooting Slow Proxy Performance** After installing a proxy server gateway, you notice a significant performance drop on your network. You have installed a single proxy server on the perimeter of your network that handles all services. Use a Web search tool to identify at least two strategies for improving performance.

4. **Do a Batch Configuration** You install a proxy server system in a midsize organization with about 100 separate hosts distributed among several subnets. You are faced with the task of configuring all client software on all 100 hosts to access the proxy so that employees can send and receive e-mail and other Internet services. Yet, you have to get everyone online within a day or two. How would you perform the batch configuration quickly? Use a Web browser to identify at least two different solutions that address this task, and then compare the features of each.

Hands-On Projects

Project 7-1: Install and Configure NetProxy

There are many proxy server programs you can install, but for the purposes of lab testing, a good way to start is to download a free program that you can keep in the lab and use as needed. NetProxy is free for single-user use. You can install the program on any Windows XP workstation. NetProxy can be downloaded from *http://download.cnet.com/* by searching on the term "NetProxy." (The most recent version is 4.03. While it's a bit old, it illustrates the basic functions of a proxy.)

The NetProxy software (and the steps that follow) both assume that the workstations on your network use reserved IP addresses in the range 192.168.0.0/24 and that they are dynamically generated by a server using Dynamic Host Control Protocol (DHCP). If the workstation on which you install NetProxy uses a different IP address, substitute your machine's actual IP address for the one NetProxy instructs you to enter by default.

1. Download NetProxy from *http://download.cnet.com*. Save the file (np403.exe) in a location you can access (e.g., My Documents).

2. Double-click the file (np403.exe) you downloaded. Follow the installation steps to install the program.

3. After the installation completes, click **Start, Run,** type **cmd** in the text box, and then press **Enter.** In the command window that opens, type **ipconfig /all**. Record this information for use later when configuring NetProxy. Close the command window when finished, or leave it open in the background.

4. Click **Start,** point to **All Programs,** point to **NetProxy,** and click **NetProxy Configuration.** The NetProxy window opens.

5. To configure NetProxy, click the **Configuration Wizard** button on the NetProxy toolbar. (This button isn't labeled, but it looks like a pair of pliers and a wrench.) The NetProxy 4.0 window opens.

6. With the information you gathered from the ipconfig command, fill out the details that apply to your Internet connection in the ISP's Server Details section. For instance, in the WWW Proxy Server text box, enter the IP address of your machine and the port on which you access the Web (this will probably be either Port 80 or 8080).

7. Fill out the rest of the boxes with the IP address of your primary DNS server, mail server names, and newsgroup server names (again, from the ipconfig command).

8. In the Connection section, click the **Connect to the Internet using a modem or ISDN adaptor** option button only if you use a dial-up modem to connect to the Net. Otherwise, leave the **Connected to the Internet permanently** option button selected.

9. Click **OK.** If you are unable to enter an address in the DNS Server box, you can still continue to configure and test NetProxy.

10. If your computer lab uses a set of IP addresses other than 192.168.0.0/24, click **Options** and click **Firewall.** (Otherwise, skip to step 18.)

11. In the Incoming Firewall Rules dialog box, click **Add.** The Add Incoming Firewall Rules dialog box opens.

7

12. In the IP address range text box, enter the IP address range your network uses. Leave **All Services** displayed in the Service box, and then click **OK**. The new address range is added to the list in the Incoming Firewall Rules dialog box.

13. Click **OK** to close the Incoming Firewall Rules dialog box and return to the NetProxy window.

14. Click **Options** and click **Logging**. The Access Logging dialog box opens.

15. Check the boxes next to **WWW proxy requests** and to any other services you want to log, and then click **OK**.

16. After you have NetProxy configured, stop any other firewall program, such as Tiny Personal Firewall, that is currently running to ensure that it doesn't interfere with NetProxy.

17. Connect to any Web site, such as *www.cengage.com/coursetechnology*. Is the Web browser's performance slower than usual?

18. Start a text editor such as Notepad and click **Start**, point to **All Programs**, point to **Accessories**, and then click **Notepad**.

19. Click **File** on the menu bar, click **Open**, and then click **All Files** on the Files of type drop-down menu in the Open dialog box. Click **Open**.

20. Navigate to the log file for NetProxy, which is contained in C:\Program Files\NetProxy4 (or in the location you installed the program). The filename ends with the extension .log and begins with a number (for example, 2002617.log). (If you cannot find a log file, click **Options** and click **Logging** from the NetProxy toolbar. In the Access Logging window, check the location specified in the Log file directory box.) Double-click the file to open it. How many log entries were created by that single Web site access? What is the difference between the different log entries? Record the answers in a lab book or word-processing file.

Project 7-2: Configure a Client to Work with a Proxy

Every client that expects to communicate via the proxy server gateway needs to be configured to work with that gateway. The most obvious example is a Web browser that will have a proxy acting on its behalf to connect to Web sites and retrieve information. Assume you have a proxy server at 192.168.0.1 running Web services on Port 8080. You'll need to configure your Web browser to work with NetProxy for your own personal use; if you're setting up a proxy in a corporate setting, you'll need to either instruct employees how to do this or do the configuration for them.

1. Double-click the **Internet Explorer** icon on your desktop.

2. Click **Tools**, and then click **Internet Options** to open the Internet Options dialog box.

3. Click the **Connections** tab to bring the Connections options to the front.

4. If you use a dial-up modem connection to connect to the Internet, click the connection in the Dial-up settings box to select it, and then click **Settings**. Because you probably connect via a LAN in your lab, click **LAN Settings**.

5. In the Local Area Network (LAN) Settings dialog box, check the **Use a proxy server for your LAN** check box, and then click **Advanced**.

6. In the Proxy Settings dialog box, type the address of your proxy server in the HTTP: text box, and then enter the port your proxy uses for HTTP service in the adjacent Port text box.

7. If you use different proxy servers for different services, repeat step 6 for each of the services you plan to use: FTP, e-mail, and so on. Otherwise, check the **Use the same proxy server for all protocols** check box.

8. If you regularly need to connect to a computer on your local network, you don't need to access that machine through the proxy server. Enter the machine's name (and any other computers' names to which you need to connect) or IP address in the Exceptions text box.

9. Click **OK** to close the Proxy Settings, Local Area Network (LAN) Settings, and Internet Options dialog boxes in succession and return to the Internet Explorer window.

10. Connect to a remote Web site, such as *www.cengage.com/coursetechnology*. When you connect to the Internet through your proxy server, what message appears in your browser's status bar?

11. Exit Internet Explorer and return to the Windows desktop.

Project 7-3: Test Proxy Server Network Address Translation (NAT)

This project assumes that you have one workstation in your lab that is running NetProxy and at least one other workstation that has a network connection to it. For the purposes of this project, we refer to the remote workstation as the "Remote Machine" and the one with the proxy software as the "Proxy Machine."

1. Start the Remote Machine and its associated firewall software. Set up logon auditing on the Remote Machine. (Make sure you activate account logon auditing.)

2. Start the Proxy Machine.

3. Make sure NetProxy is running on the Proxy Machine. To verify this, click **Start**, point to **Programs** (**All Programs** in Windows XP), point to **NetProxy**, and click **NetProxy Configuration**.

4. In the NetProxy window, click the **Enable/Disable NetProxy** button. The message "NetProxy is running" should appear in the status bar of the NetProxy window.

5. Make note of the Proxy Machine's IP address.

6. Log on to the Remote Machine from the Proxy Machine. (Usually, when you attempt to access a shared folder on the remote machine, you are prompted to log on, unless automatic logon has been enabled.)

7. Switch to the Remote Machine. View this machine's event log by clicking **Start** and clicking **Control Panel**. (In Windows 2000, click **Start**, point to **Settings**, and then click **Control Panel**.)

8. Double-click **Administrative Tools** to open the Administrative Tools window.

9. Double-click **Event Viewer** to display the Event Viewer Management Console.

10. In the left half of the Event Viewer, click **Security**.

11. Make a note of the logon from the remote computer. What machine is identified as having logged on? Record the result in your lab notebook or a word-processing program.

Running Case Projects

In this exercise, you add proxy server features to your firewall. Specifically, you learn how to:

- Configure and enable Vyatta's proxy server to manage Web requests
- Use Vyatta's blacklist and whitelist capabilities to allow or deny specific Web site requests

Student Tasks

First, we will modify the existing firewall rule set to handle the addition of traffic to and from the proxy server.

1. Log in to the Vyatta interface via the command line using "vyatta" as the username and the password you created in Chapter 4.

2. Enter **configure** and press **Enter** to enter configuration mode.

3. Enter **set firewall name eth1_local rule 20 action accept** and press **Enter**.

4. Enter **set firewall name eth1_local rule 20 description "Allow webproxy traffic through"** and press **Enter**.

5. Enter **set firewall name eth1_local rule 20 destination address** *IP address of internal NIC* and press **Enter**.

6. Enter **set firewall name eth1_local rule 20 state new enable** and press **Enter**.

7. Enter **set firewall name eth1_local rule 20 state established enable** and press **Enter**.

8. Enter **set firewall name eth1_local rule 20 state related enable** and press **Enter**.

9. Enter **set firewall name eth0_local rule 10 action accept** and press **Enter**.

10. Enter **set firewall name eth0_local rule 10 description "Allow webproxy traffic through"** and press **Enter**.

11. Enter **set firewall name eth0_local rule 10 protocol tcp** and press **Enter**.

12. Enter **set firewall name eth0_local rule 10 source port 80,443** and press **Enter**.

13. Enter **set firewall name eth0_local rule 10 destination address** *IP address of external NIC* and press **Enter**.

14. Enter **set firewall name eth0_local rule 10 state established enable** and press **Enter**.

15. Enter **set firewall name eth0_local rule 10 state related enable** and press **Enter**.

16. Enter **set firewall name eth0_local rule 20 action accept** and press **Enter**.

17. Enter **set firewall name eth0_local rule 20 description "Allow webproxy DNS requests"** and press **Enter**.

18. Enter **set firewall name eth0_local rule 20 protocol udp** and press **Enter**.

19. Enter **set firewall name eth0_local rule 20 source address** *IP address of DNS server* and press **Enter**.

20. Enter **set firewall name eth0_local rule 20 source port 53** and press **Enter**.

21. Enter **set firewall name eth0_local rule 20 destination address** *IP address of external NIC* and press **Enter**.

22. Enter **set firewall name eth0_local rule 20 state established enable** and press **Enter**.

23. Enter **set firewall name eth0_local rule 20 state related enable** and press **Enter**.

24. Enter **commit** and press **Enter** to commit the changes to memory.

25. Enter **save** and press **Enter** to permanently write the changes to the system.

Now, we will configure and enable the proxy server to manage Web requests. Note that, by default, Vyatta disables Web traffic by IP address, so we do not have to concern ourselves with that.

26. Enter **set service webproxy listen-address** *Internal NIC IP address* and press **Enter**.

27. Enter **set service webproxy url-filtering squidguard redirect-url** "http://*Internal NIC IP address*/cgi-bin/squidGuard-simple.cgi?targetclass=%t&url=%u" and press **Enter**. This command returns an error message to the user when a restricted Web site is requested. Note that the Vyatta command line may trap the question mark when you type it, offering you the help menu. If this happens, press **CTRL+v**, and then press the question mark (**?**) key.

28. Enter **commit** and press **Enter** to commit the changes.

Organizations have to make a fundamental decision regarding proxied traffic in general: do we allow all requests and block specific sites (blacklist), or do we deny all requests and allow specific sites (whitelist)? Vyatta can handle either approach through the use of the default-action command, using either the allow or the block option.

First, we will create a blacklist, and then deny access to the Facebook Web site.

29. Enter **set service webproxy url-filtering squidguard default-action allow** and press **Enter**.

30. Enter **set service webproxy url-filtering squidguard local-block facebook.com** and press **Enter**. Enter **commit** and press **Enter** to commit the changes.

Open up a Web browser on a system in the trusted network and visit a Web site other than Facebook. You will see that your browsing is not interfered with in any way. Now attempt to visit the Facebook Web site. Your request will be denied, with an error page being returned to your browser. You can add as many domain names to the blacklist as you need to, simply by repeating the local-block command used in step 30, replacing facebook.com with the domain name to be blocked.

Now, we will step through the process of creating a whitelist proxy server that will deny all Web traffic except for those Web sites specifically permitted.

31. Enter **delete service webproxy url-filtering** and press **Enter** to delete the existing URL-filtering configuration.

32. Enter **commit** to commit the changes to the production environment.

33. Enter **set service webproxy url-filtering squidguard redirect-url** "http://*Internal NIC IP address*/cgi-bin/squidGuard-simple.cgi?targetclass=%t&url=%u" and press **Enter**. This command returns an error message to the user when a restricted Web site is requested. Note that the Vyatta command line may trap the question mark when you type it, offering you the help menu. If this happens, press **CTRL+v**, and then press the question mark (**?**) key.

34. Enter **set service webproxy url-filtering squidguard default-action block** and press **Enter**.

35. Enter **commit** and press **Enter** to commit the changes to the production environment.

Visit *www.kennesaw.edu* using a Web browser on the internal, trusted network. As you will see, the traffic is denied by the proxy server because of the rule we committed in step 35. To demonstrate the effectiveness of a whitelist, we will now step through the process of creating a whitelist entry to allow Web traffic to a specific site.

36. Enter **set service webproxy url-filtering squidguard local-ok kennesaw.edu** and press **Enter**.

37. Enter **set service webproxy url-filtering squidguard local-ok google.com** and press **Enter**.

38. Enter **commit** and press **Enter** to commit the changes to the production environment.

39. Enter **save** and press **Enter** to make the changes permanent.

Visit *www.kennesaw.edu* again. Now, we are able to view the content on the KSU Web site because of the whitelist entry. To further test, visit *www.google.com* and search for "vyatta." Google will return search results, but what happens when you click any of those links?

chapter 8

Implementing the Bastion Host

After reading this chapter and completing the exercises, you will be able to:

- Describe the general requirements for installing a bastion host
- Select the optimal attributes—memory, processor speed, and operating system—for the bastion host
- Evaluate different options for positioning the bastion host, both physically and within the network
- Discuss critical components of the bastion host configuration
- Explain how to provide for backups of the bastion host operating system and data
- Establish a baseline performance level and audit procedures

Running Case: Dealing with Intruders

Rachel looked over Alex's shoulder at the firewall he was configuring. "Looks good!" she said. Alex leaned back in his chair, thankful that the long configuration session was almost over. It had literally been hours of poring over the various configuration menus, options, and settings. Under Rachel's expert tutelage, he had come a long way. "We're almost done?" he asked.

"Yep, a few more settings and we're ready to add the IDPS," Rachel replied. "Then you can test it and put it online."

"So this intrusion system you're talking about will detect and respond to various attacks to this firewall?" Alex asked, looking over at Rachel. He finally understood the foundations of the bastion firewall he was setting up, but he didn't fully grasp the need for another piece of software. "I thought you said we needed to strip this bastion firewall down to the bare bones, not load it up with unnecessary software. Doesn't the firewall itself monitor the network?"

"The firewall monitors its own activities, but it can't really detect advanced attacks," Rachel said. "It will work in cooperation with the Intrusion Detection and Prevention System that's running on the same hardware to detect advanced network attacks coming through the data stream, as well as host-based attacks aimed at the firewall itself." She pointed to the screen. "Between the two, you'll not only know that the network perimeter is secure, you'll know what it's doing to protect you. We find that once a firewall solution is successful and things quiet down, management begins to wonder about the ongoing costs of maintenance and support if there's no activity. These systems not only protect the network, they collect data on how they're protecting the network."

"I heard that!"

Rachel turned to see Meghan walking in the room, a smile on her face. "And on behalf of management," Meghan said, "I assure you that these systems will be fully funded as long as they are needed, which I estimate to be forever!"

Introduction

The effectiveness of a network security configuration depends on many things, and one of them is the bastion host that runs the firewall software or other services on the network perimeter. A **bastion host** is a system specifically designed and implemented to withstand attacks. The term **bastion** comes from a thirteenth-century French word meaning "a structure projecting outward from the main enclosure of a fortification, situated in both corners of a straight wall, facilitating active defense against assaulting troops."[1] Bastions are usually placed in the demilitarized zone (DMZ) or outside the firewall and thus must withstand direct assault from external attackers.

With the popularity of Virtual Private Networks (VPNs) discussed in Chapters 9 and 10, organizations are increasingly using the Internet for private communications. The need to position organizational data for external access requires protected archives and systems.

When serving as the host for the company's Web server, the bastion host is the organization's public face on the Internet. Because it is highly exposed on the network perimeter, a bastion host needs to be highly secured. Setting up a bastion host requires the administrator to be systematic and thorough to a higher degree than on internal systems; backups, detailed record keeping, and auditing are essential steps. In the pages that follow, you'll learn more about bastion hosts, specifically the factors to take into consideration when selecting a host machine, possible locations for the bastion host, and how to decide what functions the host should perform.

Installing a Bastion Host: General Requirements

A bastion host can be any server that hosts a Web server, e-mail server, FTP server, or other network service. However, it typically provides only one service because, as more services are offered on the bastion host, there's a greater chance that security vulnerabilities will exist in the installed applications and services.

The bastion host should present intruders with only a minimal set of resources and open ports; this bare-bones configuration reduces the chances of attack and has the extra benefit of boosting efficiency. The fewer the resources and openings on the system, the more secure the host. A simple, bare-bones server may not be what the management of your own organization has in mind, however—at least initially. You're likely to receive a request from management to "install a strong bastion host to keep out hackers." More likely, the words "bastion host" won't be used at all; you'll simply be directed to "install a firewall and keep the Web server secure." The bastion hosts don't need to contain the latest and most expensive processor/memory combinations, however. The most important requirements for a bastion host, instead, are your own level of comfort with the system, its security, and its reliability. In general, the steps you need to follow to secure a bastion host can be broken down as follows:

1. Obtain a machine with sufficient memory and processor speed.
2. Choose and install the operating system.
3. Determine where the host will fit in the network configuration and put it in a safe and controlled physical environment.
4. Enable the host to defend itself.
5. Install the services to provide or modify existing services.
6. Remove any and all services and accounts that aren't needed.
7. Back up the system and all data on it, including log files.
8. Run a security audit.
9. Connect the machine to the network.

These are the steps that will be detailed in the sections that follow. Throughout the process, you'll develop the highest level of security if you adopt an approach that can be described as "healthy paranoia." Assume that you will be attacked, that you don't know where the attack will come from, and that you cannot trust even resources with which you are familiar.

As described in earlier chapters, the concept of defense in depth requires hardening the system at multiple levels to minimize the possibility of intrusion. When moving data from the bastion host to other computers inside your network, that information will go through some of those layers. It's likely that, as described later in this chapter, because of its high security configuration, your bastion host will be placed in a particularly vulnerable location on the Demilitarized Zone and outside the internal LAN. The **Demilitarized Zone (DMZ)** is a no-man's-land between the inside and outside networks that serves as a buffer against outside attacks; it is also where some organizations place their Web servers. Log file and system data, which need to be backed up regularly, should go through the firewall that protects the internal LAN to screen them for viruses and other vulnerabilities.

As described in earlier chapters, sometimes the firewall residing in the DMZ isn't a single bastion host but more of a bastion subnet or screened subnet. By dividing key responsibilities among multiple systems—each a bastion host in its own right—we can reduce the number of tasks a single system must handle. Remember the KISS principle: Keep It Simple, Stupid!

Selecting the Host Machine

Choose a combination of machine type and software with which you are familiar and on which you can work easily if you need to. You don't want to be repairing or rebuilding a machine under pressure while learning how to operate it.

Do You Need More Than One Machine?

First, decide whether you need more than one bastion host on the perimeter. It's ideal to have one service on each bastion host, but this means that if you have a firewall program, a Web server, an FTP server, a DNS server, and an SMTP server on the perimeter, you would have to obtain and configure five separate bastion hosts. For many organizations, this isn't practical. The cost of obtaining multiple hosts might well be prohibitive. On the other hand, the risk of losing proprietary information might make it worth the expenditure.

When you're analyzing the cost of one or more bastion hosts, it's often a good idea to conduct a comprehensive risk analysis of all the resources in your organization. Even if your own company may not be able to lay out sizeable expenditures on separate hardware devices to protect every segment of your network topology, you should ask management to at least conduct a threat assessment that identifies the most valuable information you have—the information that needs to be protected by the proper bastion host or other hardware. Refer to the list of network resources you used to develop a security policy in Chapter 2. Note that you'll have to perform the usual balancing act between cost-effectiveness and security. You should get as many bastion hosts as you can afford in order to maximize security. On the other hand, you can combine two or more services on the bastion host if you need to save money.

Memory Considerations

RAM is always important when operating a server, but because the bastion host may be providing only a single service on the network, you aren't likely to need multiterabytes worth of RAM. Don't forget that, in addition to the services you provide on the bastion host, you'll probably need to operate a program that maintains, rotates (i.e., moves the current log file to a storage area and opens a new log file), and clears outdated log files. With the costs of RAM dropping on a regular basis, however, you should be able to set up a robust system with sufficient memory at a reasonable price. At the time of this printing, the industry standard for bastion host memory is between 4 GB and 8 GB of RAM at an estimated $50 to $75 per gigabyte, depending on the speed, size, and manufacturer of the memory.

Hard disk storage space should be in the multiterabyte category because you'll be accumulating vast quantities of **log files**—records detailing who accessed resources on the server and when the access attempts occurred. You'll need to review and analyze this information either manually or by making use of log file analysis software. You should also create a page file on your hard disk so that you can make use of additional memory, if needed. Currently, hard drives for rack-mounted servers range from $250 to $750 per terabyte, depending on the manufacturer, form factor (2.5" versus 3.5"), and drive speed (e.g., 7200 rpm versus 1000 rpm).

Processor Speed

Processor speed is the rate at which the logic circuitry or microprocessor within a computing device processes the basic instructions that make the device operate. You can check your computer's system information for the clock speed of your processor, which may be called the Central Processing Unit (CPU). Clock speed is expressed in GHz (gigahertz) and includes a cache speed descriptor, expressed in MHz (megahertz). Most computer systems have at least three independent caches: an **instruction cache** to speed up the processing of executable instructions, a **data cache** to speed up the retrieval and storage of stored data, and a **translation lookaside buffer** used to speed up the translation of virtual-to-physical address for both data and instructions.[2] An example of a current processor is the Intel Xeon X5570 Quad Core 2.93 GHz, 8 MB Cache, HT, 1333 MHz, meaning the processor itself runs at 2.93 GHz, with an 8 MB cache and requiring 1333 MHz memory modules. The HT stands for Hyper-Threading, Intel's proprietary multithreading function implemented in its processors. For each physical core processor (there are four present in this example), there are two virtual processors that can multithread instructions.

Because the bastion host is integral to network security, you should obtain a machine with the fastest processor you can afford. Keep in mind that the speed of the machine doesn't depend solely on the type or number of processors within it. The speed of a computer's operation on a network is also a factor of available bandwidth; a fast computer won't be able to move traffic quickly if the speed of its own Internet connection is slow.

Some security administrators believe that a slower machine used as a bastion host actually helps to deter would-be attackers because a slower machine, when it's at work, doesn't have as many resources sitting unused as a faster machine. If resources aren't available, a hacker cannot exploit them. In the real world, this doesn't mean that you should look for a slow, outdated computer to function as a bastion host; rather, it means that to keep costs down or to be able to afford multiple bastion hosts, you don't necessarily have to look for the most expensive or full-featured computer. If you are running a Web server on a bastion host, by all means get the fastest processor you can afford, so that the server will operate more smoothly and quickly on the network.

As more firewalls are required to add Secure Sockets Layer (SSL) encryption to their lists of features, as described in earlier chapters, processor speed will become even more critical so that the firewall doesn't add latency (i.e., delay) to the network.

Choosing the Operating System

Where the bastion host operating system is concerned, the most important consideration is your own familiarity with the system. If you are a UNIX person, choose UNIX, and likewise for Linux and Windows. The supervisors in your organization aren't necessarily going to concern themselves with what operating system you install: their priority is that you are able to get the machine that protects the internal network up and running and that you can maintain it smoothly.

UNIX and Linux Hosts

UNIX is the most popular operating system used to provide services on the Internet. It contains an extensive set of software tools for development and auditing, and there is plenty of online documentation explaining how to configure the various varieties.

The security patches you install must correspond to the operating system you choose. If you are using HP-UX, install HP-UX security patches; for AIX, install AIX patches, and so on. Installing security patches is no small undertaking. You might have six, eight, or even a dozen to install. It can also be time consuming and demanding to keep up with new patches as they come out. However, you can do this by visiting the operating system manufacturer's Web site on a periodic basis to check for the release of such patches. You may also want to install supplemental security software, such as TCP Wrapper and SSH.

You also need to enable logging through the **syslog** daemon, which is a standard for logging program messages; be sure to configure syslog to record messages to files. It's also useful to pick a version of UNIX that includes a utility called **chkconfig**, which reports on the services that are currently started; you can check the list of services to see if all of them are absolutely necessary or whether they should be stopped.

Windows Hosts

Windows Server 2003 and 2008 are also excellent choices for bastion host operating systems because of their reliability and widespread use as servers. If your network already uses Windows, the choice of Windows for the bastion host is a natural one.

If you plan to run Windows Server 2003 or 2008 on a bastion host that is intended to function solely as a Web server, you should download and use the Security Compliance Manager, available directly from Microsoft (*http://technet.microsoft.com/en-us/library/cc677002.aspx*). The SCM will provide a baseline configuration specifically designed for high-risk environments like bastion hosts. This application also standardizes the configuration so you can set up multiple systems identically, which is critical for creating a backup or secondary bastion host. You should also make sure the NetBIOS interface, Server service, and Workstation service are disabled, as they are not needed. Also be sure to set up logging for the following events: account logon and logoff, object access, policy changes, privilege use, and system events (restart and shutdown). Most of these options will be preset in the SCM baseline.

Keep Your Operating System Updated

Whatever system you decide on, be sure to pick a version of that system that is stable and secure. You can check the following locations for updates to your operating system:

- Windows Server (Start button, All Programs, Windows Update)
- Red Hat Linux (*www.redhat.com*)
- Linux Home Page (*www.linux.org*)
- The FreeBSD Project (*www.freebsd.org*)
- The SANS Institute's list of the Top Twenty Most Critical Internet Security Vulnerabilities, which includes subsections on UNIX and Windows vulnerabilities (*www.sans.org/top20.htm*)
- The U.S. Department of Energy's Cyber Incident Response Capability (DOE-CIRC) site (*http://doecirc.energy.gov*), which lists newly discovered security advisories right on its home page

You should observe extreme caution when using automatic updating. While it is a valuable tool for desktop use, most organizations prefer to evaluate, test, and batch updates for critical systems like online production servers. This prevents a new patch from creating a new vulnerability.

Along with making sure your bastion host's operating system has the latest patches installed, make sure your system of choice can reliably provide the services you want to make available on the public DMZ.

Table 8-1 shows the configuration of a standard high-end and a standard mid-range corporate server (*Note:* These recommendations are sized to current practices circa 2011):

High-End 2U Server ($15,000–$20,000)	Mid-Range 1U Server ($5,000–$10,000)
Chassis with room for up to eight hot swap hard drives	Quad Core Intel® Xeon X3323, 2.5 GHz, 2x3M Cache, 1333 MHz FSB
Processor (single or dual) Intel Xeon 2.66 GHz, 12M Cache, Turbo, HT, 1066 MHz, MaX Mem	8 GB DDR2, 667 MHz, 4x2 GB, dual ranked DIMMs
16 GB memory (4x4 GB) 1066 MHz, dual ranked UDIMS for two processors	Windows Server 2008 SP2, Standard includes Hyper V™
Windows Server 2008 SP2 or Red Hat Enterprise Linux	Red Hat Enterprise Linux 5.3
RAID 1, RAID 5 for PERC6i controllers, x8 chassis	Add-in SAS6iR (SATA/SAS controller) that supports 2 HD – RAID 0
PERC6i controller, PERC battery with PERC, SAS 6/iR Hot Plug 8HD	Onboard dual gigabit network adapter
Eight – 2 TB 7.2 RPM SATA 3.5 in HotPlug hard drive	DVD +/-RW drive, internal, SATA
750-watt nonredundant power supply	2x 500 GB 7.2K RPM Serial ATA 3 Gbps, 3.5-in Cabled HD
Baseboard management controller	
Broadcom 5709 Dual Port 1GbE NIC w/TOE iSCSI, PCIe-4	
DVD +/-RW, SATA Internal	
Optional: VMware VIEW Enterprise installation to enable server virtualization	Optional: VMware VIEW Enterprise installation to enable server virtualization

Table 8-1 Corporate Server Configurations

Positioning the Bastion Host

Bastion hosts sit on the perimeter of the network. They should provide a buffer between the Internet and the internal network that is being protected. That much is straightforward, but beyond that, you do have several options for locating the host, both physically and logically, within the network configuration.

Physical Location

The physical location of a bastion host is often overlooked in the process of configuring and installing it. The physical location is defined as the exact building and room in which the device is located. The room itself should be properly ventilated, with adequate cooling and a backup power system. If your organization has a specially designated server room with all the proper environmental controls (sprinklers and air conditioning) as well as the required physical security devices (deadbolt locks and alarm systems), then this is where the bastion host should be physically located. If, on the other hand, your organization does not have an isolated server room available, then at the very least, the bastion host and other critical servers should be located in a locked server cabinet that has proper ventilation and cooling and that has backup power available.

Many companies decide to co-locate Web servers and other bastion hosts off-site. Co-location occurs when a company physically hosts its server(s) in a data center that is managed by a third party. Co-location can result in greater security and improved network uptime (the time the server is online). Companies that specialize in hosting services are protected against storms and other natural disasters. They also have electrical backup systems that can keep them online in case of power outages.

Many hosting services are available. Because some are more secure than others, selecting a hosting service should not be undertaken lightly or too quickly. Be sure to get references, and get reports on the hosting service's uptime, backup resources, environmental and security protection, and everything else about the reliability of the company. The hosting service must be able to adhere to the company's stated security, legal, and regulatory requirements. How do you determine whether a host is able to meet those requirements? Here are some specific suggestions:

- Do research and ask questions. Get an idea of the host's track record—how long it has been around. Are there any financial warning signs, such as layoffs or other cutbacks?

- Pin the hosting service down on all the startup fees it is going to charge as well as other fees that might come as a surprise. The contract you sign with the host should outline additional monthly fees for data backup and recovery (often these items are included in the main fee). Also, make sure you understand whether there will be any fees for help-desk support and any fees for placing support calls to the host.

- Get a Service-Level Agreement (SLA), a document that defines an agreed-upon level of service that the host will provide, and adjust it to fit your needs. A good SLA serves as a complete. service agreement. It should address availability, response time, reliability, and monthly fees.

- Do a risk-benefit analysis. Try to quantify what you'll gain by outsourcing—how much staff time or money you will save by hiring a hosting service. Also, try to estimate how much it would cost to perform the desired function in-house.

- Ask for references. Talk to current customers; in addition, try to locate any independent software vendors (ISVs). ISVs provide hosting services and the software they then lease to end users like you. These ISVs are good places to turn for references on hosting services.

- Shop around. It's not uncommon for companies to solicit information from a dozen or more hosting services and then request full proposals from five of those companies.

Contracts typically range from 12 to 36 months, although they can be even longer. Don't get sucked into signing a long-term contract unless you're really sure of the hosting service's future.

On the downside, co-locating makes it more complicated for the administrator, who has to configure and maintain the bastion host remotely. It also extends the network perimeter into the domain of the company that is hosting the bastion host. Theoretically, this should be a highly secure network, but because it's not *your* network, you don't have ultimate control over the security measures it employs.

Network Location

A DMZ is a network of publicly accessible servers, such as Web and FTP servers, that is connected to the firewall, but that is isolated from the internal network to protect internal users from intrusions and attacks. Because it has been specially secured and is prepared to defend itself against attacks, the logical location for a bastion host is in the highly vulnerable public DMZ, as shown in Figure 8-1.

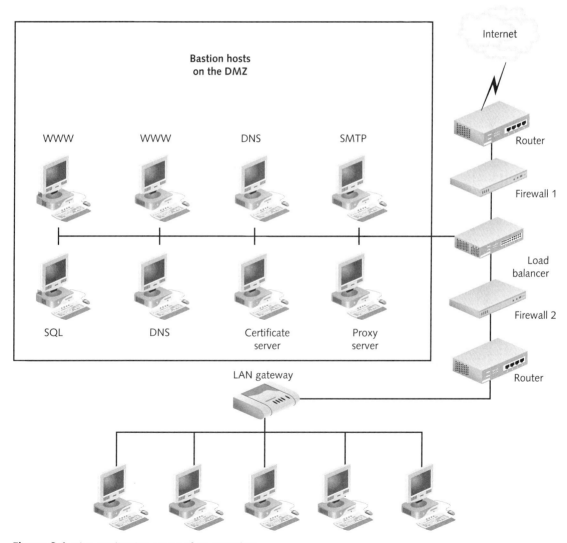

Figure 8-1 The Application Layer of an IP Packet
© Cengage Learning 2012

A bastion host can, however, be located at any point in a network that is considered vulnerable or where an extra level of security is needed. A bastion host should be part of a strategy of Defense in Depth, which calls for a network to be hardened at many different levels. Accordingly, a single hardened bastion host that is placed on the DMZ should not be relied on as the sole source of security for a network. All servers or other components of the DMZ (such as routers) should be secured as well. Ideally, if one machine in the DMZ suffers a security breach, the entire DMZ will not be compromised, only weakened, and the internal network will not be compromised, either.

Securing the Machine Itself

When you install a bastion host, you need to take special steps to protect it, both physically and in terms of the operating system. If you have an extra workstation available, consider using it as a spare server that you can connect to the network in case of disaster. Having spare equipment available is only one small-scale strategy that forms part of an organization's disaster recovery plan. Other aspects of such a plan include:

- How often you back up data, either on the bastion hosts or other hosts
- How to securely store data off-site
- Where to find temporary office space in case of disaster (ideally, you should arrange for such space before the disaster occurs)
- Hardware/software insurance you might need
- How often to test your disaster program

The availability of bastion hosts is just one aspect of disaster recovery. Strategies for data backup and recovery have to weigh the budgetary demands against the techniques (such as co-location and contracting businesses that specialize in data recovery) that can help a company get back online after a natural disaster or terrorist attack.

Hardening a Windows or Linux Server
While beyond the scope of this text, there are several online references that an industrious systems administrator can access when facing the need to harden (secure) an OS. For hardening Windows products, Microsoft hosts podcasts and TechNet discussion boards at *www.microsoft.com/events/podcasts/default .aspx* and *technet.microsoft.com*. Similarly, several vendors like IBM have support sites that promote best practices in hardening various Linux distributions—for example, *www.ibm.com/ developerworks/linux/* and *www.linux-sec.net*.

Selecting a Secure Location

Because of its prominent role in the network security configuration, you should not leave the bastion host out in the middle of an office or in a high-traffic area. It should be located in a room to which only a limited number of individuals have access. Ideally, it will be protected by an alarm system that has a battery backup and that is connected to a central alarm service that can notify the police in case of trouble. Rack-mounting servers in a lockable cabinet with security screws will provide even more protection.

Set up a password-protected screen saver on the bastion host and configure it with a short time delay so that the screen saver switches on quickly after you finish working on the machine. Use a blank screen saver, which consumes fewer resources than an animated one.

Installing the Operating System Securely

Sometimes, the most vulnerable part of a computer (regardless of whether it functions as a bastion host) is the operating system. When it comes to securing a bastion host, securing the operating system that is to run on that host is one of the most important activities you can undertake. In terms of the operating system, even if the machine comes with an operating system installed, you may want to reinstall an operating system you consider to be more secure and do so with a minimum configuration. For instance, if the installation disk gives you the option of a stripped-down installation, such as the HP-UX option "64-Bit Minimal HP-UX (English Only)," you should choose it. This option bypasses the installation of X-Windows and other unneeded items or services.

On a Windows bastion host, consider creating two partitions: one for the operating system (this should be the C: drive) and one for the Web server, DNS server, or other software you plan to run on the host (this could be the D: drive or another drive). To create a partition, you need to have administrator status on the computer. You can then open Computer Management, click Disk Management, right-click the unallocated region of a disk drive (if there is one) you want to partition, and click New Partition. Then follow the steps shown in the New Partition Wizard. (Note that if there is no unallocated space on the disk drive, the New Partition option will not appear.)

Use only the NTFS file system for file storage, because NTFS security features, such as auditing and permission-level protection, are not available on FAT file systems. Install only the most essential components, such as the Microsoft Management Console, Data Sources, and so forth.

Reinstalling the system is time consuming, but when you do the installation yourself from scratch, you gain a great deal of control and can decide exactly what you want to install.

Virus protection software should certainly be included on a bastion host.

A DNS server that is located on a bastion host in the DMZ should be configured to prohibit unauthorized zone transfers. This is usually done by default. A zone transfer (also known as AXFR) allows DNS database duplication and replication. It is a response to a DNS query for all DNS information for a domain. Since a zone transfer is one of the mechanisms that primary and secondary DNS Name servers use to update their data, an attacker can use the information to "scope out" a network and/or inject poisoned or spoofed information into a server.

Documenting Your Work

It's important to document the steps you go through to secure the machine and locate backups, Emergency Recovery Disks, and so forth. Why? If there's a system crash, you want to be able to move quickly to get the host up and running again. You don't want to consume valuable time looking for such resources. You also want to make it easy for other personnel to do the repair work if you're not there when the problem occurs. To document your work, prepare a simple word-processed document. Consider giving the document a title that will quickly tell your co-workers exactly what it contains, such as "Steps to Follow in Case a Bastion Host Crashes."

Make sure your instructions include the following information:

- Name and location of the bastion host
- The bastion host's IP address and domain name
- Bastion host operating system
- Location of backup files

- What to do in case the system crashes
- The levels of the patches (if any) that have been made to the bastion host's operating system
- Any customized scripts that have been developed to support the host

Also document how you decided which services to install on each bastion host. If you can't install a single service on each host, state why you grouped the services as you did. Important services (such as HTTP) should go on one host, whereas less important services (such as chat) should go on another. Put trusted services on one bastion host, and allocate the others to services that are less trusted.

Configuring Your Bastion Host

A security policy becomes important when deciding what role the bastion host will play. Look to your security policy to determine which resources need to be protected and which threats need to be addressed. A policy that puts an emphasis on connectivity will result in a host that has a minimum of services. For instance, consider a policy that advocates a more restrictive deny-all approach (an approach in which the firewall will block everything by default and specifically allow only those services you need on a case-by-case basis). Such an approach might call for the bastion host to function as a proxy server—a server that conceals hosts on the internal LAN by processing requests on their behalf.

The following sections describe some of the important aspects of configuring a bastion host.

Making the Host Defend Itself

Some organizations set up a **honeypot** server—a machine that is placed in the DMZ to attract hackers and direct them away from the servers being protected. It is supposed to be bait that is used to catch hackers. A honeypot is configured the same as a normal bastion host, and it appears to be a real network server containing Web, FTP, or DNS services, but it is not connected to any other machines on the network, and it does not contain any files of any value. If the honeypot machine is compromised, the rest of the DMZ—as well as the internal LAN—should remain secure. A honeypot bastion host is also referred to as a "victim machine" or a "sacrificial goat."

Some security professionals advise against using honeypots, arguing that they may attract as many attackers as they deflect. Intrusion detection and prevention systems, properly configured and implemented on the bastion host and other systems, can serve to notify you or the IT staff of possible intrusion attempts. You have a number of options for installing an IDPS system. You can place a host-based IDPS system, such as Tripwire (*www.tripwire.com*), directly on the host itself, or you can place a network-based IDS, such as Snort (*www.snort.org*), on the firewall or router that protects the bastion hosts in the DMZ.

Selecting Services to Be Provided

When you perform a fresh installation of the operating system, you have the opportunity to choose services that you'll need, such as the primary service or services, a backup utility, logging, and the like. Whether the primary service you want to run on the bastion host is a Web server, FTP server, e-mail server, or proxy server, make sure the server software is the latest version. Also make sure you install any security patches or updates that are available. Table 8-2 provides the URLs for various operating systems.

Operating System	URL
Linux	*www.linux.org*
Debian Linux	*www.debian.org*
Fedora Linux	*http://fedoraproject.org*
Red Hat Linux	*www.redhat.com*
SUSE—Commercial	*www.novell.com/linux/*
SUSE—Open	*www.opensuse.org*
Ubuntu Linux	*www.ubuntu.com*
IBM AIX	*www-03.ibm.com/systems/power/software/aix/index.html*
HP-UX	*http://h71028.www7.hp.com/enterprise/w1/en/os/hpux11i-overview.html*
Oracle Solaris	*www.oracle.com/us/products/servers-storage/solaris/index.html*
Windows Server 2003	*www.microsoft.com/windowsserver2003/default.mspx*
Windows Server 2008	*www.microsoft.com/windowsserver2008/en/us/default.aspx*

8

Table 8-2 URLs for Various Operating Systems

Whenever you install software on the bastion host, observe extreme caution; make sure you are using the latest available version of the software and that any security patches have been added to the program. For an extra measure of safety, you should consider installing the software on another workstation first to ensure that the product is secure.

Special Considerations for UNIX Systems

UNIX uses a utility called **security_patch_check**, which automates the process of analyzing security patches that are already on the system and reports patches that should be added. You should become very familiar with this utility.

On a UNIX host, you should run a **Trusted Computing Base (TCB)** check, a set of software programs that makes sure any software you're running on your system is a trusted program. You should also consider enabling some sort of system logging. On UNIX, enable inetd logging if you plan to run the inetd daemon on the server.

Log files are likely to take up a lot of room on the bastion host, and yet they are essential to monitoring network security. Be sure to provide sufficient room for log files to grow, and increase log file buffer size as much as possible. Keep in mind that a central logging server can be set up to handle logging for all critical servers on the network. Typically, a central logging server is a secure system with an extra-large storage capacity. It gives you a central location from which to search all log files for malicious activity.

Special Considerations for Windows Systems

If you are configuring a bastion host using Windows Server software, you should make use of two utilities that Microsoft has provided to help harden the systems. Microsoft Baseline Security Analyzer performs an analysis of the current Windows configuration. It identifies hotfixes and patches that are necessary and isolates vulnerabilities such as open "Guest" accounts and anonymous connections being enabled. Running the Baseline Security Analyzer after you do a clean install of the operating system on the bastion host is a good way to identify obvious vulnerabilities. Another piece of software, the Microsoft Security Assessment Tool (MSAT), allows system owners to tap into a large knowledge base of details about vulnerabilities and get advice from vendor and security experts on how to make specific Microsoft operating systems and layered products like databases and Web servers more secure.[3]

Disabling Accounts

As with most operating systems and application software, default accounts may be created during installation. Accordingly, you should delete all user accounts from the bastion host. They aren't needed because individual users should not be able to connect to the host from their workstations. Each user account on the bastion host increases the chances of a security breach.

Another way to deter hackers is to rename the administrator account. Many hackers are able to gain access to computers through administrator accounts that use the default account name "Administrator" and that are never assigned a password. Renaming such accounts and using passwords that contain at least eight alphanumeric characters, plus at least one numeric or special character, can prevent these attacks.

Disabling Unnecessary Services

One of the most important bastion host configuration tasks is the elimination of unnecessary services. These services (such as FTP, Telnet, or SMTP) listen on open ports that can provide hackers with entry points. Perhaps the most important services you should disable are those that enable the host to do routing or IP forwarding—unless, of course, the host is intended to function as a router. Also, take out hardware features you won't use, such as unneeded USB or FireWire connections. However, you may have to include some capacity to write data to an external or network drive or a DVD-RW to make a binary disk image of the bastion host, as described later in this chapter.

Table 8-3 lists the services and features that a network administrator should typically disable for UNIX and Windows systems.

Obviously, when you are stopping or removing services, you should not disable any **dependency services**—services that the system needs to function correctly. It's advisable to stop services one at a time. Each time a service is stopped, test the system to make sure it still functions properly by opening an application, copying a file, or performing another simple task. If the system runs slowly or fails to perform the task, you need to restore the service you disabled most recently. On the other hand, if the system continues to work correctly after you disable a service, don't simply move on to the next one; get in the habit of documenting every single change you make and recording how the system reacts so that you have a record you can call upon in case you have to troubleshoot that same system at a later date.

Be sure to disable any routing services on the bastion host because routing can be exploited by intruders. Any routing services that enable the bastion hosts to direct traffic to hosts on the internal network represent a security weakness. In addition, pay special attention to services that cannot be disabled. You'll have to leave them running, but make a list of such dependency services so that you can check them first in case of trouble.

UNIX Hosts	Windows Hosts
All services from within /etc/inetd.conf	Guest access account
All accounts except Administrator	All accounts except Administrator
Links to any startup scripts in the /etc/rc.d directories that start network services	Sample scripts for Internet Information Server (IIS), located in the iissamples folder in the inetpub folder; delete only if you plan to run bastion host as a Web server running IIS; otherwise disable IIS altogether
The X window system	The %SystemRoot%\system32/os2 folder
The PPP-RUN fileset	These unnecessary files in the system32 folder: %SystemRoot%\system32\ntvdm.exe %SystemRoot%\system32\krnl386.exe %SystemRoot%\system32\psxdll.dll %SystemRoot%\system32\psxss.exe %SystemRoot%\system32\posix.exe %SystemRoot%\system32\os2.exe
Any network services except those you will be running on the bastion host	Any network services except those you will be running on the bastion host
SNMP daemons; you may not be able to completely remove these daemons, but you can disable them	
The swagentd (SD-UX) daemon	
The sendmail daemon; disable only if you don't plan to run mail services on the bastion host	
The rpcbind daemon; disable only if you don't plan to run RPC services	

Table 8-3 Services and Features to Disable on a Bastion Host

Limiting Ports

For reasons that should be obvious (you want to eliminate as many points of entry to hackers as possible), you should stop traffic on all ports but the ones you actually need to provide services on the network. On a bastion host that is intended to function as a Web server, for instance, you only need to enable traffic on TCP Port 80 and Port 443 for SSL traffic. After the bastion host has been configured, you can use scanner tools like Nmap or SuperScan to scan your system for active ports. You can then close any ports that are being used by unknown or unneeded services.

Handling Backups

Having gone through the effort to harden and secure a bastion host, you should now take steps to back up the data on the machine so you can restore it if needed. If the system becomes corrupted by a virus or a worm that replicates itself throughout the system, you can restore part or all of it from scratch using the backup you've made.

The best kind of backup is a **binary drive image**, which is a mirror image of all the data on a hard disk or partition, including not only files but applications and system data. Several commercial applications are available for creating a binary drive image. These include Symantec's Norton Ghost (*www.symantec.com/norton/ghost*) and Clonezilla (*clonezilla.org*). Of course, you can also back up the system by copying all the relevant files to a disk or by using the system's built-in back-up utility, if one is available (e.g., Windows Backup Utility). A detachable DVD-RW drive or external USB drive would be ideal. You can make a backup of the system and data, and then detach the drive and store it in a safe location.

Auditing the Bastion Host

After you put the host online, the last step is to **audit** the system by testing it for vulnerabilities and evaluating its performance. The effectiveness of a bastion host configuration can be evaluated by asking yourself two questions:

- How well does the bastion host protect itself from attack? You can use one of the hacker tools mentioned earlier (Nmap or SuperScan) to research this after the machine is online.

- How well does the bastion host protect the internal LAN behind it from attack? This is something you judge by reviewing the log files for unsuccessful access attempts as well as for other possible intrusions.

You need to establish a **baseline** for system performance. A baseline is a level of performance that you consider acceptable and against which the system can be compared. The process of establishing a baseline is a form of **benchmarking**. Benchmarking requires that you check system logs, event logs, and performance information and record the information you uncover. Check the server on a daily or weekly basis after it is first installed, and compile a month's worth of log files that you can analyze. Take a snapshot of system logs (i.e., record a typical day's worth of activity in a text file) to see how the system normally runs. Print system and event logs, and store them in case you need to refer to them when testing the system in the future.

When you configure the bastion host, do not use your production servers for testing. You will not likely get your configuration perfect on the first try and you would disable functionality, so if you are using your production servers, you will be out of business. First, apply hardening actions to a server in a test environment; then, once you are fairly certain of the configuration, move your new functionality to a quality assurance server for final acceptance testing using a mock production environment. After you verify that the server is functional, perform the same steps on a production server.

Connecting the Bastion Host

After all the configuration and auditing is complete, you can finally connect the server to the network. When the bastion host is up and running, test the system and check it against your baseline level of performance to make sure it's still functioning correctly. Applications like the Performance Monitor Wizard (for Windows Server 2003) and the System Center Operations Manager (for Windows Server 2003 or 2008) can assist in keeping an eye on systems performance.

Continue to audit the host on a periodic basis—daily or weekly, depending on how much time you can devote to it. An automated service such as Security Space Security Audits (*www.securityspace .com/smysecure/index.html*) can test the system and provide you with a detailed security report.

Running Case: Able to Hack It

Rachel leaned back in her chair. It had been a long day, but the system was almost ready to go online. All they had to do was activate the IDPS and test the system. The new multi-thousand-dollar bastion firewall would go a long way toward resolving Data Mart's perimeter defense needs. "Let's call it a day, and we'll wrap it up tomorrow," Rachel said to Alex.

"Sounds good to me," Alex replied.

The next morning, Rachel came in late because she had to set up a schedule with the client with whom she would be working after Data Mart. Business is looking up, she thought, but things didn't seem so rosy when she walked into Alex's office. He was looking at the config-uration screens for the bastion host they had worked so hard on for the past two days.

"Problem," Alex said nervously.

"What is it?" Rachel asked.

"One of my techs started the bastion host and put it online last night, thinking it was just a down server," Alex replied. "We hadn't tested it, and it got hacked."

"How bad?" Rachel asked, dreading the response.

"Totaled," Alex replied. "They trashed the system configuration, encrypted the hard drive, and caused it to start attacking our other systems. One more day, and it would have been ready."

One more day and I would have been done, Rachel thought. Now it looks like we have to replicate our work for the entire last week!

Chapter Summary

- In this chapter, you learned about the requirements for successfully configuring and main-taining a bastion host. A bastion host is a specially hardened computer that is located on the network perimeter and hosts firewall software and/or publicly accessible services such as Web, FTP, and e-mail servers. Because of its exposed position, extra steps need to be taken to ensure that the bastion host is secure and that it functions reliably.

- When putting together the combination of hardware and operating system that the bastion host comprises, be sure to choose systems with which you are familiar so that you can shandle configuration and troubleshooting as the need arises. RAM is important if you plan to run a Web server, but other requirements for the bastion host are not as extensive because (aside from log analysis software) few other applications should be run on it. Processor speed also isn't the most critical consideration when choosing hardware for a bastion host.

- The bastion host should be placed on the perimeter of the network. The logical location for a bastion host that is intended to provide DNS services or publicly available services is on the DMZ. A bastion host that hosts firewall software should be in a room with limited access and with backup power and air conditioning.

- You need to decide what function the bastion host will be called upon to perform. Besides running public services, the bastion host can function as a proxy server. Some bastion hosts are set up as honeypot servers that intentionally attract intruders but that are not connected to any computers on the internal network. Log files should be recorded and reviewed on the server, and security patches that guard against buffer overflows and other problems should be installed. Any unnecessary services or accounts on the bastion host should be disabled. In particular, routing services should be disabled so that they cannot be exploited by intruders.

■ After the bastion host software has been installed and a minimal operating system is in place, you should back up all the system data so it can be restored quickly if it becomes corrupted. A binary drive image is a mirror image of all the information on a hard disk or partition. It can be created by a number of commercial applications, such as Norton Ghost.

■ Along with saving backups of the system and data on the bastion host, you need to audit the system. You should test it for vulnerabilities and evaluate its performance. First, establish a baseline for acceptable system performance. Then, regularly monitor the system to see how it compares with the baseline. Software programs are available to test the bastion host for vulnerabilities and to monitor how frequently the bastion host goes offline due to problems with the network, the operating system, or the services provided by the host.

Review Questions

1. How can you minimize the chance that security vulnerabilities will arise in a bastion host?

2. A bastion host provides only one network service, and that service is a firewall. True or False?

3. Which functions are required to a greater degree when configuring a bastion host than with other firewall-related tasks?

4. If it's ideal to run only one service on a bastion host, what are the obstacles to configuring multiple hosts on a network?

5. The speed with which a bastion host works is a function of what system component?

6. What's the purpose of going through the time and effort of documenting every step involved in bastion host configuration?

7. What type of server is placed on the DMZ to direct hackers away from bastion host servers? What are the advantages and disadvantages of this strategy?

8. What are the primary features of the "healthy paranoia" you should adopt when configuring a bastion host?

9. What are the components of a CPU's processor that describe its capabilities and speed?

10. Describe the ideal operating system for a bastion host.

11. What is a benefit of establishing a bare-bones configuration on a bastion host?

12. What is the benefit of using an application like Microsoft Security Compliance Manager? What does it do?

13. What characteristics should you look for when physically locating the bastion host?

14. What are the criteria for grouping services on the same bastion host?

15. What services should be disabled on a typical UNIX/Linux server? Windows server?

16. What are dependency services?

17. Why back up a system after you configure it?

18. What are three important things to consider when choosing a bastion host OS?

19. What should you consider when evaluating the effectiveness of the bastion host configuration during the auditing process?

20. What is a baseline, and why is it important in the context of a bastion host?

Real World Exercises

For the following five exercises, you will go to *www.dell.com* or some other online computer vendor's Web site. You will then specify and configure a bastion host server by evaluating the component described in each exercise. If using the Dell site, start by selecting **For Public Sector,** and then **Higher Education.** On the menu at the left, select **Servers** under **Systems,** and then click the green button labeled **Choose** under Rack Servers. You will see several variations of PowerEdge Rack Servers. Print your configuration when you are finished with all five exercises.

1. **Processor:** Review all the servers listed and identify the two major processor vendors used by Dell in its PowerEdge servers. Identify the three most common processors from each vendor and compare their capabilities. Use a search tool to locate these processor manufacturers' Web sites and find a complete description for each processor. Which would you prefer if cost were no object? Which seems to be the "best buy"?

2. **Memory:** Identify the range of memory size and type. Repeat the process for Exercise 1 and identify the top two vendors and the top three memory configurations for each of those vendors. Research the characteristics of each. What type and amount of memory would you select if cost were no object? What memory do you consider the best buy?

3. **Hard Drive:** Here, you have to determine two major components: configuration and drive size/speed. What different hard drive architectures do you find? Research and describe each drive configuration. Which do you prefer and why?

4. **Hard Drive Size:** Repeat the process of identifying the top two vendors and top three models from each, and then compare them. What if money were no object? What is the best buy?

5. **Specify the bastion host:** Pull it all together. Select the PowerEdge 2970 (or current comparable system) and customize it with the options you selected earlier. From what other options must you choose? Using the "best buy" option, identify each option you would select, and write a brief description of why you chose that option. Print your configuration when you have completed this exercise.

Hands-On Projects

Project 8-1: Port Scanning with SuperScan for Windows

Basic port scanning is a very simple process that takes a range of TCP/IP addresses and a range of TCP and/or UDP ports and tries to determine which ports are active at which addresses. The various tools that can be used to perform this activity provide automated controls that use a variety of mechanisms to make the connections.

1. Write down the target IP address range and the target ports provided by your instructor.

2. Start SuperScan. Your lab instructor may have placed a shortcut to SuperScan on your desktop. If that is not the case, you can use Windows Explorer to locate the file, and then double-click **SuperScan.exe,** usually found in the \Program Files\SuperScan folder on the system drive.

3. Insert the START and STOP IP address range in the Start IP and Stop IP text boxes in the IP section provided by the instructor. Then click the **right arrow** (→) next to these boxes to load your addresses into the right windowpane.

4. Click the **Host and Service Discovery** tab at the top of the window and ensure Echo Request is selected.

5. In the UDP and TCP port scan areas of this tab, either enter the Start port and End port values in the text boxes provided or select specific ports in the center area (hold Control and click to select multiple ports).

6. Select the **Scan Options** tab and ensure **Hostname lookups** is selected, as shown in Figure 8-2. Go back to the Scan tab and click the Play [▶] button to begin the scan. When SuperScan has finished running, click the **View HTML Results** button to see the final report.

7. Record the responding hostname and available TCP/IP ports.

Now that you have a list of available hosts and ports, what can you do with this information?

Project 8-2: Active Stack Fingerprinting Using Nmap

The NMap program can be used via the command line; however, the Windows version of Nmap has a Graphical User Interface (GUI) called Zenmap.

1. Make a note of the target IP address range and the target ports provided by your lab instructor.

2. Start the Nmap GUI interface by clicking the **Start** menu and selecting **All Programs.** Choose the **Zenmap** menu, and then the **Zenmap** program. Once the Zenmap GUI is running, enter the target IP address provided by the lab instructor (a single address like 192.168.2.254, a range of addresses like 192.168.2.*, or even 192.168.2.–255) in the Host window.

3. The Profile pull-down menu outlines the various types of scans the system can perform. Select **Regular Scan** as your profile. Note the Command text box shows the command-line version of the scan you are executing. Briefly review the Help file for additional details about the utility.

4. Click **Scan** to start the analysis.

5. Once the scan is complete, the TCP port, the port's state, and information about the service of that port are shown.

6. Record the information on the highest numbered port shown, its state, and its service, based on your scan.

What should you do with this information?

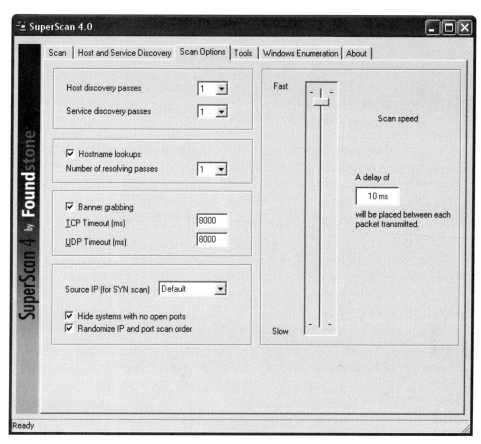

Figure 8-2 Using the LanGuard Network Security Scanner
© Cengage Learning 2012

Project 8-3: Determining Which Services Are Functioning in a Windows System

1. Select **Start, Control Panel, Classic View** (unless you are already in the classic view), double-click **Administrative Tools,** and then double-click **Services.** Note that the Extended and Standard tabs at the bottom change the view slightly.

2. Export the list of services to a .txt file by selecting **Action, Export List.** Name the document with your name and click **Save.** Open this document in a document editor like Microsoft Word.

3. You can also perform this task using the command line by clicking **Start, Run** and entering **CMD.EXE**. Then enter **tasklist /svc >c:*yourname*.txt,** where *yourname* is your last name.

4. Back in the Services list, right-click each started service and select **Properties.** Click the **Dependencies** tab. Record the dependency for as many services as your instructor desires in the services document.

5. Using a Web browser, search the Web for a site that provides insight into which functions the service provides. One of the most commonly queried services is svchost. For insight into this service, refer to the Microsoft support site at *http://support.microsoft.com/default .aspx?scid=kb;en-us;*.

6. For each service identified, determine if the service is a legitimate, needed service or an unauthorized service. If in doubt, ask your instructor. For each unauthorized or illegitimate service, right-click the service and select **Stop**. If the service has a startup type of Automatic, it will restart on the next bootup. In order to stop an unauthorized process, you must uninstall the application that requires the service or delete the associated file indicated in the Dependencies tab. Do not perform this task unless requested by your instructor.

Project 8-4: Microsoft Baseline Security Analyzer

1. Although your instructor should already have the tool installed, the home page for the MBSA is located at *www.microsoft.com/technet/security/tools/mbsahome.mspx*. You may want to check here for updates as well as other security tools and information pertaining to Microsoft operating systems and software.

2. Click **Start, All Programs, Microsoft Baseline Security Analyzer 2.1**. The application should appear.

3. This tool is capable of scanning remote machines in a network, but you will only be scanning the local machine for this lab. Click **Scan a computer**.

4. You are presented with several options pertaining to the computer that you would like to scan. The name of your computer should appear in the box labeled Computer name.

5. Click **Start Scan**. The scan finishes more quickly if no other applications are running at the same time. When the scan has finished, you should see results. Record or print these as directed by your instructor.

6. By clicking **Result details** below any of the listed vulnerabilities, a new window opens with any details about the listed issue. This can be very helpful for systems administrators. The "How to correct this" link for each vulnerability is also handy.

In reviewing the list of problems, do you see any of the same vulnerabilities that came up during the scan in the first lab? Discuss several of the most important items (the severest risks) and how fixing them could harden your system.

Running Case Projects

CASE PROJECTS

The lab component of this case exercise is so comprehensive and complex that it is included as Appendix A. The exercise presumes you have access to a computer system you can dedicate exclusively as a bastion host. For that system, you will install a bastion host firewall, and then test the system for vulnerabilities. Once the system is up and running, you can duplicate the preceding Hands-On Projects on that system to identify and remediate any issues you may find.

Endnotes

1. "Bastion." Accessed 15 January 2010 from *http://en.wikipedia.org/wiki/Bastion*.

2. "CPU cache." Accessed 15 January 2010 from *http://en.wikipedia.org/wiki/CPU_cache*.

3. "Microsoft Security Assessment Tool 4.0." Accessed 15 January 2010 from *www .microsoft.com/downloads/details.aspx?familyid=CD057D9D-86B9-4E35-9733-7ACB0-B2A3CA1 &displaylang=en*.

"There are two types of encryption: one that will prevent your sister from reading your diary and one that will prevent your government."
—*Bruce Schneier*

chapter 9

Encryption—The Foundation for the Virtual Private Network

After reading this chapter and completing the exercises, you will be able to:

- Describe the role encryption plays in firewall and VPN architectures
- Explain how digital certificates work and why they are important security tools
- Analyze the workings of SSL, PGP, and other popular encryption schemes
- Discuss Internet Protocol Security (IPSec) and identify its protocols and modes

Running Case: Secret Codes

Rachel was relieved. Yes, a member of Alex's team had placed the newly developed firewall online before it could be finalized, which resulted in it getting hacked. Fortunately, though, Rachel had selected a firewall with an autoarchive feature, which means it periodically backs up its configuration to the log server, a completely separate system. Instead of taking days to get back up and running, the new firewall was back up in minutes.

Now, Rachel was chatting with Meghan, Data Mart's COO, over coffee.

"I really like the idea of being able to securely access our information from outside the building," Meghan said. "Several of us travel frequently on business, trying to attract new customers. It would be a great advantage if we could access our data from the customers' locations."

"It's really not that difficult," Rachel said. "You have two options: you can set up a VPN server on the current firewall, or you can set up a separate VPN appliance. All you have to do then is select the encryption standard you need, AES or Triple DES, decide if you want strong authentication and whether you want synchronous or asynchronous tokens."

Meghan slowly set her coffee cup down on the table and stared at Rachel. "You lost me at 'current firewall,'" she said.

Introduction

Many firewalls can be equipped to serve as Virtual Private Network (VPN) endpoints. What a VPN is and what it can do are explained in Chapter 10. For now, you should know that a VPN allows an organization to use a relatively low-cost and unsecured network, like the Internet, to transmit confidential information. It does this by enabling encryption on the sending and receiving ends, and then encrypting parts of the IP packet. Encryption is an integral part of VPNs and is used for the following:

- Enabling the firewall to determine whether the user who wants to connect to the VPN is actually authorized to do so

- Encoding the payload of the information to maintain privacy

This chapter explains why firewalls and VPNs use encryption and how to use it in a way that complements and does not hinder the firewall. The chapter also describes encryption applications, such as Pretty Good Privacy (PGP), Secure Sockets Layer (SSL), and Internet Protocol Security (IPSec), as well as schemes that can form part of firewall and VPN architectures. By encrypting the data that passes into and out of your network, you help protect your data, which makes untrusted networks trustworthy.

Encryption Overview

Encryption is a process that turns information that is plainly readable (**plaintext**) into scrambled form (**ciphertext**) in order to preserve the authenticity, integrity, and privacy of the information that passes through the security perimeter. In other words, encryption renders information unreadable to all but the intended recipients.

Firewalls have not always been able to perform encryption-related functions. They originally focused on basic features like IP forwarding and Network Address Translation (NAT); while these approaches provided protection at the network level, they didn't account for application-level problems, such as executable code that finds its way into a system. In fact, many of the attacks upon companies both small and large—even those companies already protected by firewalls—are the result of executable code that is either tampered with before it reaches the firewall or, more commonly, makes it past the firewall in malicious e-mail attachments or HTTP downloads.

Firewall and VPN vendors add encryption to their products to provide protection against "active attacks," which are also known as **session hijacks**. These are attacks involving a communication session that has already been established between a server and a client. The hacker inserts confusing or misleading commands into packets, thus disabling the server and enabling the hacker to gain control of the session. These are different from "passive attacks," such as packet sniffing, in which a program scans for open ports that can be compromised.

As shown in Figure 9-1, the unencrypted packet is subject to modification by a hacker after being sent from point A and after being received at point B.

With encryption, however, packet integrity and confidentiality is maintained, as shown in Figure 9-2.

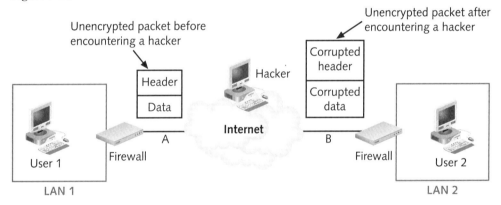

Figure 9-1 Unencrypted Packet
© Cengage Learning 2012

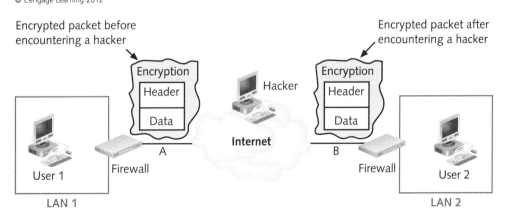

Figure 9-2 Encrypted Packet
© Cengage Learning 2012

The most obvious reason to encrypt data is to keep it confidential. Computers are often stolen for the information they contain, not the value of the hardware. According to the computer insurance agency Safeware, Inc. (*www.safeware.com*), a laptop is stolen every 12 seconds—over 2.6 million per year. In addition, the annual CSI Computer Crime and Security Survey found that in 2009 over 42 percent of surveyed companies suffered laptop or mobile device theft. Six percent of surveyed companies also reported theft of or unauthorized access to intellectual property from these losses. The studied organizations reported an average loss of over $234,000 per incident.[1] Such losses are especially hard to document or verify because many companies lose data to thieves, hackers, and disgruntled employees without even knowing it.

Principles of Crytography

Although it is not a specific application or security tool, cryptography is a sophisticated element that is often included in other information security controls. In fact, many security-related tools use embedded encryption technologies to protect sensitive information. The use of the proper cryptographic tools can ensure confidentiality by keeping private information concealed from those who do not need to see it. Alternative cryptographic methods can provide increased data integrity through a mechanism that guarantees that a message in transit has not been altered. These alternative methods create a secure message digest, or hash. In e-commerce, some cryptographic tools can be used to assure that parties to the transaction are authentic, so that they cannot later deny having participated in a transaction, a feature often called **nonrepudiation**.

Encryption is the process of converting a message into a form that cannot be read by unauthorized individuals. An encrypted message cannot be converted back to its readable form without the specific tools and knowledge used to encrypt it. The science of encryption, known as **cryptology**, actually encompasses two disciplines: cryptography and cryptanalysis. **Cryptography**—from the Greek words "kryptos," meaning "hidden," and "graphein," meaning "to write"—refers to the processes involved in encoding and decoding messages so that others cannot understand them. **Cryptanalysis**—from "analyein," meaning "to break up"—is the process of deciphering the original message (or plaintext) from an encrypted message (or ciphertext) without knowing the algorithms and keys used to perform the encryption.

Cryptology is a very complex field based on advanced mathematical concepts. The following sections provide a brief overview of the foundations of encryption and a short discussion of some of the related issues and tools in the field of information security. Those students who would like more information about cryptography may consult either H. X. Mel and D. Baker's *Cryptography Decrypted* for a general introduction, or Bruce Schneier's *Applied Cryptography: Protocols, Algorithms, and Source Code in C,* which provides a more technical tutorial.

Encryption Definitions

You can better understand the tools and functions popular in encryption security solutions if you understand some basic terminology:

Algorithm: The mathematical formula or method used to convert an unencrypted message into an encrypted message or vice versa

Cipher: The transformation of the individual components (characters, bytes, or bits) of an unencrypted message into encrypted components

Ciphertext or **cryptogram**: The encrypted or encoded message resulting from an encryption

Cryptosystem: The set of transformations necessary to convert an unencrypted message into an encrypted message

Decipher: To decrypt or convert ciphertext to plaintext

Encipher: To encrypt or convert plaintext to ciphertext

Key or **cryptovariable**: The information used in conjunction with the algorithm to create the ciphertext from the plaintext

Keyspace: The entire range of values that can possibly be used to construct an individual key

Plaintext: The original unencrypted message or the results from successful decryption

Work factor: The amount of effort (usually expressed in units of time) required to perform cryptanalysis on an encoded message

Cryptographic Notation

The notation used to describe the encryption process varies, depending on its source. The notation chosen for the discussion in this text uses the letter "M" to represent the original message, "C" to represent the resulting ciphertext, and "E" to represent the encryption process. Thus, the formula $E(M) = C$ represents the application of encryption (E) to a message (M) to create ciphertext (C).[2] In this notation scheme, the letter "D" represents the decryption or deciphering process. Thus, the formula $D[E(M)] = M$ represents the deciphering (D) of an enciphered message (E(M)), resulting in the original message (M). This could also be represented as $D[C] = M$—that is, the deciphering (D) of the ciphertext (remember that C = E(M)), resulting in the original message (M). Finally, the letter "K" is used to represent the key. Therefore, $E(M, K) = C$ represents the encrypting (E) of the message (M) with the key (K), resulting in the ciphertext (C). Similarly, $D(C,K) = D[E(M,K),K] = M$ represents deciphering the ciphertext with the key (K), resulting in the original plaintext message—or, to translate this formula even more precisely, deciphering, using the key (K), the message encrypted with the key (K) results in the original message (M).

To encrypt a plaintext set of data, you can use one of two general methods: stream or block ciphers. With the stream method, each plaintext bit is transformed into a cipher bit, one after the other. With the block cipher method, the message is divided into blocks—for example, 8-, 16-, 32-, or 64-bit blocks—and then each block is transformed using the algorithm and key. Bit stream methods most commonly use algorithm functions like XOR, whereas block methods can use XOR, transposition, or substitution, described later in this chapter.

Encryption Operations

Encryption is accomplished by using algorithms to manipulate the plaintext into the ciphertext for transmission. Some widely used encryption operations are explained in the following sections.

Common Ciphers In encryption, algorithms commonly use three functions: substitution, transposition, and XOR. In a **substitution cipher**, you substitute one value for another. For example, if your "input text" were the letters of the alphabet arranged alphabetically, you could obtain your "output text" by substituting for each message character the character that is three to the right in the alphabet, as shown here:

Input text: `ABCDEFGHIJKLMNOPQRSTUVWXYZ`

Output text: `DEFGHIJKLMNOPQRSTUVWXYZABC`

Thus, a plaintext of BERLIN becomes EHUOLQ.

This is a simple enough method by itself, but it becomes very powerful if combined with other operations. Incidentally, this type of substitution is based on a **monoalphabetic substitution,** because it uses only one alphabet. More advanced substitution ciphers use two or more alphabets and are called **polyalphabetic substitutions**. To illustrate the increasing complexity introduced by the use of a polyalphabetic substitution, consider the following input text, along with the polyalphabetic substitution ciphers:

Input text: `ABCDEFGHIJKLMNOPQRSTUVWXYZ`

Substitution cipher 1: `DEFGHIJKLMNOPQRSTUVWXYZABC`

Substitution cipher 2: `GHIJKLMNOPQRSTUVWXYZABCDEF`

Substitution cipher 3: `JKLMNOPQRSTUVWXYZABCDEFGHI`

Substitution cipher 4: `MNOPQRSTUVWXYZABCDEFGHIJKL`

As we did with the monoalphabetic example, we will match the plaintext against the substitution cipher. The difference in this example is that we will match the first letter of the plaintext against cipher 1, the second letter of the plaintext against cipher 2, and so forth. Using "TEXT" as our plaintext, we replace "T" with the corresponding value from cipher 1, "E" with the corresponding value from cipher 2, "X" with the corresponding value from cipher 3, and "T" with the corresponding value from cipher 4. The resulting ciphertext is "WKGF" This type of encryption is substantially more difficult to decipher without the algorithm. You can also easily randomize the cipher rows to create more complex substitution operations.

Another simple example of the substitution cipher is the daily cryptogram in your local newspaper, or the well-known Little Orphan Annie decoder ring. Julius Caesar reportedly created ciphertext by shifting plaintext characters three characters to the right, in which A becomes D and so on; that particular substitution cipher is known as the Caesar cipher.

Like the substitution operation, transposition is simple to understand but can be complex to decipher if properly used. Unlike the substitution cipher, the **transposition cipher** (or **permutation cipher**) rearranges the values within a block to create the ciphertext. This can be done at the bit level or at the byte (character) level. Here is an example that shows four characters being transposed at the bit level:

Plaintext: `00100101011010111001010101010100`

Key: `1 > 3, 2 > 6, 3 > 8, 4 > 1, 5 > 4, 6 > 7, 7 > 5, 8 > 2`

In other words, bit 1 moves to position 3, bit 2 moves to position 6, bit 3 moves to position 8, and so on. Bit position 1, however, is the farthest to the right, and you work from right to left.

The following shows the plaintext broken into four different 8-bit blocks (for ease of discussion) and the corresponding ciphertext after applying the key to the plaintext:

Plaintext 8-bit blocks:	00100101 01101011 10010101 01010100
Ciphertext:	11000100 01110101 10001110 10011000

To make this easier to follow, consider the following example in character transposition. As with the bit blocks, we are dealing in sets of eight characters. Also, spaces count as characters.

Plaintext: MY DOG HAS FLEAS

Key: Same as above, but characters are transposed instead of bits.

Here is the plaintext broken into 8-character blocks and the corresponding ciphertext:

Plaintext 8-character blocks:	MY DOG H AS FLEAS
Ciphertext:	GY DHM O EA SFSAL

Transposition ciphers and substitution ciphers can be used in multiple combinations to create a very secure encryption process. To make the encryption stronger (more difficult to cryptanalyze), the keys and block sizes can be made much larger (64-bit or 128-bit), resulting in substantially more complex substitutions or transpositions.

In **XOR cipher conversion**, the bit stream is subjected to a Boolean XOR function against some other data stream, typically a key stream. The symbol commonly used to represent the XOR function is " ^ ". XOR works as follows:

"0" XORed with "0" results in a "0". (0 ^ 0 = 0)

"0" XORed with "1" results in a "1". (0 ^ 1 = 1)

"1" XORed with "0" results in a "1". (1 ^ 0 = 1)

"1" XORed with "1" results in a "0". (1 ^ 1 = 0)

Simply put, if the two values are the same, you get "0"; if not, you get "1". Suppose you have a data stream in which the first byte is 01000001. If you have a key stream in which the first byte is 01011010 and you XOR the two, here is what you get:

01000001	Plaintext
01011010	Key stream
00011011	Ciphertext

This process is reversible. That is, if you XOR the ciphertext with the key stream, you get the plaintext.

Vernam Cipher Also known as the one-time pad, the Vernam cipher was developed at AT&T and uses a set of characters for encryption operations only one time and then discards it. The values from this one-time pad are added to the block of text, and the resulting sum is converted to text. When the two sets of values are added, if the resulting values exceed 26, then 26 is subtracted from the total (a process called modulo 26). The corresponding results are then converted back to text. The following example demonstrates how the Vernam cipher works:

Plaintext:	M	Y	D	O	G	H	A	S	F	L	E	A	S
Corresponding values:	13	25	04	15	07	08	01	19	06	12	05	01	19
One-time pad:	F	P	Q	R	N	S	B	I	E	H	T	Z	L
Pad corresponding values:	06	16	17	18	14	19	02	09	05	08	20	26	12

Results:

Plaintext:	13	25	4	15	7	8	1	19	6	12	5	1	19
One-time Pad	6	16	17	18	14	19	2	9	5	8	20	26	12
Sum:	19	41	21	33	21	27	3	28	11	20	25	27	31
Subtraction (modulo 26)		15		7		1		2				1	5
Ciphertext:	P	O	U	G	U	A	C	B	K	T	Y	A	E

Book or Running Key Cipher Another method, one seen in the occasional spy movie, is the use of text in a book as the algorithm to decrypt a message. The key relies on two components: (1) knowing which book to use and (2) having a list of codes representing the page number, line number, and word number of the plaintext word. For example, using a copy of a particular popular novel, one might send the following message: 67,3,1; 145,9,4;375,7,4;394,17,3. Dictionaries and thesauruses are the most popular sources as they provide every needed word, although almost any book will suffice. If the receiver knows which book is used for the preceding example, he or she goes to page 67, line 3, and selects the first word from that line; the receiver then goes to page 145, line 9, and uses the fourth word; and so forth. The resulting message "cancel operation target compromised" can then be deciphered. When using dictionaries, it is necessary to use only a page and word number. An even more sophisticated version of this cipher can use multiple books, with a new book in a particular sequence for each word or phrase.

Symmetric Encryption Each of the aforementioned encryption and decryption methods requires the same algorithm and key—a **secret key**—to be used to both encipher and decipher the message. This is known as **private key encryption**, or **symmetric encryption**. Symmetric encryption is efficient and easy to process, as long as both the sender and the receiver possess the encryption key. Of course, if either copy of the key becomes compromised, an intermediary can decrypt and read the messages. One challenge in symmetric key encryption is getting a copy of the key to the receiver, a process that must be conducted out-of-band (that is, through a channel or band different from the one carrying the ciphertext) to avoid interception. Figure 9-3 illustrates the concept of symmetric encryption.

A number of popular symmetric encryption cryptosystems are available. One of the first widely employed systems is the Data Encryption Standard (DES). DES was developed in 1977 by IBM and is based on the Data Encryption Algorithm (DEA), which uses a 64-bit

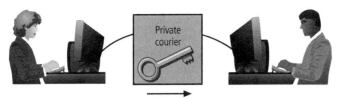

Rachel at ABC Corp. generates a secret key. She must somehow get it
to Alex at XYZ Corp. out-of-band. Once Alex has the key, Rachel can use
it to encrypt messages, and Alex can use it to decrypt and read them.

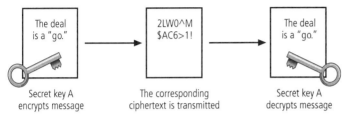

Figure 9-3 Symmetric Encryption
© Cengage Learning 2012

block size and a 56-bit key. With a 56-bit key, the algorithm has 2^{56} (more than 72 quadrillion) possible keys.

DES is a federally approved standard for nonclassified data (see *Federal Information Processing Standards Publication 46-2*). It was cracked in 1997 when Rivest-Shamir-Aldeman (RSA), the developers of a new algorithm, offered a $10,000 reward for the first person or team to crack the DEA. (You will read more about RSA later in this chapter.) Fourteen thousand users collaborated over the Internet to finally break the encryption.

Triple DES (3DES) was developed as an improvement to DES and uses as many as three keys in succession. It is substantially more secure than DES, not only because it uses as many as three keys instead of one but because it performs three different encryption operations. When it was proven that DES was not strong enough for highly classified communications, 3DES was created to provide a level of security far beyond that of standard DES. (In between, there was a 2DES; however, it was statistically shown that the double DES did not provide significantly stronger security than that of DES.) 3DES takes three 64-bit keys for an overall key length of 192 bits. Triple DES encryption is the same as that of standard DES; however, it is repeated three times. Triple DES can employ two or three keys, or it can employ a combination of steps using encryption and/or decryption in sequential steps for additional security. The most common implementations involve encrypting and decrypting with three different keys, a process that is described in the following example. 3DES employs 48 rounds in its encryption computation, generating ciphers that are approximately 2^{56} (72 quadrillion) times stronger than standard DES ciphers but require only three times longer to process. A step-by-step example of 3DES encryption is described in the following:

1. In the first operation, 3DES encrypts the message with key 1, then decrypts it with key 2, and then encrypts it with key 1 again. In cryptographic notation terms, this would be [E{D[E(M,K1)],K2},K1]. Decrypting with a different key is essentially another encryption, but it reverses the application of the traditional encryption operations.

2. In the second operation, 3DES encrypts the message with key 1, then encrypts it with key 2, and then encrypts it with key 1 again, or [E{E[E(M,K1)],K2},K1].

3. In the third operation, 3DES encrypts the message three times with three different keys: [E{E[E(M,K1)],K2},K3]. This is the most secure level of encryption possible with 3DES.

The successor to 3DES is **Advanced Encryption Standard (AES)**. Of the many ciphers that were submitted (from across the world) for consideration in the AES selection process, five finalists were chosen: MARS, RC6, Rijndael, Serpent, and Twofish. On October 2, 2000, NIST announced the selection of Rijndael as the cipher to be used as the basis for the AES, and this block cipher was approved by the Secretary of Commerce as the official federal governmental standard as of May 26, 2002. The Rinjdael Block Cipher features a variable block length and a key length of either 128, 192, or 256 bits. The AES version of Rijndael can use a system based on multiple rounds. Depending on the key size, the number of rounds varies from 9 to 13. For a 128-bit key, nine rounds plus one end round are used; for a 192-bit key, 11 rounds plus one end round are used; and for a 256-bit key, 13 rounds plus one end round are used. Once Rijndael was adopted as the AES, the ability to use variable-sized blocks was standardized to a single 128-bit block for simplicity.

There are four steps within each Rijndael round:

1. The "Byte Sub" step—Here, each byte of the block is replaced by its substitute in an S-box, which is short for "substitution box." (The S-box consists of a table of computed values, the calculation of which is beyond the scope of this text.)

2. The "Shift Row" step—Assuming the block to be made up of bytes 1 to 16, the bytes are arranged in a grid and shifted as follows:

From				To			
1	5	9	13	1	5	9	13
2	6	10	14	6	10	14	2
3	7	11	15	11	15	3	7
4	8	12	16	16	4	8	12

Other shift tables are used for larger blocks.

3. The "Mix Column" step—Here, matrix multiplication is performed; each column is multiplied by the known matrix for the 128-bit key, as shown in the following:

2	3	1	1
1	2	3	1
1	1	2	3
3	1	1	2

4. The "Add Round Key" step—This step applies the XOR function to the subkey for the current round.

The extra final round omits the Mix Column step, but is otherwise the same as a regular round."[3] In 1998, it took a special computer designed by the Electronic Frontier Foundation (*www.eff.org*) more than 56 hours to crack DES. It would take the same computer approximately 4,698,864 quintillion years (4,698,864,000,000,000,000,000,000) to crack AES.

Asymmetric Encryption Another encryption technique is **asymmetric encryption**, also known as **public key encryption**. Whereas symmetric encryption systems use the same key to both encrypt and decrypt a message, asymmetric encryption uses two different keys. Either key can be used to encrypt or decrypt the message. However, if key A is used to encrypt the message, then only key B can decrypt it; conversely, if key B is used to encrypt a message, then only key A can decrypt it. This technique is most valuable when one of the keys is private and the other is public. The public key is stored in a public location, where anyone can use it. The private key, as its name suggests, is a secret known only to the owner of the key pair.

Consider the following example, illustrated in Figure 9-4. Alex at XYZ Corporation wants to send an encrypted message to Rachel at ABC Corporation. Alex goes to a public key registry and obtains Rachel's public key. Recall the foundation of asymmetric encryption: the same key cannot be used to both encrypt and decrypt the same message. Thus, when Rachel's public key is used to encrypt the message, only her private key can be used to decrypt it, and that private key is held by Rachel alone. Similarly, if Rachel wishes to respond to Alex's message, she goes to the registry where Alex's public key is held and uses it to encrypt her message, which of course can be read only by using Alex's private key to decrypt it.

Alex at XYZ Corp. wants to send a message to Rachel at ABC Corp. Rachel stores her public key where it can be accessed by anyone. Alex retrieves her public key and uses it to create ciphertext that can only be decrypted by Rachel's private key, which she keeps secret. To respond, Rachel gets Alex's public key to encrypt her messages.

9

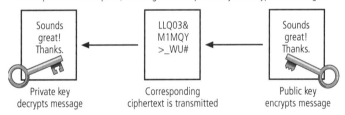

| Private key decrypts message | Corresponding ciphertext is transmitted | Public key encrypts message |

Figure 9-4 Asymmetric (Public Key) Encryption
© Cengage Learning 2012

The problem with asymmetric encryption is that it requires four keys to hold a single conversation between two parties. If four organizations want to frequently exchange messages, each must manage its own four private keys and the four public keys from each of its partners. It can be confusing to determine which public key is needed to encrypt a particular message. With more organizations in the loop, the problem grows. Also, asymmetric encryption is not as efficient in its use of CPU resources as symmetric encryption because of the extensive mathematical calculations. As a result, the hybrid system described later in this chapter is more commonly used.

Digital Signatures When the asymmetric process is reversed—the private key encrypts a (usually short) message and the public key decrypts it—the fact that the message was sent by the organization that owns the private key is difficult to refute. This nonrepudiation is the foundation of digital signatures. **Digital signatures** are encrypted messages that can be independently verified by a central facility (registry) as authentic but can also be used to prove certain characteristics of the message or file with which they are associated. They are often used in Internet software updates (see Figure 9-5). A pop-up window shows that the downloaded files did, in fact, come from the purported agency and thus can be trusted. A **digital certificate** is similar to a digital signature and asserts that a public key is associated with a particular identity (for example, that particular public key really belongs to Alex). A **certificate authority (CA)** is an agency that manages the issuance of certificates and serves as the electronic notary public to verify their origin and integrity.

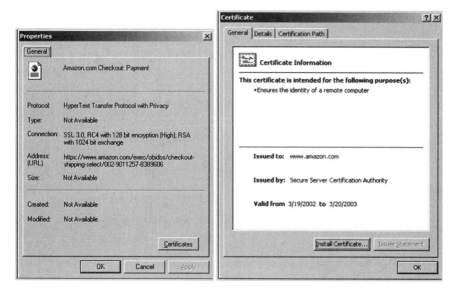

Figure 9-5 Digital Signature
© Cengage Learning 2012

RSA One of the most popular public key cryptosystems is a proprietary model named Rivest-Shamir-Aldeman (RSA), after the surnames of its developers. It is the first public key encryption algorithm developed for commercial use. RSA is very popular and has been integrated into both Microsoft Internet Explorer and Netscape Navigator. A number of extensions to the RSA algorithm exist, including RSA Encryption Scheme—Optimal Asymmetric Encryption Padding (RSAES-OAEP) and RSA Signature Scheme with Appendix—Probabilistic Signature Scheme (RSASSA-PSS). For more information as to how RSA's algorithm works, see the Wikipedia entry for RSA at *http://en.wikipedia.org/wiki/RSA*.

Public Key Infrastructure A public key infrastructure (PKI) is the entire set of hardware, software, and cryptosystems necessary to implement public key encryption. PKI systems are based on public key cryptosystems and include digital certificates and certificate authorities. Common implementations of PKI include the following:

- Systems to issue digital certificates to users and servers
- Encryption enrollment
- Key-issuing systems

- Tools for managing the key issuance
- Verification and return of certificates
- Key revocation services
- Other services associated with PKI that vendors bundle into their products

The use of cryptographic tools is made more manageable when using PKI. PKI can increase the organization's capability to protect its information assets by providing the following services:[4]

- Authentication—Permitting individuals, organizations, and Web servers to authenticate the identity of each of the parties in an Internet transaction through the use of digital certificates

- Integrity—Asserting that the content signed by a digital certificate has not been altered while in transit

- Confidentiality—Keeping information confidential by ensuring that it is not intercepted during transmission over the Internet

- Authorization—Replacing user IDs and passwords, enhancing security, and reducing some of the overhead for authorization processes and control of access privileges

- Nonrepudiation—Validating actions, making it less likely that customers or partners can later repudiate a digitally signed transaction, such as an online purchase

Hybrid Systems Pure asymmetric key encryption is not widely used except in the area of certificates. For other purposes, it is typically employed in conjunction with symmetric key encryption, creating a hybrid system. In this method, asymmetric encryption is used to exchange a symmetric key, so that two organizations can conduct quick, efficient, secure communications based on symmetric encryption.

Because symmetric encryption is more efficient than asymmetric encryption for sending messages, and because asymmetric encryption doesn't require out-of-band key exchange, asymmetric encryption can be used to transmit symmetric keys in a hybrid approach. The process is illustrated in Figure 9-6. Suppose Alex at ABC Corporation wants to communicate with Rachel at XYZ Corporation. First, Alex creates a session key. A **session key** is a symmetric key for limited-use, temporary communications. Alex encrypts a message with the session key and then gets Rachel's public key. He uses her public key to encrypt both the session key and the message that is already encrypted. Alex transmits the entire package to Rachel, who uses her private key to decrypt the package containing the session key and the encrypted message and then uses the session key to decrypt the message. Rachel can then continue the electronic conversation using only the more efficient symmetric session key.

Using Cryptographic Controls

Cryptographic controls are often misunderstood by those new to the area of information security. While modern cryptosystems can certainly generate unbreakable ciphertext, that is possible only when the proper key management infrastructure has been constructed and when the cryptosystems are operated and managed correctly. As in many InfoSec endeavors, the technical control is valuable, as long as it remains within programs that are founded on sound policy and managed with an awareness of the organization's fundamental objectives. Unfortunately, many vendors of cryptographic controls have sold products to organizations that have not

Rachel at ABC Corp. stores her public key where it can be accessed. Alex at XYZ Corp. retrieves it and uses it to encrypt his private (symmetric) key. He sends it to Rachel, who decrypts Alex's private key with her private key and then uses Alex's private key for regular communications.

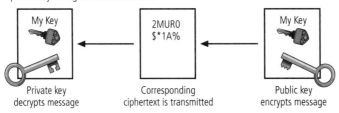

Figure 9-6 Hybrid Encryption
© Cengage Learning 2012

been able to deploy them to improve their security programs. This may be due to poor project planning, errors in executing the implementation plans, or failure to put sound policies in place before acquiring the controls. Whatever the causes, many organizations have failed to make full use of their investment in cryptographic controls.

Organizations can use cryptographic controls to support the following business areas:

- Confidentiality and integrity of e-mail and its attachments
- Authentication, confidentiality, integrity, and nonrepudiation of e-commerce transactions
- Authentication and confidentiality of remote access through VPN connections
- A higher standard of authentication when used to supplement access control systems

E-Mail Security

A number of cryptosystems have been adapted to help secure e-mail, a notoriously insecure method of communication. Some of the more popular adaptations are Secure/Multipurpose Internet Mail Extensions, Privacy Enhanced Mail, and Pretty Good Privacy.

Secure/Multipurpose Internet Mail Extensions (S/MIME) builds on the Multipurpose Internet Mail Extensions (MIME) that encode format by adding encryption and authentication via digital signatures based on public key cryptosystems. **Privacy Enhanced Mail (PEM)** has been proposed by the Internet Engineering Task Force (IETF) as a standard for public key cryptosystems. PEM uses 3DES symmetric key encryption and RSA for key exchanges and digital signatures. **Pretty Good Privacy (PGP)** was developed by Phil Zimmerman and uses the IDEA Cipher, a 128-bit symmetric key block encryption algorithm with 64-bit blocks for message encoding. Like PEM, it uses RSA for symmetric key exchange and to support digital signatures. PGP does not use a centralized certificate authority; rather, it relies on a "web of trust" model to allow its users to share key information easily, albeit with some loss in the degree of control and trust in the key information. If user A has a trusting relationship with user B, and user B has a trusting relationship with user C, then user A is presumed to have a trusting relationship with user C and can therefore exchange encrypted information with user C.

Securing the Web

Just as PGP, PEM, and S/MIME help to secure e-mail operations, a number of cryptosystems help to secure Web activity, especially transactions between customers' browsers and the Web servers at electronic commerce sites. Among the protocols used for this purpose are Secure Electronic Transactions, Secure Sockets Layer, Secure Hypertext Transfer Protocol, Secure Shell, and IP Security, which are now described.

Secure Electronic Transactions (SET) was developed by MasterCard and VISA in 1997 to provide protection from electronic payment fraud. It works by encrypting the credit card transfers with DES for encryption and RSA for key exchange, much as other algorithms do. SET provides the security for both Internet-based credit card transactions and the encryption of card swipe systems in retail stores.

Secure Sockets Layer (SSL) was developed by Netscape in 1994 to provide security for online electronic commerce transactions. It uses a number of algorithms but mainly relies on RSA for key transfer and on IDEA, DES, or 3DES for encrypted symmetric key-based data transfer. Figure 9-7 shows the certificate and SSL information that are displayed when you check out of an e-commerce site. If the Web connection does not automatically display the certificate, you can right-click in the window and select Properties to view the connection encryption and certificate properties. SSL has largely been replaced by TLS (Transport Layer Security), but many people still refer to it as SSL, and we follow that usage.

9

Figure 9-7 Digital Certificate
© Cengage Learning 2012

Secure Hypertext Transfer Protocol (SHTTP) is an encrypted solution to the unsecured version of HTTP. It provides an alternative to the aforementioned protocols and can provide secure e-commerce transactions as well as encrypted Web pages for secure data transfer over the Web using a number of different algorithms.

Secure Shell (SSH) is a popular extension to the TCP/IP protocol suite, sponsored by the IETF. It provides security for remote access connections over public networks by creating a secure and persistent connection. It provides authentication services between a client and a server and is used to secure replacement tools for terminal emulation, remote management, and file transfer applications.

IPSEC IP Security (IPSec) is the predominant cryptographic authentication and encryption protocol suite in use today. It is used to support a variety of applications, just as is SSH. A framework for security development within the TCP/IP family of protocol standards, IPSec provides application support for all uses within TCP/IP, including VPNs. This protocol combines the following cryptosystems for the following purposes:

- Diffie-Hellman key exchange for deriving key material between peers on a public network
- Public key cryptography for signing the Diffie-Hellman exchanges, to guarantee the identity of the two parties
- Bulk encryption algorithms, such as DES, for encrypting the data
- Digital certificates signed by a certificate authority to act as digital ID cards[5]

IPSec has two components: (1) the IP Security protocol itself, which specifies the information to be added to an IP packet and indicates how to encrypt packet data; and (2) the Internet Key Exchange (IKE), which uses asymmetric key exchange and negotiates the security associations.

IPSec operates in two modes: transport and tunnel. In **transport mode,** only the IP data is encrypted, not the IP headers themselves. This allows intermediate nodes to read the source and destination addresses. In **tunnel mode,** the entire IP packet is encrypted and inserted as the payload in another IP packet. This requires other systems at the beginning and end of the tunnel to act as proxies to send and receive the encrypted packets. These systems then transmit the decrypted packets to their true destinations.

IPSec and other cryptographic extensions to TCP/IP are often used to support a **virtual private network (VPN).** A VPN is a private, secure network operated over a public and insecure network. It keeps the contents of the network messages hidden from observers who may have access to public traffic. Using the VPN tunneling approach described earlier, an individual or organization can set up a network connection on the Internet and send encrypted data back and forth, using the IP-packet-within-an-IP-packet method to deliver the data safely and securely. VPN support is built into most Microsoft Server software, including Windows 2000, and client support for VPN services is included in Windows XP. While true private network services can cost hundreds of thousands of dollars to lease, configure, and maintain, a VPN can be established for much less.

Securing Authentication

A final use of cryptosystems is to provide enhanced and secure authentication. One approach to this issue is provided by **Kerberos,** named after the three-headed dog of Greek mythology ("Cerberus" in Latin) that guarded the gates to the underworld. Kerberos uses symmetric key encryption to validate an individual user's access to various network resources. It keeps a database containing the private keys of clients and servers that are in the authentication domain that it supervises. Network services running on the servers in the shared authentication domain register with Kerberos, as do clients that wish to use those services.[6] The Kerberos system knows these private keys and can authenticate one network node (client or server) to another. For example, it can authenticate a client to a print service. To understand Kerberos, think of a typical multi screen cinema. You acquire your ticket at the box office, and the ticket-taker then lets you in to the proper screen based on the contents of your ticket. Kerberos also generates temporary session keys—that is, private keys given to the two parties in a conversation. The session key is used to encrypt all communications between these two parties. Typically, a user logs into the network, is authenticated to the Kerberos system, and is then authenticated by the Kerberos system to other resources on the network.

Kerberos consists of the following three interacting services, all of which rely on a database library:

- Authentication Server (AS), which is a Kerberos server that authenticates clients and servers
- Key Distribution Center (KDC), which generates and issues session keys
- Kerberos Ticket Granting Service (TGS), which provides tickets to clients who request services

An authorization ticket is an identification card for a particular client that verifies to the server that the client is requesting services and that the client is a valid member of the Kerberos system and, therefore, authorized to receive services. The ticket consists of the client's name and network address, a ticket validation starting and ending time, and the session key, all encrypted in the private key of the target server.

9

Kerberos operates according to the following principles:

1. The KDC knows the secret keys of all clients and servers on the network.
2. The KDC initially exchanges information with the client and server by using the secret keys.
3. Kerberos authenticates a client to a requested service on a server through TGS and by issuing temporary session keys for communications between the client and the KDC, the server and the KDC, and the client and the server.
4. Communications take place between the client and server using the temporary session keys.[7]

    Figures 9-8 and 9-9 illustrate this process.

You can obtain Kerberos free of charge from MIT at *http://web.mit.edu/Kerberos/dist/index .html*. If you decide to use it, however, be aware of some concerns in its operation. If the Kerberos servers are subjected to denial-of-service attacks, no client can request (or receive) any services. If the Kerberos servers, service providers, or clients' machines become compromised, their private key information may also be compromised.

Attacks on Cryptosystems

Historically, attempts to gain unauthorized access to secure communications have used brute force attacks in which the ciphertext is repeatedly searched for clues that can lead to the algorithm's structure. These attacks are known as ciphertext attacks and involve a hacker search-

(1) User logs in to client machine (c)
(2) Client machine encrypts password to create client key (Kc)
(3) Client machine sends clear request to Kerberos TGS
(4) Kerberos TGS returns ticket consisting of:
    • Client/TGS session key for future communications between client and TGS [Kc,TGS], encrypted
      with the client's key
    • Ticket-granting ticket (TGT), which contains the client name, client address, ticket valid times,
      and the client/TGS session key, all encrypted in the TGS's private key

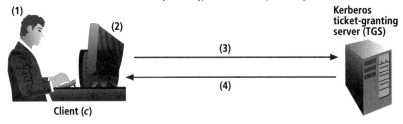

Figure 9-8 Kerberos Login
© Cengage Learning 2012

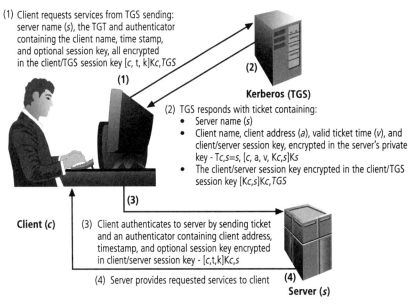

Figure 9-9 Kerberos Request for Service
© Cengage Learning 2012

ing for a common text structure, wording, or syntax in the encrypted message that can enable him or her to calculate the number of each type of letter used in the message. This process, known as frequency analysis, can be used along with published frequency patterns of various languages and can allow an experienced attacker to quickly crack almost any code if the individual has a large enough sample of the encoded text. To protect against this, modern algorithms attempt to remove the repetitive and predictable sequences of characters from the ciphertext.

Occasionally, an attacker may obtain duplicate texts, one in ciphertext and one in plaintext, which enable the individual to reverse-engineer the encryption algorithm in a **known-plaintext attack**. Alternatively, an attacker may conduct a **selected-plaintext attack** by sending the potential victim a specific text that gets forwarded to others. When the victim does encrypt and forward the message, it can be used in the attack if the attacker can acquire the outgoing encrypted version. At the very least, reverse engineering can usually lead the attacker to discover the cryptosystem that is being employed.

Publicly available encryption methods are generally released to the user community for testing of the encryption algorithm's resistance to cracking. In addition, attackers often keep themselves informed of which attack methods have failed. Although the purpose of sharing encryption methods is to develop a more secure algorithm, it has the danger of keeping attackers from wasting their time, thus freeing them up to find new weaknesses in the cryptosystem or more challenging means of obtaining encryption keys.

In general, attacks on cryptosystems fall into four general categories: man-in-the-middle, correlation, dictionary, and timing. Although these attacks have been discussed elsewhere, they are discussed here in the context of cryptosystems.

Man-in-the-Middle

A **man-in-the-middle** attack is used to intercept the transmission of a public key or even to insert a known key structure in place of the requested public key. Thus, attackers attempt to place themselves between the sender and receiver, and once they've intercepted the request for key exchanges, they send each participant a valid public key, which is known only to the attackers. To the victims of such attacks, their encrypted communication appears to be occurring normally, but, in fact, the attacker is receiving each encrypted message and decoding it (with the key given to the sending party), and then encrypting it and sending it to the originally intended recipient. Establishment of public keys with digital signatures can prevent a man-in-the-middle attack, as the attacker cannot duplicate the signatures.

Correlation Attacks

As the complexities of encryption methods have increased, so, too, have the tools and methods that cryptanalysts use to attack cryptosystems. **Correlation attacks** are collections of brute-force methods that attempt to deduce statistical relationships between the structure of the unknown key and the ciphertext that is the output of the cryptosystem. Differential and linear cryptanalysis, advanced methods of breaking codes that are beyond the scope of this discussion, have been used to mount successful attacks on block cipher encryptions such as DES. If these advanced methods can calculate the value of the public key, and if this can be achieved in a reasonable time, all messages written with that key can be decrypted. The only defense against this kind of attack is the selection of strong cryptosystems that have stood the test of time, thorough key management, and strict adherence to the best practices of cryptography in the frequency of changing keys.

Dictionary Attacks

In a **dictionary attack**, the attacker encrypts every word in a dictionary using the same cryptosystem used by the target. The attacker does this in an attempt to locate a match between the target ciphertext and the list of encrypted words from the same cryptosystem. Dictionary attacks can be successful when the ciphertext consists of relatively few characters—for example, files that contain encrypted user names and passwords. If an attacker acquires a system password file, the individual can run hundreds of thousands of potential passwords from the dictionary he or she has prepared against the stolen list. Most computer systems use a well-known one-way hash function to store passwords in such files, but this almost always allows the attacker to find at least a few matches in any stolen password file. After a match is located, the attacker has essentially identified a potential valid password for the system under attack.

Timing Attacks

In a **timing attack**, the attacker eavesdrops during a victim's session and uses statistical analysis of the user's typing patterns and inter-keystroke timings to discern sensitive session information. While timing analysis may not directly result in the decryption of sensitive data, it can be used to gain information about the encryption key and perhaps the cryptosystem in use. It may also eliminate some algorithms as possible candidates, thus narrowing the attacker's search. In this narrower field of options, the attacker can increase the odds of eventual success. Once the attacker has successfully broken an encryption, he or she may launch a **replay attack**, which is an attempt to resubmit a recording of the deciphered authentication to gain entry into a secure source.

Defending from Attacks

Encryption is a very useful tool in protecting the confidentiality of information that is in storage and/or transmission. However, it is only that—a tool in the information security administrator's arsenal of weapons against threats to information security. Frequently, unenlightened individuals describe information security exclusively in terms of encryption (and possibly firewalls and antivirus software). But encryption is simply the process of hiding the true meaning of information. Over the millennia, mankind has developed dramatically more sophisticated means of hiding information from those who should not see it. No matter how sophisticated encryption and cryptosystems have become, however, they have retained the same flaw that the first systems contained thousands of years ago: If you discover the key—that is, the method used to perform the encryption—you can determine the message. Thus, key management is not so much the management of technology as the management of people.

Encryption can protect information when it is most vulnerable, that is, when it is outside the organization's systems. Information in transit through public or leased networks is outside the organization's control. With loss of control can come loss of security. Encryption helps organizations secure information that must travel through public and leased networks by guarding the information against the efforts of those who sniff, spoof, and otherwise skulk around. As such, encryption is a vital piece of the security puzzle.

Running Case: I'll Take One of Those VPN Servers, Too

"And that's what I mean by synchronous versus asynchronous tokens," Rachel told Meghan. "More coffee?"

Their 20-minute coffee break had turned into an hour-long tutorial on encryption standards and authentication mechanisms for VPNs.

"Yes, please," Meghan said. "Now that I know what you're talking about, I think I'll leave some of the technical details to Alex, but I do think we're going to want the strong authentication. As far as the encryption standard, I think we're going to need a standard that we can not only rely on, but that we can advertise to our customers."

Meghan said this with a gleam in her eyes.

Rachel was puzzled. "Your customers? I thought we were talking about VPN support for traveling sales calls and remote employee use."

"We were," Meghan said mischievously. "But now you've given me a great idea. We can build custom client access packages that will allow our customers to access their data using a VPN connection rather than batching it and transferring it on tape. This is going to open up a whole new market for us!"

Rachel leaned back in her chair and laughed. "Glad I could help! Now about that top-of-the-line VPN server you were going to buy through us...."

Chapter Summary

- Encryption is the process of rendering information unreadable to all but the intended recipients. The purpose of encryption is to preserve the integrity and confidentiality of information and/or make the process of authenticating users more effective.

- Firewalls and VPNs use encryption to provide protection both for the data in transit and to help keep the firewall secure. Encryption of data incurs costs since it requires processing time to encrypt and decrypt the data being protected.

- The science of encryption is known as cryptology. Cryptography is the complex process of making and using codes. Applying these concealing techniques is called encryption, and decoding the ciphertext is called decryption. The process used to decrypt data when the process and/or keys are unknown is called cryptanalysis.

- Cryptographic controls are the techniques and tools used to implement cryptographic protections in networks and information systems. They are used to secure e-mail, Web access, Web applications, file transfers, and remote access procedures like VPNs. Other controls can be applied to secure the authentication processes, like Kerberos.

- Cryptographic control systems are often subject to attack. Many methods of attack have evolved, including some that use brute computational approaches and others that make use of weaknesses that are often found in the implementation of cryptographic controls. In some attacks, known as man-in-the-middle attacks, the attackers attempt to place themselves between the parties of a secured communication channel. Other attacks combine brute-force approaches like dictionary attacks and timing attacks into a so-called correlation attack.

Review Questions

1. What is cryptology?

2. What is cryptography?

3. How is encryption used to secure networks in general, and how is it used in firewalls?

4. Which aspect of digital data passing between networks is preserved by cryptography?

5. Which functions of a firewall might not be compatible with or are compromised by using encryption?

6. What problems encountered by firewalls are made worse by using encryption?

7. What name is given to an attack in which the attacker intercepts a public key exchange and acts as a go-between for the network session?

8. What name is given to an attack in which the attacker randomly guesses a key value or password through trial and error?

9. What name is given to a general type of attack where an attacker is attempting to guess a key value or password from a list of known, likely, or published possible values?

10. What is the difference between a digital signature and a digital certificate?

11. What is the main advantage of using symmetric encryption?

12. What is the advantage of using asymmetric encryption?

13. You handle security for a corporation with 10 branch offices and 5000 employees. You are tasked with issuing security keys to each of these employees. How would you handle this?

14. What is IPSec?

15. What does an IPSec policy do?

16. What is an X.509 digital certificate?

17. What protocols protect online purchases?

18. What can digital certificates authenticate that IPSec cannot?

19. Digital certificates contain digital signatures and public keys as well as detailed information about the digital certificate holder. However, the quality of all that information depends on one thing that neither you nor the digital certificate holder can control. What is it?

20. What is a hybrid security control?

Real World Exercises

1. Use an Internet browser to research Pretty Good Privacy (PGP). Peruse at least two Web sites, and then answer the following questions:

   a. Who is Phil Zimmerman, and what is his relationship to PGP?

   b. What is a web of trust? What is the alternative to a web of trust?

   c. What year was PGP released?

   d. What is the relationship between the company Network Associates and PGP?

2. Use an Internet browser to research Secure Sockets Layer (SSL). Peruse at least two Web sites, and then answer the following questions:

   a. Briefly describe SSL.

   b. How is SSL different from TLS? How is it similar?

   c. What RFC first defined the TLS/SSL protocol?

3. Use an Internet browser to research Advanced Encryption Standard (AES). Peruse at least two Web sites, and then answer the following questions:

   a. What was this cipher's name before it was adopted as the AES?

   b. When did the National Institute of Standards and Technology announce the AES?

   c. What is the AES's fixed block size? What are its possible key sizes?

4. Use an Internet browser to research symmetric encryption and asymmetric encryption. Peruse at least two Web sites for each term, and then answer the following questions:

   a. Which type of encryption can be computed more quickly?

   b. How are the two approaches the same?

   c. How are the two approaches different?

   d. How are the two approaches used together to provide a better way to do encryption?

5. Use an Internet browser to research digital signature and digital certificate. Peruse at least two Web sites for each term, and then answer the following questions:

   a. What are the typical components of a digital certificate?

   b. What international standard controls how digital certificates are used?

   c. How are digital signatures related to digital certificates?

9

Hands-On Projects

HANDS-ON PROJECTS

Project 9-1: Using Truecrypt Encryption to Protect Files

TrueCrypt is a freeware utility that allows you to harness the power of AES-256 Encryption to protect your files, whether in storage or transmission. You begin by creating containers (or volumes), which are fixed-size folders in which you can store information. The emphasis is on the word "fixed-size." It is most common to create a volume container approximately the size of (slightly smaller than, actually) the storage mechanism you plan to use—a USB flash drive or a writeable CD or DVD. Once the volume is created, logging into the volume using the TrueCrypt utility mounts the volume like a hard drive, and you simply add and remove your files as needed. Ready to send the files or move to another location? Just close the utility, and it's secured, encrypted, and portable.

Creating the TrueCrypt Container

1. This lab uses version 6.1a. Click **Start**, **All Programs**, **TrueCrypt**, **TrueCrypt**. You should see the main TrueCrypt window.

2. We begin by creating the TrueCrypt volume, the storage container used to secure the files. Click the **Create Volume** button. The TrueCrypt Volume Creation Wizard opens.

3. Make sure the **Create a file container** option is selected and click **Next**. TrueCrypt volumes can be stored in separate files or can occupy an entire drive or partition. In the next window, select **Standard TrueCrypt volume** and click **Next**. You should see the Volume Location window.

4. Now we specify where the volume will be located. Click **Select File**. Browse to My Documents, and type *yourlastname* in the **File name** text box, where you substitute your first initial and last name for *yourlastname* (e.g., mwhitman). Click **Save**. Back at the Volume Location window, click **Next**.

5. In the Encryption Options window, leave the default AES (Advanced Encryption Standard) as the encryption algorithm and RIPEMD-160 as the hash algorithm and click **Next**.

6. In the Volume Size window, you specify the size of the TrueCrypt volume. The larger the size, the longer it will take to generate the volume. Type **2** in the text box and click **Next**.

7. In the Volume Password window, you specify your password to access the file.

8. The longer your password, the more secure is the container. Type your password again in the "Confirm field." (*Note:* If you forget your password, the information stored in the container is LOST FOREVER!) The instructions below the password fields provide advice for creating a good password. Your password should not be shown in plaintext; it is shown that way here only to illustrate the exercise. Do not click "Display password" unless you are creating the volume in a private, secure location.

9. Once you have entered your password in both fields, click **Next**. If you have a weak password, TrueCrypt will warn you in a pop-up window. If it does warn you, click **Yes** to close the pop-up window.

10. In the next window, TrueCrypt will generate a random pool of values from which to draw your encryption key. Move your mouse in quick random motions for at least 30 seconds to generate a sufficiently large key pool, and then click **Format**.

11. Since we are using a small volume, it should be created within a few seconds. Click **OK** in the pop-up window indicating the volume has been successfully created, and then click **Exit**.

Using the TrueCrypt Container

12. Back at the TrueCrypt main window, select the drive to which you would like to map your volume in the top frame (e.g., Z:). In the volume area, click the **Select File** button.

13. Browse to the location you specified when creating your TrueCrypt volume (e.g., My Documents*yourlastname*) and click it, and then click **Open**.

14. Back at the TrueCrypt main window, click **Mount**. Enter your password in the field and click **OK**.

15. You can now access the volume, which appears as an empty folder from any Windows file browser or access field. As long as you are logged into the system and the drive stays mapped, the contents of the volume are accessible. If you log out or shut down the computer, the volume is resecured. The volume can be copied onto a USB drive, CD, DVD R or R/W, or to any other location. All you need is TrueCrypt installed on the system you use in order to access the file; the contents will be available. Click **Exit** to close the TrueCrypt window.

Dismounting the TrueCrypt Container

16. To close the volume and thus resecure your data, reopen the TrueCrypt main window. Select the drive to which you mapped your volume in the top frame (e.g., Z:). In the Volume area, click the **Dismount** button.

17. If you have more than one volume mounted concurrently (yes, this is possible), you can select Dismount All to close them. Click **Exit** to close the TrueCrypt window.

Project 9-2: Sending Encrypted E-Mail with iSafeguard

iSafeguard Freeware is a utility that can encrypt e-mail and digitally sign documents. This project requires two systems with Microsoft Outlook or Outlook Express configured to access two users' e-mail accounts. Setting up the e-mail accounts to free sources like Gmail, Hotmail, or Yahoo! Mail is relatively straightforward. Tutorials are available on the various sites that describe how to set up Outlook and Outlook Express to access these accounts. iSafeguard Freeware is free for personal use and may be downloaded from *www.mxcsoft.com/download.htm*. The software actually works with a wide variety of e-mail clients; however, for the purposes of this lab, we require Outlook or Outlook Express.

This lab works well with teams of two or more. Each student sets up the iSafeguard on her workstation, along with a free e-mail address and client. Then the students exchange e-mail addresses (or use e-mail addresses assigned by the instructor) and exchange passphrases.

Installing iSafeguard

1. Download and install iSafeguard on your system. Follow the installation prompts, clicking **I agree** at the User License prompt and **Next** at all other prompts. Click **Close** when finished.

Launching iSafeguard and Creating a new Profile

1. After installation completes, the software will launch. The first time you log in, you will be asked to create a new profile. iSafeguard provides three ways to log in: (1) from the Start menu; (2) from the Windows Explorer context menu; and (3) from the desktop icon. You may choose any one of the login methods.

2. As long as you are logged in, the certificates and private keys are available to you for encrypting, decrypting, signing, and verifying. You can tell that you are logged in by finding the golden lock icon on the right side of the taskbar.

3. Select the **I want to create a new profile** option. Click the **OK** button. Another dialog box asks you to choose a login name and a passphrase.

4. Choose a login name (e.g., your first-name initial and your last name, like mwhitman) and a passphrase (strong password).

5. Click the **OK** button. The next time you use the software, you will be asked to enter the login name and the passphrase that will be used to verify that you own the profile. Your profile can only be decrypted with the login name and the passphrase. The program generates a new profile for you. The default path of your profile is shown in the currently displayed dialog box.

6. Click **OK** to dismiss the dialog box. Your profile is passphrase protected. The stronger the passphrase, the better. Don't forget to make a backup copy of your profile and keep it in a safe place. Remember that if you lose your profile or forget your passphrase, you will never be able to recover your encrypted data.

Obtaining a Certificate You have successfully created your profile, but it is empty until you create a certificate (and key pair) for yourself or import other people's certificates. Upon your clicking the OK button in the iSafeguard—For Your Information dialog box, the software will launch the Certificate Generation wizard to guide you through the process of generating a new certificate. If you don't want to generate a certificate at this time, you may cancel the wizard. Remember, you need a certificate to sign and encrypt your files and e-mails.

1. Click the **Next** button to go to the next page.

2. In the Subject Information screen, enter your full name and e-mail address.

3. Click the **Next** button to go to the next page. Your full name and e-mail address will show in your final digital certificate.

4. In the Key Pair Size window, you can use one of the predefined key pair sizes or choose your own customized key pair size. Choose a Key Pair Size of 2048 and then click the **Next** button to go to the next page.

5. The next screen describes the Key Pair Expiration Date. You need to select an expiration date for your certificate. If you don't want your certificate to expire, select a year very far into the future for the expiration year. Select an expiration date, and then click the **Next** button.

6. The wizard is ready to create your certificate and key pair. Click the **Next** button to continue. It may take a few minutes to generate your key pair, depending on the size you choose. When the generation is completed, you will see the Key Pair Generation screen.

7. Click the **Finish** button to close the wizard.

Viewing the Certificate

1. Locate the golden lock icon on the taskbar.

2. Right-click the golden lock icon.

3. Select **Certificate Manager** from the pop-up menu. This will start the Certificate Manager. To see the details of the certificate, click the certificate item in the window to select it.

4. Click the **Open** button. Alternatively, double-click the certificate. The certificate viewer starts, and the General tab is shown.

5. Click the **Details** tab to find more information about the certificate. This is a standard X.509 digital certificate that includes version number, serial number, signature algorithm, etc. You now have a self-signed certificate and the associated private key; both are stored in your profile. You can use the certificate to secure files and other digital assets.

Exchanging Certificates/Public Keys If you want to securely communicate with other people, you need to exchange certificates/public keys. When you encrypt a file with a password and then send it, you will need to tell the receiver your password in order for the receiver to receive the file. This is password exchange, one form of key exchange, and you have to find a secure method to tell the receiver the password.

Otherwise, anyone who knows the password can decrypt the file. Similarly you need to exchange public keys (as part of an X.509 certificate) with your correspondents. However, your public key can be public knowledge, meaning anyone can have it. Your public key is like a lock that is used to lock data. Data locked with your public key can only be decrypted with your private key. iSafeguard allows you to give your certificate to other people easily and conveniently. You may use any of the following options to do so. For the purposes of this lab, use the first option to e-mail the certificate to your receiver.

Using Certificate Manager Context Menu

1. Start iSafeguard Certificate Manager.
2. Right-click the certificate you want to send to others.
3. Select **E-mail selected certificate** from the pop-up menu.
4. Follow your e-mail program to send the exported certificate to others.

Using Drag and Drop

1. Start iSafeguard Certificate Manager.
2. Select the certificate you want to send to others.
3. Drag the selected certificate and drop it to your e-mail program.
4. Follow your e-mail program to send the exported certificate to others.

Using Certificate Export Wizard

1. Start iSafeguard Certificate Manager.
2. Select the certificate you want to send to others.
3. Click the **Export** button.
4. Follow the wizard to export the certificate to a file.
5. Attach the certificate file to your e-mail program to send to others.

Receiving Certificates from Other People Ask your friends/correspondents to do what you just did to export their certificates. You can receive their certificates via e-mail messages or file attachments, depending on how they exported them.

Receiving a Certificate as an E-Mail Message If the certificate you received is part of an e-mail message, do the following to import the certificate to your profile:

1. Start iSafeguard Certificate Manager.
2. Select the certificate text within your e-mail program, including the beginning "-----BEGIN CERTIFICATE-----" and ending "-----END CERTIFICATE-----."
3. Drag and then drop the certificate to the iSafeguard Certificate Manager window.
4. Follow the wizard to import the certificate to your profile.

Alternatively, you can:

1. Log in if you are not currently logged in.

2. Click inside the e-mail window so that it gets the input focus.

3. Press and hold the **Ctrl** and **Shift** keys at the same time, and then press the **P** key (this is the default).

4. Follow the wizard to import the certificate to your profile.

Receiving a Certificate as an E-Mail Attachment If the certificate you received is a file attachment, you can:

1. From your e-mail program, open the attached certificate file.

2. Log in if you are not currently logged in.

3. Follow the wizard to import the certificate to your profile.

Alternatively, you can:

1. Log in if you are not currently logged in.

2. Save the attached file to your hard drive.

3. Launch Windows Explorer and locate the file you've just saved.

4. Right-click the file.

5. Select **iSafeguard**, and then **Properties** from the pop-up menu.

6. Follow the wizard to import the certificate to your profile.

Receiving a Certificate as a File If the certificate you received is a file, you can:

1. Log in if you are not currently logged in.

2. Launch Windows Explorer and locate the file that contains the certificate.

3. Right-click the file.

4. Select **iSafeguard**, and then **Properties** from the pop-up menu.

5. Follow the wizard to import the certificate to your profile.

Securing E-Mails iSafeguard Certificate Manager uses an end-to-end security model. That means that only the e-mail composer and the intended recipients can read encrypted e-mails. You prepare your e-mail the way you usually do, using Outlook Client (you should not use Word to compose your e-mail).

We will use the following hotkeys to perform some of the basic functions:

*   Ctrl+Shift+E—Encrypt the text in the focus window and place the encrypted ciphertext back in the window.

*   Ctrl+Shift+S—Sign the text in the focus window and place the signed text back in the window.

*   Ctrl+Shift+B—Sign and then encrypt the text in the focus window, and then place the signed and encrypted content back in the window.

- Ctrl+Shift+D—Decrypt the ciphertext in the focus window, and then verify the signature of the decrypted content if signed. The decrypted plaintext is placed inside the window.

- Ctrl+Shift+R—Decrypt and verify the ciphertext in the focus window and display the clear text in a viewer. The original ciphertext is left untouched.

- Ctrl+Shift+P—Display the crypto properties of the ciphertext in the focus window. The intended recipients and the signer as well as the encryption and signature algorithms, are all shown.

Signing E-Mail Messages To sign your e-mail message:

1. Log in if you are not currently logged in.
2. Compose your e-mail message using an e-mail software program.
3. Press the hotkey **Ctrl+Shift+S** or right-click the **golden lock icon** on your taskbar, then select **Focus Window**, and then **Sign**.
4. Select one message signer, and then click **OK**.
5. Send the e-mail.

Encrypting E-Mail Messages To encrypt your e-mail message:

1. Log in if you are not currently logged in.
2. Compose your e-mail message using an e-mail software program.
3. Press the hotkey **Ctrl+Shift+E** or right-click the **golden lock icon** on your taskbar, then select **Focus Window**, and then **Encrypt**.
4. Select one or more message recipients, and then click **OK**.
5. Send the e-mail.

Signing and Encrypting E-Mail Messages To sign and encrypt your e-mail message:

1. Log in if you are not currently logged in.
2. Compose your e-mail message using an e-mail software program.
3. Press the hotkey **Ctrl+Shift+B** or right-click the **golden lock icon** on your taskbar, then select **Focus Window**, and then **Sign & encrypt**.
4. Select a message signer and one or more recipients, and then click **OK**.
5. Send the e-mail.

Reading Encrypted E-Mail Messages To read your encrypted message:

1. Log in if you are not currently logged in.
2. Make sure the window that contains the ciphertext has the input focus by clicking inside the window.
3. Press the hotkey **Ctrl+Shift+R** or right-click the **golden lock icon** on your taskbar, then select **Focus Window**, and then **Read**.

Decrypting and Verifying To decrypt and verify an encoded message:

1. Log in if you are not currently logged in.

2. Make sure the window that contains the ciphertext has the input focus by clicking inside the window.

3. Press the hotkey **Ctrl+Shift+D** or right-click the **golden lock icon** on your taskbar, then select **Focus Window**, and then **Decrypt & verify**.

Checking Crypto Properties To check crypto properties:

1. Log in if you are not currently logged in.

2. Make sure the window that contains the ciphertext has the input focus by clicking inside the window.

3. Press the hotkey **Ctrl+Shift+P** or right-click the **golden lock icon** on your taskbar, then select **Focus Window**, and then **Properties**.

Running Case Projects

CASE PROJECTS

Student Tasks

In this exercise, students enable the firewall to function as a VPN server in order to allow remote users to connect to the internal network. Specifically, you learn how to:

- Enable the OpenVPN server by creating the necessary CA server and associated files
- Configure Vyatta to allow encrypted connections

1. Configure OpenVPN.

   a. Log in to the Vyatta interface via the command line using "vyatta" as the username and the password you created in Chapter 4.

   b. Type **mkdir /home/vyatta/openvpn_server_keys** and press **Enter**.

Now, we will configure and access the root account in order to install OpenVPN.

   c. Type **configure** and press **Enter**.

   d. Type **set system login user root authentication plaintext-password** *password to use for root account* and press **Enter**.

   e. Type **commit** and press **Enter**.

   f. Type **save** and press **Enter**.

   g. Switch to the root user by typing **su** and press **Enter**. When prompted for the password, enter the password you entered in Step d.

   h. Move to the /usr/share/doc/openvpn/examples/easy-rsa/2.0 directory.

    i. Type **vim vars** and press **Enter**. (*Note*: Vim is a text editor. Learning to use vim is outside the scope of this textbook, but there are multiple tutorials available on the Internet.)

    j. Edit the export KEY_DIR line, changing the $EASY_RSA/keys value to /root/ openvpn_keys. Save the file, and then exit.

    k. Type **source ./vars** and press **Enter**.

    l. Type **./clean-all** and press **Enter**.

    m. Type **./build-ca** and press **Enter**. This will begin the CA build process. Edit the default values as appropriate for your country, state, city, and organization name. Accept all other default values.

    n. Type **./build-key-server server** and press **Enter**. This will begin the server key build process. Edit the default values as appropriate for your country, state, city, and organization name. Accept all other default values.

    o. Answer **y** when asked if you want to sign the certificate.

    p. Answer **y** when asked if you want to commit the certificate request.

    q. Type **./build-key client** and press **Enter**.

    r. As with previous steps, edit the default values as necessary, accepting all other default values.

    s. Answer **y** when asked if you want to sign the certificate.

    t. Answer **y** when asked if you want to commit the certificate request.

    u. Type **./build-dh** and press **Enter**.

    v. Type **exit** and press **Enter** to leave the root account.

2. Configure Vyatta.

    a. Enter configuration mode by typing **configure** and press **Enter**.

    b. Type **set interfaces openvpn vtun0** and press **Enter**.

    c. Type **set interfaces openvpn vtun0 mode server** and press **Enter**.

    d. Type **set interfaces openvpn vtun0 server subnet** *INTERNAL NIC IP ADDRESS/ SUBNET MASK* and press **Enter**.

    e. Type **set interfaces openvpn vtun0 tls ca-cert-file /home/vyatta/openvpn_server_keys/ca.crt** and press **Enter**.

    f. Type **set interfaces openvpn vtun0 tls cert-file /home/vyatta/openvpn_server_keys/server.crt** and press **Enter**.

    g. Type **set interfaces openvpn vtun0 tls crl-file /home/vyatta/openvpn_server_keys/01.pem** and press **Enter**.

    h. Type **set interfaces openvpn vtun0 tls dh-file /home/vyatta/openvpn_server_keys/dh1024.pem** and press **Enter**.

    i. Type **set interfaces openvpn vtun0 tls key-file /home/vyatta/openvpn_server_keys/server.key** and press **Enter**.

    j. Type **commit** and press **Enter**.

    k. Type **save** and press **Enter** to save the changes.

9

Endnotes

1. Richardson, R. "CSI Computer Crime and Security Survey, 2009." Accessed 1 June 2010 from *www.gocsi.com.*

2. Ronald L. Krutz and Russell Dean Vines. *The CISSP Prep Guide: Mastering the Ten Domains of Computer Security* (New York: John Wiley and Sons, Inc. (2001): 131.

3. Savard, John (1999). "The Advanced Encryption Standard (Rijndael)" Accessed 31 March 2004 at *http://home.ecn.ab.ca/~jsavard/crypto/co040401.htm.*

4. Verisign. Understanding PKI. *Verisign Online.* Accessed 22 November 2006 from *verisign.netscape.com/security/pki/understanding.html.*

5. Cisco Systems, Inc. White Paper: IPSec. *Cisco Online,* November 21, 2000. Accessed 22 November 2006 from *www.cisco.com/en/US/tech/tk827/tk369/tech_white_papers_list.html.*

6. Jennifer G. Steiner, Clifford Neuman, and Jeffrey I. Schiller. An authentication service for open network systems (paper presented for Project Athena, March 30, 1988). Accessed 22 November 2006 from *www.scs.stanford.edu/nyu/05sp/sched/readings/kerberos.pdf.*

7. Ronald L. Krutz and Russell Dean Vines. *The CISSP Prep Guide: Mastering the Ten Domains of Computer Security.* New York: John Wiley and Sons, Inc. (2001): 40.

chapter 10

*"We all live every day in
virtual environments,
defined by our ideas."*
—Michael Crichton

Setting Up a Virtual
Private Network

After reading this chapter and completing
the exercises, you will be able to:

- Explain the components and essential operations of virtual private networks (VPNs)
- Describe the different types of VPNs
- Discuss VPN setups, such as mesh or hub-and-spoke configurations
- Select the right VPN tunneling protocol for a specific user need
- Define the process of setting up secure remote access for individual users via a VPN
- Discuss best practices for effective configuration and maintenance of VPNs

Running Case: Second Time's a Charm

Rachel looked up at the class from her seat in the last row. Alex had risen to the challenge this time. When Data Mart's chief operating officer, Meghan Sanders, indicated that she wanted to develop a VPN solution not only for Data Mart employees but also as one of the company's product lines, Alex quickly volunteered to head up the technical R&D effort. While it was risky, given his problems with Data Mart's first firewall solution, Alex was given the green light by Data Mart's CEO. He quickly proved that, when it came to VPNs, he knew what he was doing. In fact, his last job, before becoming Data Mart's chief technologist, was as team leader for a start-up VPN appliance company. That company eventually went out of business, but the experience provided Alex with the tools to make this new assignment work.

He had just spent the past hour teaching Data Mart employees how to set up and use their company-issued laptops to connect remotely to the company's new high-end VPN server. And not only had he prepared a very impressive training session, he had gone so far as to set up a remote connection so that the entire class could actually configure and test their laptops right there. When the class broke up, the employees were all set.

Alex started the presentation for his second project—the VPN solutions suite that offered a variety of data rates and options to customers for secure access to their data. The marketing staffers in the room were starting to get excited. The commissions projected for the new VPN offerings could create some very respectable paychecks for each of them. Alex quickly went over the technical details of the packages he had developed, and then Meghan stepped up and covered the pricing strategies, discounts, and services that accompanied the technical solutions.

As the first session ended, Rachel joined Meghan and Alex at the front of the room. "Alex, I'm really impressed," she said. "You've got the VPN setup down cold!"

Alex smiled for perhaps the first time since Rachel met him. "Thanks, Rachel," he said. "I feel like I'm swimming in familiar waters for the first time." He then turned to Meghan. "Since Rachel is here," he told her, "I should let you know I have some concerns about our scalability with the current appliance. It's more than capable of handling our internal needs, plus about a fourth of our clients, should they all sign on to the new program, but if it's as successful as we all hope, we'll start to push the appliance's capacity and need to think about an upgrade."

Meghan turned to Rachel. "An upgrade?" she said. "Already? We just installed it a week ago!"

Introduction

As was discussed in Chapter 9, organizations routinely combine two or more LANs to facilitate point-to-point communications over a secure line that can be accessed by no one else. Private **leased lines**—services purchased from a service provider that give the user dedicated use of a predefined bandwidth or data rate—are often used to connect remote users or branch offices to a central administrative site. However, private leased lines don't scale well; the cost of leased lines and the complexity of the technology used to support them often make this an expensive, even if more reliable, option than using the public Internet infrastructure. The growth and widespread use of the Internet have been coupled with the use of encryption technology to produce a solution for specific types of private communication channels: virtual private networks (VPNs). VPNs function like private leased lines; they encapsulate and encrypt the data being transmitted, and they use authentication to ensure that only approved users can access the VPN. However, rather than having to use an expensive leased line, VPNs provide a means of secure point-to-point communications over the public Internet. In this chapter, we examine the details of VPN operations.

VPN Components and Operations

VPNs used for e-commerce and telecommuting are now widespread. Many telecommunications companies provide VPN services. VPNs can be set up with special hardware or with firewall software that includes VPN functionality. Many firewalls have VPN systems built into them because the rules that apply to the VPN are part of the firewall's existing security policy. When set up correctly, a VPN can be a critical component in an organization's perimeter security configuration.

The goal of a VPN is to provide a cost-effective and secure way to connect business locations to one another and connect remote workers to office networks. When each remote branch office has a secure connection to the central office using a VPN, all branches can communicate via a LAN-based file-sharing protocol, such as NetBIOS or AppleTalk.

VPN Components

VPNs have two types of components: hardware devices and software that performs security-related activities. This section briefly discusses these components.

10

Each VPN connection has two endpoints. **Endpoints** are hardware and/or software components that perform the following: encryption to secure data, authentication to make sure the host requesting the data is an approved user of the VPN, and **encapsulation,** the inclusion of one data structure inside another data structure. Encapsulation helps protect the integrity of the information being sent. These endpoints could consist of a user's laptop at a remote location and an organization's VPN server (as in teleworking), or they could be two VPN appliances that establish a relatively permanent connection between two distant local area networks.

A VPN connection occurs within the context of a TCP/IP tunnel. A **tunnel** is the channel or pathway over a packet network used by the VPN that runs through the Internet from one endpoint to another. The term "tunnel" can be misleading because it implies that there is a single cable joining one endpoint to another and that no one but approved users can send or receive data using that cable. In reality, a VPN uses a virtual tunnel between two endpoints. A **virtual tunnel** is a communications path that makes use of Internet-based hosts and servers to conduct data from one network station to another, just like any other TCP/IP data transmission. While using the Internet's system of networks and servers keeps costs down and makes it relatively easy to set up a VPN, it also adds a level of uncertainty to VPN communications because so many systems are involved (see the "Benefits and Drawbacks of VPNs" section later in this chapter).

In diagrams of networks that employ VPNs, you'll often see a graphical pipe used to join the two endpoints, as shown in Figure 10-1. This very simplified picture illustrates that a VPN is essentially a communications path through the Internet that provides a heightened degree of security for two participants.

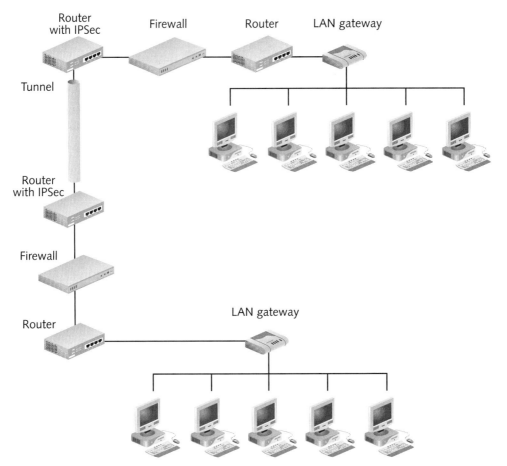

Figure 10-1 Simplified Model VPN
© Cengage Learning 2012

Figure 10-2, on the other hand, illustrates that VPNs in fact traverse the public Internet and must therefore handle the Internet's protocols and procedures. The figure shows one set of endpoints for a VPN: routers that support Internet Security Protocol (IPSec). Each LAN's communications first go to its **gateway** (the device connecting the organization's networks and equipment to the Internet), and then to its backbone network and servers.

Figure 10-2 is greatly simplified; the ISPs involved may or may not be connected to the Internet backbone, and there are probably more than three servers that lie between one LAN and the other. Not only that, more than one VPN may be involved when different offices that are part of the same organization attempt to share information. Figure 10-3 builds on this model, illustrating the complexity of the Internet environment in which VPNs are deployed.

The devices that form the endpoints of the VPN can be any of the following:

- A server running VPN protocols (e.g., IPSec)
- A VPN appliance, which is a special hardware device devoted to setting up VPN communications

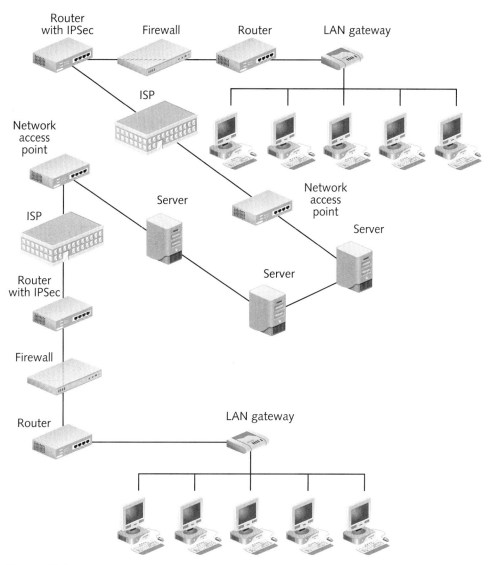

Figure 10-2 Model VPN
© Cengage Learning 2012

- A firewall/VPN combination: Many high-end firewall programs support VPN setups as part of their built-in features.

- A router-based VPN: Routers that support IPSec can be set up at the perimeter of the LANs to be connected. These are also sometimes called **IPSec concentrators**. IPSec concentrators use a complex set of security protocols to protect information, including Internet Key Exchange (IKE), which provides for the exchange of security keys between the machines in the VPN.

The final components in a VPN scenario are certificate servers, which manage certificates if that is required, and client computers that run VPN client software, which lets remote users connect to the LAN over the VPN.

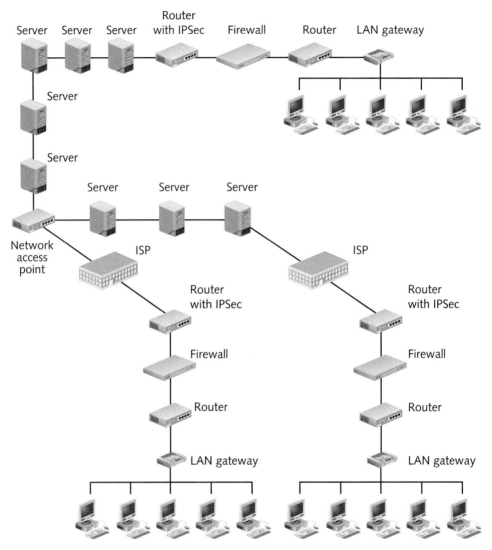

Figure 10-3 A Common VPN
© Cengage Learning 2012

Essential Activities of VPNs

Because the VPN uses the Internet to transfer information from one computer or LAN to another, the data needs to be well protected. The essential activities that protect data transmitted over a VPN are:

- IP encapsulation
- Data payload encryption
- Encrypted authentication

These are discussed in the following sections.

IP Encapsulation As you know, information that passes to and from TCP/IP-based networks travels in manageable chunks called packets. VPNs protect packets by performing IP encapsulation, the process of enclosing one packet within another one that has different IP source and destination information.

Encapsulating IP packets within other packets hides the source and destination information of the encapsulated packets; the encapsulating packet uses the source and destination addresses of the VPN gateway. The gateway might be a router that uses IPSec, a VPN appliance, or a firewall that functions as a VPN and that has a gateway set up.

What's more, because a VPN tunnel is being used, the source and destination IP addresses of the encapsulated packets can be in the private reserved blocks that are not usually routable over the Internet, such as the 10.0.0.0/8 addresses or the 192.168.0.0/16 reserved network blocks.

Data Payload Encryption One of the big benefits of using VPNs is that they can be implemented to fully or partially encrypt the data portion of the packets that are passing through them. The encryption can be accomplished in one of two ways:

- **Transport mode:** The host encrypts traffic when it is generated; the data part of packets is encrypted, but not the headers. This is commonly used for remote client-to-server communications, as in teleworking.

- **Tunnel mode:** The traffic is encrypted and decrypted in transit, somewhere between the source computer that generated it and its destination. In addition, both the header and the data portions of packets are encrypted.

The level of encryption applied by the firewall or VPN hardware device varies; the higher the number of data bits used to generate keys, the stronger the encryption. As you recall from Chapter 9, a key is the value used by the cryptographic formula or algorithm to either produce or decrypt ciphertext. The length of a key affects the strength of the encryption.

Encrypted Authentication Some VPNs use the term **encryption domain** to describe everything in the protected network and behind the gateway. The same cryptographic system that protects the information within packets can be used to authenticate computers that use the VPN. Authentication is essential because hosts in the network that receive VPN communications need to know that the host originating the communications is an approved user of the VPN.

Hosts are authenticated by exchanging long blocks of code, called keys, that are generated by complex formulas called algorithms. As you learned in Chapter 9, two types of keys can be exchanged in an encrypted transaction:

- Symmetric keys: Here, the keys are exactly the same. The two hosts exchange the same secret key to verify their identities to each other.

- Asymmetric keys: Here, each participant has two different keys: a private key and a complementary public key. The participants in the transaction exchange their public keys. Each can then use the other's public key to encrypt information, such as the body of an e-mail message. When recipients receive the encrypted messages, they can decrypt them using their private keys.

Symmetric key encryption is faster and more computationally efficient, but it is more difficult to manage because each participant must have a copy of the secret key before communication can occur. The choice and implementation of a key distribution system is another complication in setting up a VPN. For more on keys in general and symmetric/asymmetric keys, algorithms, and key distribution systems in particular, see Chapter 9.

Benefits and Drawbacks of VPNs

One of the benefits of VPNs is that they provide secure networking without the expense of establishing and maintaining leased lines. VPNs also allow the packet encryption/translation overhead to be done on dedicated systems, decreasing the load placed on production machines. Finally, VPNs allow you to control the physical setup and therefore decide upon data encryption levels—for example, whether to encrypt data at the physical level or at the application level.

VPNs do have some significant drawbacks. They are complex and, if configured improperly, can create significant network vulnerabilities. Leased lines may be more expensive, but the chance of introducing vulnerabilities is not as great because they create point-to-point connections. VPNs also make use of the unpredictable and often unreliable Internet. Multinational VPNs, in particular, can experience problems because packets being routed through various hubs can encounter slowdowns or blockages that you can neither predict nor resolve. You then have to explain to administration that the problem is occurring thousands of miles away and you'll just have to wait until it is fixed there.

Another problem involves authorization; if your VPN's authorization is not configured properly, you can easily expose the inner workings of your organization's network.

VPNs Extend Network Boundaries

High-speed Internet connections, such as cable modems and DSL lines, are changing the role of VPNs within large networks at all types of organizations. Only a few years ago, when high-speed connections were expensive and relatively hard to come by, remote users primarily used VPNs with connections created by dial-up modems connected to the organization's network. They connected to the organizational network through the VPN only for the length of the dial-up connection. Because many ISPs charged by the minute or placed restrictions on the number of hours a customer could be connected each month, the remote user was likely to hang up as soon as business was completed. Now, it's increasingly likely that the contractors, vendors, and telecommuters who connect to an organization's internal network through a VPN will have a high-speed connection that is always on. Unless you specifically place limits on how long such employees can use the VPN, they can be connected to your network around the clock. Thus, each VPN connection extends your network to a location that is out of your control, and each such connection can open up your network to intrusions, viruses, or other problems. You need to take extra care with users who connect to the VPN through always-on connections. Here are some suggestions for how to deal with the increased risk:

- *Use two or more authentication tools to identify remote users.* Multifactor authentication adds something the user possesses, such as a token or smart card, and something physically associated with the user, such as fingerprints or retinal scans. For such a system to work, each remote user would have to have a smart card reader, fingerprint reader, retinal scanner, or other (potentially expensive) device along with a computer.

- *Integrate virus protection.* Make sure each user's computer is equipped with up-to-date virus software that scans the computer continually, screening out any viruses as soon as they enter the system. After files are encapsulated, encrypted, and sent through the VPN tunnel, any viruses in those files will make it through the firewall into the organizational network. Virus-scanning software needs to be present on the network to catch any viruses, of course; however, requiring vendors, partners, or contractors to use their own antivirus software will reduce the chance of viruses entering the system in the first place.

- *Use Network Access Control (NAC).* NAC is a computer networking philosophy and a related set of protocols that are together used to evaluate the trustworthiness of a client wishing to join a network. NAC solutions vary in complexity; some check for installed antivirus software, current antivirus updates, and relevant security patches. More-sophisticated solutions can remediate identified defects by installing the appropriate items.[1]

- *Set usage limits.* It should be the organization's policy and practice to inform all VPN participants that they need to terminate VPN sessions as soon as they are done with them. Configuration of the VPN software can enforce the policy limits.

These provisions should be supported by the organization's security policies, and requirements for their enforcement should be written into any agreements with business partners or contractors. As with all security policies, they should be explained to employees and business partners during orientation and security awareness sessions.

Types of VPNs

You can set up two types of VPNs. The first type links two or more networks and is called a **site-to-site VPN**. The second type makes a network accessible to remote users who need dial-in access and is called a **client-to-site VPN**. The two types are not mutually exclusive; many large organizations link the central office to one or more branch locations using site-to-site VPNs while providing dial-in access to the central office by means of a client-to-site VPN.

Because of their cost effectiveness, VPNs are growing steadily in popularity. Accordingly, you can choose between a number of options for configuring VPNs: hardware systems, software systems, and systems that combine hardware and software. When choosing a system, keep in mind that any type of VPN, whether it consists of hardware or software or both, needs to be able to work with any number of different operating systems or types of computers.

VPN Appliances

One way to set up a VPN is to use a general-purpose hardware device such as a router that has been configured to use IPSec or another VPN protocol (see the "Tunneling Protocols Used with VPNs" section later in this chapter). Another option is to obtain a **VPN appliance**, a hardware device specially designed to serve as the endpoint for one or more VPNs and connect multiple LANs. VPN appliances can permit connections between large numbers of users or multiple networks, but they don't provide other services, such as file sharing and printing.

Most commercial VPN vendors offer a range of appliance solutions, starting at the SOHO grade, which can support 10, 25, or 50 simultaneous VPN connections along with stateful packet filtering, network address translation (NAT), and even antivirus protection. Most include some sort of Web-based interface and wizard installations. On the other end of the spectrum are products that can support up to 2000 or more concurrent VPN connections at speeds in the gigabit range.

The advantage of using appliances that leverage purpose-built hardware is illustrated in Figure 10-4. If the server goes offline or crashes (as shown in the left half of the figure), the hardware VPN appliance doesn't go offline (as shown in the right half of the figure). Additionally, hardware systems may enable you to connect more tunnels and users than comparably priced software-only systems.

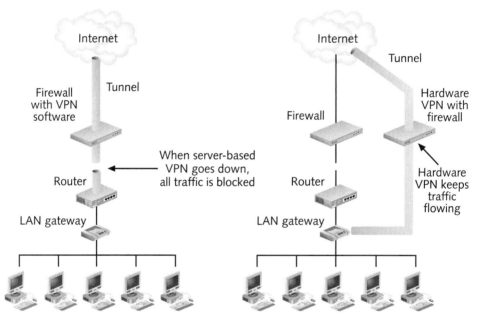

Figure 10-4 Hardware VPN
© Cengage Learning 2012

Software VPN Systems

Software VPNs are generally less expensive than hardware systems, and they tend to scale better on fast-growing networks. These products support traveling employees who need private access to an organizational LAN or intranet from any dial-up location, IT staff who need the ability to secure internal networks and partition parts of the network, and organizational partners who require secure connections to a company's data network for business collaboration.

Most high-end VPN products also use policy manager systems for enterprise-wide software distribution, policy creation, and management. Security settings for the entire organizational network using VPN can be made from the administrator's computer. Settings can be based on "role-based policies." This allows multiple configuration profiles for end users to be created; examples include "out-of-office," "at-home," or "in-office." In addition, all installations and maintenance can be performed from a single central location.

An increasingly popular alternative for remote access to Web-enabled applications is SSL-based VPNs. These make use of the SSL protocol (instead of IPSec) but only allow access to Web-enabled applications.

VPN Combinations of Hardware and Software

You may also use VPN systems that implement a VPN appliance at the central network and use client software at the remote end of each VPN connection. Most VPN concentrator appliances give users the choice of operating in one of two modes: client mode or network extension mode. In client mode, the concentrator acts as a software client, enabling users to connect to another remote network via a VPN. In network extension mode, the concentrator acts as a hardware device enabling a secure site-to-site VPN connection.

Mixed Vendor VPNs

You may have to operate a VPN system that is "mixed"—such as one, that uses hardware and software from different vendors. You might have one company that issues certificates, another that handles the client software, and another that handles the VPN termination, and so on. The challenge is to get all these pieces to communicate with one another successfully. To do this, pick a standard security protocol that is widely supported by all the devices, such as IPSec, which is described later in this chapter.

VPN Setups

10

If you have only two participants in a VPN, the configuration is relatively straightforward in terms of expense, technical difficulty, and the time involved. However, when three or more networks or individuals need to be connected, there are several options: a mesh configuration, a hub-and-spoke arrangement, or a hybrid setup.

Mesh Configuration

In a **mesh configuration**, each participant (i.e., network, router, or computer) in the VPN has an approved relationship, called a **security association (SA)**, with every other participant. In configuring the VPN, you need to specifically identify each of these participants to every other participant that uses the VPN. Before initiating a connection, each VPN hardware or software terminator checks its routing table or **SA table** to see if the other participant has an SA with it. A mesh configuration is shown in Figure 10-5.

In Figure 10-5, four separate LANs are joined in a mesh VPN. Each LAN has the ability to establish VPN communications with all of the other participants in each of the other LAN segments. If a new LAN is added to the VPN, all other VPN devices must be updated to include information about the new users in the LAN. Thus, each host can be added to the state table. In addition, every host that needs to use the VPN in each of the LANs must be equipped with sufficient memory to operate the VPN client software and to communicate with all other hosts in the VPN. The problem with VPNs is the difficulty associated with expanding the network and updating every VPN device whenever a host is added. For fast-growing networks, a hub-and-spoke configuration is preferable.

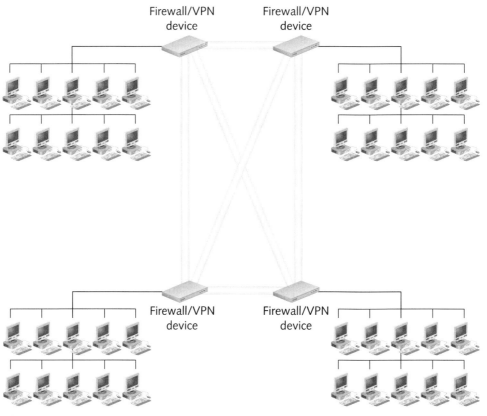

Figure 10-5 Mesh VPN
© Cengage Learning 2012

Hub-and-Spoke Configuration

In a **hub-and-spoke configuration**, a single VPN router contains records of all SAs in the VPN. Any LANs or computers that want to participate in the VPN only need to connect to the central server, not to any other machines in the VPN. This setup makes it easy to increase the size of the VPN as more branch offices or computers are added. Figure 10-6 illustrates a hub-and-spoke configuration.

In Figure 10-6, the central VPN router resides at the organization's central office because that is where the main IT staff reside. A hub-and-spoke VPN is ideally suited for communications within an organization that has a central main office and a number of branch offices.

The problem with hub-and-spoke VPNs is that the requirement that all communications flow into and out of the central router slows down communications, especially if branch offices are located on different continents. In addition, the central router must have double the bandwidth of other connections in the VPN because it must handle both inbound and outbound traffic at the same time. The high-bandwidth charge for such a router can easily amount to several thousand dollars per month. However, in a situation where all communications need to go through the central office anyway, a hub-and-spoke configuration makes sense because of the heightened security it gives to all participants.

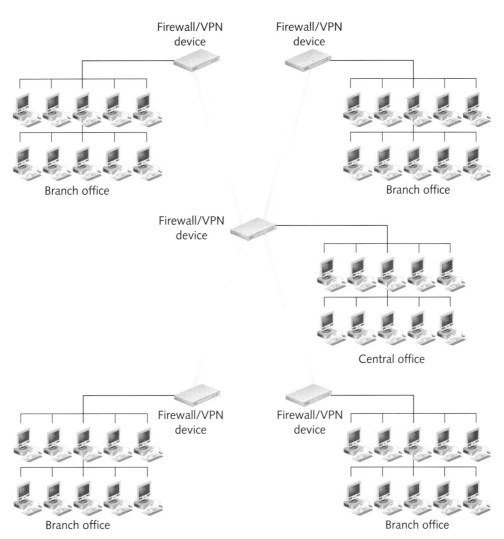

Figure 10-6 Hub-and-Spoke VPN
© Cengage Learning 2012

Hybrid Configuration

As organizations grow, a VPN that starts out as a mesh design or hub-and-spoke design often evolves into a mixture of the two. This is a common scenario, and you don't need to exclusively use one configuration or another.

Because mesh configurations tend to operate more efficiently, the central core linking the most important branches of the network should probably be a mesh configuration. However, as branch offices are added, they can be added as spokes that connect to a central VPN router at the central office.

Time-critical communications with branch offices should be part of the mesh configuration. However, far-flung offices, such as overseas branches, can be part of a hub-and-spoke configuration. A hybrid setup that combines the two configurations benefits from the strengths of each one—the scalability of the hub-and-spoke option and the speed of the mesh option. If at all possible, try to have the branch offices that participate in the VPN use the same ISP. That will minimize the number of "hops" between networks.

Configurations and Extranet and Intranet Access

Whether you use a hub-and-spoke, mesh, or hybrid configuration, creating VPNs that connect business partners and other branches of your own organization raises a number of questions and considerations.

Each end of the VPN represents an extension of your organizational network to a new location; you are, in effect, creating an **extranet**. The same security measures you take to protect your own network should be applied to the endpoints of the VPN. Each remote user or business partner should have firewalls and antivirus software enabled, for instance.

VPNs can also be used to give parts of your own organization access to other parts through an organizational **intranet**. For example, a large organization that has facilities spread across several buildings in separate locations can use a VPN to allow the IT staff in one location to monitor servers in the other location, or to allow the accounting staff to adjust the financial records or job records in a server located in another building. Leaving the VPN connection "always on" can enable an unscrupulous staff to gain access to organizational resources that they are not allowed to use. VPN users inside your organization should have usage limits and antivirus and firewall protection, just as outside users should, as indicated in Figure 10-7.

Tunneling Protocols Used with VPNs

In the past, firewalls that provided for the establishment of VPNs used **proprietary** protocols. Such firewalls would only be able to establish connections with remote LANs that used the same brand of firewall. Today, the widespread acceptance of the IPSec protocol with the Internet Key Exchange (IKE) system means that proprietary protocols are used far less often.

IPSec/IKE

IPSec is a standard for secure encrypted communications developed by the Internet Engineering Task Force (IETF). IPSec, which you learned about in detail in Chapter 7, provides for the following: encryption of the data part of packets, authentication to guarantee that packets come from valid sources, and encapsulation between two VPN hosts.

IPSec provides two security methods: Authenticated Headers (AH) and Encapsulating Security Payload (ESP). AH is used to authenticate packets, whereas ESP encrypts the data portion of packets. You can use these methods together.

IPSec can work in two different modes: transport mode and tunnel mode. Transport mode is used to provide secure communications between hosts over any range of IP addresses. Tunnel mode is used to create secure links between two private networks. Tunnel mode is the obvious choice for VPNs; however, there are some concerns about using tunnel mode in a client-to-site VPN because the IPSec protocol by itself does not provide for user

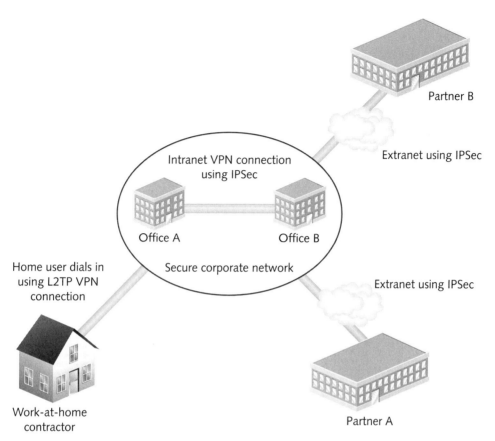

Figure 10-7 VPN for Intranets and Extranets
© Cengage Learning 2012

authentication. However, when combined with an authentication system like Kerberos, IPSec can authenticate users.

IPSec is commonly combined with IKE as a means of using public key cryptography to encrypt data between LANs or between a client and a LAN. IKE provides for the exchange of public and private keys. The key exchange is used to tell the hosts wishing to initiate a VPN connection that each is a valid user of the system. IKE can also determine which encryption protocols should be used to encrypt data that flows through the VPN tunnel. The process of establishing an IPSec/IKE VPN connection works like this:

1. The host or gateway at one end of the VPN sends a request to a host or gateway at the other end, asking to establish a connection. (Both hosts have obtained the same key, called a preshared key, from the same trusted authority.)

2. The remote host or gateway generates a random number and sends a copy of the number back to the machine that made the original request.

3. The original machine encrypts its preshared key using the random number and sends the preshared key to the remote host or gateway.

4. The remote host decrypts the preshared key and compares it to its own preshared key or, if it has multiple keys, a set of keys called a **keyring**. If the preshared key matches one of its own keys, the remote host encrypts a public key using the preshared key and sends it back to the machine that made the original request.

5. The original machine uses the public key to establish a security association (SA) between the two machines, which establishes the VPN connection.

Even though many firewalls support IPSec and IKE, they sometimes use different versions of these protocols. If your VPN uses more than one kind of firewall and you plan to implement an IPSec/IKE VPN, check with the manufacturers of those firewalls to see if their products will work with the other firewalls you have, and ask about any special configuration you have to perform.

PPTP

Point-to-Point Tunneling Protocol (PPTP) is commonly used by remote users who need to connect to a network using a dial-in modem connection. PPTP uses Microsoft Point-to-Point Encryption (MPPE) to encrypt data that passes between the remote computer and the remote access server. It's older technology than the other dial-in tunneling protocol, L2TP, but it is useful if support for older clients is needed. It's also useful because packets sent using PPTP can pass through firewalls that perform Network Address Translation (NAT)—in contrast to L2TP, which is incompatible with NAT but provides a higher level of encryption and authentication.

L2TP

Layer 2 Tunneling Protocol (L2TP) is an extension of the protocol long used to establish dial-up connections on the Internet, **Point-to-Point Protocol (PPP)**. L2TP uses IPSec rather than MPPE to encrypt data sent over PPP. It provides secure authenticated remote access by encapsulating data into packets that are sent over a PPP channel. Using L2TP, the initiating host machine makes a connection to a modem using PPP and then transmits those PPP data packets to be forwarded to another, separate remote access server. When the data reaches that remote access server, its payload is unpacked and forwarded to the destination host on the internal network.

PPP Over SSL and PPP Over SSH

Point-to-Point Protocol (PPP) over Secure Sockets Layer (SSL) and **Point-to-Point Protocol (PPP) Over Secure Shell (SSH)** are two UNIX-based methods for creating VPNs. Both combine an existing tunnel system (PPP) with a way of encrypting data in transport (SSL or SSH). As you probably know already, PPP can be used to establish a connection between two hosts over an IP-based system.

SSL is a public key encryption system used to provide secure communications over the World Wide Web (see Chapter 7 for more on SSL). SSH is the UNIX secure shell, which was developed when serious security flaws were identified in Telnet. SSH enables users to perform secure authenticated logons and encrypted communications between a client and host. SSH requires that both client and host have a secret key in advance—a **preshared key**—in order to establish a connection.

Which protocol should you use in a VPN you establish, and why? Table 10-1 lists the protocols mentioned in this section, along with situations in which they might be used.

Protocol	Recommended Use
IPSec/IKE	Rapidly becoming the protocol of choice for VPN connections of all sorts; should be used when the other protocols are not acceptable
PPTP	When a dial-up user has an old system that doesn't support L2TP and needs to use PPP to establish a VPN connection to your network
L2TP	When a dial-up user needs to establish a VPN connection with your network (L2TP provides stronger protection than PPTP.)
PPP Over SSL	When a UNIX user needs to create a VPN connection "on the fly" by connecting to the SSL port on a server
PPP Over SSH	When a UNIX user needs to create a VPN connection "on the fly" over the UNIX secure shell (SSH) and both parties know the secret key in advance

Table 10-1   VPN Protocols and Their Uses

Enabling Remote Access Connections Within VPNs

If users in disparate locations need to connect to the central network via a VPN, a remote access connection is needed. A VPN is a good way to secure communications with users who need to connect remotely by dialing into their ISP and establishing connections to the organizational network, or by using their cable or DSL Internet connections to initiate the VPN connection. To enable a remote user to connect to a VPN, you need to issue VPN client software to that user. You should also make sure the user's computer is equipped with antivirus software and a firewall. You may need to obtain a key for the remote user if you plan to use IPSec to make the VPN connection as well.

If one or more remote users who want to make a VPN connection to you reside overseas, you may encounter the problem of having to find a phone provider that will have dial-up numbers in all locations. Some providers may not cover the foreign countries you want; you may have to sign up with several different providers to obtain dial-up access from certain locations.

Configuring the Server

One step in setting up a client-to-server VPN is configuring the server to accept incoming connections. If you use a firewall-based VPN, you need to identify the client computer. The major operating systems incorporate their own methods of providing secure remote access. In Linux, you use the IP Masquerade feature built into the Linux kernel. A part of IP Masquerade, called VPN Masquerade, enables remote users to connect to the Linux-based firewall using either PPTP or IPSec.

Windows (in this example, Windows 7) includes a Wizard that makes it particularly easy to set up a workstation to make a VPN connection that will allow the individual user to connect his or her home workstation to a remote location. The system can also be set up to allow incoming VPN connections. However, if users wish to do this, they need to configure their home router/ firewalls to allow the connection. Figure 10-8 shows the initial setup window for the Windows VPN connection. Figure 10-9 shows the configuration window into which the user enters the destination address information once one of the options shown in Figure 10-8 has been specified. Figure 10-10 shows the Cisco VPN client window, Cisco being a popular VPN vendor.

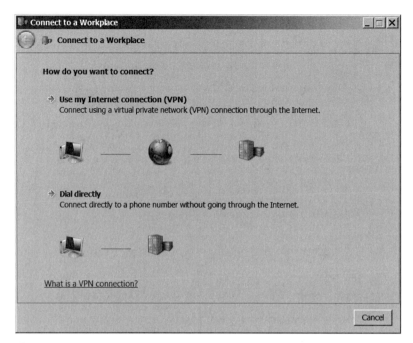

Figure 10-8 Initial Setup Window for Windows 7 VPN Connection
© Cengage Learning 2012

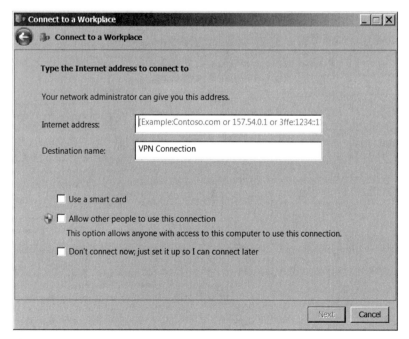

Figure 10-9 Configuration Window for Windows 7 VPN Connection
© Cengage Learning 2012

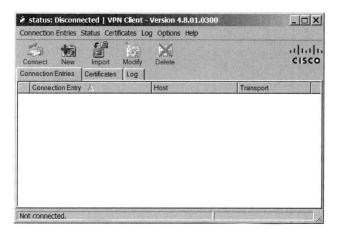

Figure 10-10 Cisco VPN Client
© Cengage Learning 2012

Configuring Clients

After you set up the server, you need to configure each client that wants to use the VPN. This involves installing and configuring VPN client software or, in the case of a Windows-to-Windows network, using the Network Connection Wizard.

The most important things to consider are whether your client software will work with all client platforms and whether the client workstation is itself protected by a firewall. All users who dial in to the LAN using a VPN extend the LAN and open up a new "hole" through which viruses and hackers can gain access. A requirement that remote users protect laptops and other computers with firewalls can be part of your organization's VPN policy.

VPN Best Practices

The successful operation of a VPN depends not only on its hardware and software components and overall configuration but also on a number of best practices. These include security policy rules that specifically apply to the VPN, the integration of firewall packet filtering with VPN traffic, and auditing the VPN to make sure it is performing acceptably.

The Need for a VPN Policy

In an organizational setting, the VPN is likely to be used by many different workers in many different locations. A VPN policy is essential for identifying who can use the VPN and for ensuring that all users know what constitutes proper use of the VPN. This can be a separate stand-alone policy, or it may be a clause within a larger security policy.

The policy should spell out who should have VPN access to your organizational network. For example, vendors might be granted access to the network through a VPN connection, but they may only be allowed to access information pertaining to their own company's accounts. The vendor VPN solution should have controls that allow the administrator to restrict where vendors can go on the organizational network. On the other hand, managers and full-time employees who access the network through a VPN while traveling should be granted more comprehensive access to network resources.

The policy should also state whether authentication is to be used and how it is to be used, whether **split tunneling** (two connections over a VPN line) is permitted, how long users can be connected using the VPN at any one session, whether virus protection is included, and so on. SANS provides a sample VPN policy in PDF format at *www.sans.org/security-resources/ policies/Virtual_Private_Network.pdf*.

Connecting from Personal Computers

One of the most troublesome aspects of allowing users remote access to an organization's internal network has to do with use of personal equipment. For example, many organizations do not provide employees or contractors a separate system to use for VPN access from home. This means that access is commonly done from the user's own computer.

In such situations, remote users must be carefully trained to understand that even when they access the organizational network from a personally owned piece of equipment, all organizational security policies (permitted use, required antivirus measures, etc.) apply during that use.

It can also be difficult for the organization's security personnel to assure that any monitoring they perform or agents they install in order to grant remote access function only during the duration of the VPN connection. After all, employees may use their own computers for entertainment and personal uses that are not allowed for a company-owned system. It would not be appropriate for a content filter or a software license metering program to block employees from such personal uses.

Packet Filtering and VPNs

When configuring a VPN, you must decide early on where data encryption and decryption will be performed in relation to packet filtering. You can do encryption and decryption either outside the packet-filtering perimeter or inside it. Figure 10-11 shows encryption and decryption outside the packet-filtering perimeter.

In the scenario shown in Figure 10-11, the firewall/VPN combination is configured to perform transport encryption. Packets are encrypted at the host as soon as they are generated. Already-encrypted packets pass through the packet filters at the perimeter of either LAN and are not filtered. In this scenario, if the LAN that generates the communications has been infected by a virus or is compromised in some way, the packets that pass through the packet filters could be infected and could then infect the destination LAN.

Figure 10-12 illustrates the alternative: encryption and decryption performed inside the packet-filtering perimeter using the tunnel method. Keep in mind that the network configurations illustrated in this figure and in Figure 10-10 depict a packet filter that is separate from the firewall (this is done for clarity of explanation). In fact, packet filtering might be done by the firewall itself; the same firewall may provide VPN services, or a separate VPN appliance may be used instead of a firewall-based VPN.

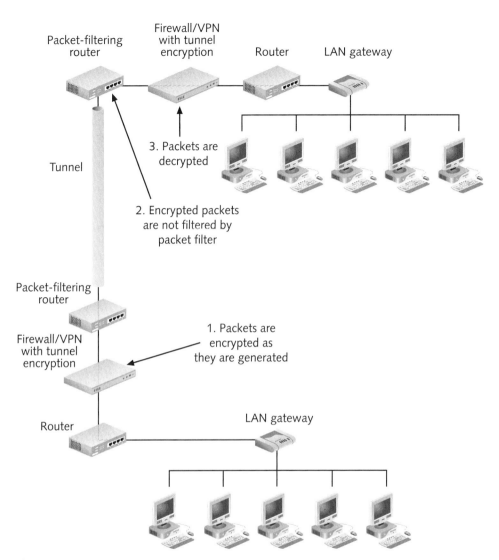

Packet-filtering
router

Firewall/VPN
with tunnel
encryption

Router

LAN gateway

3. Packets are
decrypted

Tunnel

2. Encrypted packets
are not filtered by
packet filter

Packet-filtering
router

Firewall/VPN
with tunnel
encryption

1. Packets are
encrypted as
they are generated

Router

LAN gateway

10

Figure 10-11 External Encryption
© Cengage Learning 2012

In Figure 10-12, packet filtering is performed before the data reaches the VPN. Mangled packets can be dropped before they reach the firewall/VPN, thus providing additional protection for the destination LAN.

PPTP Filters PPTP is commonly used when older clients need to connect to a network through a VPN or when a tunnel must pass through a firewall that performs NAT. For PPTP traffic to pass through the firewall, you need to set up packet-filtering rules that permit such communications. Incoming PPTP connections arrive on TCP port 1723. In addition, PPTP packets use Generic Routing Encapsulating (GRE) packets that are identified by the protocol identification number ID 47. Table 10-2 shows the filter rules that you would use for remote users at IP addresses 211.208.30.1 and 105.40.4.10.

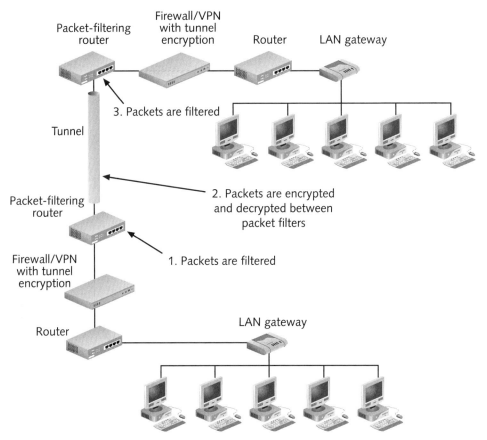

Figure 10-12 Internal Encryption
© Cengage Learning 2012

Protocol	Transport Protocol	Source IP	Source Port	Destination IP	Destination Port	Action
PPTP	TCP	211.208.30.1, 105.40.4.10	Any	Remote access server's IP address	1723	Allow
GRE	ID 47	Any		Remote access server's IP address		Allow

Table 10-2 PPTP Packet-Filtering Rule Set

L2TP and IPSec Packet-Filtering Rules

Because L2TP uses IPSec to encrypt traffic as it passes through the firewall, you need to set up packet-filtering rules that cover IPSec traffic. Table 10-3 shows the filter rules you would use for remote users at IP addresses 211.208.30.1 and 105.40.4.10.

Protocol	Transport Protocol	Source IP	Source Port	Destination IP	Destination Port	Action
IKE	UDP	211.208.30.1, 105.40.4.10	500	Remote access server's IP address	500	Allow
AH	ID 51	Any		Remote access server's IP address		
ESP	ID 50	Any		Remote access server's IP address		Allow

Table 10-3 PPTP Packet-Filtering Rule Set 2

Auditing and Testing the VPN

After the VPN is installed, you need to test the VPN client on each computer that might use the VPN. In an organization with many different workstations, this can be a time-consuming prospect. There's no easy way around this, but you can choose client software (which is installed as part of the test) that is easy for end users to install on their own to save you time and effort.

To give you an idea of how the testing of a VPN client might work, here's a step-by-step scenario:

1. Issue VPN client software and a certificate to the remote user.

2. Call the remote user on the phone and lead him or her through the process of installing the software and storing the certificate.

3. If you are using IPSec, verify with the remote user that the IPSec policies are the same on both the remote user's machine and on your VPN gateway.

4. Tell the user to start up the VPN software and connect to your gateway. (Hopefully, you'll be able to remain on the phone while the end user connects, but if the remote user has only one telephone line and a dial-up connection to the Internet, you may have to communicate by e-mail.)

5. If there are any problems connecting to the gateway, tell the remote user to write down or report the error message exactly to help you correctly diagnose the problem.

6. After the connection is established, the remote user should authenticate by entering his or her username and password when prompted to do so.

After the testing of the client is done, you need to check the VPN to make sure files are being transferred at an acceptable rate and that all parts of the VPN remain online when needed. To give you an idea of how the testing of file transferring might work, here's a step-by-step scenario:

1. After the remote user connects to your network, tell him or her to start up a Web browser and connect to your server.

2. Enter the username and password needed to access the server when prompted.

3. Locate the files to be transferred.

4. Copy the files from the organizational network to the remote user's computer (or vice versa).

5. Keep track of how long the file transfers take.

6. Open the files after they are transferred to make sure they transferred completely and work correctly.

7. The remote user should disconnect from the organizational network when he or she is finished transferring files.

If part of the network goes down frequently, switch to another ISP—preferably, an ISP that also serves another part of the VPN. If you find yourself needing to switch to another ISP, consider asking the various ISPs the following questions to help determine which ones can help you and which ones cannot:

- How often does your network go offline?
- Do you have back-up servers that will keep customers like me online if the primary server goes down?
- Do you have back-up power supplies in case of a power outage?
- How far are you from the network backbone? (Two or three hops is considered close; the closer to the backbone the ISP is, the faster the connection.)

Running Case: Thinking Ahead

Rachel smiled. When Meghan expressed shock that the newly installed VPN appliance might soon need an upgrade, Rachel's first reaction was cautious. "Let's wait and see," she said. But something about the tone of Alex's voice caught Meghan's attention. She turned to him and said "What did you have in mind, Alex?"

Alex reached into his briefcase and pulled out a neatly prepared report. "I've got preliminary numbers on capacity and demand based on your marketing projections," he told Meghan. "If your numbers are accurate, and I have no reason to doubt they are, this system will be paid for in totality by the time we've landed our 20th client, and that's even if they all buy the basic package. Purchasing another unit identical to this one at that time won't incur a major capital investment, since it will be paid for by the time we've landed our 50th customer, and the two appliances together will serve every customer we have at the premium level, plus all our internal users. I would advise, however, that we start planning for a dedicated, smaller unit just for internal use, to improve our integration with the current firewall rules. The customers and the employees have different rule sets, and if we set up different appliances, it will make management of the firewall and VPN integration easier."

Meghan saw the excited look on Alex's face. She reached out and patted him on the shoulder. "Alex, my friend, that's the most animated I've seen you in years. If Rachel agrees, and I have a sneaking suspicion she will, I'm going to recommend that we cut you loose to handle these new technologies as you see fit."

She looked over at Rachel.

"I agree, Alex," Meghan replied. "Go for it!"

Chapter Summary

- The growth and widespread use of the Internet has been coupled with the use of encryption technology to produce a solution for specific types of private communication channels: virtual private networks (VPNs). VPNs provide a means of secure point-to-point communications over the public Internet.

- VPNs are used for e-commerce and telecommuting and are becoming widespread. VPNs can be set up with special hardware or with firewall software that includes VPN functionality. Many firewalls have VPN systems built into them, and VPN is a critical component in an organization's perimeter security configuration.

- Because the VPN uses the Internet to transfer information from one computer or LAN to another, the data needs to be well protected. The essential activities that protect data transmitted over a VPN are: IP encapsulation, data payload encryption, and encrypted authentication.

- There are two general types of VPN, site-to-site and client-to-site, and these are not necessarily mutually exclusive. One way to set up a VPN is to use a hardware device such as a router that has been configured to provide a VPN protocol. You can also use a VPN appliance or run VPN software on a general-purpose server.

- VPN implementations may evolve from configurations that are either a mesh or a hub-and-spoke architecture becoming a more complex, hybrid setup. In a mesh configuration, each participant in the VPN has an approved relationship with every other participant. In a hub-and-spoke configuration, a single, central VPN router contains records of all associations in the VPN, and any other participants only need to connect to the central server, not to any other machines in the VPN. As organizations grow, a VPN that starts out as a mesh design or hub-and-spoke design often evolves into a mixture of the two.

- Firewalls that use proprietary protocols can only establish connections with remote LANs that use the same brand of firewall. Today, the widespread acceptance of the IPSec protocol with the Internet Key Exchange (IKE) system means that proprietary protocols are used far less often. IPSec provides two security methods: Authenticated Headers (AH) and Encapsulating Security Payload (ESP). AH is used to authenticate packets, whereas ESP encrypts the data portion of packets. You can use these methods together.

- Point-to-Point Tunneling Protocol (PPTP) is commonly used by remote users who need to connect to a network using a dial-in modem connection. Layer 2 Tunneling Protocol (L2TP) is an extension of the protocol long used to establish dial-up connections on the Internet, Point-to-Point Protocol (PPP).

- Point-to-Point Protocol (PPP) over Secure Sockets Layer (SSL) and Point-to-Point Protocol (PPP) over Secure Shell (SSH) are two UNIX-based methods for creating VPNs. Both combine an existing tunnel system (PPP) with a way of encrypting data in transport (SSL or SSH).

- A VPN is a good way to secure communications with users who need to connect remotely by dialing into their ISP, or who use their cable or DSL Internet connections to initiate the VPN connection. To enable a remote user to connect to a VPN, you need to issue VPN client software to that user. You should make sure the user's computer is equipped with antivirus software and a firewall. You may need to obtain a key for the remote user if you plan to use IPSec to make the VPN connection as well.

■ The successful operation of a VPN depends not only on its hardware and software components and overall configuration but on a number of best practices. These include security policy rules that specifically apply to the VPN, the integration of firewall packet filtering with VPN traffic, and auditing the VPN to make sure it is performing acceptably.

Review Questions

1. What do VPNs do that firewalls cannot do?

2. What are the disadvantages of using leased lines to set up a private network?

3. What are the disadvantages of using a VPN instead of a leased line?

4. Why would you choose a VPN that is built into a firewall rather than a VPN appliance or a router?

5. In the context of VPNs, why is the term *tunnel* misleading?

6. What is the downside of using a proprietary VPN protocol?

7. Why is authentication an essential part of a VPN?

8. What are the ways that participants in a VPN can be authenticated?

9. Which of the VPN protocols discussed in this chapter provide for client-to-site authentication?

10. What are the benefits of setting up a VPN rather than using a leased line?

11. What special considerations need to be made when setting up a multinational VPN?

12. Why would you consider purchasing a VPN appliance rather than installing less expensive VPN software?

13. Aside from the fact that they're less expensive, under what circumstances does using a software VPN give you an advantage over a VPN appliance?

14. Define and describe a mesh VPN configuration.

15. Under what circumstances is a mesh VPN configuration most useful?

16. Define and describe a hub-and-spoke VPN configuration.

17. When is a hub-and-spoke VPN configuration most useful?

18. Which VPN protocol is most widely used today?

19. Tunnel mode seems like the obvious choice in using IPSec to secure communications through a VPN tunnel; what's the potential drawback to using it?

20. PPTP is an older VPN protocol that is mainly used with older client computers, but it has one advantage over the more recent L2TP. What is that advantage?

Real World Exercises

1. You have been hired by a small company that has set up a VPN. The VPN is used by two business partners with which the company needs to communicate on a regular basis. You set up a simple mesh configuration, going from office to office to do the initial configuration, which includes SA table listings for all devices in the VPN. The VPN operates smoothly until your company purchases another business that has branch offices located overseas. You are given the assignment of expanding the VPN to include the new employees. You are told that all internal LANs should be able to communicate with one another and are told in confidence that more acquisitions may be in store. You are happy about the prospect of traveling overseas to extend the VPN, but the prospect of updating four or more VPN devices around the world on a regular basis seems impractical. What should you do to help the VPN grow?

2. Your company (the same one from the previous exercise) does indeed follow through with the purchase of a distribution center located in another state. You are told, however, that only the central office and one branch office will need to communicate with the distribution center, to send delivery instructions and maintain shipping records. You are told that speed is of the essence in getting updated records, particularly at budget time each spring. What is the best way to expand this VPN?

3. Once the expanded VPN mentioned in the previous exercise is up and running, you notice significant slowdowns in communications, particularly with one Asian branch office. What are your options for speeding up communications with this single office? Give two alternatives.

4. Your VPN uses transport mode to send traffic to other VPN participants. The network administrator of one of the LANs in the VPN e-mails you an alert stating that his network has been infected with the W32.Storm virus. Because all communications between your LAN and the other LAN go through a VPN, you feel reasonably confident that you won't be infected. Nevertheless, the next day a computer on your machine reports that its antivirus software has isolated the same virus. How could this have happened, and what steps can you take to reduce the chances of it happening again?

5. Using an Internet search engine, look up the term "split tunneling." Be sure to read at least two definitions, and then write your own definition of this term. What kinds of attacks can split tunneling help prevent?

10

Hands-On Projects

In this chapter, you will set up a VPN connection to access a Microsoft VPN server (PC or Server configured to receive VPN clients) and then access a client on the internal network using the Remote Desktop Protocol (RDP). Both of these systems must be preconfigured for these exercises to work. You may choose to set up the RDP on any two computers yourself, but the VPN setup requires a server setup.

Project 10-1: A VPN Connection with Microsoft VPN Client
Set Up the Microsoft VPN Client on the Internet PC

1. To use the Microsoft VPN Client, first the server must have a valid account preconfigured. Ask your instructor for this information. Record it where you can locate it later.

2. You must create at least one connection entry, which identifies the following information:

   • The VPN device (the remote server) to access.

   • Preshared keys—The IPSec group to which the system administrator assigned you. Your group determines how you access and use the remote network. For example, it specifies access hours, number of simultaneous logins, user authentication method, and the IPSec algorithms your VPN Client uses.

   • Certificates—The name of the certificate you are using for authentication.

   • Optional parameters that govern VPN Client operation and connection to the remote network.

3. You can create multiple connection entries if you use your VPN Client to connect to multiple networks (though not simultaneously) or if you belong to more than one VPN remote access group.

4. Use the following procedure to create a new connection entry.

5. Choose **Start, All Programs, Accessories, Communications, New Connection Wizard.** You should see the Wizard begin.

6. Click **Next.** The New Connection Wizard starts and displays the available options. Select the **Connect to the network at my workplace** radio button. Click **Next.**

7. In the Network Connection window, select **Virtual Private Network connection.** Click **Next.**

8. In the **Company Name** field, type a unique name for this connection—for example, *yourlastname* VPNLab. Click **Next.**

9. In the VPN Server Selection window, enter the IP address for the VPN Server (i.e., 10.10.10.5) and click **Next.** You may be asked if you want to use a smart card. Click **Do not use my smart card** if asked and click **Next.**

10. Click the **Add a shortcut to this connection to my desktop** option, and then click **Finish** in the next window.

11. Open **My Network Places** (in Vista, open **Network,** and the current network connections will be displayed), and then click **View Network Connections** on the left-side menu.

12. Right-click the **VPNLab** connection you just created and click **Properties.** Here, you can modify the configuration of the VPN connection.

13. If you are logged into a Windows domain and want to use the same credentials for both the local login and the VPN connection, you can specify this in the Security tab. Close the properties window when you have finished reviewing it.

Connecting to the VPN Server

14. From your system, connect to the VPN Server by double-clicking the VPN Connection icon you created earlier.

15. Connect to the VPN and attempt to connect to the Internal Web Server by opening a Web browser and entering a URL (e.g., *www.cengage.com/coursetechnology*). Is your connection successful? Record your findings.

16. Attempt to connect to another Web location. Is your connection successful? Why or why not?

Project 10-2: Remote Access with Microsoft Remote Desktop Protocol

To accomplish this lab, you need one computer designated as host (the computer containing the files you wish to access) and one computer designated as remote (the computer on which you will use RDP to connect to the host). This exercise is run from the computer running Windows XP, Vista, or 7. Both computers must be connected to the Internet through a network or VPN connection.

Setting up Remote Desktop

1. On the computer designated as host, click **Start**, click **Control Panel**, double-click **System**, and then click the **Remote** tab. In the window, select the **Allow users to connect remotely to this computer** check box.

2. Record the computer name, and then click **OK**.

3. Set Windows Firewall up to allow exceptions. Click **Start**, **Control Panel**, and then double-click **Windows Firewall**. Make sure the Don't allow exceptions check box is not selected.

4. Click the **Exceptions** tab and check the **Remote Desktop** check box if it is not already selected. Click **OK**. The host is ready to accept remote connection requests.

5. The next step is to permit individual users to access the host. If the intended user does not already have an account, you must create one. Open **Control Panel**, select **Administrative Tools**, and then select **Computer Management**. Open **Local Users and Groups** and look for the Remote Desktop Users group under the Groups listing.

6. Add any users you want to access the host using RDP by opening the **Remote Desktop Users** group and clicking the **Add** button, and then clicking the **Advanced** button. In the **Select Users** window, click the **Find now** button and select the user you wish to add.

7. Click the **OK** button.

8. Click **OK** in the **Select Users** window and the **Remote Desktop Users Properties** window.

Connecting the Remote Computer to the Host

9. On the remote computer, click **Start**, **All Programs**, **Accessories**, **Communications**, and then click **Remote Desktop Connection**.

10

10. If you cannot find the Remote Desktop Connection menu option, you will need to download and add it by going to Windows Update and searching on Remote Desktop Connection Software Download (i.e., *www.microsoft.com/windowsxp/downloads/tools/rdclientdl.mspx*). Follow the instructions to install it.

11. If you wish your remote computer drives mapped on the host computer, select the **Options** button to display a number of different tabs.

12. Click the **Local Resources** tab, and then click **Disk drives** in the Local Devices and Resources area.

13. If you don't see drives under Local devices and resources, click the **More** button and you'll see them with expanded options.

14. If you plan to connect to this computer on a regular basis, you can enter the computer name, enter your username on the General tab, and have the remote computer save it for you. Otherwise, click the **Options** button again.

15. In the Computer box described earlier, type the name of your host computer, which you recorded earlier, and then click **Connect**. If the user indeed selected disk drives in Steps 13 and 14, the Remote Desktop Connection Security Warning dialog box appears, telling the user that the local disk drives will be available to the remote computer. Click **OK** to continue.

16. When the **Log On to Windows** dialog box appears, enter a legitimate username and password, and then click **OK**.

17. The Remote Desktop window opens, and you should see a window showing the desktop of the remote host computer.

18. To end your Remote Desktop session, click **Start,** and then click **Log Off** at the bottom of the Start menu. When prompted, click **Log Off.**

Endnotes

1. Kadrich, M. *Endpoint Security*. Boston: Addison-Wesley (2007).

Setting Up and Operating a Software Firewall

In this appendix, you set up the Endian Community Firewall, another open-source, software-based firewall, to function as a bastion firewall. To successfully complete this appendix, you need a system on which you can install the Endian software, with the following minimum specifications:

1 GHz processor

512 MB RAM

8 GB HD

2 Network cards, minimum 10/100

In addition, you need a separate system to function as an internal network client. Lastly, you need a hardware switch device to connect the internal network client to the firewall. Alternatively, you can connect the internal network client directly to the internal NIC on the firewall through the use of a crossover cable.

Although you worked from the command line for the end-of-chapter exercises, you will make extensive use of the Endian Web interface to complete this appendix.

Install and Configure Firewall

1. Download the Endian Firewall Community 2.4 ISO from the Endian Web site, located at *www.endian.com/en/community/download/*. After the downloading is complete, burn the ISO to a CD.

2. Power on the system to be used, directing it to boot from the CD. (*Note:* All drive contents will be erased!)

3. Accept the default values on install, with the exception of using an RS-232 cable to connect to the system. In this case, deny the option.

4. The install process will continue, partitioning the disk drive and installing the necessary software.

5. When prompted, replace the default IP address and subnet mask provided by the installer with the IP address/subnet mask to be used for the GREEN, or internal, interface.

6. Once configuration is complete, allow the system to reboot.

7. Connect your internal network client, using either the switch or crossover cable.

8. Open a Web browser on the client and point it to https://<IP address of GREEN interface>:10443 (for example, https://10.10.10.1:10443). You will be presented with the Endian Web interface, which you will use to finish configuration. Click the >>> button to begin the process.

9. Select the language and time zone to use, and then click the >>> button.

10. Click the check box to accept the license, and then click the >>> button.

11. Answer **no** when asked if you want to restore a backup, and then click the >>> button.

12. Change the admin and root passwords to values of your choosing, and then click the >>> button.

13. Choose the appropriate value for the RED interface, and then click the >>> button.

14. Choose **None** for the network zones option, and then click the >>> button.

15. Ensure the presented values are correct for the GREEN interface, and then click the >>> button. (*Note:* Configuration of the RED interface will vary, based on your lab environment details. See your instructor for setup specifics for your network.)

16. Enter the DNS server IP addresses supplied by your instructor. If you have only a single DNS server address available, supply that address in both fields, and then click the >>> button.

17. Skip the configuration of the default admin mail address by clicking the >>> button.

18. Click the **OK, apply configuration** button to apply the new settings.

19. After a brief delay, you will be prompted for login credentials. Use the username "admin" (without quotes) and the admin password you supplied in Step 12.

Modify Default Firewall Rule Sets

In the end-of-chapter exercises, you had to manually create rule sets to allow basic outbound traffic types, such as DNS, HTTP, and HTTPS. Endian installs default rule sets to allow these types of outbound traffic (as well as other types), but it does not enable the outbound firewall by default. In this section, review the default rule sets, disable some of them, and activate the outbound firewall.

1. From your internal network client, use your Web browser to access the Endian GUI, as done previously. When prompted for credentials, use the username "admin" (without quotes) and the admin password configured earlier.

2. From the main horizontal menu, select the **Firewall** link, and then select the **Outgoing traffic** link from the vertical menu on the left side of the page. You should now see the complete outbound traffic rule set for all zones.

3. Disable the IMAP and IMAPs rules by clicking the green check box in the Actions area for each rule. Click the **Apply** button that appears in the green dialog box at the top of the page. You have now disabled IMAP and IMAPs outbound traffic for the network.

4. To verify that HTTP traffic is being permitted, open a Web browser and visit a Web site you frequent—for example, *www.kennesaw.edu*. You should be able to view content from that Web site with no problems.

5. To verify that the Endian GUI and rule set management are functioning properly, disable the HTTP and HTTPS rules by clicking the green check box in the Actions area for each rule. Click the **Apply** button that appears in the green dialog box at the top of the page. You have now disabled HTTP and HTTPS outbound traffic. To verify this, use the other Web browser to reload the page you originally visited. Your browser should now time out on the request.

6. Re enable the rules by clicking the green check box in the Actions area for each rule. Click the **Apply** button that appears in the green dialog box at the top of the page. You have now enabled HTTP and HTTPS outbound traffic for the network.

Enable SSH Access to the Firewall

By default, SSH access to the Endian firewall is disabled. In this section, you enable SSH access to the firewall from the GREEN interface, and then restrict that access to a specified IP address on our internal, trusted network.

1. From your internal network client, use your Web browser to access the Endian GUI, as done previously (for example, https://10.10.10.1:10443). When prompted for credentials, use the username "admin" (without quotes) and the admin password configured earlier.

2. From the main horizontal menu, select the **System** link, and then select the **SSH access** link from the vertical menu on the left side of the page. You should now see the page that allows you to modify SSH access settings.

3. Click the button to enable SSH access. Leave the default values, and then click the **Save** button to commit the changes and enable the service.

4. To verify that SSH traffic is being allowed, use your internal network client to initiate an SSH connection to the firewall's GREEN interface address. If you don't already have an SSH client installed on the system, several excellent open-source clients are available for download, such as PuTTY (*www.putty.org*). When prompted, accept the certificate warning, and then authenticate, using "root" (without quotes) as the user and the root password you entered earlier in this appendix. You should now be connected remotely to the firewall at the command line.

5. Type **exit** and press **Return** to close the SSH session.

6. You now enter rules to restrict SSH access to a single IP address from our internal, trusted network. First, create a rule to allow traffic from the IP address, and then create a rule to deny traffic from all other sources in the GREEN interface.

7. From the main horizontal menu, select the **Firewall** link, and then select the **System access** link from the vertical menu on the left side of the page. You should now see the current rule set, which should be empty.

8. Click the **Add a new system access rule** link.

9. In the Source address text box, type the IP address of your internal system client—for example, 10.10.10.5.

10. Select **GREEN** in the Source interface box.

11. Select **SSH** from the Service pull-down list.

12. Select **Allow** from the Action pull-down list, and then supply a descriptive comment in the Remark text box—for example, "Allow SSH to FW."

13. Click the **Add Rule** button to complete the process. After you are returned to the summary page, you should see the new rule listed.

14. Click the **Add a new system access rule** link. This time, leave the Source address blank and select **GREEN** in the Source interface box.

15. Select **SSH** from the Service pull-down list.

16. Select **Deny** from the Action pull-down list and supply a descriptive comment in the Remark text box—for example, "Deny SSH to FW from GREEN interface." Ensure that the value in the Position pull-down list is set to Last.

17. Click the **Add Rule** button to complete the process.

18. After you are returned to the summary page, you should see the new rule listed. Ensure that the rule to allow SSH traffic from the trusted IP address is listed *before* the deny rule, and then click the **Apply** button that appears in the green dialog box at the top of the page.

19. Verify SSH connectivity using your SSH client, as you did earlier. To ensure that the rules are working as desired, you can temporarily disable the Allow rule in the GUI, and then attempt to connect. This time, the connection will time out.

Web Proxy Server Configuration

By default, proxy services in the Endian firewall are disabled. In this section, you enable the Web proxy service. You first disable the default HTTP and HTTPS outbound traffic rules, and then configure the desired Web proxy features.

1. From your internal network client, use your Web browser to access the Endian GUI, as done previously. When prompted for credentials, use the username "admin" (without quotes) and the admin password configured earlier.

2. From the main horizontal menu, select the **Firewall** link, and then select the **Outgoing traffic** link from the vertical menu on the left side of the page. You should now see the page that allows you to modify the outgoing traffic rule sets.

3. Click the green check box next to the HTTP and HTTPS rule sets to uncheck each of the rules, and then click the **Apply** button that appears in the green dialog box at the top of the page.

4. Verify the denial of HTTP traffic by opening a Web browser and visiting your favorite Web site—for example, *www.kennesaw.edu*. The browser request should time out.

5. From the main horizontal menu, select the **Proxy** link, and then select the **HTTP** link from the vertical menu on the left side of the page. You should now see the Configuration page that allows you to modify HTTP proxy settings.

6. Click the button to enable the HTTP proxy.

7. After the page reloads, select the **not transparent** option for the GREEN interface.

8. Expand the **Log settings**, and then check each of the logging options to fully enable logging for the proxy.

9. Click the **Save** button to complete the HTTP proxy server process.

10. You will now set up a "blacklist" that will allow all Web traffic except to the site(s) we specify. Select the **Contentfilter** option on the horizontal submenu.

11. Click the **Create a Profile** link to add a new filtering profile.

12. Type **Web filtering** in the Profile Name field.

13. Click the **Custom black-and-whitelists** bar to expand and display options.

14. Type **kennesaw.edu** in the Block the following sites text box.

15. Click the **Save profile** button to save your work.

16. Click the **Access Policy** option on the horizontal submenu.

17. Click the **Add access policy** link to add a new access policy.

18. Leave all default values selected on the page, changing only the Filter profile value to use the Web-filtering profile we just built.

19. Click the **Create policy** button to save your work, and then click the **Apply** button that appears in the green dialog box at the top of the page.

20. Change your Web browser settings to require the use of the Web proxy browser. The steps to complete this will vary based on your particular Web browser.

21. Verify the allowance of HTTP traffic by opening a Web browser and visiting your favorite Web site. The browser request returns content from the Web site.

22. Verify the denial of HTTP traffic to the kennesaw.edu domain by entering *www.kennesaw.edu* in the browser's URL window. The Web proxy should return a message that the site has been blocked.

23. You will now change from the "blacklist" to a "whitelist" that will prohibit all Web traffic except to the site(s) you specify. Click the **Contentfilter** option on the horizontal submenu.

24. Click the pencil icon to the right of the Web-filtering profile you built earlier.

25. Enter the IP address of the GREEN interface, along with "kennesaw.edu" (without quotes) in the Allow the following sites text box, one entry per line.

26. Remove the kennesaw.edu entry from the Block the following sites text box and replace it with two asterisks (**).

27. Click the **Update profile** button to save the changes, and then click the **Apply** button that appears in the green dialog box at the top of the page. The proxy server will restart.

28. Verify the allowance of HTTP traffic to the kennesaw.edu domain by opening a Web browser and entering *www.kennesaw.edu* in the browser's URL window. The browser request should get content from the Web site.

29. Verify the denial of HTTP traffic to all other domains by trying to visit two or three of your favorite Web sites. In all cases, the Web proxy should return a message that the site has been blocked.

VPN Server Configuration

In this section, you enable the VPN server to allow remote user connections, and you set up a user account to which you grant VPN access privileges.

1. From your internal network client, use your Web browser to access the Endian GUI, as done previously. When prompted for credentials, use the username "admin" (without quotes) and the admin password configured earlier.

2. From the main horizontal menu, select the **VPN** link, and then select the **OpenVPN server** link from the vertical menu on the left side of the page. You should now see the page that allows you to configure the global settings for the VPN server.

3. Click the check box to enable the OpenVPN server.

4. Enter the beginning and ending IP addresses of the range of addresses to be assigned by the OpenVPN server—for example, 10.10.10.50 for the beginning address and 10.10.10.60 for the ending address.

5. Click the **Save and restart** button to save your work and start the OpenVPN server.

6. After the OpenVPN server starts, click the **Accounts** link on the horizontal submenu.

7. Click the **Add account** button to add a new VPN user.

8. Type **testuser** in the Username field.

9. Type **password** in the Password field and the Verify password field.

10. Click the **Save** button to add the new user.

11. Click the **Restart OpenVPN server** button to apply the changes and restart the OpenVPN server.

Glossary

/etc/passwd Encrypted file in which Linux stores passwords.

AAA services Authentication, authorization, and accounting.

access control list (ACL) A method of implementing technical specifications which utilizes user access lists, matrices, and capability tables to govern the rights and privileges of users.

access control matrix A combination of tables and lists, in which organizational assets are listed along the column headers, while users are listed along the row headers. The resulting matrix contains access control lists in columns for a particular device or asset, while a row contains the capability table for a particular user.

accountability Documenting the activities of the authorized individual and systems.

accuracy Indicates that information is free from mistakes or errors, and has the value that the end user expects.

acknowledgment (ACK) flag Part of a data packet's flag section that, when set, signifies that the destination computer has received the packets that were previously sent.

Advanced Encryption Standard (AES) The successor to 3DES.

algorithm The mathematical formula or method used to convert an unencrypted message into an encrypted message, or vice versa.

application-layer gateway A device that controls the way applications inside the network access external networks by setting up proxy services.

application-level gateway See "proxy server."

application proxy See "proxy server."

asset Anything that has value for the organization.

asymmetric encryption See "public key encryption."

asynchronous token A hardware component used in authentication that employs a cryptographic process and a challenge-response dialogue to validate an identity.

attack An act or action that takes advantage of a vulnerability to compromise a controlled system.

attack profile A detailed description of the activities that occur during an attack.

attack scenario end case The final result of the business impact analysis, which utilizes attack success scenarios to estimate the cost of the best, worst, and most likely cases.

audit The record (usually as a log file) of authentication and authorization activities.

authentication The act of confirming the identity of a potential user.

authentication, authorization, and accounting (AAA) server A server, used in a centralized authentication setup, that alleviates the need to provide each server on the network with a separate database of usernames and passwords, each of which would have to be updated individually each time a password changed or a user was added.

authenticity The quality or state of being genuine or original, rather than a reproduction or fabrication.

Information is authentic when it is the information that was originally created, placed, stored, or transferred.

authorization Determining which actions that entity can perform in that physical or logical area.

availability Enables authorized users—persons or computer systems—to access information without interference or obstruction, and to receive it in the required format.

average lifetime How long a connection to a host lasts.

back door Vulnerability created in a system by a virus or worm which allows the attacker to access the system at will with special privileges.

baseline A level of performance that you consider acceptable and that the system can be compared against.

bastion host Computer in a network that is fortified against illegal entry and attack because it is exposed to external networks so it can screen the internal network from security exposure. It is typically the only computer an organization allows to be addressed directly from outside the network.

benchmarking A business process that makes a comparison of current practices against those used by other organizations or groups of organizations, perhaps a trade association or industry group.

binary drive image A mirror image of all the data on a hard disk or partition, which includes not only files but applications and system data.

biometrics The use of retinal scans, fingerprints, and the like for authentication.

blackout A lengthy complete loss of power.

boot-up password Password that must be entered to complete the process of starting up a computer.

boot virus A virus that infects the key operating system files located in a computer's boot sector.

brownout A prolonged drop in voltage.

brute force attack The application of computing and network resources to try every possible combination of options of a password.

buffer overflow An application error that occurs when more data is sent to a buffer than it can handle.

business continuity (BC) plan A method that ensures that critical business functions continue, if a catastrophic incident or disaster occurs.

business continuity planning Activities that prepare an organization to reestablish critical business operations during a disaster that affects operations at the primary site.

business impact analysis (BIA) An investigation and assessment of the impact that various attacks can have on an organization.

cache The storage of frequently accessed data on a disk, or a reference to the storage media or location itself.

caching Storing frequently accessed data on disk.

capability table A type of access control list that specifies which subjects and objects users or groups can access. In some systems, capability tables are called user profiles or user policies.

centralized authentication service A form of authentication in which a centralized server handles identification, authentication, authorization, and accountability.

certificate authority (CA) Agency that manages the issuance of certificates and serves as the electronic notary public to verify their origin and integrity.

champion A senior executive who promotes a project and ensures that it is supported, both financially and administratively, at the highest levels of the organization.

chief information officer (CIO) This individual is often the senior technology officer and is primarily responsible for advising the chief executive officer, president, or company owner on the strategic planning that affects the management of information in the organization.

chief information security officer (CISO) The individual primarily responsible for the assessment, management, and implementation of information security in the organization. The CISO usually reports directly to the CIO, although in larger organizations it is not uncommon for one or more layers of management to exist between the two.

Chkconfig A *NIX utility used for maintaining the runtime status of system services.

C.I.A. triangle A concept developed by the computer security industry that has been the industry standard since the development of the mainframe. It is based on the three characteristics of information that make it valuable to organizations: confidentiality, integrity, and availability.

cipher The transformation of the individual components (characters, bytes, or bits) of an unencrypted message into encrypted components.

ciphertext The encrypted or encoded message resulting from an encryption.

circuit-level gateway A type of firewall that works at the Session layer of the OSI model, filtering internal traffic that leaves the network being protected.

client authentication Authentication method similar to user authentication but with the addition of usage limits.

client-to-site VPN One of two different types of VPNs. This type makes a network accessible to remote users who need dial-in access.

communications security The protection of an organization's communications media, technology, and content.

computer virus A type of malicious code that runs inside another program on a computer.

concurrent connections The number of connections made to hosts in the internal network at any one time.

confidentiality Exists when information is protected from disclosure or exposure to unauthorized individuals or systems. This means that only those with the rights and privileges to access the information are able to do so.

configuration file A text file or other form of storage local to a system that contains the setting options needed to configure a program or an operating system component to operate in the intended fashion.

configuration rules The specific instructions entered into a security system, to regulate how it reacts to the data it receives.

Content Vectoring Protocol (CVP) Protocol that enables firewalls to work with virus-scanning applications so certain content can be filtered out.

contingency plan A method prepared by the organization to anticipate, react to, and recover from events that threaten the security of information and information assets in the organization, and, subsequently, to restore the organization to normal modes of business operations.

controls Security mechanisms, policies, or procedures that can successfully counter attacks, reduce risk, resolve vulnerabilities, and generally improve the security within an organization.

correlation attack Collection of brute force methods that attempt to deduce statistical relationships between the structure of the unknown key and the ciphertext that is the output of the cryptosystem. If these advanced approaches can calculate the value of the public key, and if this can be achieved in a reasonable time, all messages written with that key can be decrypted.

countermeasures See "controls."

cracker An individual who "cracks" or removes software protection that is designed to prevent unauthorized duplication.

cracking Attempting to reverse-calculate a password.

crisis management The actions taken during and after a disaster.

critical resource A software- or hardware-related item that is indispensable to the operation of a device or program.

cryptanalysis The process of deciphering the original message from an encrypted message, without knowing the algorithms and keys used to perform the encryption.

cryptogram See "ciphertext."

cryptography The processes involved in encoding and decoding messages so that others cannot understand them.

cryptology The science of encryption, which actually encompasses the two disciplines of cryptography and cryptanalysis.

cryptosystem The set of transformations necessary to convert an unencrypted message into an encrypted message.

cryptovariable See "key."

cyberactivist See "hacktivist."

cyberterrorism Activities conducted by individuals for the purpose of hacking systems to conduct terrorist activities through network or Internet pathways.

data cache A local data storage facility that is usually very close to the place where it will be used in a computation. Inside a processor, this will be a dedicated memory location adjacent to the computational registers in the processor. In disk subsystems, this may be a memory area in the controller that is used to stage what the system thinks is most likely to be requested next.

data custodians Individuals responsible for the storage, maintenance, and protection of the data owner's information. The custodian could be a dedicated position, or it may be an additional responsibility of a systems administrator or other technology manager.

datagram A data packet, the basic quantum of network data, which contains two types of information: the header and the data.

data owners Those responsible for the security and use of a particular set of information. Usually members of senior management and sometimes even CIOs, data owners usually determine the level of data classification associated with the data, and work with subordinate managers to oversee the day-to-day administration of that data.

data users End users who work with the information to perform their daily jobs supporting the mission of the organization.

decipher To decrypt or convert ciphertext to plaintext.

de facto standards Standards that are informal or part of an organizational culture.

defense in depth One of the basic tenets of security architectures; the layered implementation of security.

de jure standards Standards that are published, scrutinized, and ratified by a group.

demilitarized zone (DMZ) A computer or small subnetwork between an organization's trusted internal network and an untrusted, external network.

denial-of-service (DoS) An attack in which the attacker sends a large number of connection or information requests to a target. So many requests are made that the target system cannot handle them along with other, legitimate requests for service. The system may crash or may simply be unable to perform ordinary functions.

dependency services Services that a system needs to function correctly.

dictionary attack A variation on the brute force attack, this attack narrows the field by selecting specific target accounts and using a list of commonly used passwords (the dictionary) instead of random combinations.

digital certificate Similar to a digital signature, it asserts that a public key is associated with a particular identity.

digital signature An encrypted code attached to files that are exchanged during a transaction so that each party can verify the other's identity.

direct attack An attack in which a hacker uses a personal computer to break into a system.

disaster recovery (DR) plan A method that addresses the preparation for and recovery from a disaster, whether natural or human-made.

disaster recovery planning The preparation for and recovery from a disaster, whether natural or human-made.

distributed denial-of-service (DDoS) A coordinated attack in which streams of requests are launched against a target from many locations at the same time. Most DDoS attacks

are preceded by a preparation phase in which many systems, perhaps thousands, are compromised.

distributed firewalls An environment in which firewalls are installed at all endpoints of the network, including the remote computers that connect to the network through VPNs.

encapsulation The inclusion of one type of data structure or encoding process inside another data structure or encoding process to facilitate transmission over a network.

encipher To encrypt or convert plaintext to ciphertext.

encryption The process of converting a message into a form that cannot be read by unauthorized individuals.

encryption domain Phrase used to describe everything in the protected network and behind the gateway of a VPN.

endpoint Hardware devices or software modules that perform encryption to secure data, authentication to make sure the host requesting the data is an approved user of the VPN, and encapsulation to protect the integrity of the information being sent.

end users Those who will be most directly affected by new implementations and changes to existing systems. Ideally, a selection of users from various departments, levels, and degrees of technical knowledge who assist a project team in focusing on the application of realistic controls applied in ways that do not disrupt the essential business activities they seek to safeguard.

enterprise information security policy (EISP) An executive-level document that guides the development, implementation, and management of the security program. It is based on and directly supports the mission, vision, and direction of the organization and sets the strategic direction, scope, and tone for all security efforts.

environmental management Measures taken to reduce risks to the physical environment where IT assets and resources are stored.

exploit To take advantage of a weakness in the defenses of an asset; also refers to a packaged attack that leverages a weakness to cause a loss to an asset.

extranet An extension of the corporate network to a new location.

fault Complete loss of power for a moment.

firewall In general, anything, whether hardware or software (or a combination of hardware and software), that can filter the transmission of packets of digital information as they attempt to pass through a boundary of a network.

fragment Packet that is part of a larger, whole packet.

gateway A system that joins one device or network to another device or network and controls access between the two.

Generally Accepted System Security Principles (GASSP) A set of security and information management practices put forth by the International Information Security Foundation (I2SF).

hackers The classic perpetrators of espionage or trespass, these are people who use and create computer software to gain access to information illegally.

hacktivist Someone who interferes with or disrupts systems to protest the operations, policies, or actions of an organization or government agency.

header The first part of a datagram, which consists of general information about the size of the packet, the protocol that was used to send it, and the IP address of both the source computer and its destination.

heartbeat network Network that monitors the operation of the primary firewall and synchronizes state table connections so the two, or more, firewalls have the same information at any given time.

high availability A system or network of systems designed to have maximum possible uptime.

hole A port, machine, or other vulnerable computer through which hackers can gain entry.

honeypot Decoy system designed to lure potential attackers away from critical systems. It is also known as a decoy, lure, or fly-trap.

hot standby System in which one or more auxiliary or failover firewalls are configured to take over all traffic if the primary firewall fails.

hub-and-spoke configuration Arrangement in which a single VPN router contains records of all SAs in the VPN. Any LANs or computers that want to participate in the VPN need only connect to the central server, not to any other machines in the VPN.

hybrid firewall Firewall that combines several different security technologies, such as packet filtering, application-level gateways, and VPNs.

identification Obtaining the identity of the entity requesting access to a logical or physical area.

incident Any clearly identified attack on the organization's information assets that would threaten the assets' confidentiality, integrity, or availability.

incident response (IR) The set of activities taken to plan for, detect, and correct the impact of an incident that affects the confidently, integrity, or availability of information assets.

incident response (IR) plan A method that addresses the identification, classification, response to, and recovery from an incident.

indirect attack An attack in which a system is compromised and used to attack other systems.

information security (InfoSec) The protection of information and its critical elements, including the systems and hardware that use, store, and transmit that information.

information security policy A set of rules that provides for the protection of the information assets of the organization.

instruction cache A local memory store in the processor that holds the next one or few instructions that are the most likely to be executed. They are stored in this way so as to be ready, if needed, with very little delay before execution commences.

integrity Indicates that information remains whole, complete, and uncorrupted. The integrity of information is threatened when the information is exposed to corruption, damage, destruction, or other disruption of its authentic state.

intellectual property (IP) The control of ideas and innovation, an important part of the value of assets that organizations control.

intranet A private network contained within an organization.

IP forwarding Process that causes all requests to a certain Internet Protocol address to be redirected to an alternate, specified IP address.

IPSec concentrators Routers that support IPSec that are set up at the perimeter of connected LANs.

IP security (IPSec) Primary and now dominant cryptographic authentication and encryption product of the IETF's IP Protocol Security Working Group. It provides application support for all uses within TCP/IP, including VPNs.

issue-specific security policy (ISSP) A statement of the organization's position that instructs employees on the proper use of technologies and processes as they pertain to a specific issue.

JavaScript A scripted programming language that is widely used to enable automation tasks on Web-based information systems.

Kerberos Authentication system that uses symmetric key encryption to validate an individual user's access to various network resources.

key The information used in conjunction with the algorithm to create the ciphertext from the plaintext.

keyring A centralized store of encryption keys, often in the possession of an individual and stored in a secured file on a specific computer system.

keyspace The entire range of values that can possibly be used to construct an individual key.

known-plaintext attack Scheme in which an attacker obtains duplicate texts, one in ciphertext and one in plaintext, which then enables the individual to reverse-engineer the encryption algorithm.

lattice-based access control A form of access control in which users are assigned a matrix of authorizations for various areas of access.

Layer 2 Tunneling Protocol (L2TP) An extension of the Point-to-Point Protocol (PPP).

layer four switches Network devices with the intelligence to make routing decisions based on source and destination IP address or port numbers as specified in layer four of the OSI reference model.

leased lines Point-to-point communications used by organizations to join two or more LANs. These lines are often used to connect remote users or branch offices to a central administrative site.

least privilege The information security principle by which employees are provided access to the minimal amount of information for the least duration of time necessary for them to perform their jobs.

likelihood The possibility or probability of unwanted action on an information asset.

load balancing The practice of balancing the load placed on a device so that it is handled by two or more devices.

load sharing The practice of configuring two or more devices to share the total traffic load. Each device in a load-sharing setup is active at the same time.

local authentication the most common form of authentication, in which a server maintains a local file of usernames and passwords that it refers to for matching the username-password pair being supplied by a client.

log file Records of events such as logon attempts and accesses to files.

macro virus Virus that is embedded in the automatically executing macro code common in word processors, spreadsheets, and database applications.

mail bomb A form of e-mail attack that is also a DoS attack in which an attacker routes large quantities of e-mail to the target system.

maintenance hook *See* "back door."

malicious code Software deliberately designed to cause a system or a program to act in a way that is not the intention of the system's owner or operator. Usually this code is designed to steal information or to make the system follow future commands from the attacker and become a "bot" or "zombie" system.

malicious software *See* "malicious code."

malware *See* "malicious code."

managerial guidance A type of systems-specific policy created by management to guide the implementation and configuration of technology, as well as to regulate the behavior of people in the organization.

man-in-the-middle In this well-known type of attack, an attacker monitors (or sniffs) packets from the network, modifies them using IP spoofing techniques, and inserts them back into the network, allowing the attacker to eavesdrop as well as to change, delete, reroute, add, forge, or divert data.

Mandatory Access Control (MAC) A set of mandatory controls implemented by the organization to regulate access to information. It is typically centrally controlled and implemented, and is a requirement in some settings.

McCumber Cube A comprehensive model for information security that is becoming the evaluation standard for the security of information systems. It provides a graphical description of the architectural approach widely used in computer and information security. The McCumber Cube uses a representation in three dimensions of a 3×3×3 cube with 27 cells representing areas that must be addressed to secure today's information systems.

mesh configuration VPN arrangement in which each participant in the VPN has an approved relationship with every other participant.

mission A written statement of an organization's purpose.

mission-critical Refers to an integral, key part of an organization's core operations.

monoalphabetic substitution Substitution cipher that utilizes only one alphabet.

need to know The information security principle by which employees are provided access to the amount of information that is required for them to perform their jobs.

network load balancing (NLB) A method of using multiple systems to take process service requests in such a way as to reduce the risk of any one system getting overloaded.

network security The protection of networking components, connections, and contents.

nonrepudiation A method used to ensure that parties to the transaction are authentic, so that they cannot later deny having participated in a transaction.

object of an attack A computer that is the entity being attacked.

Open Platform for Security (OPSEC) model Design with the capability to extend functionality and integrate virus scanning and other functions into its set of abilities.

operations security The protection of the details of a particular operation or series of activities.

packets Small, manageable chunks of data that computers use to communicate with one another.

packet filter Hardware or software that is designed to block or allow transmission of packets of information based on criteria such as port, IP address, and protocol.

packet header *See* "header."

packet monkeys Script kiddies who use automated exploits to engage in distributed denial-of-service attacks.

parameter Criterion used by proxy servers, firewalls, and similar devices to filter content and control access.

password attack Repeatedly guessing passwords to commonly used accounts.

permutation cipher *See* "transposition cipher."

personal security The protection of the people who are authorized to access the organization and its operations.

phreaker One who hacks the public telephone network to make free calls or disrupt services.

physical security The protection of the physical items, objects, or areas of an organization from unauthorized access and misuse.

plaintext An original unencrypted message, or the results from successful decryption.

Point-to-Point Protocol (PPP) Protocol long used to establish dial-up connections on the Internet.

Point-to-Point Protocol (PPP) over Secure Shell (SSH) A UNIX-based method for creating VPNs.

Point-to-Point Protocol (PPP) over Secure Sockets Layer (SSL) A UNIX-based method for creating VPNs.

Point-to-Point Tunneling Protocol (PPTP) A protocol commonly used by remote users who need to connect to a network using a dial-in modem connection.

policy A set of guidelines or instructions that an organization's senior management implements to regulate the activities of the members of the organization who make decisions, take actions, and perform other duties.

polyalphabetic substitution Substitution cipher that utilizes two or more alphabets.

possession The ownership or control of some object or item of information. Information is said to be in one's possession if one obtains it, independent of format or other characteristics.

power irregularities Variations in the 120-volt, 60-cycle power provided to most businesses through a 15- or 20-amp circuit.

pre-shared key An encryption key that is used by multiple parties and through some out-of-band, secured channel.

Pretty Good Privacy (PGP) Method to secure e-mail that was developed by Phil Zimmerman and uses the IDEA Cipher, a 128-bit symmetric key block encryption algorithm with 64-bit blocks for message encoding.

Privacy Enhanced Mail (PEM) A method to secure e-mail proposed by the Internet Engineering Task Force (IETF) as a standard that will function with public key cryptosystems. It uses 3DES symmetric key encryption and RSA for key exchanges and digital signatures.

private key Used in some encrypted communications by a recipient to decode a message encoded using their public key. This key is not shared publicly.

private key encryption A method of encrypting communications that utilizes the same algorithm and secret key to both encipher and decipher a message.

project team Group responsible for designing and implementing information security projects. It should consist of a number of individuals who are experienced in one or multiple facets of the vast array of required technical and nontechnical areas.

proprietary Privately owned.

proxy server Network device that makes high-level application connections on behalf of internal hosts and other machines.

proxy service See "proxy server."

public key encryption An encryption system that utilizes two different keys to encrypt and decrypt a message. Either key can be used to encrypt or decrypt the message. However, if one key is used to encrypt the message, then only the other key can decrypt it.

Remote Authentication Dial-In User Service (RADIUS) Common protocol used to provide dial-in authentication.

replay attack An attempt to resubmit a recording of a deciphered authentication to gain entry into a secure source.

residual risk The amount of risk that remains after an organization takes precautions, implements controls and safeguards, and performs other security activities.

reverse proxy A service that acts as a proxy for inbound connections.

risk The state of being unsecure, either partially or totally, and thus susceptible to attack, as in "at risk."

risk appetite The amount of risk an organization chooses to live with, also called risk tolerance.

risk assessment specialists Individuals who understand financial risk assessment techniques, the value of organizational assets, and the security methods to be used.

risk management The processes used to identify, assess, and control the risks that may cause losses to assets.

risk tolerance See "risk appetite."

role-based access controls (RBAC) Nondiscretionary access controls that are tied to the role that a particular user performs in an organization.

rootkit A collection of software tools and a recipe used to gain control of a system by bypassing its legitimate security controls.

routing tables Maps used by routing devices that match externally known IP addresses to internal, hidden IP addresses.

rule base List of rules kept by a firewall which it uses to evaluate data packets.

rule-based access controls A form of discretionary access controls where actions are taken based on rules established by a central authority.

safeguards See "controls."

sag A momentary low voltage.

salt A randomly generated value used by Linux when encrypting passwords in the /etc/passwd file.

SA table Routing table kept by each VPN hardware or software terminator in a VPN network to verify approved relationships.

scalable Capable of growing and maintaining effectiveness.

script kiddies Hackers of limited skill who use expertly written software to attack a system.

secret key A private key used to both encipher and decipher a message.

Secure Electronic Transactions (SET) Cryptosystem developed by MasterCard and VISA in 1997 to provide protection from electronic payment fraud. It works by encrypting the credit card transfers with DES for encryption and RSA for key exchange.

Secure Hypertext Transfer Protocol (SHTTP) Encrypted solution to the unsecured version of HTTP. It can provide secure e-commerce transactions as well as encrypted Web pages for secure data transfer over the Web.

Secure/Multipurpose Internet Mail Extensions (S/MIME) Cryptosystem that builds on the Multipurpose Internet Mail Extensions (MIME) encoding format by adding encryption and authentication via digital signatures based on public key cryptosystems

Secure Shell (SSH) Popular extension to the TCP/IP protocol suite, sponsored by the IETF. It provides security for remote access connections over public networks by creating a secure and persistent connection.

Secure Sockets Layer (SSL) Cryptosystem developed by Netscape in 1994 to provide security for online electronic commerce transactions.

security association (SA) An approved relationship between two participants in a VPN.

security blueprint The basis for the design, selection, and implementation of all security program elements, including policy implementation, ongoing policy management, risk management programs, education and training programs, technological controls, and maintenance of the security program.

security education, training, and awareness (SETA) A control measure designed to reduce the incidences of accidental security breaches by employees.

security framework An outline of the overall information security strategy and a roadmap for planned changes to the organization's information security environment.

security_patch_check A UNIX utility that automates the process of analyzing security patches that are already on a system and reports patches that should be added.

security perimeter Defines the boundary between the outer limit of an organization's security and the beginning of the outside world, protecting all internal systems from outside threats.

security policy In general, a set of rules that protect an organization's assets.

security policy developers Individuals who understand the organizational culture, existing policies, and requirements for developing and implementing successful policies.

security professionals Dedicated, trained, and well-educated specialists in all aspects of information security, both technical and nontechnical.

selected-plaintext attack Scheme in which an attacker sends the potential victim a specific text that they are sure the victim will forward to others. When the victim does encrypt and forward the message, it can be used in the attack, if the attacker can acquire the outgoing encrypted version. At the very least, reverse engineering can usually lead the attacker to discover the cryptosystem that is being employed.

separation of duties The information security principle by which more than one individual is responsible for a particular information asset, process, or task.

session authentication Authentication method that requires authentication whenever a client system attempts to connect to a network resource and establish a session (a period when communications are exchanged).

session hijacks Attacks involving a communication session that has already been established between a server and a client. The hacker inserts confusing or misleading commands into packets, thus disabling the server and enabling the hacker to gain control of the session.

session key A symmetric key for limited-use, temporary communications.

shadow password system A feature of the Linux operating system that enables the secure storage of passwords.

shoulder surfing A technique used to gather information one is not authorized to have, by looking over another individual's shoulder or viewing the information from a distance, in a public or semipublic setting.

site-to-site VPN One of two different types of VPNs. This type links two or more networks.

sniffer A program or device that can monitor data traveling over a network.

social engineering The process of using social skills to convince people to reveal access credentials or other valuable information to an attacker.

socket The combination of a sender's full address (network address plus port) and a receiver's address (network address plus port).

SOCKS A set of protocols that enable proxy server access to applications without an assigned proxy server.

software piracy The unlawful use or duplication of software-based intellectual property.

source routing Technique in which the originator of a packet can attempt to partially or completely control the path through the network to the destination.

spam Unsolicited commercial e-mail.

specific sign-on System type in which clients must authenticate each time they access a server or use a service on the protected network.

spike A momentary increase in voltage levels.

split tunneling Two connections over a VPN line.

spoofing A technique used to gain unauthorized access to computers, wherein the intruder sends messages whose IP address indicates to the recipient that the messages are coming from a trusted host.

standards A set of guidelines that, although they have the same compliance requirements as policies, are more detailed descriptions of what must be done to comply with policy.

standard sign-on System type in which the client, after being successfully authenticated, is allowed to access whatever resources the user needs or perform any desired functions.

stateful packet filtering A packet-filtering method that can do everything a stateless packet filter can, while additionally maintaining a record of the state of a connection.

stateless packet filtering The simplest packet-filtering method, also called static packet filtering, reviews packet header content and makes decisions on whether to allow or drop the packets based on whether a connection has actually been established between an external host and an internal one.

static IP address The assignment of a dedicated IP address to a device using a manual process, compared to the more common practice of using the Dynamic Host Control Protocol (DHCP) to automatically assign IP addresses from an available pool of addresses.

strategic planning Process of moving the organization toward its vision.

strong authentication An authentication method that utilizes two different forms of confirming the proposed identity.

subject of an attack A computer that is used as an active tool to conduct an attack.

substitution cipher Encryption algorithm in which one value is substituted for another value.

supervisor password A higher-level password used to gain access to the BIOS setup program or to change the BIOS password.

surge A prolonged increase in voltage levels.

symmetric encryption *See* "private key encryption."

synchronous token A hardware component used in authentication that employs a cryptographic process combined with a clock to validate an identity.

syslog A *NIX standard for logging program messages.

systems, networks, and storage administrators Individuals with the primary responsibility for administering the systems, storage, and networks that house and provide access to the organization's information.

task-based access controls (TBAC) Nondiscretionary access controls based on tasks assigned.

team leader A project manager, who may be a departmental line manager or staff unit manager, who understands project management, personnel management, and information security technical requirements.

technical specifications A type of systems-specific policy a systems administrator may need to create in order to implement managerial policy. These specifications translate managerial intent into an enforceable technical approach for each type of equipment.

Terminal Access Controller Access Control System Plus (TACACS+) Commonly called "tac-plus," this is the latest and strongest version of a set of authentication protocols developed by Cisco Systems. It replaces its less secure predecessor protocols, TACACS and XTACACS.

threat In the context of information security, an object, person, or other entity that represents a constant danger to an asset.

threat agent An object, person, or other entity that launches an attack in order to damage or steal an organization's information or physical asset.

Ticket-granting server (TGS) Part of a Kerberos system; a server which, upon receiving a ticket-granting ticket (TGT) from a client, grants a session ticket and forwards it to the server holding the requested file or service. The client is then granted access to that resource.

Ticket-granting ticket (TGT) A session key generated by a Kerberos system that the client presents to a ticket-granting server (TGS) as part of the process of gaining access to system resources.

timing attack An attack technique that works by measuring the time required to access a Web page and deducing that the user has visited the site before by the presence of the page in the browser's cache.

token Physical object such as a smart card or other kind of physical item used to offer a more stringent level of authentication in which users need to have something in order to gain access.

translation lookaside buffer A specific form of cache memory on the processor that maps physical and virtual memory spaces to allow more rapid translation of memory addresses to make page swapping more effective.

transport mode One of two modes in which IPSec operates. In this mode, only the IP data is encrypted—not the IP headers themselves.

transposition cipher Encryption algorithm in which the values within a block are rearranged to create the ciphertext. This can be done at the bit level or at the byte (character) level.

trap door See "back door."

Triple DES (3DES) An improvement to DES that uses as many as three keys in succession, making it substantially more secure than DES.

Trojan horse A software program that reveals its designed behavior only when activated. Trojan horses are frequently disguised as helpful, interesting, or necessary pieces of software.

Trusted Computing Base (TCB) The collection of all hardware, firmware, and software components critical to the security of the system. Any vulnerabilities in the TCB will threaten the security of the entire system.

tunnel A channel or pathway over a packet network used by a VPN that runs through the Internet from one endpoint to another.

tunnel mode One of two modes in which IPSec operates. In this mode, the entire IP packet is encrypted and inserted as the payload in another IP packet.

URI Filtering Protocol server A server that filters and processes requests for URIs and that can work in conjunction with firewalls.

URL redirection Direction of clients to a different Web server based on the host being requested.

U.S. Department of Defense (DOD) classification scheme A data classification model used most often by the U.S. military and which relies on a more complex categorization system than those used by most corporations.

user authentication Act of confirming the identity of a potential user of a system before granting access to protected resources.

utility The quality or state of information having value for some purpose or end. To have utility, information must be in a format meaningful to the end user.

virtual private network (VPN) A private, secure network operated over a public and insecure network.

virtual tunnel A communications path that makes use of Internet-based hosts and servers to conduct data from one network station to another.

viruses Segments of code that perform malicious actions.

vision A written statement of the organization's long-term goals.

VPN appliance A hardware device specially designed to terminate VPNs and join multiple LANs.

vulnerability An identified weakness in a controlled system, where controls are not present or are no longer effective.

well-known vulnerabilities Vulnerabilities that have been examined, documented, and published.

work factor The amount of effort (usually expressed in units of time) required to perform cryptanalysis on an encoded message.

worms Malicious programs that replicate themselves constantly, without requiring another program to provide a safe environment for replication.

XOR cipher conversion Encryption algorithm in which the bit stream is subjected to a Boolean XOR function against some other data stream, typically a key stream.

zombies/bots Compromised machines that are directed during a distributed denial-of-service (usually by a transmitted command) to participate in the attack.

Index

bastion host (*Continued*)
  installing, 239–240
  machine for, 240–243
    choosing operating system for,
      241, 247
    keeping operating system
      updated, 242–243
    memory considerations,
      240–241
    number needed, 240
    processor speed, 241
    UNIX and Linux hosts, 242
    Windows hosts, 242
  network location of, 245–246
  physical location of, 244–246
BC (business continuity), 51, 61
benchmarking, 252
benefits
  of proxy servers, 214–219
    blocking URLs, 215–216
    concealing internal clients,
      214–215
    content filtering, 216–217
    e-mail proxy protection, 217
    ensuring security, 217–219
    improving performance, 217
    providing user authentication, 219
    redirecting URLs, 219
  of VPNs, 300
BGP (Border Gateway Protocol), 200
BIA (business impact analysis), 53–56
  assessment of potential damage, 55–56
  business unit analysis, 55
  classification of subordinate plans, 56
  identifying and prioritizing threats
    and attacks, 54–55
  scenarios of successful attacks, 55
binary drive image, 251
biometrics, 75
blackouts, 17
Block all Internet access option, 171
Block pop-up windows option, 27
Block reported attack site option, 28
Block reported web forgeries option, 28
book cipher, 268
Boot Hard Disk option, 136
boot virus, 17
Border Gateway Protocol (BGP), 200
bots, 20
brownout, 17
brute force, compromising passwords, 19
buffer overflow
  attacks using, 22–23
  vulnerabilities, of proxy servers, 223
business continuity (BC), 51, 61
business continuity planning,
  developing programs for, 58–59

business impact analysis. *See* BIA
business needs, 6

C

CA (certificate authority), 272
Cache Array Routing Protocol
  (CARP), 121
caching, 100, 217
Cancel option, 27–28, 167, 170–171
capability table, 40, 70
CARP (Cache Array Routing Protocol),
  121
CD/DVD Images, 135
Central Processing Unit (CPU), 241
centralization, providing with firewall,
  106
centralized authentication, 78–82
  comparison of
    filtering characteristics, 82
    NAT characteristics, 82
    proxy characteristics, 82
    strength of security, 81–82
  vs. decentralized access controls, 73
  Kerberos system, 79–80
  RADIUS, 81
  TACACS+, 80–81
CERT/CC (Computer Emergency
  Response Team Coordination
  Center), 48
certificate authority (CA), 272
Certificate Manager option, 286
certificate-based authentication, 84
Champion role, 7
Change scope for this entry option, 167
Check for Baselines option, 90
chief information officer (CIO), 7
chief information security officer
  (CISO), 7
chief security officer (CSO), 7
chkconfig utility, 242
Choose button, 255
C.I.A. triangle, 3
CIO (chief information officer), 7
cipher, 264
ciphertext, 265
circuit gateways, 118, 224
CISO (chief information security
  officer), 7
Clear history when Firefox closes
  option, 28
client authentication, firewall
  authentication methods, 77
client configurations, for proxy servers,
  220–221
client-to-site VPN, 301
Close option, 27, 64, 169, 285
CMD.EXE, 257

CNSS (U.S. Committee on National
  Systems Security) Security Model,
  4–5
Command Prompt, 133–134
commercial-grade firewalls
  appliances, 120
  systems, 120–121
Committee on National Systems
  Security, U.S. (CNSS) Security
  Model, 4–5
Common Vulnerabilities and Exposures
  (CVE), 47
communications security (ComSec), 3, 70
Company Name field, 320
components
  of firewalls, 102–103
  of VPNs, 295–298
Computer Emergency Response Team
  Coordination Center (CERT/CC), 48
Computer Management option, 321
Computer Security Institute (CSI), 12
computer security policies, identifying
  for local computer, 63–64
Computer Security Resource Center
  (CSRC), 42
computer viruses, 17
ComSec (communications security), 3, 70
confidentiality, of information, 4
Configuration rules, 41
Configuration Wizard, 231
configurations for VPNs, 303–306
  and extranet and intranet access, 306
  hub-and-spoke configuration, 304–305
  hybrid configuration, 305–306
  mesh configuration, 303–304
Connect option, 322
Connect to the Internet using a modem
  or ISDN adaptor option, 231
Connect to the network at my
  workplace option, 320
Connected to the Internet permanently
  option, 231
connections, average lifetime of, 190
Connections tab, 232
connectivity-based firewalls, 182–183
content filtering
  with firewalls, 200–202
  with proxy servers, 216–217
Content tab, 27
Content Vectoring Protocol (CVP), 201
contingency plan, 51
Control Panel, 168–169, 233, 321
controls, 9
correlation attacks, on cryptosystems, 279
countermeasures, 9
CPU (Central Processing Unit), 241
cracker, 17

IRP (incident response planning), 56–57

ISA (Internet Security and Acceleration Server), 121, 192, 215, 226

iSafeguard, sending encrypted e-mail with, 285–290

ISMS (information security management system), 42

ISO (information security officer), 7

ISO (International Standards Organization), 35, 41

ISO 27000 Series, 41–42

ISP (Internet Service Provider), 121, 227

ISSP (Issue-Specific Security Policy), 37–39

ISVs (independent software vendors), 244

IT (information technology), 3

K

KDC (Key Distribution Center), 80, 277

Keep until option, 27

Kerberos system, 79–80, 276

Key Distribution Center (KDC), 80, 277

keyring, 308

keys, 265

keyspace, 265

known-plaintext attack, 278

L

L2TP (Layer 2 Tunneling Protocol), for VPNs, 308, 314–315

LAN (Local Area Network), 232–233

Layer 2 Tunneling Protocol (L2TP), for VPNs, 308, 314–315

layer four switches, 200

LDAP (Lightweight Directory Access Protocol), 164

learning mode, 171

leased lines, 294

least privilege principle, 69

Level, Framework of SETA, 50

level of performance, baseline, 252

Lightweight Directory Access Protocol (LDAP), 164

likelihood, 9

limitations, of firewalls, 130

Linux, for bastion host, 242

load balancing, for firewalls, 200

Load images automatically option, 27

Local Area Network (LAN), 232–233

Local Resources tab, 322

Local Security Policy option, 169

Local Users and Groups folder, 321

Lock after _minutes of inactivity option, 171

Log dropped packets box, 168

Log files, 217, 240

Log Off option, 322

Log On to Windows option, 322

Log successful connections box, 168

logging, 232

M

MAC (Mandatory Access Control)
data classification model, 70–71
layer firewalls, 118–119
security clearances, 71–72

macro virus, 17

mail bombing, e-mail attacks, 21

maintenance hook, 17

malicious code, attacks using, 17–18

malicious software, 17

malware, 17

Managerial Guidance SysSPs, 40

Mandatory Access Control. See MAC

man-in-middle attacks
on cryptosystems, 279
using, 20–21

MBSA (Microsoft Baseline Security Analyzer), 92–94, 258

McCumber Cube, 4

megahertz (MHz), 241

memory considerations, for bastion host, 240–241

Memory exercise, 255

mesh configuration, for VPNs, 303–304

MHz (megahertz), 241

Microsoft Baseline Security Analyzer (MBSA), 92–94, 258

Microsoft ISA (Internet Security & Acceleration Server), 226

Microsoft Point-to-Point Encryption (MPPE), 308

Microsoft Remote Desktop protocol, setting up, 321–322

Microsoft Security Assessment Tool (MSAT), 250

Microsoft Security Compliance Manager, 88–92
baseline templates for
installing, 90–91
modifying and applying, 91–92
installing, 88–90

Microsoft VPN Client, setting up, 321

MIME (Multipurpose Internet Mail Extensions), 274

misconceptions about firewalls, 100

mission policy, 36

mission-critical, firewalls, 200

mkdir /home/vyatta/ openvpn_server_keys, 290

MMC console, 64

monoalphabetic substitution, 266

More button, 322

Mount option, 284

Mozilla Firefox, 27

MPPE (Microsoft Point-to-Point Encryption), 308

MSAT (Microsoft Security Assessment Tool), 250

Multipurpose Internet Mail Extensions (MIME), 274

My Network Places, 320

My network (subnet) only, 167

N

NAC (Network Access Control), 301

NAT (Network Address Translation), 131, 140, 210, 228, 263, 302, 308
characteristics of RADIUS, 82
characteristics of TACACS+, 82
in firewalls, 185–189
overview, 112–114
testing for with proxy server, 233

National Institute of Standards and Technology security models. See NIST security models

Need to know principle, 70

NetProxy, installing and configuring, 231–232

Netstat application, 133–134

Network Access Control (NAC), 301

Network Address Translation. See NAT

Network and Internet Connections option, 168

Network Connections option, 168

Network Interface Card (NIC), 119, 128

Network load balancing (NLB), 223

network location, of bastion host, 245–246

Network News Transfer Protocol (NNTP), 153

Network option, 136, 320

network security, 3

New button, 136

Next option, 89, 93, 136, 169–170, 283–286, 320

NIC (Network Interface Card), 119, 128

NIST (National Institute of Standards and Technology) security models, 42–47
SP 800-14, 45
SP 800-41 Rev. 1, 45
SP 800-53 A, Jul 2008, 46
SP 800-53 Rev. 3, 45–46
special publications of, 47

NLB (Network load balancing), 223

Nmap, active stack fingerprinting using, 256–257

NNTP (Network News Transfer Protocol), 153